HEIRS
of the
FOUNDERS

ALSO BY H.W. BRANDS
AVAILABLE FROM RANDOM HOUSE
LARGE PRINT

The General vs. the President

HEIRS
of the
FOUNDERS

The Epic Rivalry of Henry Clay,

John Calhoun and Daniel Webster,

the Second Generation of

American Giants

H. W. BRANDS

RANDOM HOUSE
LARGE PRINT

Cover design by Michael J. Windsor
Cover paintings (details): John C. Calhoun by
Arthur E. Schmalz Conrad; Daniel Webster by
Adrian S. Lamb; Henry Clay by Allen Cox. All
courtesy of the U.S. Senate Collection.

Portrait of Daniel Webster by Francis Alexander
(1835, oil on canvas) courtesy of the National
Portrait Gallery, Smithsonian Institution;
bequest of Mrs. John Hay Whitney. All other
images courtesy of the Library of Congress.

The Library of Congress has established a
Cataloging-in-Publication record for this title.

ISBN: 978-1-9848-3362-4

www.randomhouse.com/largeprint

FIRST LARGE PRINT EDITION

Printed in the United States of America

10 9 8 7 6 5 4 3 2 1

This Large Print edition published in accord
with the standards of the N.A.V.H.

Contents

PART SIX
The Fatal Compromise
485

HEIRS
of the
FOUNDERS

Prologue

JANUARY 1850

The marvelous news from the West was the last thing Henry Clay had wanted to hear. Gold! Gold in California! It set the pulse of America racing; it sent a hundred thousand brave souls to that far-off land to make their fortunes. It hastened the day when the institutions of American democracy, and not merely the American flag, would be planted on the Pacific shore. And it meant that Henry Clay—aging, ailing Henry Clay—must leave Ashland, his home and refuge at Lexington, Kentucky, and once more make the long journey to Washington.

Five years he had been at home. Five years he had sought and eventually found solace from ambition definitively frustrated. He would never be president. The White House would never be more than a place for him to visit. No one had come closer to its portal more often than he. No one had a better claim to the knowledge, temperament and character required of its residents. But the American people were fickle and easily swayed, and at the crucial moments they had turned from him to others.

He had learned to accept his fate. A statesman did what he **could** in his country's service, not what he **would**. And it was for his country that he felt so dispirited by the news from California. Whatever it would cost him personally—in effort expended, health further compromised, obloquy endured—it would cost the Union more. Henry Clay had been born amid the American Revolution and come of age with the Constitution; for his entire adult life the Union had been his guiding star. Twice he had steered the Union between the Scylla of jealous states' rights and the Charybdis of rampant centralism. But the turbulent seas of democracy grew more tempestuous with each passing decade. And the gold fever whipped them higher still, for the sudden peopling of California compelled Congress to rule on the fate of slavery in the new American West. California sought admission to the Union as a free state. The North demanded California's admission, and would probably get it. What would the South demand in return? And what would the competing demands do to the creaking hull and strained rigging of the American ship of state?

The genius of Henry Clay was a knack for compromise, for finding formulas neither side loved but both sides could live with. He had conjured one such formula in the Missouri crisis of 1820, and another in the South Carolina crisis of 1833. The genius of American democracy was its ability to muddle through crises—to accept answers as tentative and let principle nod to expedience. Henry Clay had been criticized for pliant principles, but he pleaded the higher aim of preserving the Union, the guarantor of American democracy. Democracy was a work in progress, never perfect but never finished. Given time, democracy would find a way forward.

California's gold meant democracy might not have time. With everyone else, Henry Clay had supposed that filling the territories acquired from Mexico in the recent war would take decades. The Louisiana territory had been American for half a century and wasn't a tenth full. Clay, though a slaveholder, was an emancipationist at heart: he judged slavery a curse and looked to the day when the Southern economy would outgrow slavery, as the Northern economy had done. A few decades, no more time than had already passed since the Missouri Compromise, was all that was needed.

Clay knew **he** didn't have a few decades. He would be lucky to last a few years. But if he could somehow conjure another compromise, he might give the Union the time it required.

JOHN C. CALHOUN had less time than Henry Clay. His consumption—tuberculosis—was more advanced than Clay's. He might have months; he might have weeks. Some days he couldn't get out of bed. His voice, for decades the trumpet of the South, could barely rise above a whisper.

Upon the news from California, his thoughts turned to Henry Clay. The two had entered the House of Representatives together amid the troubles that sparked the War of 1812. For years they had worked in harness, defending and bolstering the country their generation had inherited from America's founders. But ambition drove them apart, like sons contesting control of an estate they were supposed to share. Clay was the elder, in years and seniority, yet Calhoun had gifts of intellect and guile Clay couldn't match. It was the guile that surprised most people, including Clay, who puzzled at Calhoun's ability to advance himself—and get past Clay—without appearing to try.

But it was the intellect that brought Calhoun down. Or maybe it was the ambition, disguised as intellect. Calhoun's political strength was his base in South Carolina, yet his strength was also his weakness. Other states insisted on what they considered their sovereign rights vis-à-vis the national government, but none were so vigilant and quick to take offense as South Carolina. The founders had left deliberately vague where the boundary lay between state and national authority; similarly blurred was who would determine the boundary and how it would be enforced. They knew that any explicit answer might wreck their experiment in self-government before it got fairly started; they left to their heirs to find a solution the country could live with. The task had been the work of Calhoun's—and Clay's—lifetime.

South Carolina had registered particular umbrage at a tariff that harmed planters in the state. Those planters sought an advocate, and they discovered one in John Calhoun. He penned an exegesis that would have made a medieval scholastic proud, investing South Carolina with the exclusive authority to determine its rights and privileges. The planters applauded; their respect for Calhoun grew. So did Calhoun's own regard for his skills as an interpreter of the Constitution and a shaper of America's destiny.

But he found he had mounted a tiger. South Carolina pushed its case to the brink of armed conflict with the national government. Calhoun took alarm: for his state, for the country, for his political future. He worked with Henry Clay to defuse the crisis; characteristically, each man claimed credit for averting civil war.

Yet where the nation honored Clay, the man of the Union, it suspected Calhoun, the guardian of his state. In serving South Carolina, Calhoun tainted himself in the eyes of America. Those who had watched him for years—and they were many, for in his prime he was one of the most arresting figures in Washington, tall and straight, with curling auburn hair and eyes of the fiercest blue—increasingly detected a change in him. His defense of states' rights, and especially of the right most important to Southern planters, the right to own slaves, became a monomania. Where other defenders of slavery were content to call it a necessary evil, essential to the operation of the Southern economy but nothing to boast of, Calhoun pronounced it a positive good, an ornament of the South's superior culture. As his national reputation diminished, and with it his hopes for national office, he retreated into state and section, which honored him the more. He became a Miltonian figure: rather than serve in heaven, he determined to reign in hell.

And now he found himself confronting Henry Clay again. Clay would save the Union, if he could. Calhoun would wreck the Union, if that's what it cost to preserve slavery and states' rights.

Coughing, Calhoun reckoned his body might stand one final battle. He would defeat Henry Clay once and for all. Or he would die trying.

DANIEL WEBSTER WAS two months older than John Calhoun and five years younger than Henry Clay. But he looked a decade younger than either man. He had never felt the responsibility that weighed on them: Clay for the Union, Calhoun for the South. Nor had ambition driven him as hard as it drove them. At least not until now.

In an age of orators Daniel Webster had no peers. Henry Clay's words danced and laughed, setting to sound the Kentuckian's open, engaging personality. Clay won arguments less often than he won followers; the Henry Clay Clubs that sprang up around the country revealed but the tip of his celebrity. John Calhoun's speeches impressed all and intimidated many; his tightly marshaled arguments advanced like a Roman phalanx across the field of political battle.

But Daniel Webster had a way with words that seemed almost supernatural. Indeed, some said he must have struck a bargain with the devil to acquire such a gift. He perfected the art of persuasion in the courtroom and became the most sought after, and generously compensated, advocate of his era. The stern justices of the Supreme Court were no match for Webster; at the conclusion of his argument for Dartmouth College in a landmark case, even John Marshall—**John Marshall!**—wept. When Webster spoke in Congress, Washington stopped what it was doing and hurried to hear him.

Yet Webster was profligate: with his talents, his time, his earnings. Things came too easily to him. It was said of Webster that he must be a fraud: no one could be as great as he looked. "God-like Daniel," people called him, and it went to his head.

His most important speeches he prepared carefully, but lesser ones—lesser for him yet beyond mere mortals—he tossed off with scarcely a thought. As much as he earned, he spent even more. He was always in debt and in need of the income his law practice supplied. He wasn't above taking discreet payments from powerful people whose interests he promoted in Congress.

He had the caliber to be president but not the true aim. He had come close to the White House almost by accident. Yet of the three towering figures of the age—Clay, Calhoun and Webster were spoken of as the "great triumvirate," not always admiringly—he was the only one, in 1850, who retained a chance of reaching the summit of American politics. Which was to say, as the California crisis loomed, that from a personal perspective Daniel Webster had the most to lose.

He could easily lose it all. His Massachusetts constituents had long loved him, but the abolitionist movement was powerful in the state, and its leaders were demanding that he share their intolerance of slavery. Many abolitionists had no more devotion to the Union than the most secessionist Southerners did, if the Union required toleration of slavery. Siding with them risked making Webster as much a pariah outside New England as John Calhoun had become outside the South. Yet opposing them, and taking an uncompromising stand for the Union—beside Henry

Clay—could cost him his political base and possibly his livelihood.

Throughout his career Webster had dodged difficult choices, and gotten away with it. His silver tongue had talked him out of one cul-de-sac after another. But he had never faced a test like this. He would have to speak as he had never spoken. He could make John Marshall weep, but to hold his home base and maintain his hopes for the presidency—to sustain his section without imperiling the Union—Daniel Webster might have to go back to the devil for a second mortgage on his soul.

PART ONE

The Spirit of '76

It is the war of the Revolution revived. We are again struggling for our liberty and independence.

—JOHN CALHOUN, 1812

1

GEORGE GLEIG HAD seen thousands of soldiers in battle, but he had never seen any perform more disgracefully than the Americans assigned to defend Washington in the summer of 1814. "No troops could behave worse than they did," wrote Gleig, an officer with a British force attacking the American capital. "The skirmishers were driven in as soon as attacked, the first line gave way without offering the slightest resistance, and the left of the main body was broken within half an hour after it was seriously engaged." The British hadn't dreamed that their assault would proceed so swiftly; they had barely engaged the defenders before the path to the city lay wide open.

The British commander, General Robert Ross, sent a flag of truce from the edge of Washington. But the bearer of the flag was fired upon from a window of a house, and his horse was killed beneath him. "You will easily believe that conduct so unjustifiable, so direct a breach of the law of nations, roused the indignation of every individual, from the General himself down to the private soldier," George Gleig continued. "All thoughts of accommodation were instantly laid aside; the troops advanced forthwith into the town, and having first put to the sword all who were found in the house from which the shots were fired, and reduced it to ashes, they proceeded, without a moment's delay, to burn and destroy every thing in the most distant degree connected with the government. In this general devastation were included the Senate-house"— the Capitol—"the President's place, an extensive dock-yard and arsenal, barracks for two or three thousand men, several large store-houses filled with naval and military stores, some hundreds of cannon of different descriptions, and nearly twenty thousand stand of small arms."

A spirit of righteous retribution moved the British in their sack of Washington, for earlier in the war American troops had gratuitously torched British government buildings in York, Canada. "All this was as it should be," George Gleig said of the British reprisal. "And had the arm of vengeance been extended no farther, there would not have been room given for so much as a whisper of disapprobation. But unfortunately it did not stop here. A noble library, several printing offices, and all the national archives were likewise committed to the flames, which, though no doubt the property of government, might better have been spared."

Years later Gleig recalled the awesome spectacle of Washington afire. Night was falling as the last of the British regiments marched into the city. "The blazing of houses, ships, and stores, the report of exploding magazines, and the crash of falling roofs informed them, as they proceeded, of what was going forward. You can conceive nothing finer than the sight which met them as they drew near to the town. The sky was brilliantly illumined by the different conflagrations; and a dark red light was thrown upon the road, sufficient to permit each man to view distinctly his comrade's face. Except the burning of St. Sebastian's"—in Spain during the Peninsular War—"I do not recollect to have witnessed, at any period of my life, a scene more striking or more sublime."

THE BURNING OF Washington made Henry Clay look a fool. He had spearheaded the campaign in Congress in favor of the war against Britain and predicted a rapid victory. His drumbeating had started as soon as he entered the House of Representatives in 1811, when he earned the unprecedented—and never repeated—distinction of being made speaker of the House on his first day in the chamber. American grievances against

Britain dated to the Revolutionary War. Britain had been slow to honor the treaty that ended that war, retaining posts near the Great Lakes, obstructing American commerce, and generally according the United States little of the respect due the independent nation America had become. The troubles escalated when war broke out between Britain and France in the early 1790s. American merchants and shipowners argued that they ought to be able to trade with both countries, since America was a neutral. But neither Britain nor France bought the argument, even as each continued to purchase the goods the Americans were selling, while trying to prevent the other from doing so. British ships seized American vessels bound for France and confiscated their cargoes; French seized American ships bound for Britain.

The American government complained, although the direction of the complaints depended on which party held power. The founders had uniformly decried parties as baleful manifestations of the selfish opportunism that had characterized British politics and prompted America's bolt from the empire; they prayed their infant republic would be spared. But the new federal government was scarcely up and running before parties began to form, and the first divisive issue was the European war. Thomas Jefferson looked favorably on France, contending that revolution was usually a good thing and that France, having aided America in America's hour of need, deserved American support now. A faction, then a party, of like-minded Francophiles coalesced around Jefferson and called themselves Republicans. Alexander Hamilton preferred Britain, citing ties of commerce and cultural affinity and detesting revolution on principle. American Anglophiles followed Hamilton and called themselves Federalists.

When the Federalists were in power the finger of American blame for ship seizures pointed at France. Indeed the Federalist administration of John Adams fought an undeclared naval war against France over the issue. When the Republicans took charge, Britain bore the brunt of American anger. The administration of Thomas Jefferson attempted diplomacy, then an embargo of American foreign trade, to end the seizures. Neither worked, and the seizures continued into the administration of Republican James Madison, who held the presidency when Henry Clay became House speaker.

A second issue intensified American anger at Britain. The British navy was desperate for seamen, and its officers had orders to man their vessels by any means possible. Service in the British navy was notoriously hard, and British sailors were chronically tempted to jump ship. Some did so in American ports, where British craft resupplied, and disappeared into the wharf-side populations. Not infrequently they then signed on with American merchantmen. British officers, alert to the practice, intercepted American vessels when they could and reclaimed the deserters.

The searches and seizures alone rankled Americans, as violations of American sovereignty. Even more infuriating was the British habit of seizing sailors who had never been in the British navy, on specious claims that they had been. This was nothing less than kidnapping and was condemned by Americans as intolerable.

The British provocations grew more egregious over time. In 1807 a British warship fired on an American navy vessel, the **Chesapeake,** within sight of the Virginia shore. The commander of the British vessel had called for the **Chesapeake** to stop and allow a British search party to board. The American commander refused, and the British officer ordered his gunners to blast a broadside into the unready American ship. Three Americans were killed and more than a dozen wounded, including the commander.

The attack outraged American opinion. Americans were shrewd enough to realize that the owners and captains of merchant vessels were making a gamble when they put to sea against the British; sometimes the gamble paid off and sometimes it didn't. But an attack against a ship of the U.S. navy was an affront to the entire country.

Still another issue angered Americans toward Britain. From bases in Canada, British traders provisioned Indians living in the American Northwest.

The provisions included weapons some of the tribes used to attack American settlements and kill American citizens. Westerners (in particular) resented the British role in the violence, and many demanded that Canada be seized and the British evicted from their last North American redoubt.

HENRY CLAY WAS one of those Westerners, by adoption. His birthplace was Hanover County, Virginia, and his earliest memories included the looting of his boyhood home by British soldiers during the Revolutionary War. The image would stick in his head as he grew older and dispose him to think the worst of Britain. More important at the time was the death that same year—1781—of his father, a Baptist minister and middling planter. Clay's mother inherited the farm and a score of slaves; Henry and his brothers got two slaves each. Henry's mother remarried, and Henry's stepfather moved the family to Richmond, where he introduced Henry to George Wythe, a prominent jurist, signer of the Declaration of Independence, delegate to the Constitutional Convention, and mentor of Thomas Jefferson. Wythe saw promise in young Clay akin to what he had seen in Jefferson, and he made Clay his personal secretary. Clay read law in Wythe's office and was admitted to the Virginia bar in 1797. He was twenty years old.

Richmond was thick with lawyers, leaving little

room for a novice, even one with friends like George
Wythe. So Clay did what generations of ambitious
young Americans had done and would do: he
headed west. Kentucky had been part of Virginia
until 1792, by which time the trans-Appalachian
portion of the Old Dominion had attained sufficient population to qualify for admission to the
Union as a state of its own. It also had gravity
working on behalf of statehood. In the 1790s, and
indeed until the introduction of steamboat service
on America's rivers, the West began at the apex
of the Appalachians. Cargoes floated downstream
with ease and upstream with expense; rivers that
flowed to the Mississippi made Westerners of
the farmers and merchants who lived in their
valleys.

Henry Clay crossed the mountains and became
a Westerner. He settled in Lexington and commenced trying lawsuits, probating wills, drafting
contracts and contesting them, and arranging the
purchase and sale of real estate and other property,
including slaves. Currency in the West was scarce,
and his clients often paid in land or horses. He
acquired a farm he called Ashland, for the trees
there. He married Lucretia Hart, a daughter of one
of Kentucky's earliest settlers. Neighbors pointed
him out as one of their community's most promising young men.

Yet he stepped on toes. Kentucky's first try at a
constitution didn't suit all the important political

actors in the state, and various groups supported a new constitutional convention. Clay joined them, and in doing so challenged the state's single most powerful interest. Slaveholders feared that a convention might threaten slavery in Kentucky. The existing constitution prohibited the legislature from tampering with the institution; certain proponents of a convention wanted to undo this prohibition. Northern states were freeing their slaves, and some Kentuckians thought their state should follow suit.

Clay agreed with the emancipationists, despite being a slaveholder himself. He thought slavery did harm to masters as well as slaves. The latter lacked freedom, the former pride in honest labor. "All America acknowledges the existence of slavery to be an evil," he declared, "which while it deprives the slave of the best gift of heaven, in the end injures the master too, by laying waste his lands, enabling him to live indolently, and thus contracting all the vices generated by a state of idleness." Kentucky had a chance to start anew, to rid the state of this curse. "If it be this enormous evil, the sooner we attempt its destruction the better," he said.

Yet Clay was a realist. The dismantling of slavery must be gradual, even if it should begin at once. Otherwise slaveholders would be unfairly divested of their property in slaves, and elderly slaves thrown out of their homes and onto an uncaring world.

Gradual emancipation was unfolding in several Northern states; Kentucky should try something similar.

Clay won his skirmish yet lost the battle. A convention was called, but it left the safeguards around slavery in Kentucky in place. In fact it reinforced them, by withdrawing from Kentucky's free blacks the right to vote. Clay had hoped to push slavery toward dissolution. He still held that hope, but he realized the struggle would be harder than he had thought.

HE RAN FOR office as a Republican. His choice of the Republicans reflected his admiration for Thomas Jefferson, his animus toward Britain, and his judgment that the Republicans were the party of the future. Jefferson and the Republicans swept into office in Washington just as Clay was testing the political waters in Lexington; Kentucky Republicans fared comparably well. Clay jumped aboard.

He wore his Republicanism on his sleeve and defended it with vigor. He won election to the Kentucky legislature and tussled with remnant Federalists there. One, Humphrey Marshall, ridiculed Clay for slavish devotion to Jefferson. Clay called Marshall a poltroon; Marshall pronounced Clay a liar. Clay demanded a duel; Marshall obliged. The affair followed the punctilious code of honor of the venerable practice, specifying the ground rules with lawyerly precision:

1. Each gentleman will take his station at ten paces distance from the other, and will stand as may suit his choice, with his arms hanging down, and after the words Attention! Fire! both may fire at their leisure.
2. A snap or flash shall be equivalent to a fire.
3. If one should fire before the other, he who fires first shall stand in the position in which he was when he fired, except that he may let his arms fall down by his side.
4. A violation of the above rules by either of the parties (accidents excepted) shall subject the offender to instant death.

Clay was no duelist. He lacked pistols and had to borrow them. He didn't shoot often enough to have any confidence in his ability to hit his antagonist. But he had been called a liar and must go forward. Dueling was illegal in Kentucky, as it was in most states, but authorities in one state rarely pursued duelists into another. For this reason Clay and Marshall traveled to Ohio to settle their dispute. On the appointed day the two, with their seconds, some friends and a surgeon crossed the Ohio River near Louisville and repaired to a level spot on the north bank. The ten paces were taken and the duelists assumed their positions. "Attention! Fire!" was called out.

Each man fired. Marshall's first shot missed Clay completely. Clay's ball nicked Marshall, who had turned sideways to shoot, in the abdomen. The rules said nothing about how many shots would be exchanged. The practice was to keep firing until one or both could no longer fire or until they agreed that injured honor had been assuaged.

Marshall and Clay weren't finished. They reloaded. Marshall fired again, once more missing Clay. Clay took aim and pulled the trigger. "My damned pistol snapped," he said in disgust afterward. Under the rules, this counted as Clay's second shot.

They reloaded again. Marshall fired a third time, hitting Clay in the fleshy part of his thigh but sparing the bone. Clay's third shot missed Marshall.

Clay wanted another round. But Marshall had had enough. So had the seconds, whose job included bringing their principals home alive, when possible. They talked Clay into accepting an end to the matter.

Because the purpose of duels was to demonstrate courage and devotion to honor, seconds typically concluded their function by delivering a report. The seconds in this duel filed theirs with Kentucky's newspapers. "We deem it justice to both the gentlemen to pronounce their conduct on the occasion cool, determined and brave in the highest degree," they declared.

Clay's fellow Republicans were more enthusiastic. "Worthy Friend!" hailed one. "Your firmness and courage is admitted now by all parties. I feel happy to hear of the heroism with which you acted." Their mutual enemies would take the lesson. "This will serve to stop the mouths of all snivel faced Tories."

IN FACT IT did nothing of the sort. Clay continued to tangle with Federalists, including Joseph Daveiss, who had been appointed by John Adams to be United States district attorney for Kentucky. Clay and Daveiss regularly traded barbs in newspapers, and they went toe-to-toe in the courtroom. Clay had engaged to defend former vice president Aaron Burr, who had survived his own duel, with Alexander Hamilton, but whose political career hadn't long outlived Hamilton's death in that duel. Daveiss got it into his head that Burr was engaged in treasonous activity designed to separate the West from the United States. Thomas Jefferson dismissed the charges against Burr as too monstrous to believe. Clay shared Jefferson's opinion. He also valued the opportunity to represent a famous client in a high-profile case.

Clay defended Burr before a grand jury Daveiss

had summoned. He ripped into Daveiss for waging partisan war against Burr. "You have heard of inquisitions in Europe," Clay said. "You have heard of the screws and tortures made use of in the dens of despotism, to extort confession; of the dark conclaves and caucuses, for the purpose of twisting some incoherent expression into evidence of guilt. Is not the project of the attorney for the United States a similar object of terror?" Clay professed faith in the jurors' ability to see through Daveiss's conspiracy mongering. "All the art of the attorney will not effect his purpose."

Clay won the case, and then some. The grand jury not only refused to indict Burr; it joined locals in treating Burr as a Republican hero. A ball was held in his honor, with Republicans coming from miles around to congratulate Burr and Clay on defeating Daveiss and malicious Federalism.

Within months, though, Clay wished he had never met Burr. Jefferson received new information that caused him to change his mind entirely about his erstwhile number two. The president himself now leveled against Burr the very charge Clay had ridiculed as Inquisition-like. Jefferson didn't immediately share the new evidence, but Clay deemed it prudent to take the word of Jefferson against that of Burr. "It seems that we have been much mistaken about Burr," Clay wrote to Thomas Hart, his brother-in-law. He hoped his friends would accept that he had made an honest mistake. He concluded that the best thing for him to do was to keep his head down until the furor passed.

OR UNTIL ANOTHER furor took its place. War has long been a rite of passage, with new generations feeling a need to prove their courage and earn the right to supplant their elders. Clay's generation grew up on the hero tales of the American Revolution—the stories of boldness in the political arena and valor on the battlefield. Often implicit in the stories, as in the stories of every generation of elders, was skepticism that the younger generation had what it took to match the elders' feats. Where was the George Washington of the younger set, the general who could smite the British as Washington had done at Yorktown? Where were the Patrick Henry and Thomas Jefferson, whose words inspired a nation and brought down an empire? Where the James Madison and Alexander Hamilton, the framers of a new government for the new nation?

Henry Clay had heard the stories and felt the skepticism. He was burdened with no conspicuous sense of personal inferiority, but he reckoned that an ambitious young politician could do worse than demand that the country complete the work commenced by the generation of the founders. Britain had been the enemy then; Britain would be the enemy now. Clay didn't fancy himself another Washington; military service didn't appeal. But he could emulate Patrick Henry, the great orator of American independence, and could dream of following Jefferson into political leadership, perhaps even to the White House.

He argued for war from the moment he took up the gavel as House speaker. Congressional Federalists, representing the commercial classes of America in opposition to war, asserted that the British seizures of American ships were a mere tactic in Britain's struggle against France, and not an existential threat to America. Clay rejoined that the Federalists couldn't be more wrong. "The real cause of British aggression is not to distress an enemy but to destroy a rival," he said. British merchants and shippers saw America as a mortal rival in the trade of the Atlantic region, and were bent on its destruction. The Federalists gravely underestimated Britain's malevolence. "She sickens at your prosperity and beholds in your growth—your sails spread on every ocean, and your numerous seamen—the foundations of a power which, at no very distant day, is to make her tremble for naval superiority."

Clay's words grew sharper with passing time. "All hope of honorable accommodation is at an end," he told the House in April 1812. "Where is the motive for longer delay? The final step ought to be taken, and that step is war." Faint hearts feared for

America's safety. Yet courage dictated focusing not on what might befall America but on what had befallen it already. British policies systematically worked to America's mortal harm. "They violate the rights, and wound deeply the best interests, of the whole American people. If we yield to them, at this time, the cause may be considered as abandoned. There will be no rallying point hereafter." American patience had been pushed to the limit; the crisis allowed but one resolution. "It is by open and manly war only that we can get through it with honor and advantage to the country. Our wrongs have been great; our cause is just; and if we are decided and firm, success is inevitable. Let war therefore be forthwith proclaimed against England."

2

JOHN CALHOUN COULDN'T have agreed more. Calhoun was a scion of the clans of Scots-Irish who had settled the upcountry of the Carolinas in the eighteenth century. The immigrants, who included the parents of Andrew Jackson, were men and women hungry enough in Ulster to consider emigration, resourceful enough to make the journey across the ocean, and pugnacious enough to seize and hold plots of ground in a region still claimed by Indian tribes. The Scots-Irish were said to keep the Sabbath and anything else they laid hold of; in America this started with the land they made their own. Calhoun's father fought in the French and Indian War and then in the American Revolutionary War; after independence he won election to the South Carolina legislature. He opposed the Constitution of 1787 on grounds that it stole authority from South Carolina. He lost that argument but never changed his mind.

His son John was the fourth of five children. The boy was born six months after the Battle of Yorktown, and he was thirteen when his father died. The death appeared to foreclose a career as anything but a farmer tending the property on which his widowed mother lived. But John was an avid reader of whatever printed matter he could find, and he began to imagine the world beyond his fence and a life past the plow. A brother back from Charleston sang the praises of city life, spurring Calhoun's ambitions further. His mother recognized his drive and arranged the family finances to fund his education. He prepped in Georgia and entered Yale College at the age of twenty. He was older than his classmates, at least the ones from the North. Afterward remarking that Southern boys often entered college later than Northern boys, he contended that they benefited from the delay. The Southerners developed their character before they developed their intellect. "At the North you overvalue the intellect," he said. "At the South we rely upon character. And if ever there should be a collision that shall test the strength of the two sections, you will find that character is stronger than intellect, and will carry the day."

Yale was foreign in other respects to a Southerner of Jeffersonian sentiments. Calhoun endured an Independence Day oration by the brother of Yale's president, lamenting the decline of the republic under the Republicans. "We have now reached the consummation of democratic blockheadedness," Theodore Dwight declared. "We have a country governed by blockheads and knaves. The ties of marriage, with all its felicities, are severed and destroyed. Our wives and our daughters are thrown into the stews. Our children are cast into the world from the breast and forgotten. Filial piety is extinguished, and our surnames, the only mark of distinction among families, are abolished. Can the imagination paint any thing more dreadful this side of hell?"

Calhoun's displacement to Connecticut confirmed his attachment to South Carolina. To a cousin at home he described himself as "far removed from his native land." This friend had evinced envy of Calhoun's career as a student. Calhoun set him straight. "Your opinion of the pleasures of a collegiate life is too exalted," he wrote. "Day after day presents the same unvariegated scenes, a tiresome sameness. Books, books, books engross our whole time and attention. Call up to your mind a student, and trace him through one day of his existence. Let it be a winter's day. Begin when the morning bell, ere yet the sun has dispelled the darkness, summons him to the chapel. In vain the warm bed entices to indulgence and the piercing cold forbids to rise; rise he must. He riseth, and hastily having thrown on his clothes, half frozen, he repairs to chapel. He spends the day in

poring over long and abstruse mathematical dem-
onstrations. The sun now sinks below the western
horizon. All the world retires to rest, the student
alone excepted. To him rest is a stranger. When
now day has surrendered its dominions to night,
not contented with that time nature has allotted to man to labour, he trims his lamp and sits
down to study. He studies till the clock strikes
twelve. Pale and meager, with a shattered constitution, he retires to bed. His sleep is short and
interrupted. Again the bell rings, he rises again
and again goes the same round."

Yet books became Calhoun's friends, and intellectual arguments his passion. After graduation
from Yale he moved to Litchfield, Connecticut,
where America's first law school had been operating for two decades. He spent a year at Litchfield,
then repatriated to South Carolina, landing in
Abbeville, in the western part of the state.

He was preparing to take the bar examination
when the British assault on the **Chesapeake** sent
waves of patriotic outrage rolling across America.
An angry crowd gathered in Abbeville, and the
young man gave his first public speech. The neighbors were impressed enough to ask that he draft
a series of resolutions summarizing their grievances against Britain. The assignment called to
Calhoun's mind the work of Jefferson in drafting
the Declaration of Independence three decades
earlier, and he poured himself into it. "When on

our coasts, and almost in sight of our capital," he proclaimed on behalf of Abbeville, "our citizens, by her brutal violence, are murdered; a public armed vessel wholly disabled; the American Eagle struck and insulted; when unheard of indignities and outrage are offered to a humane, just, patriotic and powerful nation, every tongue should be raised to denounce the insult; every arm be stretched to avenge the injury; there should be one burst of national indignation." The resolutions followed: that Abbeville abhorred the assault on the **Chesapeake,** that anyone who didn't share Abbeville's abhorrence should be regarded as an enemy of the United States, that all who allowed partisanship to dilute their outrage were equally culpable, that men of military age should rally to the national colors.

The document was just what the patriotic citizens of Abbeville and its district desired, and at first opportunity they elected Calhoun to the South Carolina legislature. Two years later, still angry at the British and impressed by Calhoun, they nominated him for Congress.

BY THEN HE had fallen in love. Floride Colhoun was the daughter of John E. Colhoun, a cousin of Calhoun's father and a distinguished figure in South Carolina politics until his sudden death in 1802. Calhoun, a traditionalist in affairs of the heart, cultivated the mother before approaching the daughter. He was also waiting for the daughter to grow up. Floride was ten when her father died and Calhoun began writing to the widow. Topics ranged from family matters to politics. Gradually references to Floride crept into his letters. Mrs. Colhoun encouraged his suit, to his delight. "I know not how to express my gratitude for that almost maternal regard which you have always exercised towards me," he wrote. "Such is the warmth of affection which I feel towards you that I can scarcely refrain from addressing you by the endearing epithet of mother. I hope the time will not be long when I may with propriety use it."

Floride responded as Calhoun and her mother hoped, and in due course she and Calhoun were engaged. His anticipation knew no bounds. "I rejoice, my dearest Floride, that the period is fast approaching when it will be no longer necessary to address you through the cold medium of a letter," he wrote in September 1810, when she was eighteen. Floride and her mother were in Newport, Rhode Island, where they annually escaped the heat and disease of South Carolina's summer. "At furthest it cannot be much longer than a month before I shall behold the dearest object of my hopes and desires." He extolled the life they were about to commence together. "To be united in mutual virtuous love is the first and best bliss that God has permitted to our natures. My dearest one, may our love strengthen with each returning day, may it ripen and mellow with our years, and may it end in immortal joys."

Floride appreciated her fiancé's gushings, as befitted the bride-to-be. But she also had a practical side, one that took a close interest in her husband's career. Calhoun addressed this as well. "I am much involved in business at present," he explained. "Court commences in two weeks, and in a week the election for Congress will take place. My opponent is Gen. Elmore of Laurens, but it is thought that I will succeed by a large majority."

HE DID SUCCEED, and handsomely. He and Floride married. He left for Washington to make his wife and constituents proud.

Appointed by Henry Clay to the House committee on foreign relations, Calhoun picked up the thread he had started spinning in his Abbeville resolutions. His committee colleagues recognized his gift for argumentation, and as the mood of the House grew ever more anti-British, they assigned him the drafting of a statement summarizing the indictment against Britain.

Calhoun began by condemning Britain for waging "a desolating war upon our unprotected commerce." Yet British insults touched far more than commerce; they traduced American honor and independence. Would the United States defend itself against foreign aggression? Would the American government insist on the rights of its citizens? Or would it let Britain essentially recolonize the country? Congress must take a stand, Calhoun declared. "We have borne with injury until forbearance has ceased to be a virtue. The sovereignty and independence of these states, purchased and sanctified by the blood of our fathers, from whom we received them, not for ourselves only but as the inheritance of our posterity, are deliberately and systematically violated." The injury and violations must cease. "It is the sacred duty of Congress to call forth the patriotism and resources of the country." Calhoun urged his colleagues to gird the country for war. Ten thousand new army regulars should be enlisted, fifty thousand volunteers recruited, the state militias readied for action, the navy rounded into fighting trim, and American merchant vessels armed. By these means, and with God's aid, America would teach Britain a lesson it wouldn't forget.

HENRY CLAY, JOHN Calhoun and the other advocates of war were called "war hawks." The phrase had originated with Thomas Jefferson as a scornful label for the Federalists who wanted a fight with France in the 1790s. Yet when the Federalists employed it a decade later against Republicans who sought to battle Britain, Clay and the others didn't object, and war hawks they became.

The war hawks controlled Congress but not completely. Their opponents included a man who held the rare distinction of having bested Patrick Henry in rhetorical combat. John Randolph cut an oddly striking figure. A bookstore owner in Charleston, South Carolina, recalled encountering Randolph one morning in his shop. "A tall, gawky-looking, flaxen-haired stripling, apparently of the age of sixteen or eighteen, with complexion of a good parchment color, beardless chin, and as much assumed self-consequence as any two-footed animal I ever saw," the bookseller described Randolph, who acted as though he owned the store and perhaps the city. "I handed him from the shelves volume after volume, which he tumbled carelessly over and handed back again. At length he hit upon something that struck his fancy—my eye happened to be fixed upon his face at that moment—and never did I witness so sudden, so perfect a change of the human countenance. That which was before dull and heavy, in a moment became animated, and flashed with the brightest beams of intellect." Randolph had a companion that morning, a distinguished-looking, elderly fellow. Randolph slapped him on the shoulder and said, "Jack, look at this!" The bookseller concluded, "I was young then, but I never can forget the thought that rushed upon my mind at the moment, which was that he was the most impudent youth I ever saw."

John Randolph, of Roanoke, Virginia, was in fact twenty-three. His appearance consistently belied his years. Not long after his Charleston visit he was elected to Congress. He presented himself to the House clerk to claim his seat, and the clerk, wondering if the young man before him met the constitutional threshold of twenty-five, asked his age. Randolph disdained to answer, saying haughtily, "Go, sir, and ask my constituents. They sent me here."

Randolph's family was among Virginia's proudest.

He boasted descent from Pocahontas, and he and his brother split forty thousand acres and several hundred slaves upon their father's death. The land John Randolph always cherished. "Johnny, all this land belongs to you and your brother," his mother told him one day on a ride about the property. "It is your father's inheritance. When you get to be a man you must not sell your land: it is the first step to ruin for a boy to part with his father's home. Be sure to keep it as long as you live. Keep your land and your land will keep you."

But the land did **not** keep him. Tobacco exhausted the soil, with each year's crop yielding less than the year before. Virginia produced little in the way of consumer goods; in colonial times its planters depended on trade with England to support the lifestyle they desired. The annual trading ship from London brought clothing, furniture, books, wines and other items, and it carried away tobacco. But the tobacco dwindled while the purchases didn't, and debts rose. John Randolph inherited a London debt from his father, along with the land and slaves, and the yield from the land hardly allowed him to carry the debt, let alone extinguish it.

Others shared his condition. American independence freed some of the planters from their British debt burden, namely those who preferred dependence on merchants of New England and the North. Randolph couldn't abide Yankees, and he stubbornly insisted on maintaining his British ties. Yet both groups of planters struggled, and Virginia grew poor. Randolph had traveled enough to know that others lived better than Virginians. "I passed the night in Farrarville, in an apartment which, in England, would not have been thought fit for my servant," he wrote while touring the state. "Nor on the Continent did he ever occupy so mean a one. Wherever I stop it is the same: walls black and filthy; bed and furniture sordid; furniture scanty and mean, generally broken; no mirror; no fire-irons. In short, dirt and discomfort universally prevail." The educated classes couldn't be bothered to improve things. "Poverty stalking through the land, while we are engaged in political metaphysics, and, amidst our filth and vermin, like the Spaniards and Portuguese, look down with contempt on other nations, England and France especially."

The Randolph family slaves were a burden of a different sort. "I want not a single negro for any other purpose than his immediate emancipation," Randolph's brother declared. "I shudder when I think that such an insignificant animal as I am is invested with this monstrous, this horrid power." Randolph had a higher opinion of himself, but he shared his brother's horror of slavery. Like many other slaveholders of the day, including Thomas Jefferson and Henry Clay, he judged slavery corruptive of all it touched, demeaning slaveholders as well as slaves. He looked forward to the time when Virginia would be rid of the curse. He hoped his own day of deliverance would be sooner.

But two things barred its coming. The first was his debt. His plantation required the labor of its slaves to keep his creditors from foreclosing. Randolph lacked the wherewithal to free his slaves; they were collateral for his debt. His creditors would seize the slaves, and Randolph's plantation, before they would let the slaves go. The second problem was the general difficulty freed slaves encountered. Emancipation broke slave families apart, because slaves often married across plantation lines. And free blacks found themselves competing in the labor market with slaves, in which competition they couldn't win without reducing their living standard to that of the slaves.

RANDOLPH ENTERED POLITICS as an ally of Jefferson, who happened to be a kinsman, and as a foe of John Adams and the Federalists who then controlled Congress. Randolph's family name sufficed to win him nomination for the Roanoke seat in the House. The campaign proved a referendum on Federalist policies, including the Alien and Sedition Acts of 1798, which, amid the undeclared naval war with France, outlawed much dissent against the Adams administration. Patrick Henry gave a speech in Randolph's district in support of

Adams and the Federalists. Henry had grown old since immortalizing himself with the words "Give me liberty or give me death!" but his speech summoned the echoes of those early days, and when he finished he collapsed into the arms of friends "like the sun setting in his glory," one of them recounted.

Until this moment John Randolph had never spoken in public. No one knew if he had the talent; he himself hardly suspected it. But when he opened his mouth in reply to Henry, the words poured forth with ease and eloquence. He complimented Henry, affirming what Virginia owed him for his candor and long service, and then proceeded to eviscerate him. He declared the Alien and Sedition Acts an affront to the rights of Americans; more important, the noxious measures were an assault on the rights of Virginians. If Virginians allowed the laws to stand, they would surrender all that the blood of the Revolution had cost them. They would have swapped the tyranny of King George III for that of King John I. And Patrick Henry would have been complicit in the betrayal.

Randolph's reply to Henry caught a wave of Republican opposition to the Alien and Sedition Acts, which had triggered America's first constitutional crisis. Jefferson, at that time Adams's vice president, and James Madison, the author of the Bill of Rights, covertly drafted resolutions against the acts. These resolutions, or resolves, were adopted by the legislatures of Kentucky and Virginia respectively. In the late 1790s the Supreme Court had yet to assert the judiciary's right to assess the constitutionality of congressional statutes; in the silence of the court, the Kentucky and Virginia resolutions claimed that right for the states. They also claimed the states' right to nullify—prevent the enforcement of—laws the states judged invalid.

Jefferson rode the wave of opposition into the White House; Randolph and a majority of Republicans rode it into Congress. The Alien and Sedition Acts were allowed to expire, and the crisis ended, though not before giving other states ideas about how federal power might be resisted.

Randolph became Jefferson's lieutenant in the House, as chair of the ways and means committee. But though the views of the two men ran parallel, their temperaments and philosophies diverged. Jefferson was a democrat, an advocate of the ordinary people of America. Randolph was an elitist, a believer in government by the best. Jefferson favored small government, fearing that big government would trample the rights of the people. Randolph's complaint against big government was that it threatened the rights of Virginia.

The break occurred during Jefferson's second term. Some said the precipitant was Jefferson's selection of Madison over Randolph as his secretary of state and heir apparent. Randolph himself said—perhaps facetiously: with Randolph one could never be sure—that the cause was a victory he won over Jefferson in a game of chess. A more likely trigger was the growing belligerence of the Republicans toward Britain. Randolph, the tory at heart, preferred Britain over France in the struggle between those two countries. Randolph detested what the French Revolution had done to France and what its principles might do to America. The French Revolution had inspired the slaves of Haiti to rise up and massacre their masters; the slaves of America might do the same. Randolph disapproved of slavery as an institution, but he didn't want to be murdered in his bed. Britain's fight against France, he felt, was the fight of reason against unreason, of order against chaos.

This feeling inspired Randolph's response to Henry Clay and John Calhoun. Randolph resisted a Republican war against Britain in 1812 as ardently as Republicans had resisted the Federalist war against France in the 1790s. He castigated Clay and Calhoun as ambitious men eager to magnify slights into occasion for armed conflict. He accused them of deliberately downplaying the expense of a war; the American people would never agree to a war if they knew how much it was going to cost them. Randolph said there were such things as just, defensive wars; he could support a military response to the actual injuries the United States had suffered at British hands. But what the war hawks advocated, with their talk of taking Canada, was a war of naked aggression.

War power had ruined the Federalists, Randolph declared, and it would ruin the Republicans. "Soon or late, some mania seizes upon its possessors; they fall from the dizzy heights through the giddiness of their own heads." A recent massacre by Indians of settlers in the Northwest had angered Americans across the country. The war advocates blamed the British, for providing the weapons used by the Indians in the attack. If the allegation was true, Randolph said, it required a response. But he didn't believe the allegation, and the war hawks had produced no evidence. Randolph thought the tale a pretext for a seizure of Indian land, and for gouging by war profiteers. "No sooner was the report laid on the table than the vultures were flocking around their prey, the carcass of a great military establishment."

The war hawks predicted swift victory; Randolph forecast defeat. He noted that the United States had no answer to the British navy. While Western militia forces were invading Canada and taking Indian land, the Eastern seaboard, where most Americans lived, would be open to attack. "The coast is to be left defenseless whilst men of the interior are reveling in conquest and spoil." There were just wars, Randolph repeated, but the war the Republicans projected was nothing of the sort. And he wanted no part of it.

4

JOHN CALHOUN KNEW Randolph by reputation, and he had heard that Randolph was a dangerous man to cross. Once Randolph took a dislike to another lawmaker, he spared no effort to ridicule and embarrass him. Randolph was too much the elitist to move bills through the House, where successful legislating required a democratic touch. But he could obstruct, for he knew the intricacies of House procedure and could talk forever. No one liked him; many feared him. When Randolph rose to speak, other members stopped what they were doing. If they sensed he was looking their way, they froze and made themselves as inconspicuous as possible. None could match him for insult, and none wanted to try. If his baleful gaze and wicked tongue passed them by, they breathed again and went back to their reading or correspondence.

Calhoun was not deterred. Standing erect and proud, he rebutted Randolph point by point.

Randolph had branded Calhoun and his allies warmongers. Nothing could be further from the truth, Calhoun declared. "War, in this country, ought never to be resorted to but when it is clearly justifiable and necessary." And now it was both. Britain continued to kidnap American seamen and hijack American ships. "The evil still grows, and in each succeeding year swells in extent and pretension beyond the preceding." The question confronting the House reduced to a single point: "Which shall we do, abandon or defend our own commercial and maritime rights, and the personal liberties of our citizens employed in exercising them?" Honor dictated the latter. "War is the only means of redress."

Randolph had complained of the expense of a war and said the American people would not be willing to pay for it. "Why not?" rejoined Calhoun. "Is it a want of capacity? What, with one million tons of shipping, a trade of near $100,000,000, manufactures of $150,000,000, and agriculture of thrice that amount, shall we be told the country wants capacity to raise and support ten thousand or fifteen thousand additional regulars?" Plainly the country had the ability to pay. What about the willingness? "Is not the course a just and necessary one? Shall we, then, utter this libel on the nation?" Would Randolph put a price on American honor? Calhoun would not. "I am not versed in this calcu-lating policy. I cannot dare to measure, in shillings and pence, the misery, the stripes, and the slavery of our impressed seamen." Randolph had distinguished between a defensive war and an offensive war. Calhoun answered that in the present case this was splitting things too finely. "By his system, if you receive a blow on the breast, you dare not return it on the head; you are obliged to measure and return it on the precise point on which it was received. If you do not proceed with mathematical accuracy, it ceases to be self-defense; it becomes an unprovoked attack." Britain was already warring on America; the United States was free to defend itself however and wherever it chose. Only a fool would think otherwise.

CALHOUN WAS REPLYING to John Randolph, but he was also speaking to an audience beyond the House of Representatives. Foremost of his absent listeners was James Madison, who was leaning toward war but hadn't quite made the decision. The president initially asked Congress for funds to ready the United States for war, should matters come to that. Reiterating the war hawks' indictment of Britain, Madison told the lawmakers, "With this evidence of hostile inflexibility in trampling on rights which no independent nation can relinquish, Congress will feel the duty of putting the United States into an armor and an attitude demanded by the crisis." He urged the lawmakers to approve measures that would fill out the ranks of the regular army, mobilize the state militias, manufacture more weapons and build more warships. Madison added an item that would be hotly contested during the following decades: tariff protection for American manufactures. "We should not be left in unnecessary dependence on external supplies," the president said.

When the British insults continued, Madison went further. In June 1812 he announced that he had had enough of Britain and its arrogance. "The conduct of her government presents a series of acts hostile to the United States as an independent and neutral nation," he told Congress in a special message. Impressment continued, with the number of Americans stolen from their ships running into the thousands. American trade had been ruined. "Our commerce has been plundered in every sea." On the Western frontier, British officials encouraged the Indians to "a warfare which is known to spare neither age nor sex and to be distinguished by features peculiarly shocking to humanity." Diplomacy had failed. "Our moderation and conciliation have had no other effect than to encourage perseverance and to enlarge pretensions." Americans saw their rights and interests affronted daily. "We behold, in fine, on the side of Great Britain a state of war against the United States, and on the side of the United States a state of peace toward Great Britain."

In later decades an indictment like Madison's against Britain would have culminated in a presidential request for a war declaration. But no president had ever asked Congress for a war declaration, and Madison wasn't sure he should. As one of the framers of the Constitution, he took very seriously the prerogatives of the legislature on this subject. He made the case for war, then concluded simply that the issue was "a solemn question which the Constitution wisely confides to the legislative department of the Government."

JOHN CALHOUN KNEW exactly what to do with Madison's message. Calhoun, as head of the House foreign relations committee, took it upon himself to convert the president's statement into a resolution for war. "If long forbearance under injuries ought ever to be considered a virtue in any nation, it is one which peculiarly becomes the United States," Calhoun wrote. "No people ever had stronger motives to cherish peace; none have ever cherished it with greater sincerity and zeal." But forbearance had its limits. "The period has now arrived when the United States must support their character and station among the nations of the earth or submit to the most shameful degradation."

Calhoun cast his resolution as a second Declaration of Independence. "The United States must act as an independent nation, and assert their rights, and avenge their wrongs," he said. "The contest which is now forced on the United States is radically a contest for their sovereignty and independence." The American Revolution had won Americans their freedom from Britain; the contest at hand would confirm that freedom. "Your committee, believing that the free born sons of America are worthy to enjoy the liberty which their fathers purchased at the price of so much blood and treasure, and seeing in the measures adopted by Great Britain a course commenced and persisted in, which must lead to a loss of national character and independence, feel no hesitation in advising resistance by force, in which the Americans of the present day will prove to the enemy and to the world that we have not only inherited that liberty which our fathers gave us, but also the will and power to maintain it. . . . Your committee recommend an immediate appeal to arms."

5

DANIEL WEBSTER ARRIVED in Washington too late to stop the rush to war. He was busy building a law practice and hadn't time to bother about American honor and British perfidy. A son of the rocky soil of New England, a child of a home where money was always scarce, he had only just found the key to society's cash drawer and wouldn't deny himself. But when his own business intersected the nation's business—when his clients complained that the policies of the Republicans in Washington were ruining them—he found his way to politics.

He brought to his new calling a love for the written and spoken word. The written word had entranced him first. "I do not remember when or by whom I was taught to read, because I cannot and never could recollect a time when I could not read the Bible," Webster remarked in middle age. But he did recall something else. "I remember one occurrence that shews the value then attached to books. The close of the year had brought the next year's almanac. This was an acquisition. A page was devoted to each month, and on the top of each page were four lines of poetry—some moral, some sentimental, some ludicrous. The almanac came in the morning, and before night my brother and myself were masters of its content—at least of its poetry and its anecdotes. We went to bed upon it, but awaking long before the morning light, we had a difference of recollection about one word, in the third line of April's poetry. We could not settle it by argument, and there was no umpire. But the fact could be ascertained by inspection of the book. I arose, groped my way to the kitchen, lighted a candle, proceeded to a distant room in search of the almanac, found it, and brought it away. The disputed passage was examined. I believe I was found to be in the wrong, and blew out my candle and went to bed. But the consequences of my error had been well nigh serious. It was about two o'clock in the morning, and just as I was again going to sleep, I thought I saw signs of light in the room I had visited. I sprang out of bed, ran to the door, opened the room, and it was all on fire. I had let fall a spark or touched the light to some thing that had communicated fire to a parcel of cotton clothes; they had communicated it to the furniture and to the sides of the room, and the flames had already begun to shew themselves through the ceiling, in the chamber above.

A pretty earnest cry soon brought the household together. By great good luck, we escaped. Two or three minutes more and we should all have been in danger of burning."

The house was saved by the quick action of Webster's father, but the boy never forgot the incident. And when his own house burned in his adulthood, he wondered if fire had some strange affinity for him. He wondered, too, if fate had marked him for an early grave. He was the youngest of his father's five sons, by two wives, and one of ten children. Before he turned fifty, he was the only survivor among the siblings. Had he been specially spared? Or was the scythe of death slinging toward him unseen?

His father's farm was on the frontier of English settlement in the Americas. "When he had built his log cabin and lighted his fire," Webster wrote, "his smoke ascended nearer to the north star than that of any other of his Majesty's New England subjects. His nearest civilized neighbor on the north was at Montreal"—in French Canada.

Education was haphazard in rural New Hampshire. The teachers in the town schools knew the rudiments but often little more. Had Daniel been hardier, he might have left school at the same young age as his siblings, but his puny physique and chronic ailments augured a short life if spent farming or engaged in other manly work. His father set him on a different path. "On the 25th of May, 1796, he mounted his horse, put me on another, carried me to Exeter, and placed me in Phillips Academy." Daniel was fourteen. "I had never been from home before, and the change overpowered me. I hardly remained master of my own senses, among ninety boys who had seen so much more and appeared to know so much more than I did."

Yet he proved a good student, in all subjects but rhetoric. "I could not make a declamation. I could not speak before the school. The kind and excellent Buckminster"—his teacher—"sought especially to persuade me to perform the exercise of declamation, like other boys, but I could not do it. Many a piece did I commit to memory, and recite and rehearse, in my own room, over and over again; yet, when the day came, when the school collected to hear declamations, when my name was called and I saw all eyes turned to my seat, I could not raise myself from it. Sometimes the instructors frowned, sometimes they smiled. Mr. Buckminster always pressed and entreated most winningly that I would venture. But I could never command sufficient resolution. When the occasion was over, I went home and wept bitter tears of mortification."

The kind Buckminster passed him nonetheless, and Webster entered Dartmouth College. His speech paralysis eventually eased. "I delivered two or three occasional addresses, which were published," he recounted. "I trust they are forgotten. They were in very bad taste." But they whetted his appetite for what speaking could accomplish and pointed him toward the practice of law. On graduation he moved to Massachusetts to find an office in which to apprentice. A lawyer named Christopher Gore took him in. Gore allowed time to observe the attorneys at the Boston bar. Webster kept notes. "T. P. is now about 55 years old, of pretty large stature and rather inclining to corpulency," he recorded. "His manner is steady, forcible, and perfectly perspicuous. He does not address the jury as a mechanical body to be put in motion by mechanical means. He appeals to them as men, and as having minds capable of receiving the ideas in his own. Of course he never harangues; he knows by the juror's countenance when he is convinced, and therefore never disgusts him by arguing that of which he is already sensible or which he knows it is impossible to impress. He is not content with shining on occasions; he will shine every where. As no cause is too great, none is too small for him. He knows the great benefit of understanding small circumstances. It is not enough for him that he has learned the leading points in a cause; he will know every thing."

Webster imagined himself before the juries, shining bright and knowing everything. He dissected the logic and dramaturgy of two other lawyers: "P. begins with common maxims, and his course to the particular subject, and the particular conclusion, brightens and shines more and more clearly to its end. D. begins with the particular position which he intends to support. Darkness surrounds him. No one knows the path by which he arrived at his conclusion. Around him, however, is a circle of light when he opens his mouth. Like a conflagration seen at a distance, the evening mist may intervene between it and the eye of the observer, though the blaze ascend to the sky and cannot but be seen."

THE YOUNG MAN from the northern frontier hungered for success; he hungered for fame; he hungered for life. And he hungered for money, the sine qua non of the others. "The first and greatest circumstance in my case is poverty," he lamented to a Dartmouth friend. "The next a little spice of ambition for professional respectability, and the last, a strong wish to 'live while I live.'" With his brother Ezekiel he shared his emerging philosophy. "I never heard what particular substance Archimedes wished his desired fulcrum to be, resting on which he was going to move the world, but if his design had been to move every thing in it, he would have wished it **cash**. Cash, of all things of a perishable nature, is worth the most—it deserves the most toil. It ever did, does and ever will constitute the real, unavoidable aristocracy that exists and must exist in society." In another letter to Ezekiel he moaned, "Money is scarce as love."

His hunger for money tempted him from his chosen path. He had almost completed his legal studies when he received an offer of a clerkship in the court of common pleas in Hillsborough County, near the family home. The annual salary was fifteen hundred dollars. "This was equal to a presidential election," Webster recalled. "It seemed to me very great." His father had finagled to win his son the preference and was gratified that he had prevailed. "Its possession would make the family easy."

Webster couldn't wait to accept the offer. "I certainly considered it a great prize myself, and was ready to abandon my profession for it." Already the hunger in his soul was abating.

He went to receive the congratulations of his mentor, Christopher Gore. He got a cold slap instead. "Mr. Gore peremptorily shut me out from this opening paradise." Gore told Webster he was meant for greater things. A clerkship and its salary seemed grand to a young man who rarely had two nickels to rub together, but if he quit the law and took the clerk job, he would never rise higher. Besides, the clerkship was a political post that could be taken away as easily as it might be given. "Go on and finish your studies," Gore said. "You are poor enough, but there are greater evils than poverty. Live on no man's favor. What bread you do eat, let it be the bread of independence. Pursue your profession. Make yourself useful to your friends and a little formidable to your enemies, and you have nothing to fear."

Webster slunk away. He gradually reconciled himself to accepting Gore's advice. But he had to break the news to his father. "I knew it would strike him like a thunder bolt. He had long had this office in view for me; its income would make him, and make us all, easy and comfortable. His health was bad and growing worse. His sons were all gone from him. This office would bring me home and it would bring also comfort and competency to all the house."

Snow covered the roads of New Hampshire. Webster hitched a ride on a farmer's sleigh to the vicinity of the homestead. He made the final stretch on foot. "It was evening," he recalled. "My father was sitting before his fire and received me with manifest joy. He looked feebler than I had ever seen him, but his countenance lighted up on seeing his **Clerk** stand before him."

Webster had feared a loss of his nerve, and now a wave of panic swept over him. "I felt as if I could die, or fly," he said. "I could hardly breathe."

But he summoned his courage and described his thinking, as influenced by Gore. He recited his prospects as a lawyer and his hopes for greater earnings than a clerk could ever make. Meanwhile he monitored his father's reaction. "I proceeded in this strain till he exhibited signs of amazement, it having occurred to him, at length, that I might be serious."

The old man wanted a direct answer. "Do you intend to decline this office?"

Webster said he did. He had higher aims than a clerkship. "I mean to use my tongue in the courts, not my pen; to be an actor, not a register of other men's actions. I hope yet, sir, to astonish your honor, in your own court, by my professional attainments."

Webster would never find a judge or a jury harder to read than his father in that moment. "I thought he was angry. He rocked his chair slightly. A flash went over an eye softened by age but still black as jet."

The old man delivered his verdict, which wasn't so much a verdict as an observation and a warning. "Well, my son, your mother has always said that you would come to something, or nothing. She was not sure which. I think you are now about settling that doubt for her."

WEBSTER FINISHED HIS studies and in 1807 commenced a law practice in Portsmouth. The city lived on the seaborne trade that entered its harbor, but in the year of Jefferson's embargo it was dying from want of that trade. In the coastal cities of New England, the embargo reminded

the older residents of the British blockade of
Boston after the Boston Tea Party. Boston and its
hinterland had faced the specter of starvation and
had responded with the battles of Lexington
and Concord. New England amid the embargo
was in a similarly aggrieved and potentially revolutionary mood.

The suffering of Webster's clients became his own
suffering. They couldn't pay their bills to him, and
they stopped bringing him their business. In his
hurry to make money, he had taken fliers in local
banks and land schemes; his investments soured
and set his creditors on his trail. His desire to live
to the full had led him to Madeira's fine wines; his
wine merchant was among his dunners.

"I am so particularly pushed that I find it necessary to take some measures to raise cash," he wrote
to Ezekiel in 1810. Ezekiel was a lawyer too now and
an occasional business partner; Webster asked him
to discount a note and take out a new mortgage on
some property to facilitate cash flow. Ezekiel did
what he could, but the problem persisted. "After
counting up all my means, I find I shall come
up short unless I receive something from above,"
Webster told Ezekiel in 1811. And heaven hadn't
been helpful of late. "My debts are not paid; I am
undone. . . . If you have a dollar, you must send it.
Give me strength this time to slay the Philistines."

Ezekiel drew the line. He had his own debts,
and he realized that a dollar sent to Daniel would

be a dollar gone forever. The Philistines remained unvanquished.

So Webster lit into the Republicans. His political interests until this point had been modest, shaped but not fired by the Federalism of his father, Christopher Gore and most of his clients. But as Henry Clay, John Calhoun and the other war hawks in Washington carried America to war, Webster discovered in himself a new talent and passion. Beleaguered as Webster's neighbors and clients had felt under the embargo, they expected worse from a war. Any lingering British compunction about seizing American ships would vanish with the Republicans' war declaration, which passed Congress on June 18, 1812.

Webster had been invited to deliver a Fourth of July address at Brentwood in Rockingham County. Word of the war declaration arrived while he was preparing his remarks, and it rang like a death knell across the New England countryside. He sharpened his language and delivered a riposte that thrilled his listeners and prompted a group of antiwar Federalists to ask him to write a protest, or memorial, that they could dispatch to President Madison.

Webster made the case for New England. "We regard commerce as a great and essential interest," he said. "It is not only in itself a leading pursuit, but it is most intimately blended with all our other interests and occupations." New England wasn't

Virginia or Pennsylvania; its inhabitants couldn't live like the farming peoples of those states. "Habits arising naturally from our local situation and the nature of our soil and products, and now confirmed by the usage of two centuries, are not to be changed." Where other regions looked to the soil for sustenance, New England looked to the sea.

The Constitution charged the central government with defending the people and promoting their welfare. The people were the ones who determined whether the government was doing its duty. New Englanders would make that determination for New England. "We hold the right of judging for ourselves," Webster said. The present judgment was not favorable. "When we assented to the national Constitution, it was among other (but none more important) reasons to the end that our commerce might be better protected and the farther extended." The Republican policies of the last several years had had precisely the opposite effect.

Webster was edging onto dangerous ground in saying that the government at Washington had reneged on what New England had given its assent to. What New England had given, New England could take away. Yet he pushed further out. The embargo and now the war had not simply failed to protect New England's commerce; they had effectively destroyed it. This was not at all what the region had agreed to in ratifying the Constitution. "We originally saw nothing, and can now see nothing, either in the letter or the spirit of the national compact which makes it our duty to acquiesce in a system tending to compel us to abandon our natural and accustomed pursuits."

Webster was a lawyer, a professional accustomed to fine distinctions among words. He understood that in calling the Constitution a "compact," he gave precedence to the states that had ratified it, rather than the people identified in its preamble. The language of compact was the language of the Kentucky and Virginia resolutions of 1798, against the Alien and Sedition Acts. It was language that claimed the right of nullification. It was language that might lead beyond nullification to secession.

Webster dismissed the Republicans' assertion that impressment amounted to a casus belli. "The number of these cases has been extravagantly exaggerated," he said. Moreover, the problem was nothing new. "This evil of impressment, however great it may be, is at least not greater now than it was in the time of Washington. That great man did not, however, deem it an evil to be remedied by war." Webster added the observation that the loudest cries against impressment came from Western states that sent the fewest men to sea. Something was fishy here.

He returned to the matter of allegiance and issued a threat. "We are, sir, from principle and habit attached to the union of the states. But our attachment is to the substance and not to the form." The substance was everything. "If the time should ever arrive when this union shall be holden together by nothing but the authority of law, when its incorporating, vital principle shall become extinct, when its principal exercises shall consist in acts of power and authority, not of protection and beneficence, when it shall lose the strong bond which it hath hitherto had in the public affection, and when, consequently, we shall be one not in interest and mutual regard but in name and form only—we, sir, shall look on that hour as the closing scene of our country's prosperity."

In that hour might come a separation. New England would not leave the Union lightly, Webster said. "We shrink from the separation of the states, as an event fraught with incalculable evils." But the Republicans' persistence in misguided policies could bring the country to that. "If a separation of the states ever should take place, it will be on some occasion when one portion of the country undertakes to control, to regulate and to sacrifice the interest of another." Such an occasion was dangerously nigh. "The present course of measures will prove most prejudicial and ruinous to the country."

———

WEBSTER'S ROCKINGHAM MEMORIAL electrified New England and marked its author as an
audacious champion of the region's rights. The
voters of Webster's congressional district were
delighted to send him to Washington to do
battle on their behalf.

He made the journey south in the spring of
1813 with the cries of his constituents' pain in his
ears. **"Curse this Government!"** one man wrote.
"I would march at 6 days notice for Washington,
if I could get any body to go with me; and enough
I could if I had but a commission"—as a militia
officer. "I would swear upon the **altar** never to
return till Madison was buried under the ruins of
the capitol." Times were harder than they had ever
been, this struggling farmer said. "We are all here
in **misery;** the distress of this part of the country
is inconceivable, already starving and **starved.** A
woman and 2 children are already dead of the
famine as I am informed. Many are sick and fam-
ishing from want. God preserve us or we shall
all die."

The approach to the capital city showed little
sign of prosperity or importance. "It has not the
wealth nor the people which I expected," Webster
wrote to a friend. "From Baltimore to this place,
the whole distance, almost, you travel through
woods and in a worse road than you ever saw.
There are two or three plantations looking toler-

ably well; all the rest is a desert. It never entered into your imagination that roads could be so bad as I have found them this side of New York."

He took the measure of Washington and its denizens. "I went yesterday to make my bow to the president," he recorded soon after his arrival. "I did not like his looks, any better than I like his administration." Webster's colleagues in the House were full of bluster. "Speaker Clay made a vehement speech." The topic was unimportant, rendering the vehemence ridiculous. "Calhoun made a long speech"—on the same irrelevant subject. Webster noted several errors of fact in Calhoun's disquisition. He was pleased to observe that a solid Federalist had put the Republicans in their place. "Sheffey demolished all this nonsense, in a very sensible argument, and strewed the dust of the fabric over those who had raised it."

The Republicans had declared war promising quick success. Webster wasn't unhappy to observe that the war was proving them wrong. "Public business seems to be in a state of languishment," he wrote. "The president and the chairman of the Ways and Means, sick; Mr. Gallatin"—the treasury secretary—"gone; the heads of the departments that remain not supposed to be in the most perfect amity. The Senate very much inclined to have its own course; the House reluctantly engaging in taxes; the Commander in Chief resigned. At the same time, the enemy is in great force down the Bay, has possessed himself of Hampton and threatens Norfolk. Canada not quite conquered. No money in the treasury, and our expenses going on, at this moment, as is well ascertained, at the rate of 6 millions and a fraction per month!"

6

WEBSTER'S PRÉCIS OF the fighting scarcely scratched the surface of a war gone badly awry. The war hawks had predicted the easy conquest of Canada. "The militia of Kentucky are alone competent to place Montreal and Upper Canada at your feet," Henry Clay boasted to his fellow lawmakers. Clay couldn't have been more wrong. A largely militia force under William Hull invaded Canada with high expectations, but it was repulsed by British and Indian forces, whose counterattack so terrified Hull that he surrendered Detroit without a shot being fired. Hull went on to order the evacuation of Fort Dearborn, on the future site of Chicago. Amid the evacuation more than eighty Americans were massacred by pro-British Potawatomie Indians.

A second attempt at capturing Canada began with an attack across the Niagara River near the great falls. It ended as soon as it started, with the rout of the Americans at Queenston Heights. A third try, a thrust north from Lake Champlain, fizzled when militia troops refused to fight beyond America's borders.

Far from adding to American territory, the war soon found American forces fighting to keep from losing American ground. William Henry Harrison took over from Hull, who was court-martialed for cowardice, convicted and sentenced to death, only to be reprieved by Madison. Harrison rallied his troops and in 1813 moved against the British and their Shawnee allies, led by Tecumseh. He recaptured Detroit before crossing a short distance into Canada, where he defeated the Anglo-Indian allies and killed Tecumseh at the Battle of the Thames.

Harrison's victory eased the threat to the American Northwest, but it did nothing to secure the Atlantic seaboard. The British navy dominated America's small fleet, strangling American commerce and ferrying British troops to undefended points along the coast. The only thing that prevented a full-scale British invasion was London's continuing concern about the war against France. But that conflict ended in the spring of 1814 with the defeat of Napoleon. British ships and troops were transferred to the American theater and immediately began making their presence felt. In August the British squadron to which George Gleig was attached ascended the Chesapeake and landed the force that smashed the feckless defenders of Washington, rampaged about the city and burned the principal government buildings. Congress was not in session, sparing Clay, Calhoun and the other war hawks the ignominy of having to flee the enemy they had scorned. But Madison and his administration were forced to take refuge in Virginia. The only person who gained reputation that dark day was Dolley Madison, the president's wife, who rescued a revered portrait of George Washington before the White House was torched.

JOHN CALHOUN REALIZED he had some explaining to do. He didn't blame himself for having oversold the war. And he couldn't blame the soldiers without seeming unpatriotic. So he blamed the Federalists. "Party spirit is more violent than I ever knew," he told a friend. "In what it will terminate is impossible to conjecture." Calhoun decried the threat of secession from Daniel Webster and other spokesmen for New England. They were criminally hindering the war effort and giving aid and comfort to the enemy. Calhoun vowed to stay the course. "My resolve is taken. No menace, no threat of disunion shall shake me." Calhoun would become the high priest of sectionalism, but at this early date he identified with the nation. "I by no means despair of the destiny of our nation or government," he said. "National greatness and perfection are of slow growth, often checked, often to appearance destroyed." But the underlying strength remained. "The intelligence, the virtue and the tone of public sentiment are too great in this country to permit its freedom to be destroyed by either domestic or foreign foes."

Calhoun would construct a philosophy demanding respect for political minorities, but while he was in the majority, he demanded that the minority sit down and shut up. He distinguished between two species of opposition. "When it is simply the result of that diversity in the structure of our intellect which conducts to different conclusions on the same subject, and is confined within those bounds which love of country and political honesty prescribe, it is one of the most useful guardians of liberty," he told the House. But too often it took a different form. "Combined with faction and ambition, it bursts those limits within which it may usefully act, and becomes the first of evils." The latter variety, which Calhoun called "factious opposition," sought not the good of the country but the good of the opposition. "The fiercest and most ungovernable passions of our nature—ambition, pride, rivalry and hate— enter into its dangerous composition, made all the more so by its power of delusion, by which its projects against government are covered in most instances, even to the eyes of its victims, by the specious show of patriotism."

Calhoun regretted that factious opposition marked the Federalists' resistance to the administration's war measures. "What is it at this moment?" he asked rhetorically of the Federalists' strategy. "Withhold the laws; withhold the loans; withhold the men who are to fight our battles; or, in other words, to destroy public faith and deliver the country unarmed to the mercy of the enemy." The Federalists were engaged in nothing less than "moral treason," the form of disloyalty "which in all ages and countries ever proved the most deadly foe to freedom."

Calhoun called on every member of Congress to act with the Republican majority while the war lasted. Nothing less than the fate of the republic hung in the balance.

"It is the war of the Revolution revived," he said, repeating the battle cry of the war hawks. "We are again struggling for our liberty and independence." Americans must pull together as they had pulled together in 1776. "The enemy stands ready and eagerly watches to seize any opportunity which our feebleness or division may present to realize his gigantic schemes of conquest." America must show no weakness; Congress must act as one.

7

D ANIEL WEBSTER SHOOK his head, disbelieving that Calhoun and the Republicans could cling to the policies that had been shown so wanting by the course of the war. The administration appeared to have learned nothing from the country's humiliation. "It continues to go on in its old party path, to revolve around its party center and to draw all its heat and its light, its animation and its being, from party sources," he said. "The measure of ability with which the war has been conducted is about equal to the measure of prudence with which it was declared, and the success of the issue, without a change of auspices, will probably be proportionate to both." The burning of Washington made undeniable the administration's ineptness. "It invited the enemy to the conflict. It is attacked, two years after, in the center of the nation, on the very threshold of the Capitol, and even there is found unarmed and unprepared."

Webster predicted that the Republicans, having sown the wind, would reap the whirlwind. "We are here on the eve of great events," he told Ezekiel in November 1814. "I expect a blow up soon. My opinion is that within sixty days the government will cease to pay even secretaries, clerks and members of Congress. This I expect, and when it comes, we are wound up. Every thing is in confusion here." The administration was weighing a conscription bill, to bolster the army. The mere mention had raised hackles and fears, and the bill hadn't come before the full House. "If it does, it will cause a storm such as was never witnessed here," Webster said. "In short, if peace does not come this winter, the government will die in its own weakness."

The prospect grew worse. A British force of hardened veterans of the Napoleonic wars was being transported to New Orleans to commence a drive up the Mississippi. If successful, the campaign would split the United States in two along the great river and possibly dispossess America of upper Louisiana.

Or the fault might open where New England abutted New York. While the British invading force neared New Orleans, a group of New England Federalists gathered at Hartford, Connecticut. Bitter, alienated and convinced that the government that demanded their loyalty was failing to serve their interests, they reprised the mood of the Continental Congress in 1776. Webster and others, by their characterization of the Constitution as a revocable compact, furnished the philosophical basis for a New England declaration of independence; the misery described by Webster's constituents supplied the emotional impetus for a secessionist bolt. No agenda had been published for the Hartford convention, and even after the meetings began, no one outside knew what was happening within, for the sessions were closed and secret. But friends of the Union expected nothing good.

The government's war policy was caught in a vicious downward spiral. Popular enthusiasm for the war hadn't survived the early reverses; the burning of Washington depressed morale to levels that reminded old-timers of the winter of Valley Forge. The army dwindled as enlistments expired, and the government, unable to persuade lenders to put more of their money at risk, lacked funds to entice new recruits. The shrinking of the army caused morale to plummet further. The British would surely capture New Orleans and the Mississippi River. Lenders grew still leerier; recruitments fell the more.

In its extremity the administration did turn to a military draft. If young men wouldn't volunteer to defend the country, they could be compelled to do so. The administration sent a conscription bill to Congress. The Senate approved the measure, but with a conspicuous lack of enthusiasm. Even the Republicans in the upper house understood how unpopular conscription was.

In the House the bill ran into Daniel Webster. John Randolph had lost his seat in the 1812 elections, causing Clay and Calhoun to think that the opposition would be weakened. But Webster proved a more formidable antagonist than the Virginian. In the first place, Webster was a Federalist, with an opposition party behind him. In the second, he spoke for New England, the Federalist stronghold. In the third, he spoke with power, unlike Randolph, who could cut and thrust but rarely compel. When Webster rose, his colleagues listened not out of self-defense, as they did with Randolph, but for self-improvement. They might learn something. Their beliefs might be challenged, their emotions stirred. And they might witness a heavy blow landed against the Republican leadership.

Webster threw haymakers from the start of his speech against the conscription bill. "It is an attempt to exercise the power of forcing the free men of this country into the ranks of an army for the general purposes of war," he said. As such it was tyrannical and unconstitutional. Never had the national government attempted such a thing, for the good reason that it was beyond the bounds of the authority conferred on Congress by the Constitution. The Constitution gave Congress the power to raise armies but not to dragoon the unwilling. If a war was so unpopular that honest men refused to enlist—as the present war was—Congress could not make them do so. Webster offered an analogy. "Congress has the power to borrow money. How is it to exercise this power? Is it confined to voluntary loans?" By the reasoning behind the conscription bill, it was not. "Congress might resort to a **forced** loan. It might take the money of any man by force and give him in exchange exchequer notes or certificates of stock." This was absurd, as even the Republicans would admit. But it was no more absurd than their logic behind conscription. Indeed it was less absurd, for it dealt with inanimate money rather than actual lives. "A compulsory loan is not to be compared, in point of enormity, with a compulsory military service," Webster said.

Conscription orders would rend the heart of the country. "Who shall describe the distress and anguish which they will spread over those hills and valleys where men have heretofore been accustomed to labor and to rest in security and happiness?" The administration's bill proposed a lottery among the eligible. Webster asked the House to envision its operation. "Anticipate the scene, sir, when the class shall assemble to stand its draft, and to throw the dice for blood. What a group of wives and mothers and sisters, of helpless age and helpless infancy, shall gather round the theatre of this horrible lottery, as if the stroke of death were to fall from heaven before their eyes on a father, a brother, a son or a husband." And the stroke of death it would be, given the administration's incompetence. "Under present prospects of the continuance of the war, not one half of them on whom your conscription shall fall will ever return to tell the tale of their sufferings. They will perish of disease and pestilence, or they will leave their bones to whiten in fields beyond the frontier."

WEBSTER'S SPEECH BROUGHT the conscription bill to a clattering halt. Members imagined having to answer to those wives and mothers when they returned to their districts, having to defend this self-inflicted form of impressment when they sought reelection. Senators were shielded from popular wrath by their six-year terms of office and especially by the state legislatures, which in that era chose them. For Republican senators, party discipline counted more heavily than popular sentiments. Hence the bill's success in the Senate. But members of the House stood before voters every other year and directly. For them the unpopularity of a draft mattered more. Hence the bill's failure in the House when rank-and-file Republicans abandoned the party leadership.

Webster was pleased with his victory. He valued the respect in which he had come to be regarded by his allies and his opponents. He didn't deny that the Republicans' mishandling of the war created opportunities for Federalists like himself.

But as the new year began, reports from the West were so disturbing as to give even him pause. "We hear that the British are near New Orleans," he wrote to Ezekiel in early January 1815. "I have no doubt the British will take it." Webster couldn't tell what would become of the country. "The present state of things cannot last long," he said. "When or where or what the change will be, is known only to the all-seeing eye of heaven."

PART TWO

To Build a Nation

We are not legislating for this moment only, or for
the present generation, or for the present populated
limits of these states; but our acts must embrace
a wider scope, reaching northwestwardly to the
Pacific and more southwardly to the river Del Norte.
Imagine this extent of territory covered with sixty,
or seventy, or an hundred millions of people.

—HENRY CLAY, 1818

8

GEORGE GLEIG WAS a member of the British force that approached New Orleans. Full of themselves after the sack of Washington, Gleig and the British expected little trouble from the motley army Andrew Jackson, the American commander, had gathered in front of the city. "From the General down to the youngest drum-boy, a confident anticipation of success seemed to pervade all ranks," Gleig recounted. Intelligence added to the British confidence. Deserters from the American lines spoke of the fright and despondency that pervaded the city. "They assured us that there were not at present 5,000 soldiers in the state; that the principal inhabitants had long ago left the place; that such as remained were ready to join us as soon as we should appear among them; and that, therefore, we might lay our account with a speedy and bloodless conquest." The city would be a great prize. "The same persons likewise dilated upon the wealth and importance of the town, upon the large quantity of government stores there collected, and the rich booty which would reward its capture."

The Mississippi River below New Orleans was infamously treacherous, besides being fortified against shipborne assault. The British accordingly chose an oblique approach, via Lakes Borgne and Pontchartrain. The operation proceeded smoothly. "The place where we landed was as wild as it is possible to imagine," Gleig recorded. "Wherever we looked, nothing was to be seen except one huge marsh, covered with tall reeds; not a house, nor a vestige of human industry could be discovered; and even of trees there were but a few growing upon the banks of the creek. Yet it was such a spot as, above all others, favored our operations. No eye could watch us, or report our arrival to the American general."

The British edged closer to their objective, coming out on the Mississippi below New Orleans but above the last American fort. "Looking up towards the town, which we at this time faced, the marsh is upon your right, and the river upon your left," Gleig wrote. "Close to the latter runs the main road, following the course of the stream all the way to New Orleans. Between the road and the water is thrown up a lofty and strong embankment, resembling the dykes in Holland and meant to serve a similar purpose, by means of which the Mississippi is prevented from overflowing its banks and the entire flat is preserved from inundation. But the attention of the stranger is irresistibly drawn away from every other object to contemplate the magnificence of this noble river. Pouring along at the prodigious rate of four miles an hour, an immense body of water is spread out before you, measuring a full mile across and nearly a hundred fathoms in depth."

What Gleig and the British didn't realize was that Andrew Jackson now had the British precisely where he wanted them: pinned between the marsh and the river. They discovered their predicament soon enough. The British had made camp and were preparing to settle in for the night. "About half-past seven o'clock, the attention of several individuals was drawn to a large vessel, which seemed to be stealing up the river till she came opposite to our camp, when her anchor was dropped and her sails leisurely furled," Gleig recalled. "At first we were doubtful whether she might not be one of our own cruisers which had passed the fort unobserved and had arrived to render her assistance in our future operations. To satisfy this doubt, she was repeatedly hailed; but returning no answer, an alarm immediately spread through the bivouac, and all thought of sleep was laid aside. Several musket shots were now fired at her with the design of exacting a reply, of which no notice was taken; till at length having fastened all her sails and swung her broad-side towards us, we could distinctly hear some one cry out in a commanding voice, 'Give them this for the honour of America.' The words were instantly followed by the flashes of her guns, and a deadly shower of grape swept down numbers in the camp."

It occurred to the British that they had fallen into Jackson's trap. Between the marsh and the river, they could only go forward toward his well-defended lines or back whence they had come. The latter course was never considered. This was the army that had defeated Napoleon; it would not retreat before a frontier general who had fought enemies no more formidable than Indians. So forward the British went.

They learned that Americans held different ideas of warfare than Europeans did. The British closed upon the American lines until the pickets of the two sides were within sight of each other. The British awaited the main battle; the Americans did not. "While two European armies remain inactively facing each other, the out-posts of neither are molested, unless a direct attack upon the main body be intended," Gleig explained. "Nay, so far is this tacit good understanding carried that I have myself beheld French and English sentinels not more than twenty yards apart. But the Americans entertained no such chivalrous notions. An enemy was to them an enemy, whether alone or in the midst of five thousand companions, and they therefore counted the death of every individual as so much taken from the strength of the whole. In point of fact, they no doubt reasoned correctly, but to us at least it appeared an ungenerous return to barbarity. Whenever they could approach unperceived within proper distance of our watch fires, six or eight riflemen would fire amongst the party that sat round them, while one or two, stealing as close to each sentinel as a regard to their own safety would permit, acted the part of assassins rather than of soldiers and attempted to murder them in cold blood."

The British commander, Edward Pakenham, ordered his men to erect batteries. This they did with great skill and energy, working around the clock until thirty big guns were brought to bear against the American defenses. The job was finished on the last night of 1814. The next day dawned gloomy, but brightened as the morning wore on. Gleig and the British were surprised to see the Americans celebrating the New Year. "The different regiments were upon parade, and being dressed in holiday suits, presented a really fine appearance," Gleig wrote. "Mounted officers were riding backwards and forwards through the ranks, bands were playing, and colours floating in the air. In a word, all seemed jollity and gala."

Pakenham gave the order to fire. "Our batteries opened, and the face of affairs was instantly changed. The ranks were broken; the different corps dispersing, fled in all directions, while the utmost terror and disorder appeared to prevail. Instead of nicely dressed lines, nothing but confused crowds could now be observed; nor was it without much difficulty that order was finally restored."

When it was, American guns answered the British fire, and a tremendous artillery battle ensued, lasting the entire day. The British matched the Americans salvo for salvo until the late afternoon, when the invaders ran short of ammunition. Jackson's cannoneers, sensing the British weakness, redoubled their efforts, pounding the British with fire from guns mounted in front of them, guns on ships in the river, and guns on the river's far bank. The British were forced to abandon the batteries they had established with such effort and fall back to more defensible lines.

Pakenham realized time was working against him. More American troops were arriving in Jackson's camp each day; the British force was as large as it was going to get. Pakenham resolved on a bold stroke. He would divide his army, sending part across the river to capture the American batteries there; just as it succeeded, his main force would assault the American lines. Crossing the river required getting boats from Lake Pontchartrain to the Mississippi, which in turn required digging a canal between the two bodies of water. Once more the British bent their backs to hard labor; by January 6 they had succeeded well enough to start the transit of the boats from the lake to the river. By the following day the boats were ready to launch into the great stream.

That night the British parties assigned to cross the river set out. They intended to surprise the American artillery crews and capture the guns. They would send up a rocket signaling success and would turn the guns against Jackson's line. On the rocket signal, the main body of the British would charge the American front. The old confidence returned to Gleig and his fellows. "Our numbers amounted now to little short of eight thousand men, a force which, in almost any other quarter of America, would have been irresistible," Gleig said. Reports and rumors placed the American troops at perhaps three times that many, but the Americans were known to lack experience and presumed to lack discipline.

The British plan faltered even before the battle commenced. The boats encountered a current stronger than their helmsmen and rowers had ever experienced. The craft were swept downstream, leaving the soldiers miles to march once they landed. Pakenham awaited the signal that the American guns had been taken. The signal didn't come. He waited longer. Still no signal. Yet with his main army already in motion, he couldn't well call off the battle. And his pride as a British soldier wouldn't allow it. Daylight revealed the approach of the British to the Americans, who commenced a withering fire. The front ranks of the British troops suffered terribly. "They were mowed down by hundreds," Gleig wrote.

Pakenham gave the order to charge, hoping the units across the river would achieve their objective at any moment. The result was one of the most appalling disasters in British military history. The redcoats marched into the teeth of Jackson's guns. Row after row went down, yet the line pressed forward until it reached the American fortifications. Ladders had been assigned to the assault teams but had been abandoned under the duress of the deadly fire. "To scale the parapet without ladders was impossible," Gleig wrote. "Some few, indeed, by mounting upon another's shoulders, succeeded in entering the works, but these were instantly overpowered, most of them killed, and the rest taken; while as many as stood without were exposed to a sweeping fire, which cut them down by whole companies. It was in vain that the most obstinate courage was displayed. They fell by the hands of men whom they absolutely did not see; for the Americans, without so much as lifting their faces above the rampart, swung their firelocks by one arm over the wall and discharged them directly upon their heads. The whole of the guns, likewise, from the opposite bank"—the ones that were supposed to have been captured—"kept up a well directed and deadly cannonade upon their flank; and thus were they destroyed without an opportunity being given of displaying their valour."

Pakenham did what he could to rally his men. Galloping conspicuously to and fro, he shouted at the troops to follow him against the American lines. In the act, he was hit in the leg by an American musket ball, which killed his horse and threw him to the ground. He seized another horse and remounted, only to be hit by another ball, this time fatally. Two other British generals took up where Pakenham had left off; they were quickly wounded and had to be carried off the field. "All was now confusion and dismay," Gleig recorded. "Without leaders, ignorant of what was to be done, the troops first halted and then began to retire, till finally the retreat was changed into a flight, and they quitted the ground in the utmost disorder."

The battle ended with the British army broken and the Americans in complete command of the field. Yet it wasn't until the following day that the extent of Britain's debacle became apparent. The senior surviving British officer requested a truce so that the two sides could bury their dead. Jackson consented. George Gleig accompanied one of the British burial crews onto the battlefield. "Of all the sights I ever witnessed, that which met me there was beyond comparison the most shocking and the most humiliating," he wrote. "Within the small compass of a few hundred yards were gathered nearly a thousand bodies, all of them arrayed in British uniforms. Not a single American was among them; all were English."

9

THE AMERICAN VICTORY at New Orleans was so astonishing as to appear miraculous. Jackson's army killed, wounded or captured more than two thousand British soldiers while losing fewer than one hundred of its own. The British abandoned their design on New Orleans and the Mississippi Valley and sailed away in disgrace. Overnight Jackson became an American hero, the towering figure in an otherwise dismal war. Americans spoke of Jackson as the second George Washington, and New Orleans as the sequel to Yorktown. Before the battle the republican experiment had seemed on the brink of dissolution; after the battle it stood strong and glorious.

Henry Clay's fortunes turned a handspring on the news of the victory. Clay had grown as dispirited as anyone by the first two years of the war. He might have questioned his own judgment in bringing on the conflict, but instead he blamed the president. "Mr. Madison is wholly unfit for the storms of war," Clay wrote to a confidant. "Nature has cast him in too benevolent a mold. Admirably adapted to the tranquil scenes of peace, blending all the mild and amiable virtues, he is not fit for the rough and rude blasts which the conflicts of nations generate."

Yet Madison **was** the president, and the de facto leader of the Republican party. Clay had no choice but to make do. Consequently when, in early 1814, Madison asked him to join a peace commission to negotiate an end to the war, Clay couldn't say no. It was a shrewd appointment on the president's part. Clay had played a large role in getting the country into the war; now he would have to take responsibility for getting the country out of it. At this time nearly everyone in the United States thought the country would be lucky to escape the war with its territory intact and its honor no more than bruised. The heady hopes of Clay and the others that Canada would fall into America's grasp had proven delusional; Madison wanted to ensure that the chief delusionist signed the treaty that said it wasn't going to happen.

Clay had his own calculations. He couldn't plausibly turn down the assignment, and he supposed that it would confer gravitas on a young man eager to better himself in the political world. As speaker of the House, Clay was commonly accounted the second most powerful man in the American government. Having taken the measure of the man ahead of him—and having concluded that James Madison had nothing on Henry Clay—he let himself think he might become president in the fullness of time. The peace commission promised a path. A peace commissioner would gain diplomatic experience that would qualify him to become secretary of state, and secretaries of state had shown a habit of becoming president. Secretary Jefferson had become President Jefferson; Secretary Madison had become President Madison; Secretary James Monroe was being groomed to be President Monroe. Secretary Clay . . . ?

The peace commission, which included John Quincy Adams, recently American minister to Russia, and Albert Gallatin, secretary of the treasury, found little to do at first. The British, fresh from their defeat of Napoleon, were conspicuously uninterested in any terms the Americans could accept. "We were prepared, by the events which occurred in Europe, by the temper manifested in English pamphlets and prints, and by the well known arrogance of the British character, for the most extravagant propositions to be brought forward in our negotiations," Clay informed Monroe in a confidential letter. "Unhappily we have not been disappointed in this expectation." Britain's envoys refused even to discuss the issues that had prompted the war. "The prospect of peace has vanished," Clay said.

Peace was elusive even among the American commissioners. John Quincy Adams found fault in all men, and the better he knew them, the more fault he found. His acquaintance with Clay had been slight; as it improved, his opinion of Clay did not. James Gallatin was the teenage son of Albert Gallatin, who had brought the boy along to take notes and make copies. James also kept a diary. "Mr. Adams in a very bad temper," he wrote not long after the negotiations began. "Mr. Clay annoys him. Father pours oil on the troubled waters." The sniping continued. "Clay uses strong language to Adams, and Adams returns the compliment," James wrote. "Father looks calmly on with a twinkle in his eye." On another day: "Mr. Adams and Mr. Clay object to everything except what they suggest themselves. Father remains calm but firm and does all he can to keep peace."

To a degree surprising in a diplomat, Adams could be deficient in basic tact. "We had been three hours in conference with the British plenipotentiaries," Adams wrote to his wife. "And it had been perhaps the most unpleasant one that we have held with them. We had returned home, and were in session conversing together upon what had been passing in the conference, when Mr. Clay remarked that Mr. Goulburn"—of the British party—"was a man of much **irritation. Irritability,** said I, is the word, Mr. Clay: **irritability.** And then, fixing him with an earnest look, and a tone of voice between seriousness and jest, I added 'like somebody else that I know.'" Clay laughed off the gibe before returning it: "Aye, that we do; all know him, and none better than yourself."

Adams's chronic complaint was that Clay—and the other members of the commission—failed to take their assignment as seriously as he did. "I dined again at the table-d'hôte at one," Adams wrote in his diary. "The other gentlemen dined together, at four. They sit after dinner and drink bad wine and smoke cigars, which neither suits my habits nor my health, and absorbs time which I cannot spare. I find it impossible, even with the most rigorous economy of time, to do half the writing that I ought."

Eventually the British got down to business, and serious negotiations commenced. They lasted until December, when, on Christmas Eve, the two sides' commissioners put their names to the Treaty of Ghent, the essence of which was a return to the status quo ante bellum. Neither side gained or lost territory; neither side won or surrendered rights. The British didn't forswear seizing neutral ships; they didn't abandon the principle of impressment. But they no longer required either against the United States now that the war with France was over. The Americans didn't win Canada, but neither did they surrender land of their own.

"The terms of this instrument are undoubtedly not such as our country expected at the commencement of the war," Clay reported to Monroe the day after the signing. This was a striking understatement from one of those most responsible for raising the initial American expectations. "Judged of, however, by the actual condition of things, so far as it is known to us, they cannot be pronounced very unfavorable. We lose no territory, I think no honor."

ANDREW JACKSON DIDN'T get the word. No one west of the Atlantic did for several weeks after the Ghent signing. In the interim, Jackson rewrote the treaty, as it came to be interpreted by Americans. Nearly everyone in America had expected grim tidings from New Orleans; instead they received news of the tremendous victory. And then arrived the ship from Europe bearing the treaty. The sequence of events prompted many Americans to conclude—emotionally if not intellectually—that the triumph at New Orleans had forced the British to come to terms. Interpreted before New Orleans, the treaty had declared the war a draw; after New Orleans it made America the winner.

It made winners as well of Henry Clay and John Calhoun. The leaders of the war hawks, lately on the defensive, now basked in the glow of victory. They quietly forgot their promises of Canada falling easily into American hands and focused on their defense of American rights and honor. They had stood up for America, and been vindicated. What more could Americans ask of their leaders?

Clay benefited particularly from the turn of mood. He had braced himself, at the time of the signing of the treaty, for searching questions from disappointed constituents. Instead he came home to celebrations. Supporters in Washington, Philadelphia and Lexington held dinners and parades in his honor. Kentucky voters gave him back his seat in Congress, where he resumed his duties as House speaker. In the House he praised the war against the faint hearts who had called it into question. The war's declaration had been just, he said, and though the most optimistic expectations accompanying the war's start hadn't been borne out, this was due to circumstances that had changed during the war. "France was annihilated, blotted out of the map of Europe; the vast power wielded by Bonaparte existed no longer," Clay explained. Suddenly fighting alone against Britain, the United States had held the most powerful empire on earth to a draw. "Let any man look at the degraded condition of this country before the war—the scorn of the universe, the contempt of ourselves—and tell me if we have gained nothing by the war. What is our present situation? Respectability and character abroad, security and confidence at home." Clay was proud to own his part in this result. "I gave a vote for the declaration of war. I exerted all the little influence and talents I could command to make the war. The war was made. It is terminated. And I declare, with perfect sincerity, if it had been permitted to me to lift the veil of futurity and to have seen the precise series of events which has occurred, my vote would have been unchanged."

10

Y ET FOR ALL his talk of doing things the
same way again, Clay learned much from
the war. He had entered politics a traditional
Republican, enamored of the small-government,
states' rights philosophy of the party's founder,
Jefferson. But his Republicanism had included
a belligerent streak, which accounted for his
emergence as the leader of the war hawks. The
belligerent streak by itself tested the Republican
philosophy, for war is an exercise of government
power beyond almost any other, and the power
exercised is that of the central government, not
the states. The experience of this particular war
convinced Clay of the need for a broader view of
government power.

The revelation was most striking in the realm of
finance. Clay had been a boy when Congress first
debated and then approved a national bank, the
Bank of the United States. Brainchild of Alexander
Hamilton, the bank became an adjunct of the

federal treasury and the manager of federal funds, as well as the overseer of what at the time passed for monetary policy. Republicans decried the bank as unconstitutional and illustrative of the stranglehold the propertied classes would impose on the ordinary people of America if allowed. Corporate charters in those days typically expired after a set period; the bank's 1791 charter ran out in 1811. By then the Republicans controlled Congress and the presidency, and they surprised no one by refusing to renew the charter.

Then came the War of 1812, which changed many Republican minds, including Henry Clay's. The war created strains the treasury had never experienced, and those strains were transmitted to the state banks that held the treasury's accounts. In many cases the state banks buckled, throwing the system of revenues and expenditures into disarray. By war's end even Clay, who had staunchly opposed renewal of the national bank's charter, concluded that a new national bank was necessary.

The rethinking required justification, because it represented a complete reversal of his former stance. Clay acknowledged his change of mind, although he imputed it to altered conditions. "The Constitution, it is true, never changes; it is always the same," he told the House in 1816. "But the force of circumstances and the lights of experience may evolve to the fallible persons charged with its administration." In 1811, America had been at peace; the modest resources and powers of state banks had sufficed for the nation's fiscal needs. Within a year the country had gone to war, and suddenly the government found itself having to make unprecedented transfers from one region to another—from the East Coast, for example, where taxes were collected, to the Western frontier, where the army was deployed. Without a national bank, the funds had to be transferred from one state bank to another and another, with the chain of institutions being no stronger than its weakest link. As the weak links gave way, evil ripples racked the system as a whole. The war effort suffered badly. Soldiers weren't paid; suppliers were shortchanged; lenders ran away from the government. "The state of the currency was such that no thinking man could contemplate it without the most serious alarm," Clay said. "It threatened general distress, if it did not ultimately lead to convulsion and subversion of the government."

The nation had survived the war, but it might not survive another without reform of its finances, Clay said. Beyond this, he cited aspects of the constitutional argument for a national bank that had seemed uncompelling to him previously. In Clay's time the federal government issued only metal money: gold and silver coins, called specie. Paper currency was the responsibility of banks, which promised to redeem their notes in specie. But some banks' promises were more reliable than others, and the value of their notes differed accordingly. The promise of the Bank of the United States had been the most reliable of all; its notes had served as a national currency. Clay now judged the bank's reputation and notes necessary to the nation's general welfare. "The want of a general medium is every where felt. Exchange varies continually not only between different parts of the Union but between different parts of the same state, and even different parts of the same city." The fluctuations and uncertainty inhibited commerce and investment and weakened the Union. Reestablishing the national bank would have the opposite, beneficial effects.

CONGRESS WAS PERSUADED, and in 1816 it established the second Bank of the United States, with a new twenty-year charter. Clay then turned to a second item in what he was beginning to conceive as his nation-building agenda. Republicans had long looked skeptically on federal spending for internal improvements, as roads, bridges, canals and other aspects of transportation were collectively called. Their objections were both constitutional and fiscal. The constitutional complaint was that road building exceeded the federal charter; if people wanted public roads, they should look to the states. The fiscal complaint was that federal roads required federal taxes, which shouldn't be higher than absolutely necessary.

Most Republicans continued to oppose a federal role in internal improvements, but not Henry Clay. And he dissented from the orthodoxy on grounds that made the states' rights men especially queasy. "What was the object of the convention in framing the Constitution?" he asked the House rhetorically, referring to the Philadelphia meeting in 1787. "The leading object was **Union**." Clay cited a letter written by George Washington that accompanied the Constitution as it was sent to the states for ratification, in which Washington had proclaimed as the greatest of American interests "the consolidation of our Union, in which is involved our prosperity, felicity, safety, perhaps our national existence." Speaking in his own voice, Clay continued, "Union and peace were the great objects of the framers of this Constitution, and should be kept steadily in view in the interpretation of any clause of it. And where it is susceptible of various interpretations, that construction should be preferred which promotes the objects of the framers of the Constitution." Turning to his specific subject, Clay read from the Constitution itself: "Congress shall have power to establish post offices and post roads." That is, Congress could appropriate funds to build post roads, it could award contracts, it could purchase land for the roads, and so on. To this none could reasonably object, Clay said. Nor could a reasonable man object when, once the post roads had been built, they were opened to people and purposes other than mail carriers and the transport of mail.

Returning to his theme of Union, Clay observed that nothing promoted union like easy transport and communication. Already the states that traded with one another, whose inhabitants traveled from one to the other, felt an affinity not shared by those who didn't. The larger the realm of trade and travel, the broader the affinity. Moreover, said Clay, members of Congress must think not merely about the current generation and the country as it then existed but about future generations and the country as it would become. "We are not legislating for this moment only, or for the present generation, or for the present populated limits of these states; but our acts must embrace a wider scope, reaching northwestwardly to the Pacific and more southwardly to the river Del Norte"— the Rio Grande. "Imagine this extent of territory covered with sixty, or seventy, or an hundred millions of people." Clay hoped that the moral sentiments that bound Americans together now would persist. But one day they might weaken. Congress must plan for that moment. "The man who does not look forward to another state of things, when physical causes will have their influence, is unworthy of having a place here." Physical causes—the force of gravity on flowing streams, the discouragement of distance—would tear the nation apart unless the government moved to counteract it. Well-built roads, bridges and canals would counteract the rending forces. "Could then a better basis for the union, a stronger tie to connect the various parts of the country together, be conceived?"

Clay remarked that better roads would provide for the common defense by facilitating the transport of troops and provisions in the event of war. Nothing was more obviously authorized by the Constitution, whose preamble used that very phrase—"the common defense." Clay considered how certain campaigns of the recent war would have differed had American troops been able to move more swiftly from one threatened spot to another. Military intelligence, the knowledge of where an enemy was and where he might strike, would be more rapidly disseminated over better roads.

Clay reminded his fellow members, many of whom were lawyers, that they should interpret the Constitution not as lawyers but as public servants. "You are not to look at that instrument with the eye of an ingenious advocate, who is seeking to screen from merited punishment a convicted felon. You are to take into the view the great destinies of our country."

CLAY'S QUEST FOR internal improvements would be a continuing battle. Congress had funded the Cumberland Road, from the Potomac River to the Ohio, in the first decade of the nineteenth century; the road was extended in later installments. But other projects, including those in a measure Clay promoted in 1817, to be underwritten by profits from the new Bank of the United States, failed to overcome resistance from unreconstructed Republicans, from Easterners who refused to support projects that benefited the West primarily, and from stakeholders in businesses that benefited from existing transportation routes and modes.

The third front in Clay's nation-building campaign saw fighting that proved the most dangerous of all. The American Revolution had originated in disputes over taxes, including import duties, or tariffs. Tariffs were an attractive source of revenue for governments, for two reasons. They were essentially sales taxes and consequently could be avoided by those most stubbornly opposed, by the expedient of not purchasing the goods on which the tariff was levied. And they could be conveniently collected at a few ports of entry. But tariffs were complicated as well. They could be devised to maximize revenue, or they could be designed to discourage imports. In the latter case rates would be high, deterring importers; in the former they would be lower, encouraging imports while taking a small bite from each.

Henry Clay favored high rates. His goal was not revenue but deterrence, although he phrased it more positively, as protection of American producers, principally manufacturers, from foreign competition. He justified protection as a way to diversify and strengthen the American economy, as well as to reduce the entanglements that had spawned the recent war. America had historically been a supplier of raw materials to Britain and other countries, he told the House. This arrangement had suited America when its population was small and its talents few. But times had changed. The country had grown to nearly ten million inhabitants, and its talents had multiplied commensurately. "A new epoch has arisen, and it becomes us deliberately to contemplate our own actual condition, and the relations which are likely to exist between us and the other parts of the world." Evidence of the new order abounded. Cotton glutted the market, with American production outpacing European consumption. Tobacco had passed its peak, with prices falling similarly. So long as American producers depended on European consumers, the problem would get worse. The American economy must become more self-contained, more self-reliant. Instead of selling raw cotton to England to be made into cloth and clothing that England then sold back to America, American planters should sell their cotton to American textile makers, who would produce the finished goods to sell to American consumers.

Clay compared the national economy to a household. Isaac Shelby was a Revolutionary War hero, the first governor of Kentucky and a beloved figure in the state's history. Clay held him up as a model of economic self-reliance. Taking his listeners on a mental visit to Shelby's Lincoln County farm, Clay explained, "You will behold every member of his family clad with the produce of their own hands and usefully employed, the spinning wheel and the loom in motion by day-break. With what pleasure will his wife carry you into her neat dairy, lead you into her store-house and point to the table cloths, the sheets, the counterpanes which lie on this shelf for her daughter Sally, or that for Nancy, all prepared in advance, by her provident care, for the day of their respective marriages." Clay contrasted this thriving model with the sorry state of the farmer who produced solely for commerce, made nothing for himself or his family, and so relied on merchants and manufacturers. "You will find **him** perhaps in the tavern, or at the shop at the cross-roads. He is engaged with the rum-grog on the table, taking depositions to make out some case of usury or fraud. Or perhaps he is furnishing to his lawyer the materials to prepare a long bill of injunction in some intricate case. The sheriff is hovering about his farm to serve some new writ. On court days (he never misses attending them) you will find him eagerly collecting his witnesses to defend himself against the merchants' and doctors' bills. Go to his house, and after a short and giddy period, when his wife and daughters have flirted about the country in their calico and muslin frocks, what a scene of discomfort and distress is presented to you there."

Clay's metaphor got the better of him here; he wasn't contending that Americans should spin their thread and weave their cloth themselves individually. But they should spin and weave for themselves collectively, and not depend on British textile makers. Clay identified three inventors as having created the modern era of economics: Richard Arkwright, the father of the spinning frame; Eli Whitney, crafter of the cotton gin; and Robert Fulton, builder of the first successful steamboat. The second and third were Americans, and Clay thought this proportion indicative of America's industrial promise. But the promise had to be nurtured. The American government must protect young industries from predatory competition. The appropriate means was the tariff.

The most advanced economic thinking of the day took the opposite view. Adam Smith had won converts in Britain to free trade, and their views were echoed by American shippers and others interested in trade for trade's sake. When American industry matured, Clay said, free trade might be appropriate. But for now its chief result was to enrich British producers at the expense of American consumers. And at the cost of American self-reliance. "The truth is, and it is in vain to disguise it, that we are a sort of independent colonies of England—politically free, commercially slaves," Clay said. Advocates of free trade asserted that it made Americans better off by bringing them foreign goods produced more cheaply than Americans could produce those goods. This reasoning was facile and myopic, Clay rejoined. "If the governing consideration were cheapness, if national independence were to weigh nothing, if honor nothing, why not subsidize foreign powers to defend us? Why not hire Swiss or Hessian mercenaries to protect us?" Clay observed that the advocates of free trade didn't practice themselves what they preached to others. The British demanded the right to sell their manufactures in America while barring American grain from being sold in Britain. Nor was Britain alone. "All other countries but our own exclude by high duties, or absolute prohibitions, whatever they can respectively produce within themselves." The free traders were not realists but utopians. "They tell us of what has never existed, does not exist and perhaps never will exist."

The advocates of free trade argued that it would make the world more peaceful. Clay saw scant evidence of this effect. Just the opposite had occurred in the genesis of the late war. America's overseas trade had prompted the British to try to stifle it, compelling America's eventual belligerent response. Trade competition begot trade wars, which spawned wars of lead and powder. "Foreign commerce is the great source of foreign wars," Clay summarized. And once war broke out, a country that relied on trade would find that trade cut off, as had happened to the United States in the war against Britain. Dependence on foreign commerce was dangerous. Conversely, cultivation of **domestic** commerce would have positive effects. Southern producers of cotton currently looked to Liverpool for their markets. Let them look to Philadelphia and New York. Mutually beneficial ties would knit North to South.

The protected world of Clay's vision clashed against the unprotected world he actually witnessed. He recounted a visit to New England. "In passing along the highway, one frequently sees large and spacious buildings, with the glass broken out of the windows, the shutters hanging in ruinous disorder, without any appearance of activity, and enveloped in solitary gloom. Upon inquiring what they are, you are almost always informed that they were some cotton or other factory, which their proprietors could no longer keep in motion against the overwhelming pressure of foreign competition."

The pressure wouldn't ease, Clay said, nor the American economy fulfill its natural promise, until the government took steps to protect American industry.

11

CLAY WOULD CODIFY his program of a national bank, internal improvements and a protective tariff as the "American system." The intended implication was that those who opposed it opposed American interests. This claim elicited reactions that ranged from assent to ridicule to threats of violence. The program enjoyed early support from John Calhoun, but within a decade Calhoun would become its mortal enemy. Daniel Webster, who had been the foe of Clay and Calhoun on the war, would become Clay's ally against Calhoun. Clay's program would split the Republican party, creating a new party and giving the old party a new name.

Daniel Webster sided with Clay for philosophical reasons, but also because Webster needed a new political home. As great a political boon as the victory at New Orleans had been for Clay, it had been a disaster for Webster. His criticism of the war had seemed prescient while the war went badly, and his denunciation of Madison and the war hawks had been within the bounds of acceptable politics. But the war's glorious end cast a retrospective shadow over Webster's opposition, implicating his judgment, certainly, and perhaps his patriotism.

Making matters worse—much worse—was the seditious air that hung over the Hartford convention. When the participants finally went public, they proposed nothing more provocative than some amendments to the Constitution, which, given the constitutional requirement of approval by three-quarters of the states, stood no chance of adoption. But the reports of secessionist mutterings among the more extreme Federalists persisted and, amid the celebrations following the victory at New Orleans, sounded treasonous. The Federalists had been on hard times since John Adams's loss to Thomas Jefferson in 1800; the jarring juxtaposition of Hartford defeatism and the New Orleans triumph guaranteed their oblivion.

Webster had to find a new party, perhaps a new career. He resumed his law practice, but in a different locale. "I have settled my purpose to remove from New Hampshire in the course of the summer," he wrote to his brother in the spring of 1816. "I have thought of Boston, New York and Albany. On the whole I shall probably go to Boston, although I am not without some inducements to go into the state of New York. Our New England prosperity and importance are passing away. This is fact. The events of the times, the policy of England, the consequences of our war, and the Ghent Treaty have bereft us of our commerce, the great source of our wealth." He did go to Boston, which, if it wasn't the hub it had been, remained the capital of New England. Boston would forgive his Federalism and his flirtation with disunion, even if the rest of the country might not.

NOR DID IT hurt Webster's law prospects that the last of the great Federalists presided over the highest law court in the land. John Marshall's Federalism gave Alexander Hamilton an afterlife, and it did so in ways that vexed and infuriated Hamilton's great rival Jefferson, and Jefferson's followers. In the process it strengthened the nation—as distinct from the separate states—in ways neither Hamilton nor Jefferson could have envisioned.

Marshall landed his first blow against Jefferson in 1803, in the case of **Marbury v. Madison**. William Marbury had been appointed a justice of the peace for the District of Columbia in the waning days of the Adams administration, but he hadn't received his commission by the time Jefferson took office. Jefferson saw no reason to deliver the commission, and consequently withheld it. Marbury sued James

Madison, the secretary of state and thereby the official responsible for delivering commissions, and the case reached the Supreme Court. Marshall and the court ruled against Marbury, pleasing Jefferson, but they did so on ground that outraged the president and most Republicans. Marshall held that the statute under which Marbury had been appointed was unconstitutional and thus void. The Supreme Court had never declared a federal statute unconstitutional; the very idea flabbergasted lawyers, elected officials and the public alike. Interested parties scoured the Constitution to find the basis of Marshall's reasoning and came up short. Precedent from the prehistory of the Constitution—the British common law—pointed in just the opposite direction.

Marshall's genius in the case lay not in the reasoning, dubious as it was, but in the execution. He asserted an abstract principle while forestalling those in power from doing any more than objecting abstractly. If he had ordered Madison to deliver Marbury's commission, Madison, with Jefferson's support, would simply have refused. Marshall and the court would have been weakened, Jefferson and the executive branch strengthened. Instead Marshall gave Jefferson the immediate victory while claiming authority that would be exercised over the long term. In fact, the Supreme Court never again during Marshall's lifetime negated a federal law. Not until the 1850s would Marshall's precedent be reprised. But by then it would have acquired the legitimacy that comes from half a century's standing.

Another case vexed Jefferson more personally. Following the president's conversion to the belief that Aaron Burr was a scoundrel and a traitor, Burr was arrested and brought to trial for treason. The judge in the trial was none other than John Marshall, in his capacity as a circuit judge. In those days the Supreme Court didn't attract enough business to employ the justices full time; when the high court was idle, they heard cases in various circuit courts. Burr's alleged crime took place in the jurisdiction of the Richmond court of Marshall. Jefferson made the Burr case a test of executive authority; he threw the whole weight of his administration against Burr. Burr defended himself with an artfulness that turned Jefferson blue in the face, but he might still have been convicted had Marshall not put his thumb on the scale of justice. Burr didn't bother trying to prove his innocence; instead he argued that the prosecution had failed to meet the constitutional standard for a treason conviction: namely the testimony of two eyewitnesses to the same treasonous act, defined as levying war on the United States or giving aid and comfort to America's enemies during time of war, or a confession. Burr certainly didn't confess, and the prosecution couldn't supply the required witnesses. Marshall might have let the case go to the jury, but instead he directed an acquittal, on account of the lack of the constitutionally required evidence. Burr got off, to Jefferson's chagrin, and prosecutions for treason became all but unheard of in American law.

MARSHALL OUTLASTED JEFFERSON'S presidency. He was still directing the court when Daniel Webster argued a case before it in 1818. The case involved Dartmouth College, which had received its charter from King George III before American independence and had operated for decades as a private institution. After a dispute arose among the administrators of the college, the New Hampshire legislature stepped in and asserted authority to amend the charter. The college sued, and the plaintiffs enlisted Webster, an alumnus as well as a lawyer with a rising reputation. Eventually the case reached the Supreme Court.

Chauncey Goodrich was a professor at Yale College and a skeptic on Webster. "I was told that in arguing the case at Exeter, New Hampshire, he had left the whole court-room in tears at the conclusion of his speech," Goodrich recalled. "This, I confess, struck me unpleasantly—any attempt at pathos on a purely legal question like this seemed hardly in good taste." Nor would it have any effect on the final outcome. "Whatever may have seemed appropriate in defending the college

at home, and on her own ground," Goodrich told himself, "there will be no appeal to the feelings of Judge Marshall and his associates at Washington."

Goodrich traveled to Washington to see Webster foiled. "The Supreme Court of the United States held its session, that winter, in a mean apartment of moderate size—the capitol not having been rebuilt after its destruction in 1814," he recounted. "The audience, when the case came on, was, therefore, small, consisting chiefly of legal men, the elite of the profession throughout the country."

Webster commenced his argument. Goodrich was surprised that he spoke calmly and evenly, scarcely raising his voice. He spoke, as well, without effort, rarely glancing at notes. And he spoke at length, for four hours.

He had the entire attention of his audience, including the justices of the court. "I observed that Judge Story, at the opening of the case, had prepared himself, pen in hand, as if to take copious minutes," Goodrich recalled. "Hour after hour I saw him fixed in the same attitude, but, so far as I could perceive, with not a note on his paper. The argument closed, and **I could not discover that he had taken a single note**. Others around me remarked the same thing, and it was among the **on dits** of Washington that a friend spoke to him of the fact with surprise, when the judge remarked, 'Every thing was so clear, and so easy to remember, that not a note seemed necessary.'"

Webster concluded, apparently, and stood silent. The courtroom was silent too, for a long moment.

Then Webster turned to face John Marshall squarely. "This, sir, is my case. It is the case not merely of that humble institution; it is the case of every college in our land. It is more. It is the case of every eleemosynary institution throughout our country—of all those great charities founded by the piety of our ancestors to alleviate human misery and scatter blessings along the pathway of life. It is more! It is, in some sense, the case of every man among us who has property of which he may be stripped, for the question is simply this: Shall our state legislatures be allowed to take that which is not their own, to turn it from its original use and apply it to such ends or purposes as they in their discretion shall see fit?"

He paused again. "Sir, you may destroy this little institution. It is weak. It is in your hands. I know it is one of the lesser lights in the literary horizon of our country. You may put it out. But if you do so, you must carry through your work! You must extinguish, one after another, all those greater lights of science which, for more than a century, have thrown their radiance over our land!"

He paused a last time. "It is, sir, as I have said, a small college. And yet there are those who love it."

Finally Webster's feelings came to the surface. "His lips quivered," Chauncey Goodrich observed. "His firm cheeks trembled with emotion;

his eyes were filled with tears; his voice choked, and he seemed struggling to the utmost simply to gain that mastery over himself which might save him from an unmanly burst of feeling."

The court was swept away. Goodrich recorded the tableau: "Chief Justice Marshall, with his tall and gaunt figure bent over, as if to catch the slightest whisper, the deep furrows of his cheek expanded with emotion, and his eyes suffused with tears; Mr. Justice Washington at his side, with his small and emaciated frame and countenance more like marble than I ever saw on any other human being, leaning forward with an eager, troubled look; and the remainder of the court, at the two extremities, pressing, as it were, toward a single point, while the audience below were wrapping themselves round in closer folds beneath the bench, to catch each look and every movement of the speaker's face."

Gradually Webster recovered himself. He had a few final words for the chief justice. "Sir, I know not how others may feel"—here he glanced at the opposition—"but for myself, when I see my alma mater surrounded, like Caesar in the senate house, by those who are reiterating stab after stab, I would not, for this right hand, have her turn to me and say, **Et tu quoque mi fili! And thou too, my son!**"

THE COURT RULED in Webster's favor, accepting his argument that a contract was inviolate under the Constitution. It ruled in his favor in other cases he argued as well. **McCulloch v. Maryland** involved the constitutionality of the 1816 charter of the new Bank of the United States, and of the right of states to tax or otherwise regulate the bank. Webster was enlisted by the bank to defend the charter and refute a claim by Maryland of authority to tax the bank. He essayed the former by construing broadly the meaning and purpose of the Constitution. That document granted Congress certain powers explicitly, but others implicitly. "The grant of powers itself necessarily implies the grant of all usual and suitable means for the execution of the powers granted," Webster told the court. "Congress may declare war; it may consequently carry on war, by armies and navies and other suitable means and methods of warfare." The counsel for Maryland had noted that nowhere did the Constitution mention a bank. Nor was there evidence that the framers even thought of a bank. Webster conceded the point, but drew an opposite conclusion. "It is not enough to say that it does not appear that a bank was in the contemplation of the framers of the constitution. It was not their intention, in these cases, to enumerate particulars." The Constitution was a sketch, an outline, not a detailed rendering. "The true view of the subject is that if it be a fit instrument to an authorized purpose, it may be used, not being specially prohibited."

This was a broad, bold claim, directly affronting the understanding of many of those who voted to ratify the Constitution only after being assured that its power was limited to what was written in the text. Webster went further in creatively construing some of what **was** written in the text. Interpretations of the Constitution often hung on how the phrase "necessary and proper" was parsed in the clause granting Congress the authority to "make all laws which shall be necessary and proper" for executing the enumerated powers. Strict constructionists emphasized "necessary," while broad constructionists stressed "proper." Webster sided with the latter by waving away the former. "These words, 'necessary and proper,' in such an instrument, are probably to be considered synonymous," he said. "Necessary powers must here intend such powers as are suitable and fitted to the subject; such as are best and most useful in relation to the end proposed. If this not be so, and if Congress could use no means but such as were absolutely indispensable to the existence of a granted power, the government would hardly exist; at least, it would be wholly inadequate to the purposes of its formation." He applied his logic to the bank in question. "A bank is a proper and suitable instrument to assist in the operations of the government, in the collection and disbursement of the revenue, in the occasional anticipations of taxes and imposts, and in the regulation of the actual currency, as being part of the trade and exchange between the states."

He proceeded to the question of whether a state could tax the bank. By no means, he declared. "If the states may tax the bank, to what extent shall they tax it, and where shall they stop? An unlimited power to tax involves, necessarily, a power to destroy, because there is a limit beyond which no institution and no property can bear taxation. A question of constitutional power can hardly be made to depend on a question of more or less. If the states may tax, they have no limit but their discretion; and the bank, therefore, must depend on the discretion of the state governments for its existence. This consequence is inevitable."

The crux of the issue was the matter of sovereignty. "The bank cannot exist, nor can any bank established by Congress exist, if this right to tax it exists in the state governments. One or the other must be surrendered; and a surrender on the part of the government of the United States would be a giving up of those fundamental and essential powers without which the government cannot be maintained." The whole purpose of the Constitution was to create a government above and beyond the state governments. The current case gave the court an opportunity to affirm what the framers intended. "Nothing can be plainer than that, if the law of Congress establishing the bank be a constitutional act, it must have its full and complete effects. Its operation cannot be either defeated or impeded by acts of state legislation. To hold otherwise would be to declare that Congress can only exercise its constitutional powers subject to the controlling discretion, and under the sufferance, of the state governments." This was patently not the intention of the founders. Maryland must give way.

THE COURT ACCEPTED Webster's argument. It upheld the federal law chartering the bank and effectively adopted Webster's synonymizing of "necessary" and "proper." And it struck down the Maryland law taxing the bank. On this point John Marshall paid Webster the high compliment of stealing his language. "The power to tax involves the power to destroy," Marshall wrote for the court.

Webster and Marshall collaborated on other expansions of federal authority, most notably in the case of **Gibbons v. Ogden**. Webster defended steamboat operator Thomas Gibbons against a New York law inhibiting his operations. Webster argued that the clause of the Constitution granting Congress the authority to regulate commerce among the states was exclusive, precluding state regulations. Marshall agreed, and another precedent for the growth of federal power was established.

Alexander Hamilton, the founder of the Federalist party, was long dead, and the party itself had disbanded, but the nation-building spirit of Federalism lived in the work of Webster and Marshall. The arrangement suited Marshall, who held his federal judgeship for life, but it left Webster, who hankered to return to political office, at loose ends. The dying gasp of the Federalists had come in the election of 1816, in which James Monroe defeated Rufus King of New York by the electoral margin of 183 to 34. King's drubbing demoralized the remnants of his party; never again would the Federalists mount a national campaign.

Monroe proposed a victory tour of the country. Webster suggested including New England on the itinerary. Virginia Republicans had rarely been seen in New England, and Webster thought a presidential visit would reassure a region recently alienated from the rest of the country. It would also help rehabilitate Webster, an architect of that alienation. The tour was a triumph. A Boston paper christened the dawning age the "era of good feelings" for its presumptive lack of party strife.

THE LABEL STUCK but the good feelings didn't. They dissipated under a strain that would characterize American politics for the next forty years. The admission of states beyond the original thirteen, from Vermont in 1791 to Alabama in 1819, had occurred without particular challenge or rancor. The Northwest Ordinance of 1787 established the Ohio River as the boundary between slavery and freedom, and the admission of states had proceeded accordingly. But Missouri lay outside the realm of the Ohio River boundary, being west of the Mississippi River. It would be the first state created from the Louisiana Purchase aside from Louisiana, which had been uncontroversially admitted as a slave state on account of its deep Southern location and the many slaves left there from French and Spanish times.

Missouri's geography was perceptually ambiguous. To Northerners, Missouri appeared a natural extension of the North. It was immediately across the Mississippi from Illinois, a free state. To Southerners, it seemed Southern. It lay almost entirely below the latitude of the Mason-Dixon Line and hence no farther north than Virginia.

Slavery existed in Missouri Territory. No law had prevented slaveholders from taking their slaves there, and planters found the bottomlands on the Mississippi's west bank conducive to cotton culture. As elsewhere, the presence of slavery discouraged settlement by non-slaveholding farmers, who had difficulty competing on production costs. Slaveholders dominated the politics of the territory, and they hoped Missouri would become a slave state.

James Tallmadge of New York had other ideas. When a bill that would enable the inhabitants of Missouri to write a state constitution came before the House of Representatives in 1819, Tallmadge proposed an amendment directing that new slaves not be allowed into Missouri and that slave children there become free at the age of twenty-five. Missouri could enter the Union as a slave state, but its slavery would gradually disappear.

The Tallmadge amendment passed the House, where Northern representatives outnumbered Southern representatives, but it stalled in the Senate, where the two regions were evenly balanced. The opponents of the amendment argued not only that it would harm the South and threaten the future of slavery but also that it was unconstitutional.

The Constitution gave no power to Congress to restrict slavery in the states, which was a matter for the states themselves to settle, each for itself. The supporters of the amendment rejoined that Missouri was not yet a state and that Congress **did** have authority over federal territories.

The disagreement—between the House and the Senate, between North and South, between the opposing views of congressional authority—prevented admission of Missouri in 1819. But the population of the territory continued to grow, the demands of its residents for a state government became more insistent, and the Missouri issue festered in the national mind. The era of good feelings proclaimed just two years earlier threatened to degenerate into a season of very bad feelings. If anything, the Federalist demise that had allowed the pronouncement of such an era made the animosity more intense, for in the absence of party divisions the split over Missouri became explicitly sectional. Northerners newly resented the Constitution's three-fifths compromise, which counted 60 percent of slaves toward representation in the House of Representatives and implicitly in the electoral college, though none of the slaves voted. Southerners, who had nevertheless lost their majority in the House, accused the North of wanting to destroy the institution on which their economy was based, and of perverting the Constitution to do so. Angry talk of secession, lately heard in New England, rattled around the South.

The question returned to Congress with the opening of the 1820 session. "The Missouri subject monopolizes all our conversation, all our thoughts and for three weeks at least to come will all our time," Henry Clay wrote to a friend that January. "No body seems to think or care about any thing else." To another correspondent he declared, "It is a most unhappy question, awakening sectional feelings and exasperating them to the highest degree. The words **civil war** and **disunion** are uttered almost without emotion, and a senator of the United States, in his place, as I understand, said the other day that he would rather have both than fail in the resolution." To yet another acquaintance Clay explained his view of the Tallmadge amendment: "I think the Constitution perfectly clear against the proposed restriction." But he acknowledged that others differed, and their views would have to be taken into account. He thought they **could** be taken into account. "I incline to believe that it will yet be arranged by a compromise. At all events you know I never despair of the Republic."

The compromise Clay had in mind involved Maine, which fortuitously was seeking to separate from Massachusetts. If the admission of Maine, a free state, could be linked to the admission of slave state Missouri, then both North and South could claim partial victory. Neither would be happy, but neither would be so **un**happy as to attempt mortal harm against the Union. A statesman, at this fraught juncture, could ask for no more.

Crafting the compromise would not be easy. Tempers were high, principles passionately held. As a first step Clay tried to soften support in the House for Tallmadge-like restrictions on slavery in Missouri. He guessed that the South would adamantly resist restrictions on the freedom of states to chart their own course on slavery. Allow that Congress could tell Missouri what to do about slavery, and Congress would soon be telling Virginia and South Carolina what to do.

In early February, Clay took on the subject of restriction. Reporting of speeches in Congress was haphazard during this period, and his remarks were not transcribed. Neither did he write them out for publication, as members often did when they wanted their speeches preserved for posterity. In this case the lack of a paper trail suited Clay, who, recognizing the sensitivity of the subject, was willing for his words to waft away after his listeners heard them. Yet some of those present considered his speech on the Missouri question one of the greatest he ever uttered. "Everyone felt the electricity of his mind," a newsman present recalled. "His elocution was so rapid, his argumentation so restless, and his manner so vehement and impetuous, that I believe none were unmoved, and but few retired unconvinced."

This reporter was too generous. Clay contended that the proposed restriction was not simply unconstitutional but imprudent. Clinging, at least in public, to the notion that slaveholders would eventually agree with him that slavery injured them as well as their slaves, he argued that the spread of slavery could actually advance the cause of emancipation. Where slaves competed with free white labor, he contended, they would eventually lose out. Free workers had incentives to become more productive; slaves had nothing of the sort. Moreover, Northern resistance to the spread of slavery needlessly alarmed the South, which would become more attached to the institution and less likely to heed reason and enlightened self-interest and emancipate its slaves voluntarily.

If the reporter thought Clay's argument changed many minds among the opponents of slavery, he was mistaken. It was not even certain that Clay himself believed his argument. But it put a gloss of respectability on the compromise he sought. Some antislavery men would have to vote for Missouri's admission, and they would have to go home and explain their votes to skeptical constituents. Clay showed them how.

More important was Clay's deftness in maneuvering the legislation he desired through Congress. He let the Senate take the lead, and in mid-February the upper house approved a bill that would grant statehood to Maine and authorize Missouri to write a constitution without restrictions on slavery. In a new twist, an amendment offered by Jesse Thomas of Illinois to the Missouri part of the package extended the Ohio River westward, so to speak, by making the latitude of 36°30′—roughly that of the mouth of the Ohio—a dividing line between free territory to the north and slave territory to the south. Missouri was an exception, in that most of the state would lie above the specified latitude. But it would be the only exception, and the line that divided slavery from freedom would extend west as far as the American writ ran.

The Thomas amendment was a nod to the North. By it the South renounced slavery in most of the Louisiana Purchase. But it wasn't a painful renunciation, for almost no one believed slavery would ever be profitable on the barren plains that constituted most of the region. There was considerable doubt that agriculture of any sort would be profitable there. Southern members of Congress supposed they were giving away little.

Yet the Thomas amendment had political significance for Northern opponents of slavery. They could claim they had kept slavery out of most of the Louisiana Purchase. And they had gotten the South to accept the principle that Congress could bar slavery from federal territories.

The Thomas amendment had the greatest value for Henry Clay. The strength of the antislavery forces in the House had grown; no longer content with the timetable of the Tallmadge amendment, the Northern bloc insisted on a substitute proposed by John Taylor of New York that would emancipate at birth all children of Missouri slaves. Clay knew the Taylor substitute would never receive the approval of the Senate. But he let the House vote it through, believing he could finagle something in reconciliation talks between the two houses.

Which was precisely what he did. He packed the reconciliation committee with House members amenable to compromise, and with his blessing they dropped Taylor's emancipation scheme in favor of Thomas's line. The South got Missouri with slaves and the lower portion of the Louisiana Purchase; the North got Maine and upper Louisiana. And Henry Clay got a solution to the slave question he hoped would last for decades.

"The settlement of the Missouri question I think a happy thing," Clay wrote in early March, the day after the compromise received the signature of President Monroe. "And I believe the arrangement which has been made a very good one."

NOT EVERYONE AGREED. Northern antislavery activists condemned the intrusion of slavery into the American West. Southern zealots decried any restriction on slavery's future. Yet Clay appreciated that anger at the margins was the cost, even the measure, of any meaningful compromise. He hoped the anger would dissipate with time. And time was precisely what the Missouri Compromise bought. The West was large; generations would pass before settlement outran the Missouri Compromise line. Clay hoped the slavery question would be answered definitively before then.

John Randolph was one of those unhappy with the compromise. After the House had endorsed the package, Randolph moved to reconsider it. The Virginian opposed the restriction on the prerogatives of the states, even ones not yet called into being; he also resented Henry Clay, who had defeated him over the war with Britain and was defeating him again. Clay declared the hour too late for reconsideration, which he scheduled for the next day. Overnight Clay set the wheels of the House turning to dispatch the approved bill to the Senate. At the opening the next morning Randolph renewed his motion. Clay ruled it out of order until the quotidian business of the House was disposed of. Randolph fumed, helpless against the speaker. Eventually the petitions of the day were exhausted. Randolph moved once more for reconsideration. Clay blithely responded that the motion came too late: the approved bill had gone to the Senate. Randolph cried foul and demanded that the House vote to overrule the speaker. Amid the uproar the compromise bill returned from the Senate, enacted and sealed. Clay so informed the House, to Randolph's still greater outrage.

Thomas Jefferson's reaction to Clay's compromise was less personal and more trenchant. Jefferson had retired from politics on leaving the presidency; of late he rarely stirred from Monticello. By his own testimony he had gladly surrendered responsibility for the nation's welfare to men like Clay. "I had for a long time ceased to read the newspapers or pay any attention to public affairs, confident they were in good hands, and content to be a passenger in our bark to the shore from which I am not distant," he wrote to a friend in April 1820. But the Missouri dispute snapped him out of his complacency. "This momentous question, like a fire bell in the night, awakened and filled me with terror. I considered it at once as the knell of the Union." Clay's compromise gave Jefferson some comfort on the slave controversy, but not a lot. "It is hushed indeed for the moment, but this is a reprieve only, not a final sentence." What Clay found appealing about the Missouri bargain, Jefferson deemed a danger. "A geographical line, coinciding with a marked principle, moral and political, once conceived and held up to the angry passions of men, will never be obliterated, and every new irritation will mark it deeper and deeper."

Jefferson reflected on the broad issue of slavery, as it shaped the nation and touched him personally. "I can say with conscious truth that there is not a man on earth who would sacrifice more than I would to relieve us from this heavy reproach, in any practicable way. The cession of that kind of property, for so it is misnamed, is a bagatelle which would not cost me in a second thought, if, in that way, a general emancipation and expatriation could be effected; and, gradually, and with due sacrifices, I think it might be. But, as it is, we have the wolf by the ear, and we can neither hold him, nor safely let him go. Justice is in one scale, and self-preservation in the other."

Jefferson feared that the great work of his life was being undone. "I regret that I am now to die in the belief that the useless sacrifice of themselves by the generation of '76, to acquire self government and happiness to their country, is to be thrown away by the unwise and unworthy passions of their sons, and that my only consolation is to be that I live not to weep over it."

T HE MISSOURI QUESTION wasn't the only thing that spoiled the good feelings of James Monroe's presidency. A panic seized the financial system in 1819 and spread to the larger economy, afflicting every section of the country. "The years 1819 and '20 were a period of gloom and agony," Thomas Hart Benton recalled later. Benton was a direct beneficiary of Clay's work on Missouri; he was one of the first two men elected to the Senate from the new state, in 1821. As a Missourian he was well placed to witness the searing effects of the panic, which hit the West hardest of all. "No money, either gold or silver; no paper convertible into specie; no measure or standard of value left remaining. . . . No price for property or produce. No sales but those of the sheriff and the marshal. No purchasers at execution sales but the creditor or some hoarder of money. No employment for industry; no demand for labor; no sale for the product of the farm. No sound of the hammer but that of the auctioneer, knocking down property. . . . No medium of exchange but depreciated paper; no change, even, but little bits of foul paper, marked by so many cents and signed by some tradesman, barber or innkeeper. Exchanges deranged to the extent of fifty or one hundred per cent. DISTRESS, the universal cry of the people. RELIEF, the universal demand thundered at the doors of all legislatures, state and federal."

Henry Clay fared far better than the millions who lost jobs, lost farms, lost homes, lost hope. Yet the panic caught him holding bad debt, which left him exposed when his debtors defaulted. He liquidated property and cut deals with creditors where he could, but it wasn't enough. A dispassionate calculation convinced him he couldn't afford to continue in politics. He announced he would not seek reelection in 1820.

He began reckoning how he might recoup his fortunes, or at least stay out of debtors' prison. He formed a new law practice. "The subscribers have associated themselves together in the practice of the LAW in the Courts at Lexington," he and partner Greenberry Ridgely advertised in the **Kentucky Reporter**. "Engagements entered into by either will be attended to by both, as far as practicable. One or both of them may be generally found in the room adjoining the Athenaeum at the Kentucky Hotel."

He tested new methods of getting profits from his farm. The crash caused prices for most commodities to plummet, but one that held promise was hemp, used for making rope. A correspondent sent him a news clipping about a novel method of converting the crop to fiber. Clay responded, "The information which you have had the goodness thus to communicate comes very seasonably, for after having almost abandoned the culture of hemp in this fine region of country to which it is so well adapted, ever since the termination of the late war, the farmers are beginning again to turn their attention considerably to it, and it bears a better price at this time than any other produce of the land." The letter Clay had received identified a machine that processed the hemp more efficiently than other devices. "What would be the probable cost?" he inquired. "I wish to procure one."

To FOCUS ON his business affairs, he resigned as speaker of the House before his congressional term ended. He expected to play a minor role in the session that ran until March 1821, when the new Congress would be sworn in.

But the House had gotten used to his leadership, and it floundered for lack of his guidance. The Missouri question arose again when the drafters of that new state's constitution included a provision forbidding the entry of free blacks. The ban reflected slaveholders' perception that free blacks were an anomaly that undermined the slave system, which rested on the principle that blacks in America were meant to be slaves. When black slaves encountered blacks who were **not** slaves, they started to get unsettling ideas. Existing slave states were making manumission more difficult, in part to keep their numbers of free blacks low. Missouri sought to avoid the problem by keeping free blacks out.

But Northern opponents of slavery took the ban as an insult, not to mention a violation of the clause of the Constitution guaranteeing that the citizens of each state be accorded the rights of citizens in all states. Blacks were citizens in some Northern states and so could not be barred from entering Missouri. The Missouri Compromise had slipped through Congress with the help of Clay's dexterity; now it seemed on the verge of unraveling. And the new House leadership could do nothing to stop it.

So Clay stepped into the breach. He got himself appointed chairman of a special committee to address the issue. One by one he buttonholed the members and made his plea for the Union. In due course the committee proposed that Missouri be made a state on the condition that its legislature never adopt a law barring the entry of any class of citizens of other states. Clay was hardly alone in recognizing the cosmetic nature of the condition.

Missouri could accept it, become a state, and then write whatever laws it wanted. Congress had no power over state laws; only the federal courts did. But cosmetics serve a purpose, and this brand gave cover to Northerners with antislavery constituents. Not enough cover, as things proved: Clay's measure was defeated when it came before the House.

A new complication developed. The demise of the Federalists left James Monroe without an opponent in the 1820 election. The states submitted their electoral votes, but Congress still had to count them. Missouri sent three votes for Monroe, asserting that having written its constitution, it was already a state. Southern members of Congress generally supported Missouri's claim and wanted to accept its votes. Most Northerners did not. All realized that the difference wouldn't affect the outcome of the election: Monroe was going to be elected nearly unanimously in either case. But a decision in the matter would have consequences for Missouri. If its votes were counted, its claim to statehood would be strengthened. If they were rejected, the claim would suffer.

In Clay's decade in Congress he had learned that distraction undid more good intentions than any other influence. He refused to let the House get distracted by a lengthy debate over counting the electoral votes. He proposed an unprecedented solution. Two counts would be taken, one with Missouri's votes, the other without. If the discrepancy did not affect the identity of the winner, both results would be reported to the president of the Senate, who would then announce the winner.

Clay's plan provoked an outcry. Opponents of Missouri's admission objected that it would give de facto approval to that admission, rewarding the scoundrels who had flouted the clear intent of Congress in the original compromise. Constitutional purists spluttered that it mocked the charter's straightforward directions for counting the electoral votes. John Randolph condemned it as more of Clay's high-handedness.

But the House approved, and the Senate too, and Clay's solution went forward. James Monroe was duly elected with either 228 or 231 electoral votes. John Quincy Adams, the runner-up, received 1 vote.

Though the result got Clay and the country no closer to a solution to the larger Missouri problem, at least it carried them no further away. Yet he still couldn't see a clear path to the end. "This Missouri storm is threatening to sweep every thing before it," he wrote to an associate. "Unhappy subject! Every attempt to settle it has yet failed." But he wouldn't give up. "I still cherish, perhaps vainly, hopes." Some in the House suggested putting off action on Missouri until the next Congress. Clay refused to entertain the idea, not least because he knew he wouldn't be in Congress then. "Put off the question!" he said. "No! I would as soon sleep amidst the conflagration of a city, under the vain persuasion that in the morning, when I awoke, it would be time enough to endeavor to extinguish the flames."

WILLIAM HENRY SPARKS was a guest in the House when Clay made a final effort to douse the fire. Writing decades later, Sparks recalled the moment. "About him was gathered the talent of the Senate and the House," Sparks said. "The lobbies and galleries were filled to overflowing." Clay dominated the scene. "How grandly he towered up over those seated about him! Dressed in a full suit of black, his hair combed closely down to his head, displaying its magnificent proportions, with his piercing gray eyes fixed upon those of the Speaker, he poured out, in fervid words, the wisdom of his wonderful mind and the deep feelings of his great heart. . . . All the majesty of his nature seemed as a halo emanating from his person and features as, turning to those grouped about him, and then to the House, his words, warm and persuasive, flowing as a stream of melody, with his hand lifted from his desk, he said: 'I wish that my country should be prosperous and her government perpetual. I am in my soul assured that no other can ever afford the same protection to human liberty and insure the same amount. Leave the North to her laws and her institutions.

Extend the same conciliating charity to the South and West. Their people, as yours, know best their wants, know best their interests. Let them provide for their own. Our system is one of compromises. And in the spirit of harmony come together; in the spirit of brothers compromise any and every jarring sentiment which may arise in the progress of the country. There is security in this; there is peace and fraternal union. Thus we may, we shall, go on to cover this entire continent with prosperous states and a contented, self-governed and happy people.'"

In Sparks's memory, Clay's performance worked a miracle. "There was oil upon the waters, and the turbulent waves went down. Men who had been estranged and angered for many months met and, with friendly smiles, greeted each other again. The ladies in the gallery above rose up as if by a common impulse to look down, with smiles, upon the great commoner. One whose silvered hair, parted smoothly and modestly upon her aged forehead, fell in two massy folds behind her ears, clasped her hands and audibly uttered, 'God bless him.'"

The reality was rougher than Sparks recalled, but only a little. Clay's previously rejected cosmetic proposal became the fallback as the session raced toward its close. The Senate and the House agreed to admit Missouri on the condition that the state's legislature promise that it would never adopt legislation abridging the rights of any citizens of any states. The votes were close. Some Northerners still objected to admitting Missouri with slaves at all. Southerners complained about the demeaning condition extorted from Missouri. Missouri lawmakers, in their turn, gave the required promise even as they denied the authority of Congress to require it.

Clay didn't care about the margin, only the result. Failure would have meant disaster. "No human being could have anticipated the consequences of the exclusion from the Union of Missouri for any length of time," he told a friend. "My firm conviction is, founded upon a knowledge of several powerful forces operating in the West, that one of them would have been an attempt at separation of some, and ultimately all, of the Western states from the confederacy."

The crisis had passed, though not the underlying danger. "Wisdom and prudence may keep us united a long time, I hope for ever. But there are natural causes tending towards disseverance." The work of statesmen, of the builders of the American nation, was never done.

PART THREE

The People's Government

It is, sir, the people's Constitution, the people's
government; made for the people; made by
the people; and answerable to the people.

—DANIEL WEBSTER, 1830

JOHN CALHOUN BECAME war secretary because Henry Clay didn't want the job. James Monroe, on entering the White House—which in fact was still blackened from the British torch—attempted something unique in American history: one-party rule. Self-identifying Federalists had largely vanished; Republicans were everywhere. But some were more Republican than others, with differences owing to the interests of the different sections of the country. To keep all happy, Monroe spread the wealth of his patronage. In constructing his cabinet, he sought regional balance. The North must be represented; likewise the South and the West. To the North he looked for his secretary of state, choosing John Quincy Adams. Adams had special gifts for the post, having apprenticed in diplomacy under his father, John Adams, and spent many years abroad. But his appointment also reflected Monroe's desire to drive a nail through the coffin of Federalism by poaching a famous son of New England, Federalism's last redoubt. In tapping Adams for secretary of state, Monroe effectively made him heir apparent to the presidency. Monroe calculated that he could always change his mind, but for now the appointment allayed concerns that Virginia would never relinquish the White House.

William Crawford was given the treasury. Crawford was a Georgian of talent and ambition. He had been secretary of war under James Madison and then secretary of the treasury. Monroe deemed it prudent to keep him at the treasury, where his experience would help right the nation's postwar finances and ensure the success of the new Bank of the United States. Crawford's appointment would please the South.

To honor the West, Monroe looked to Henry Clay. Clay's leading role in starting and then ending the War of 1812 made him a natural for war secretary. Clay had been offered the job before, by Madison, and had declined. Monroe renewed the offer; Clay again declined. He might have accepted the state department, the plum of the cabinet appointments. He might even have taken the treasury, which would surely play a large role in the coming years. But the war department looked a backwater, with no war in the offing. Clay kept his job as speaker of the House.

Monroe scoured the West again. He considered Andrew Jackson, now the most famous Westerner in America. But the general let him know his work in the field wasn't finished. Monroe turned to Isaac Shelby, Clay's model of Kentucky success. But Shelby was old and found his farm as appealing as Clay had described it, and declined the offer.

Despairing of getting a Westerner, Monroe settled for John Calhoun. Although from South Carolina, Calhoun was often seen as a proxy for Westerner Clay. Calhoun's positions on the war mirrored Clay's; he was an ardent supporter of Clay's program of internal improvements, tariff protection and the national bank. And Calhoun, unlike Clay, considered the post of war secretary a promotion. When Monroe made the offer, Calhoun accepted.

HE DIDN'T REALIZE what he was getting into. The world knew Andrew Jackson as the hero of New Orleans. Washington insiders knew a bit more: that Jackson was headstrong, that he interpreted orders from his political superiors as suggestions, and that he despised the British and everything associated with them. What neither the Washington crowd collectively nor John Calhoun individually knew was just how headstrong Jackson was, how thoroughly he resented the intrusion of politics into his work as defender of America's southwestern frontier, and how broadly he perceived the machinations of Britain.

During the war, Jackson had exceeded orders and attacked Spanish positions in Florida. The Madison administration thought two enemies— Britain and the Indian alliance backed by the British—were quite enough; Jackson was cautioned not to antagonize the Spanish. But Jackson concluded that he couldn't secure his flanks against the British and the Indians if the Spanish, who favored both groups over the Americans, allowed them refuge and staging grounds in Florida. Jackson attacked Pensacola and dealt a humiliating blow to the Spanish there. The saving grace for the administration was precisely that Jackson had exceeded orders. Spain, which was no more eager for war with America than the American government was for war with Spain, was able to treat the attack as an error rather than a deliberate affront.

Jackson left Pensacola to fight the British at New Orleans. But he continued to deem Spanish Florida a threat to American security. Spanish control over Florida was notional at best. Seminole Indians raided American settlements north of the Florida border and fled south to escape reprisal. Escaped slaves from American plantations vanished into the Florida swamps and forests. British merchants, some doubling as agents of the British government, provisioned and sometimes provoked the Indians. Pirates waylaid vessels from harbors on the Florida coast. Jackson concluded that America would never be secure until Florida was America's.

James Monroe came to the same conclusion
more slowly. Rounding out America's southern
border by taking Florida had been an obvious
goal for American policy since the acquisition of
Louisiana, but Spain was in no mood to give it
up. Most of Central and South America had risen
in revolt against Spanish rule, with success that
varied from region to region. The revolts followed
the battering of Spanish pride and sovereignty by
Napoleon, and the Spanish monarchy couldn't
cede Florida without further, perhaps fatal, loss of
prestige.

Yet what Spain wouldn't cede might be taken
from it forcibly. Jackson knew this, and Monroe
eventually concurred. The president pursued a
two-track policy. He authorized John Quincy
Adams as secretary of state to engage the Spanish in
diplomatic negotiations, and he allowed, without
expressly authorizing, Jackson to demonstrate that
the Spanish couldn't hold Florida if negotiations
failed. Jackson wrote Monroe a letter explaining what should be done. The general proposed
a punitive expedition into Florida, nominally
against the marauding Seminoles. But he would
keep marching until he had taken the whole place.
"This done, it puts all opposition down, secures our
citizens a complete indemnity, and saves us from a
war with Great Britain or some of the continental
powers combined with Spain."

The part that most intrigued Monroe came

next. "This can be done without implicating the government," Jackson said. "Let it be signified to me through any channel, say Mr. J. Rhea"—John Rhea of Tennessee—"that the possession of the Floridas would be desirable to the United States, and in sixty days it will be accomplished."

MONROE'S RESPONSE TO Jackson's offer became a matter of subsequent dispute, a dispute that centered on John Calhoun. "I was sick in bed and could not read it," Monroe recalled of Jackson's letter, in a letter to Calhoun. "You were either present or came in immediately afterwards, and I handed it to you for perusal. After reading it, you replaced it, with a remark that it required my attention, or would require an answer, but without any notice of its contents. Mr. Crawford came in soon afterwards, and I handed it also to him for perusal. He read it and returned it in like manner." Monroe added, "I never showed it to any other person." And that was that. "The letter was laid aside and forgotten by me, and I never read it until after the conclusion of the war."

Jackson remembered things differently. "In accordance with the advice of Mr. Calhoun, and availing himself of the suggestion contained in the letter, Mr. Monroe sent for Mr. John Rhea (then a member of Congress), showed him the confidential letter, and requested him to answer it," Jackson wrote in defense of his actions. Referring to himself in the third person, he continued, "In conformity with this request, Mr. Rhea did answer the letter and informed General Jackson that the President had shown him the confidential letter, and requested him to state that he approved of its suggestions." Unfortunately for Jackson's case, he didn't save the letter, as he explained. Sometime after he received the letter, he and Rhea were in Washington together. "Mr. Rhea called on General Jackson, as he said, at the request of Mr. Monroe, and begged him on his return home to burn his reply. He said the President feared that by the death of General Jackson or some other accident, it might fall into the hands of those who would make an improper use of it." Jackson said he did as Monroe requested.

The reason the matter was being argued years later was that after Jackson did what he claimed Monroe and Calhoun had authorized him to do—seize Florida by force—the president felt obliged to disown the general's action. Jackson's campaign affronted the Spanish, with whom Monroe was still publicly trying to negotiate. Jackson insulted the British as well, by seizing two British subjects in company with the Indians he was fighting and executing them for inciting war against the United States. If Monroe took responsibility for Jackson's actions, he might compel the British, the Spanish or both to declare war on the United States. Better to blame an unruly general.

Jackson had invited such blame by saying that his Florida campaign needn't implicate the administration. And if the chastisement had been simply for the benefit of the Spanish and the British, Jackson shouldn't have objected. But he caught wind that the finger-pointing had a domestic audience. Some members of the administration were portraying him as a general drunk with blood. Jackson's sources identified the principal culprit as William Crawford, who was known to have ambitions to succeed Monroe as president and thus had a motive to slander Jackson, a likely rival.

In fact it was Calhoun who led the critics. "Mr. Calhoun is extremely dissatisfied with General Jackson's proceedings in Florida," John Quincy Adams wrote in his diary after a meeting in which the administration weighed its response to the Spanish and British protests. "Thinks Jackson's object was to produce a war for the sake of commanding an expedition against Mexico, and that we shall certainly have a Spanish war." Calhoun judged that Jackson was uncontrollable. "He has violated his orders, and upon his own arbitrary will set all authority at defiance," Calhoun said, according to Adams.

15

CALHOUN BORROWED TROUBLE with Jackson by his criticism. But it was a long-term debt. In the moment, in correspondence with the general, Calhoun gave no clue of what he was saying behind the closed doors of the cabinet. Jackson, far from suspecting Calhoun, thought the war secretary was defending him. Calhoun would keep his secret from Jackson for more than a decade.

Meanwhile there was politics to tend to. Presidential elections had grown decreasingly competitive since 1800. Each succession had been an anointing, each reelection a waltz. But 1824 promised to be different. For the first time the country would choose a president who had not taken an adult part in the American Revolution. William Crawford was the favorite of the congressional Republican caucus, which had chosen the party's previous candidates. Yet the caucus now wielded less power than in those earlier elections. The spirit of democracy was catching hold in America. In the days of George Washington, the electorate was quite small; women and nonwhites generally couldn't vote, and even among white men, property and residency requirements restricted the franchise to the wealthy and rooted. But the electorate expanded with the emergence of the West, where new states lured settlers with the promise of easy voting rights. The old states countered by reducing their restrictions, lest they lose residents to the frontier democracies. By the 1820s nearly all white men could vote.

And though they still didn't vote directly for presidential candidates, they voted more often for the presidential electors than before, as state legislatures relinquished that prerogative. Presidential elections became popularity contests, with the most successful candidates being those who touched a chord in the ordinary farmers, mechanics and crossroads merchants who increasingly held president-making power. When the founding generation of Americans had made George Washington president, no one asked him to be a man of the people. But when Andrew Jackson, John Quincy Adams, William Crawford, Henry Clay and John Calhoun jockeyed for position in 1824, being a man of the people—or appearing to be—was a political prerequisite.

———

THE CAMPAIGN COMMENCED early. Some observers dated the start to the beginning of Monroe's presidency, in maneuverings within the cabinet. But the politicking remained intramural until Monroe's second term, when the several hopefuls made their candidacies known. Jackson was nominated by unofficial bodies of Republicans in Tennessee and Pennsylvania. The general declined to accept the nomination, but he also declined to refuse it. He adopted the position that he would not seek the presidency, but if the people called him to serve, he would answer the call as he had answered the call to military service.

The administration insiders—Crawford, Adams and Calhoun—signaled their availability to backers in various states, who then campaigned on their behalf. Crawford appeared to have the advantage. The longtime treasury secretary had employed the patronage that came with his office to build a network of loyalists. Yet the ranks of his friends were almost equaled by the ranks of his enemies. Some disliked him personally; his prickly temperament had involved him in multiple duels. In one he killed his antagonist; in another he caught a bullet in his wrist that disabled his hand for many months. More than a few Crawford skeptics perceived corruption in the patronage he conferred on his favorites. At times the other candidates presented themselves as the best placed to block Crawford, and their appeals drew support. But the Georgian cast himself as the candidate of the South, and with the apparent lapse of the Virginia dynasty of Washington, Jefferson, Madison and Monroe, much of the South responded positively.

Adams ran directly against Crawford, on a comparably regional basis. The South was the most coherently influential region of the country, but New England came a close second, and many in New England and elsewhere judged that America had had enough of Southern presidents. Who better to break the Southern hold than the son of the only non-Southern president so far? Adams was his own worst enemy in the contest for support among politicos in the various states; his patent self-righteousness put people off. Yet he was capable and experienced, and he gradually gained momentum.

Calhoun was the Hamlet of the bunch. Egregious ambition was held against any candidate; it was the chief complaint against Crawford. But Calhoun erred in the other direction. Some days he actively sought the presidency, by conversation and correspondence; other days he seemed not to care. His was the most cerebral of the campaigns; his arguments for himself, like his arguments for the nation-building agenda he shared with Clay, clicked into place logically and securely. But they didn't inspire people. This was a serious handicap, for in the emerging age of democracy, people wanted to be inspired.

———

OF THE CHIEF contenders, Henry Clay ran the campaign that one day would seem the most modern, for he actually gave speeches on his own behalf. Andrew Jackson's call-to-duty diffidence was but a slightly exaggerated version of what was expected of candidates generally. The presidency was a gift of the people, bestowed on whom the people chose. Potential recipients were supposed to sit quietly and wait until the gift was bestowed on them. Everyone understood that this was a fiction; candidates were allowed, indeed expected, to work behind the scenes to win the top job in American politics. But the work had to be invisible, or at any rate easily overlooked. Speeches on behalf of oneself were almost disqualifying offenses.

Clay, however, was a member of Congress, having returned to the House in 1823, and been reelected speaker, after stabilizing his finances at home. Crawford, Adams and Calhoun were not members. Jackson had been sent to the Senate by Tennessee in 1823, but he was no orator and didn't pretend to be one. Clay was accounted one of the two best orators on Capitol Hill, the other being Daniel Webster and the order depending on listeners' tastes. Clay actively joined debates in the House, and while his remarks involved issues before the chamber, they simultaneously served as campaign speeches.

In January 1824 he resumed his nation-building efforts. The national bank was up and running, though its reputation had suffered a setback in the financial panic. It had received the blessing of John Marshall and the Supreme Court, and its charter wouldn't have to be renewed for another decade. Clay devoted little breath to its necessity and virtues. But the other elements of his three-part program—internal improvements and tariff protection—gave him plenty to talk about. Opinions on the former, Clay asserted, were essentially judgments about the meaning and destiny of the republic. Opponents of improvements, men who argued that the national government couldn't or shouldn't take responsibility for the roads and canals that would knit the country together, were ill-begotten sons of the Articles of Confederation, the failed system thankfully supplanted by the Constitution of 1787. "This is the characteristic difference between the two systems of government, of which we should never lose sight," Clay told the House. "Interpreted in the one way"—that of the Articles—"we shall relapse into the feebleness and debility of the old confederacy. In the other, we shall escape from its evils and fulfill the great purposes which the enlightened framers of the existing Constitution intended to effectuate."

Clay endorsed tariff protection as the sole way to lead the country out of its lingering lethargy and establish prosperity on a sound footing. "Two classes of politicians divide the country," he said. "According to the system of one, the produce of foreign industry should be subjected to no other impost than such as may be necessary to provide a public revenue." The second class perceived a higher and more beneficial role for tariffs. "They would so adjust and arrange the duties on foreign fabrics"—the topic then before the House—"as to afford a gradual but adequate protection to American industry and lessen our dependence on foreign nations by securing a certain, and ultimately a cheaper and better, supply of our own wants from our abundant resources." The lack of an enlightened tariff policy was the cause of the continuing distress of the country, Clay said. America had allowed itself to grow dependent on foreign suppliers. The British government, at the behest of British private interests, targeted American markets with precise and telling effect. The American government, by its low-tariff policy, had abetted Britain's offensive. Such folly must cease and be reversed.

In this speech Clay introduced his patriotic label for his program. "Are we doomed to behold our industry languish and decay yet more and more?" he asked. By no means. "There is a remedy, and that remedy consists in modifying our foreign policy and adopting a genuine American system." Soon Clay was capitalizing "American System." He elaborated: "We must naturalize the arts"—the industrial arts—"in our country, and we must naturalize them by the only means which the wisdom of nations has yet discovered to be effectual: by adequate protection against the otherwise overwhelming influence of foreigners." Opponents of protection argued that American industry would arise of itself, if simply left alone. Clay rebutted by contending that American industry was **not** being left alone. Britain's predatory policies were the furthest thing from laissez-faire. The American System, as it applied to tariffs, was nothing more than a leveling of the playing field. "The cause is the cause of the country, and it must and will prevail."

EVEN WHILE GIVING what amounted to campaign speeches from the floor of the House, Clay worked the levers of politics. He talked daily with members of Congress and others in Washington, and he corresponded with leading and useful figures in the states. He did his best to prevent the Republican caucus from choosing the party's nominee. His objection lay partly in his perception that the caucus smacked of an outdated elitism, and partly in his realization that he wouldn't be the nominee of the caucus. Not that he admitted disadvantage in any level fight. "My friends are perfectly willing fairly to submit my pretensions, whatever they may be, to a caucus composed of the great body of the Republican party in Congress, or indeed to a caucus composed of all the members of Congress, without reference to party," he told a New York ally. "They believe that any practical decision to which a caucus, composed in either of those modes, would come **must** be favorable to me." But he suspected that the Republican caucus would be unfairly stacked in favor of William Crawford. And so he worked to sabotage it. "There will be none," he declared encouragingly to his New York friend, speaking of a caucus. "You must discredit all assertions to the contrary."

He talked down the Crawford candidacy directly. "Be assured that the Crawford interest is in the greatest confusion and despondency," Clay wrote to a supporter in January 1824. "His partisans continue to assert that there will be a caucus here, but they do not themselves believe it." Clay had done a head count of Republicans. "There are 181 members against a caucus, 68 for one, and the residue doubtful." Crawford's plan was doomed. **"There cannot be any caucus here."**

In fact there was a caucus, but it drew only the minority Clay predicted, and its outcome left him hopeful. "The contemplated meeting of Mr. Crawford's partisans took place last night," he wrote in February. "The whole week, indeed I may say the session, had been employed by them in the endeavor to collect together as many as possible. Pretensions, threats, coaxing, entreaties were unsparingly used. These conjoint means brought together sixty-six persons!" Predictably they had nominated Crawford, who, Clay contended, had been discredited by their measly numbers. "Mr. Crawford never could have been elected president, but if he ever stood any chance the **mere fact** of such a nomination, with its train of necessary consequences, must inevitably destroy all his prospects."

Surveying the field, Clay forecast that no candidate would win a majority of the electors. The race, therefore, would go to the House of Representatives. "You may rely upon it," he told a Virginia confidant, "that you will have, as your next president, Adams, Jackson or myself. You will have in Virginia to choose between those three evils. It is madness, it is perfect infatuation, to think at this time of any body else." Clay's Virginia friend thought Crawford still had a chance. Clay responded that Crawford was too weak in the House. "Mr. Crawford cannot be elected, whoever may be," Clay said. "If he, Adams and Jackson go into the House, Adams will be elected. If he, Adams and I go into the House, he will still not be elected."

JOHN CALHOUN'S CAMPAIGN never surmounted his indecisiveness. He positioned himself among Southerners as the anti-Crawford candidate, and to those put off by the whiff of corruption downwind of Crawford, Calhoun seemed an upright alternative. But the Crawford patronage paid off especially in the South, and when the Georgian won the Republican caucus, such as it was, Calhoun's prospects dimmed.

They darkened further as those of Andrew Jackson improved. Pennsylvania was viewed as an important test. Both Calhoun and Jackson were running outside their home regions, with implications for the countrywide vote. A groundswell for Jackson grew into a tidal wave, and the general carried the state's convention of Republicans with 124 votes out of 125. At the time it was small comfort to Calhoun that he was the choice of a large majority to be vice president.

Henry Clay read the Pennsylvania results as an obituary to Calhoun's presidential hopes. "Mr. Calhoun will be dropt in a few days," Clay predicted. "The course of events in Pennsylvania has rendered that inevitable." Yet he suspected that Calhoun was already making other plans. "It is rumored that he means to lend his support to General Jackson."

16

JOHN QUINCY ADAMS considered himself
above the intriguing of the other candidates,
particularly John Calhoun and William
Crawford. "The organization of newspaper support for Mr. Crawford throughout the Union
is very extensive, and is managed with much
address," Adams wrote in his diary. "Democracy,
Economy and Reform are the watch-words for his
recruiting service—Democracy to be used against
me, Economy against Calhoun, and Reform
against both. Calhoun is organizing a counter-
system of newspaper artillery, and his Washington
Republican is already working powerfully in his
favor. These engines will counteract each other,
but I shall be a mark for both sides, and, having
no counter-fire upon them, what can happen
but that I must fall? This fall may be the happi-
est event that could befall me, and I but fervently
ask that my mind may be disciplined to whatever
betide me."

Adams definitely held himself above the barbarous practice of dueling, and when the tussling between Crawford and Calhoun produced a duel between two of their supporters, he shook his head in disapproving wonder. "This feud has become a sort of historical incident," he wrote. "It originated in the rivalry between Crawford and Calhoun for the presidential succession; began by some vulgar abuse upon each other in newspapers, in consequence of which Cumming challenged McDuffie before the last session of Congress, and came here last winter during the session to fight him." William Cumming was a Crawford man from Georgia, George McDuffie a South Carolinian for Calhoun. "The meeting was then postponed to thirty days after the close of the session of Congress, when they met, and McDuffie was shot in the back." More abuse, threats, challenges and shots followed. "Never was such a burlesque upon duels since the practice existed," Adams tut-tutted. At least Calhoun had the decency to disapprove, backhandedly. "Calhoun does not talk of it with pleasure, but says Cumming is subject to hereditary insanity from his mother."

Adams ascribed base motives to Calhoun. When critics of the army and of government spending advocated closing the military academy at West Point, Adams attributed Calhoun's defense of the institution—an understandable reaction from a secretary of war—to his desire to employ the patronage involved toward his presidential ambitions. When Adams proposed a presidential statement warning the European powers against intervening in the independence struggle of Spain's Latin American colonies, and James Monroe expressed concern at the reaction of the Europeans, Calhoun fanned the fears of the president and others in the cabinet. "Calhoun stimulates the panic," Adams wrote. Again and again Adams encountered resistance from Calhoun—"who in all his movements of every kind has an eye to himself," Adams wrote. Adams eventually inured himself to what he deemed Calhoun's double-dealing—"the professions of friendship and the acts of insidious hostility"—but it didn't improve his opinion of the war secretary, and he was happy when Calhoun's campaign fizzled.

THE CONTEST AMONG the four remaining candidates intensified during the summer of 1824. Momentum favored Andrew Jackson as new voters signaled their preference for the political outsider. William Crawford, the original front-runner, lost even more ground when a cerebral thrombosis laid him low and cast doubt over his future health. John Quincy Adams worked to hold New England. Henry Clay counted on Westerners not smitten by Jackson, on Southern defectors from Crawford, on former Federalists drawn to his American System, and on anyone else he could charm or persuade.

The election took place over several weeks in the fall, with eighteen states letting voters choose the electors and six sticking with legislative selection. The popular tally favored Jackson, with more than 150,000 votes. Adams finished second with somewhat fewer than 115,000. Crawford and Clay together garnered 90,000. These results gave Jackson bragging rights to a plurality of the popular vote but nothing near a majority. Not that it mattered, for the only tally that counted was of the electors. Here again Jackson ran first, with 99 votes, and Adams second with 84. Crawford got 41 and Clay 37.

The final figure—Clay's 37 electors—was the crucial one. The absence of an electoral majority dictated that the race would go to the House of Representatives. Clay's failure to edge Crawford for third place meant that Clay would not be a candidate there. The Twelfth Amendment specifies that in the absence of a majority winner in the electoral vote, the top three candidates proceed to a House runoff, in which each state's delegation casts a single vote. In the House, Clay would have had a good chance of becoming president. Many of Adams's New England supporters viewed Jackson with incomprehension and alarm; if convinced that Adams couldn't beat Jackson, they might well have accepted Clay. This now could not happen.

Yet if he couldn't be king, he might be kingmaker. Clay too eyed Jackson with distrust; he also saw Jackson as a usurper of his title as the champion of the West. The electoral votes hadn't been officially tallied before Clay began working to keep Jackson out of the White House and get Adams in. His conscience rested easy in his doing so, for he judged Adams more qualified than Jackson to be president. His ambition seconded the decision, for Adams would be a less challenging act to follow in the White House than Jackson. Clay's hopes of becoming president had been deferred, not eliminated.

Adams's conscience had to struggle more than Clay's to justify their alliance. This was partly because Adams's conscience struggled with most things, but also because Adams had spent much of the previous decade finding fault with Clay. "Clay's conduct has always been hostile to me, and generally insidious," he wrote in his diary. "From the time of the Ghent negotiations I have been in the way of his ambitions, and by himself and his subordinates he has done all in his power to put me out of it." A dispute arose over who had said what at Ghent about an aspect of the negotiations of particular interest to Westerners. Adams blamed Clay for misrepresentation. "Clay's conduct throughout this affair towards me has been that of an envious rival—a fellow-servant whispering tales into the ear of the common master. He has been seven years circulating this poison against me in the West."

Yet as the election drew nearer, Adams began to think an accommodation with Clay might be necessary. John Calhoun, upon realizing he had no chance at the presidency, had indicated he would accept the vice presidency. Unspoken was the quid pro quo: that if one of the remaining presidential candidates announced his support for Calhoun as vice president, that candidate would receive Calhoun's endorsement and likely the votes of Calhoun's followers. Some of Adams's backers were suggesting a similar accommodation between Adams and Henry Clay, with the former to become president and the latter secretary of state. Some of Adams's opponents declared indignantly that the fix was already in: a deal had been struck by an Adams agent, a bargain presumably revealing that Adams, thought to be an ethical exemplar, was as corrupt as the rest. Adams reflected that if he had made such a deal, which he had not, it wouldn't have been corrupt at all. "Nor is there anything in it unconstitutional, illegal or dishonorable," he said. "The friends of every one of the candidates have sought to gain strength for their favorite by coalition with the friends of others."

By the time the electoral vote was known, Adams's conversion was complete. A Kentucky congressman named Robert Letcher dropped by to sound Adams out. "Letcher wished to know what my sentiments towards Clay were," Adams recorded. "And I told him without disguise that I harbored no hostility against him; that whatever of difference there had been between us had arisen altogether from him and not from me."

Letcher responded in a similar soothing vein. "He was sure Clay felt now no hostility to me," Adams wrote. "He had spoken respectfully of me, and was a man of sincerity." Yet Adams was able to draw nothing concrete from the conversation. "Letcher did not profess to have any authority from Clay for what he said, and he made no definite propositions. He spoke of his interview with me as altogether confidential."

Letcher returned a week later. "The object appeared to me to be to convince me of the importance of obtaining an election in the House of Representatives at the first ballot," Adams wrote in his diary. The last time a race had gone to the House was after the election of 1800, and the machinations then had riven the Republican party. Most Republicans in 1824 wanted to avert a reprise, though some suggested that John Calhoun, who had received a majority of the electors for vice president, favored a standoff that would make him president on March 4, 1825. It was not clear that this would actually happen; the Constitution was vague on the point. But the sober thinkers in

the party wished nothing to do with any such scenario, and most favored an early-ballot resolution.

The holiday season had come to the capital,
and Adams attended dinners and receptions at
which Clay was also present. The two spoke only
in passing until, at a New Year's Day reception at
the White House, Robert Letcher asked Adams
if he was going back to the state department afterward. Adams said he was. Letcher followed him
and said it was time that he—Adams—and Clay
should have a conversation. "I told him I would
very readily, and whenever it might suit the convenience of Mr. Clay," Adams wrote.

That evening Adams encountered Clay again, at
a dinner in honor of the Marquis de Lafayette, the
Revolutionary War hero and America's favorite
Frenchman. "He told me that he should be glad
to have with me soon some confidential conversation upon public affairs," Adams wrote. "I said I
should be happy to have it whenever it might suit
his convenience."

The meeting took place a week later. "Mr. Clay
came at six and spent the evening with me in a
long conversation explanatory of the past and
prospective of the future. He said that the time
was drawing near when the choice must be made
in the House of Representatives of a president
from the three candidates presented by the electoral
college; that he had been much urged and solicited
with regard to the part in that transaction that he

should take, and had not been five minutes landed at his lodgings before he had been applied to by a friend of Mr. Crawford's, in a manner so gross that it had disgusted him; that some of my friends also, disclaiming, indeed, to have any authority from me, had repeatedly applied to him, directly or indirectly, urging considerations personal to himself as motives to his cause. He had thought it best to reserve for some time his determination to himself: first, to give a decent time for his own funeral solemnities as a candidate; and, secondly, to prepare and predispose all his friends to a state of neutrality between the three candidates who would be before the House, so that they might be free ultimately to take that course which might be most conducive to the public interest." Enough time had now passed, Clay said. "He wished me, as far as I might think proper, to satisfy him with regard to some principles of great public importance, but without any personal considerations for himself." Clay stated forthrightly his position on the presidential contest. "Between General Jackson, Mr. Crawford and myself, he had no hesitation in saying that his preference would be for me."

Adams's diary entry ceases abruptly at this point. He left the remaining half of the page blank, as though he intended to write more. His handwriting was small, and in half a page he could have written much more. In fact he could have written very much more, for the following three pages are blank also. But he never did. Perhaps he became distracted; Henry Clay was not his only visitor during this tense period. Perhaps he decided that the rest of his conversation with Clay was better unrecorded.

CLAY KEPT NO diary. His letters for this period reveal the slow dying of his presidential hopes, which had continued to flicker until the electoral votes were formally counted. He had come very close. One more state—Louisiana, for instance—and he would have edged William Crawford and advanced to the House, where his chances would have been quite good. "Thirty one members out of 58 met and agreed upon a ticket for me," Clay wrote to a confidant, Peter Porter, regarding the Louisiana legislature, which chose that state's electors. "Two other friends were expected to arrive before the election. After the meeting, two of my friends went to the country and having got overturned from a gig were unable to attend. The two that were expected did not arrive. Three deserted, in consequence of false rumors; and with all these disadvantages the coalition between Jackson's friends and Adams' was only able to carry their joint ticket by 30 to 28."

Clay put his best face on the result. "I laugh off and bear with unaffected fortitude our defeat," he told Porter. "We have no reproaches to make ourselves, and it is a source of high satisfaction that my character has not suffered but been elevated by the whole canvass."

He didn't take long to decide that Adams would make a better president than Jackson. "What, I should ask, should be the distinguishing characteristic of an American statesman?" he wrote rhetorically in a letter to a New York supporter who had inquired as to his preference between Adams and Jackson. "Should it not be a devotion to civil liberty? Is it then compatible with that principle, to elect a man whose sole recommendation rests on military pretensions? I therefore say to you unequivocally that I can not, consistently with my own principles, support a military man."

Yet he found himself besieged by the backers of each of the three finalists. "My position in relation to the friends of the three returned candidates is singular enough and often to me very amusing," he explained to Francis Blair of Kentucky. "In the first place they all believe that my friends have the power of deciding the question, and that I have the power of controlling my friends. Acting upon this supposition in the same hour, I am sometimes touched gently on the shoulder by a friend (for example) of General Jackson, who will thus address me: 'My dear sir, all our dependence is on you; don't disappoint us; you know our partiality was for you next to the Hero; and how much we want a western president.' Immediately after, a friend of Mr. Crawford will accost me: 'The hopes of the Republican party are concentrated on you. For God's sake preserve it. If you had been returned instead of Mr. Crawford every man of us would have supported you to the last hour. We consider him and you as the only genuine Republican candidates.' Next a friend of Mr. Adams comes with tears in his eyes: 'Mr. Adams has always had the greatest respect for you and admiration for your talents. There is no station to which they are not equal. Most undoubtedly you were the second choice of New England. And I pray you to consider seriously whether the public good and your own future interests do not point most distinctly to the choice which you ought to make.' "

Clay told Blair that Adams would be his choice over Jackson. Adams was the safer choice for the country. "The principal difference between them is that in the election of Mr. Adams we shall not by the example inflict any wound upon the character of our institutions; but I should much fear hereafter, if not during the present generation, that the elevation of the general would give to the military spirit a stimulus and a confidence that might lead to the most pernicious results."

Clay's friends echoed his concern about the ill effects of a Jackson presidency. "While I respect General Jackson for his military qualifications, I doubt whether he has any political information and experience that fit him for the office," Peter Porter remarked. "But my great objection to him is that he is by nature a **Tyrant**. I mean no unworthy imputation, for I believe him to be a man of the purest honor and integrity, but his habits as well as native disposition have always been to consider the law and his own notions of justice as synonymous. As watchful Republicans I should think we were committing, to say the least of it, a great indiscretion in placing the whole military and civil power of the country in such hands."

17

THE MORE CLAY thought about it, the more Jackson's military background bothered him. At the end of January 1825 he wrote again to Francis Blair, explaining that the Jackson men had turned against him with a vengeance. "I am a deserter from democracy," he said they were saying of him. "A giant at intrigue. Have sold the West—sold myself—defeating General Jackson's election to leave open the Western pretensions that I may hereafter fill them myself." Clay contended that the attacks told much about the attackers. "The knaves cannot comprehend how a man can be honest. They cannot conceive that I should have solemnly interrogated my conscience and asked it to tell me seriously what I ought to do. That it should have enjoined me not to establish the dangerous precedent of elevating, in this early stage of the Republic, a Military Chieftain merely because he has won a great victory." Blair understood that Clay was referring to the Battle of

New Orleans, not Jackson's plurality in the election. Clay repeated that Adams was hardly ideal. "Mr. Adams, you know well, I should never have selected if at liberty to draw from the whole mass of our citizens for a president." But Adams was the lesser evil. "There is no danger in his elevation now or in time to come. Not so of his competitor, of whom I cannot believe that killing 2500 Englishmen at New Orleans qualifies for the various, difficult and complicated duties of the chief magistrate."

Clay liked the phrase "military chieftain" enough to use it in another letter, to Francis Brooke. "As a friend of liberty, and to the permanence of our institutions," he wrote, "I cannot consent, in this early stage of their existence, by contributing to the elevation of a military chieftain, to give the strongest guaranty that this republic will march in the fatal road which has conducted every other republic to ruin."

Clay didn't tell Brooke to publish this letter. Neither did he tell him not to. Two weeks later it appeared in the Washington **National Intelligencer**. It came to Jackson's attention shortly thereafter. From that moment Jackson conceived a hatred for Clay he would carry to the end of his life.

Jackson responded with a letter to an ally, expecting him to ensure its publication, as he did. "I am well aware that this term 'military chieftain' has, for some time past, been a cant phrase with Mr.

Clay and certain of his friends," Jackson wrote. He professed puzzlement as to what the term was supposed to mean. He acknowledged that he had served as major general of the Tennessee militia and led his troops into battle against Britain. "Does this constitute the character of a 'military chieftain'?" he asked. He said he had been honored to defend his country at New Orleans, and by the patriotic courage of his soldiers had dealt the British a sound defeat. "If this constitutes me as a 'military chieftain,' I am one." Jackson sneered at Clay for even raising the issue. "Mr. Clay has never yet risked himself for his country. He has never sacrificed his repose nor made an effort to repel an invading foe." All Clay did was talk—and talk and talk. "Demagogues, I am persuaded, have in times past done more injury to the cause of freedom and the rights of man than ever did a military chieftain."

JACKSON'S SLAP AT Clay was accompanied by others from Jackson's supporters. A Philadelphia paper printed an unsigned letter to the editor: "Dear sir: I take up my pen to inform you of one of the most disgraceful transactions that ever covered with infamy the Republican ranks. . . . For some time past the friends of Clay have hinted that they, like the Swiss, would fight for those who would pay best. Overtures were said to have been made by the friends of Adams to the friends of Clay, offering him the appointment of secretary of state for his aid to elect Adams. And the friends of Clay gave this information to the friends of Jackson and hinted that if the friends of Jackson would offer the same price they would close with them." Jackson's friends had rejected the offer at once, the masked writer said. The writer said he had supposed the Adams group would do the same. "I was of opinion, when I first heard of this transaction, that men professing any honorable principle could not, or would not, be transferred, like the planter does his negroes or the farmer his team and horses." He had been wrong. "It is now ascertained to a certainty that Henry Clay has transferred his interest to John Quincy Adams. As a consideration of this abandonment of duty to his constituents, it is said and believed, should this unhappy coalition prevail, Clay is to be appointed secretary of state."

Clay could ignore the whispered slanders of a backroom bargain, but this published libel required a response. He issued a "card"—a paid notice printed in a newspaper—as soon as he read the accusing letter. He said he believed the author to be a member of Pennsylvania's delegation in the House. He didn't mention the name George Kremer, a first-term congressman, but rumors already had. Clay offered Kremer an exit. "I believe it to be a forgery," he said. But should Kremer not disavow the scurrilous sentiments and language, Clay demanded satisfaction. "If it be genuine, I pronounce the member, whoever he may be, a base and infamous calumniator, a dastard and a liar; and if he unveil himself and avow his name I will hold him responsible, as I here admit myself to be, to all the laws which govern and regulate the conduct of men of honor."

The escalation of charge and rebuttal electrified Washington and rattled the country. Not since the Hamilton-Burr affair had a government official of such eminence as Clay been so close to a duel. The frisson intensified when Kremer published a card of his own, identifying himself and repeating the charge of his first letter. Adopting the third-person construction, he wrote, "George Kremer holds himself ready to prove, to the satisfaction of unprejudiced minds, enough to satisfy them of the accuracy of the statements which are contained in that letter."

Clay's friends urged him to reconsider. A duel would demonstrate his bravery, but it wouldn't disprove the charge of a deal with Adams. He let himself be persuaded to pursue another tack. He called for an investigation by the House. He and Kremer were both members and subject to its discipline. Kremer's lie had wounded not Henry Clay alone but the House as a whole.

Kremer agreed to the investigation. A special committee was formed, and it invited Kremer to

furnish substantiating evidence. He thereupon
changed his mind. He denounced the committee
and investigation as unconstitutional, and he said
he would rely on the American people to determine the truth in the matter.

The committee looked to Clay for guidance. He
declared that he took Kremer's failure to provide
evidence as proof that he had no evidence. This
was the satisfaction he really wanted. He was willing to let the matter drop.

THE KREMER AFFAIR caused Clay to conclude that the Jacksonians were thinking far
ahead. They were fighting not just the present
campaign but the next one and the one after that.
Nor were the Jackson men alone. "The batteries
of some of the friends of every man who would
now be president, or who four or eight years
hence would be president, are directed against me,
with only the exception of those of Mr. Adams,"
Clay told Francis Brooke. "Some of the friends of
General Jackson, Mr. Crawford, Mr. Calhoun and
Mr. Clinton"—DeWitt Clinton of New York—
"with very different ultimate ends agree for the
present to unite in assailing me." His opponents
hoped to accomplish one of two things: to keep
him out of the Adams cabinet or to tarnish him
if he accepted an Adams offer.

Clay assured Brooke the strategy would fail. "If Mr. Adams is elected, I know not who will be his cabinet. I know not whether I shall be offered a place in it or not. If there should be an offer, I shall decide upon it when it may be made, according to my sense of duty." But he wouldn't let his opponents dictate his course. "Most certainly, if an office should be offered to me under the new administration, and I should be induced to think that I ought to accept it, I shall not be deterred from accepting it either by the denunciations of open or secret enemies, or the hypocrisy of pretended friends."

"MAY THE BLESSING of God rest upon the event of this day!" wrote John Quincy Adams in his diary on February 9. The count of states in the House had yielded thirteen for him, seven for Jackson and four for Crawford. His majority made him the next president of the United States.

Clay reacted differently. "The 'long agony' was terminated yesterday, and Mr. Adams was elected on the first ballot," he wrote to Francis Brooke. "Exertions to defeat or even to delay the result, of the most strenuous kind, were made up to the last moment." Clay thought the institutions of government had functioned well. "Without referring to the issue of the election, the manner in which the whole scene was exhibited in the House of Representatives was creditable to our institutions and our country."

The agony of Clay's friends hadn't ended, though. Several days later the news still hadn't reached Kentucky, where John Crittenden feared for Clay's life. "I have seen the abuse that has been heaped upon you in some of the newspapers, and your card in the Intelligencer," Crittenden wrote. "I confess that I feel some apprehension for you. There are about you a thousand desperadoes, political and military, following at the heels of leaders and living upon expectations, that would think it a most honorable service to fasten a quarrel upon Mr. Clay and shoot him. And this card of yours, evincing such a spontaneous and uncalculating spirit of gallantry, will be a signal, I fear, for some of these fellows to gather about you and to endeavor to provoke you to some extremity. For God's sake, be on your guard."

It was good advice, for the Jacksonians were livid at their hero's loss, and they blamed Clay. They got help from backers of John Calhoun. During the week after the decision in the House, John Quincy Adams received a visit from a man named Sullivan, who said he had been speaking with friends of Calhoun. Sullivan told Adams what they had said: "That if Mr. Clay should be appointed Secretary of State, a determined opposition to the Administration would be organized from the outset; that the opposition would use the name of General Jackson as its head; that the Administration would be supported only by the New England states—New York being doubtful, the West much divided and strongly favoring Jackson as a Western man, Virginia already in opposition, and all the South decidedly adverse." The Calhoun men had gone on to name their price for not abetting this sabotage: Calhoun loyalists filling the cabinet, including South Carolinian Joel Poinsett as secretary of state.

"I asked Sullivan with whom he had held these conversations," Adams recorded. "He said, with Calhoun himself, and with Poinsett." Adams could hardly believe the boldness of the shakedown. "I told Sullivan that I would some day call on him to testify to these facts in a court of justice."

Sullivan said Adams surely wouldn't do that.

"I insisted that I would," Adams continued, "and told him that I would find it necessary under this threatened opposition of Mr. Calhoun, between him and me; that I had no doubt Mr. Calhoun, in holding this language to him, intended that it should come to me, and that its object was to intimidate me and deter me from the nomination of Mr. Clay."

Sullivan said that if called to testify, he would refuse to answer.

"I said his refusal to answer would be as good for me as the answer itself," Adams wrote.

Sullivan said he couldn't betray a private conversation. He said he had already said too much. Calhoun had enjoined him to say nothing of it to Adams.

Adams let Sullivan off the hook, but he didn't believe him. "I said this altered the case, and he might consider my declared intention of calling on him to testify publicly to these facts as withdrawn. I nevertheless believed Mr. Calhoun had intended he should report to me his threats of opposition in the event of Mr. Clay's appointment."

THE NEXT DAY Adams met with Clay. They spoke for half an hour, and Adams offered him the post of secretary of state. Clay thanked him for the offer and said he would think it over and consult his friends.

Their opinions differed as to whether he should take it. "On the one hand it was said that if I took it, that fact would be treated as conclusive evidence of the imputations which have been made against me," Clay wrote to Francis Brooke. "On the other hand it was urged that whether I accepted or declined the office, I should not escape severe animadversion; that in the latter contingency, it would be said that the patriotic Mr. Kremer, by an exposure of the corrupt arrangement, had prevented its consummation; that the very object of propagating the calumny would be accomplished;

that, conscious of my own purity of intentions, I ought not to give the weight of a feather to Mr. Kremer's affair." Clay explained to Brooke that the latter arguments had overcome the former, both among his friends and in himself. Consequently he was accepting Adams's offer.

NEWS OF THE appointment sent the Jacksonians into a frenzy. A "corrupt bargain," they called it, repeating the phrase until it admitted of no doubt in their minds as to its veracity or the malevolence of the deed it described.

Jackson himself was equally certain he had been robbed. His grievance against Clay grew. "The **Judas** of the West has closed the contract and will receive the thirty pieces of silver," he said of Clay. "His end will be the same."

Henry Clay's experience as a diplomat could be summarized, to 1825, by his service on the American peace commission at Ghent. Yet his interests in foreign policy ranged more broadly. His advocacy of protectionism reflected a theory of international trade; his opponents might dispute his conclusions, but they couldn't deny the careful thought that went into them. As a war hawk he had weighed the relative dangers of war and peace in the challenge he espoused to the greatest empire in the world.

But it was Clay's support for anticolonial revolutions in Latin America and in the Ottoman empire that set him apart from the rest of his generation in Washington. During the second decade of the nineteenth century, nationalists across Central and South America sought to win from Spain what the Americans had won from Britain in the 1770s and 1780s. Clay lauded the rebels in speech after speech and urged, at a minimum, American recognition of the independent governments they proclaimed. The spirit of liberty that had inspired Americans in 1776 now inspired freedom lovers to America's south, he said. Americans would be false to their truest ideals not to offer aid and comfort. The Ottoman empire was a greater stretch, but when Greek rebels raised the flag of revolt, Clay pleaded on their behalf as well. Ancient Greece was the birthplace of democracy; the United States was its modern home. If self-government could be restored in Greece, he said, self-government everywhere would be strengthened. Americans owed it to the Greeks, and to themselves, to lend a hand.

John Quincy Adams, as Monroe's secretary of state, rejected Clay's advice. In an address on the forty-fifth anniversary of the Declaration of Independence, Adams proclaimed a policy of benevolent restraint. "Wherever the standard of freedom and independence has been or shall be unfurled, there will her heart, her benedictions and her prayers be," he said of America. "But she goes not abroad in search of monsters to destroy. She is the well-wisher to the freedom and independence of all. She is the champion and vindicator only of her own." Americans should focus on perfecting their own institutions. This was America's highest task. "She well knows that by once enlisting under other banners than her own, were they even the banners of foreign independence, she would involve herself beyond the power of extrication in all the wars of interest and intrigue, of individual avarice, envy and ambition, which assume the colors and usurp the standards of freedom." America would lose its way in the chase for power. "She might become the dictatress of the world; she would be no longer the ruler of her own spirit."

A speech by a secretary of state was important, but a presidential message carried more weight. So Adams arranged for James Monroe to address the same subject in his annual message to Congress and the American people two years later. By then several of the Latin American independence movements had achieved tentative success; what they feared was an effort by Spain, perhaps in league with France or other European powers, to restore Spanish control. Britain frowned on the idea, preferring free access to the markets of the Latin American republics. The British government proposed a joint statement by Britain and the United States that the two countries opposed any restoration of European control in the Americas, as well as any new colonization by Europeans. Russia was creeping down from Alaska toward the Oregon country, which the British and the Americans wanted to divide between themselves. Adams considered the British offer and concluded that Monroe should make the statement on America's own. "It would be more candid, as well as more dignified, to avow our own principles explicitly to Russia and France, than to come in as a cock-boat in the wake of the British man-of-war," he told the cabinet.

The statement Adams crafted was delivered by Monroe in December 1823. The outcome of the struggle in Greece still pended; Monroe promised the nationalists there America's good wishes. But he offered them nothing more. And in so refraining, he drew a line between the Old World and the New. America would not meddle in Europe, he said, and the Europeans must not meddle in the Americas. "The American continents, by the free and independent condition which they have assumed and maintain, are henceforth not to be considered as subjects for future colonization by any European powers," Monroe said. "We should consider any attempt on their part to extend their system to any portion of this hemisphere as dangerous to our peace and safety." The American republics must remain free and independent. "We could not view any interposition for the purpose of oppressing them or controlling in any other manner their destiny, by any European power, in any other light than as the manifestation of an unfriendly disposition toward the United States."

NOT FOR DECADES would Monroe's statement be called a "doctrine" of American foreign policy. But it served its purpose of promoting hemispheric solidarity, and it prompted plans to hold a meeting of representatives of the American republics in Panama in 1826. Adams by now was president and Clay secretary of state; both supported American attendance, Clay with particular enthusiasm.

The idea provoked the ire of Southern members of Congress. Liberation in Latin America included the abolition of slavery, and the Southerners refused to lend legitimacy to any such movement. Moreover, Haiti would send a delegation to the Panama meeting. Founded in a bloody slave revolt against white masters, independent Haiti was the nightmare that haunted Southern sleep. For representatives of the United States government merely to sit beside Haitian delegates would give American slaves murderous thoughts, Southerners contended. Congress couldn't keep the president from sending a delegation, but it could withhold funding for the trip. Southerners threw one roadblock after another in the administration's way; debate in the House and the Senate raged heavy and hot.

John Randolph was as contrary as ever, and he took particular pleasure in stymieing the Adams administration. Randolph loathed John Quincy Adams for being a New Englander and therefore everything a Virginian detested, and he resented Henry Clay for his federalism and the slights Randolph had suffered from Clay's political deftness. Randolph had been elevated to the Senate by Virginia Jacksonians who wished to register their anger at what Adams and Clay had done to their hero. He reached the upper house too late to try to block the confirmation of Clay as secretary of state, but the missed opportunity merely caused his bile to build. In the spring of 1826, amid the Panama controversy, he outdid himself in venomous attack. He tried to filibuster the administration's request and failed. "After twenty-six hours' exertion, it was time to give in," Randolph told the Senate, according to an account circulated shortly afterward. "I was defeated—horse, foot and dragoons—cut up and clean broke down by the coalition of Blifil and Black George, by the combination, unheard of till then, of the Puritan with the black-leg."

Had Randolph stopped after his first pair of analogies, nothing might have come of his remarks. The references were from Henry Fielding's **Tom Jones;** neither character was admirable but neither a monster. Yet perhaps Randolph thought his literary mot would be lost on his listeners, and he added the line about the Puritan and the blackleg. Adams couldn't particularly object to being called a Puritan; he had been called much worse. But Clay wouldn't stand for being labeled a blackleg: a swindler, a forger, a pickpocket.

Clay wasn't present, but when Randolph's words were related to him, he reacted at once. The sum of Randolph's remarks implied, in context, that Clay had manufactured evidence submitted in support of the administration's request; punctuated with the epithet "blackleg," the imputation of dishonorable behavior was inescapable. Clay couldn't let the insult pass. "Your unprovoked attack of my character in the Senate of the United States on yesterday allows me no other alternative than that of demanding personal satisfaction," he told Randolph in a note. "The necessity of any preliminary discussions or explanations being superseded by the notoriety and the indisputable existence of the injury to which I refer, my friend General Jesup, who will present you this note, is fully authorized by me forthwith to agree to the arrangements suited to the interview proposed."

Randolph responded with some of the hairsplitting his rivals had come to expect of him. He denied Clay's right to challenge anything he had said on the floor of the Senate. Clay was a member of the executive branch, and the Constitution separated the powers of the executive from those of the legislative branch. Yet he went on to say he would not hide behind senatorial privilege. "Colonel Tattnall of Georgia, the bearer of this letter, is authorized to arrange with General Jesup, the bearer of Mr. Clay's challenge, the terms of the meeting to which Mr. Randolph is invited by that note," Randolph said.

Beneath the formality lay some confusion as to what, exactly, Randolph had said in his speech. No one had taken a transcript, and Randolph, who prided himself on his extemporaneous skills, had put nothing in writing. Journalists re-created the speech from memory. Randolph later admitted using the terms "Puritan" and "blackleg," but he said he was expressing an opinion rather than stating a fact.

Thomas Benton was in the Senate when Randolph spoke. The Missourian was an orator, though not of Randolph's caliber; more important, he was a duelist, with experience of actionable words. "I heard it all," Benton said of Randolph's speech, "and though sharp and cutting, I think it might have been heard, had he been present, without any manifestation of resentment by Mr. Clay." Benton didn't recall anything about Blifil and Black George. "As to the expression, 'blackleg and puritan,' it was merely a sarcasm to strike by antithesis." Benton became involved in the affair as a friend of Randolph, and though he tried to get Randolph to explain that the offending phrase was merely a rhetorical flourish, Randolph refused. Randolph didn't deny to Benton that he had been speaking for effect. But he held his constitutional ground, saying he would not explain to any member of the executive branch words spoken on the floor of the Senate.

Preparations for the duel went forward. Randolph insisted that it take place in Virginia, despite Virginia's law against dueling. If he died, he wanted his blood to nourish the soil of his native state. Yet he concluded, after having done nothing to avert the duel, that he didn't want to shed the blood of his opponent. "The night before the duel, Mr. Randolph sent for me in the evening," James Hamilton recalled. Hamilton was a Jackson Republican from South Carolina and a Randolph friend. "I found him calm but in a singularly kind and confiding mood. He told me he had something on his mind to tell me. He then remarked, 'Hamilton, I have determined to receive, without returning, Clay's fire. Nothing shall induce me to harm a hair of his head. I will not make his wife a widow nor his children orphans. Their tears would be shed over his grave, but when the sod of Virginia rests on my bosom, there is not in this wide world one individual to pay this tribute upon mine.' His eyes filled, and, resting his head upon his hand, we remained some moments silent."

Hamilton tried to change Randolph's mind. "My dear friend," he said, "I deeply regret that you have mentioned this subject to me, for you call upon me to go to the field and see you shot down." Randolph would not be moved. Hamilton then went to Edward Tattnall, Randolph's second, and took him to Randolph's room. "Mr. Randolph, I am told that you have determined not to return Mr. Clay's fire," Tattnall said. "I must say to you, my dear sir, if I am only to go out to see you shot down, you must find some other friend."

Randolph remained adamant. Nothing

Hamilton or Tattnall might say could alter his intent, he declared. Yet at the end of the conversation, he seemed to soften. "Well, Tattnall," he said, "I promise you one thing. If I see the devil in Clay's eye, and that with malice prepense he means to take my life, I may change my mind."

On the same evening Thomas Benton visited Henry Clay. "The family were in the parlor, company present, and some of it stayed late," Benton recalled. "The youngest child, I believe James, went to sleep on the sofa." Lucretia Clay appeared to know nothing of the impending duel and conversed in a friendly manner. Benton, a Jackson man despite having shot and been shot at by Jackson in a gunfight a few years earlier, had been at odds with Clay since the 1824 election. He wanted to straighten things out. "When all were gone, and she also had left the parlor, I did what I came for and said to Mr. Clay that, notwithstanding our late political differences, my personal feelings toward him were the same as formerly, and that, in whatever concerned his life or honor, my best wishes were with him. He expressed his gratification at the visit and said it was what he would have expected of me."

The duel was scheduled for late afternoon the following day, a Saturday. The parties crossed the Potomac at the Little Falls bridge, above Georgetown, and found a secluded spot on the west bank of the river. "I shall never forget this scene as long as I live," James Hamilton recalled later. "It has been my misfortune to witness several duels, but I never saw one, at least in its sequel, so deeply affecting. The sun was just setting behind the blue hills of Randolph's own Virginia. Here were two of the most extraordinary men our country in its prodigality had produced, about to meet in mortal combat. While Tattnall was loading Randolph's pistol, I approached my friend, I believed for the last time. I took his hand; there was not in its touch the quivering of one pulsation. He turned to me and said, 'Clay is calm but not vindictive. I hold my purpose, Hamilton, in any event; remember this.'"

Tattnall set the hair trigger on Randolph's pistol, making it easier to fire. Randolph objected that he never used a hair trigger. And he especially didn't want to use it on this occasion, because he was wearing gloves. "The trigger may fly before I know where I am," he said.

This was just what happened. As the duelists took their positions, Randolph's pistol fired by accident, while it was pointed at the ground.

Clay could have protested and claimed a breach of the dueling code. He might have counted Randolph's fire as a first shot. But he did not. He allowed Randolph to receive a freshly loaded pistol. They took their positions, ten paces apart.

On the word, Clay fired. He missed Randolph, the bullet scattering gravel and dirt beyond

Randolph's feet. Randolph fired simultaneously. He missed also, with his ball splintering a stump behind Clay.

"The moment came for me to interpose," Thomas Benton recalled. Benton had been privy to Randolph's intention not to fire at Clay, and he wondered what had changed his mind. "I went in among the parties and offered my mediation, but nothing could be done. Mr. Clay said, with that wave of the hand with which he was accustomed to put away a trifle, 'This is child's play!' and required another fire. Mr. Randolph also demanded another fire."

The seconds readied another brace of pistols. Benton meanwhile spoke to Randolph. He urged him to end the affair. "But I found him more determined than I had ever seen him, and for the first time impatient, and seemingly annoyed and dissatisfied. The accidental fire of his pistol played upon his feelings. He was doubly chagrined at it, both as a circumstance susceptible in itself of an unfair interpretation, and as having been the immediate and controlling cause of his firing at Mr. Clay. He regretted the fire the instant it was over." He said he had not aimed to kill Clay, but only to disable him and spoil his aim. He added, "I would not have seen him fall mortally, or even doubtfully wounded, for all the land that is watered by the King of Floods and his tributary streams."

With that he returned to his firing position

opposite Clay. The signal was given again. Clay fired and his ball passed through Randolph's coat without hitting him. Randolph fired into the air, declaring, "I do not fire at you, Mr. Clay."

Randolph immediately stepped forward to meet Clay. He put out his hand to receive that of his adversary. "You owe me a coat, Mr. Clay," he said with a smile.

Clay took the hand. "I am glad the debt is no greater," he said.

ROCHESTER HAD OFTEN boasted of being the boomtown of upstate New York, the "Young Lion of the West." But in October 1825, its horizons expanded dramatically: Rochester became a city of the world. Its residents celebrated appropriately. "Such was the enthusiasm of the people that at two o'clock, eight handsome uniform companies were in arms, and an immense concourse of people had assembled," recorded William Stone, the official chronicler of the event. A small flotilla arrived from the west, on a newly completed canal. A local boat called the **Young Lion of the West** hailed the **Pioneer,** at the front of the arriving group. A dialogue between the captains ensued:

Question.—Who comes there?
Answer.—Your Brothers from the West, on
  the waters of the Great Lakes.

Q.—By what means have they been diverted
so far from their natural course?

A.—By the channel of the Grand Erie Canal.

Q.—By whose authority, and by whom, was
a work of such magnitude accomplished?

A.—By the authority and by the enterprise
of the patriotic People of the State of New
York.

The opening of the Erie Canal was the greatest event in the history of New York. Dreamed
of during colonial times, endorsed by George
Washington, projected and surveyed by boost-
ers and engineers since American independence,
funded and fought over by politicians for a decade,
begun in the aftermath of the War of 1812, completed in the fiftieth anniversary year of the battles
of Lexington and Concord, the Erie Canal transformed the economic geography of the eastern
half of North America. With 360 miles of channel,
forty feet wide and four feet deep; scores of dams
and locks, which raised and lowered boats over
ridges and hills; and aqueducts that spanned rivers
and creeks, giving the impression that the boats
they carried were soaring through the air, the Erie
Canal defeated the force of gravity that had compelled farmers west of the Appalachian chain to
send their produce west and south, down the Ohio
and Mississippi to New Orleans and the Gulf of
Mexico, even when that produce was bound for

the markets of the East. From the moment of the canal's 1825 opening, transport costs for wheat, corn, pigs, lumber, iron and everything else from the interior fell by as much as 90 percent. The canal reordered the leading cities of America. New York City surpassed New Orleans as America's first port, and it eclipsed Philadelphia as the nation's financial hub.

The business and political classes of New York saw what was coming and made the most of it. To announce the linking of Lake Erie to the Atlantic, they arranged an artillery salute that spanned the five hundred miles from Buffalo to New York City. At ten o'clock in the morning of October 26, 1825, just as the flotilla left Lake Erie and entered the canal, a cannon fired. The report was heard a few miles to the east, and the sound signaled a cannon there to fire. This discharge caused another discharge farther east, then another and another and another, the full length of the canal. At Albany, where the canal met the Hudson River, the artillery salute turned south, arriving at New York City a mere eighty-two minutes after it began and completing the most rapid long-distance communication in human history until then. For good measure, an echoing salute was sent in the opposite direction, and the thousand-mile call-and-response was accomplished in less than three hours.

Every town and village on the new canal was as

thrilled as Rochester at the prospect of traffic that would make them all rich. Albany outdid itself. "Twenty-four pieces of cannon were planted on the pier," William Stone recorded, "from which a grand salute was fired as the boats passed from the Canal into the basin, down which they proceeded, towed by yawls manned by twenty-four masters of vessels, and cheered onward by bands of music, and the huzzas of thousands of rejoicing citizens, who crowded the wharves, the south bridge, the vessels, and a double line of Canal boats, which extended through the whole length of the basin."

But New York City, suddenly the gateway to the American West, was the most delirious. "All attempts at description must be utterly in vain," Stone declared. Enormous crowds lined the route of a congratulatory parade. The harbor shone in unexampled glory. "Never before has been presented to the sight a fleet so beautiful as that which then graced our waters. The numerous array of steam-boats and barges, proudly breasting the billows and dashing on their way regardless of opposing winds and tides; the flags of all nations, and banners of every hue, streaming splendidly in the breeze; the dense columns of black smoke ever and anon sent up from the boats, now partially obscuring the view, and now spreading widely over the sky and softening down the glare of light and color; the roar of cannon from the various forts, accompanied by heavy volumes of white smoke, contrasting finely with the smoke from the steam-boats; the crowds of happy beings who thronged the decks, and the voice of whose joy was mingled with the sound of music, and not unfrequently drowned by the hissing of the steam; all these, and a thousand other circumstances, awakened an interest so intense, that 'the eye could not be satisfied with seeing, nor the ear with hearing.'"

An orgy of illuminations—fireworks—climaxed the festivities. "Such rockets were never before seen in New York. They were uncommonly large. Now they shot forth alternately showers of fiery serpents and dragons, 'gorgons, and hydras, and chimeras dire,' and now they burst forth and rained down showers of stars, floating in the atmosphere like balls of liquid silver. The volcanic eruption of fire-balls and rockets with which this exhibition was concluded, afforded a spectacle of vast beauty and sublimity. They were sent up apparently from the rear of the Hall"—City Hall—"to a great height, diverging like rays from a common centre, then floating for a moment like meteors of the brightest light, and falling over in a graceful curve, presenting a scene magnificent and enchanting."

William Stone was exhausted at the end but still enthralled. "Thus passed a day so glorious to the state and city, and so deeply interesting to the countless thousands who were permitted to behold and mingle in its exhibitions. We have before said that all attempts at description must be utterly in vain. Others can comprehend the greatness of the occasion; the Grand Canal is completed, and the waters of Lake Erie have been borne upon its surface, and mingled with the Ocean."

THE OPENING OF the Erie Canal stood as proxy for a series of events that launched America into the modern era. Canals had existed since colonial times, but in the first half of the nineteenth century they spread and ramified until they formed a network of watery avenues that linked cities and towns, farms and villages across much of the eastern United States. The steamboat further improved water transport; demonstrated by Robert Fulton in the initial decade of the century, the steamboat grew sufficiently safe and reliable to allow shippers to overcome the current of rivers and send goods economically upstream as well as down. In time the steamboats would be enlarged and altered for ocean travel, finally supplanting sailing vessels in the second half of the nineteenth century. Steam power was meanwhile applied to land travel. The first railroads appeared in America in the 1830s; within two decades they crisscrossed the East.

By then America's industrial revolution would be well begun. Manufacturing had been part of American existence since colonial days, with power provided by human and animal muscle and falling water. But the application of steam power to the production process triggered a surge in output. Textile looms, stamping presses and machine tools fashioned products far faster and at lower cost than they had been made before. The reduced costs generated broader demand, which in turn inspired additional investment in new equipment. A virtuous circle of growth developed, with the effects spilling over into the cities and regions where the labor-saving devices were located.

Strikingly—and fatefully—most of the industrial development occurred in the North. The saving of labor had little appeal in slave-based economies, where labor was a fixed cost rather than a variable one. The economy of the South grew, but by extension rather than by transformation. In essence, Georgia replicated itself in Alabama and Mississippi; Tennessee was another North Carolina. The additive growth of the South couldn't match the multiplicative growth of the North, and by the 1820s it was clear to objective observers that the South would fall further and further behind in wealth and population.

Travelers on the Ohio River, the boundary between North and South west of Pennsylvania, often noted the disparity between the degrees of economic development on the opposite banks of the river. On the north shore, the river towns of Ohio and Indiana bustled and throbbed, and the farms between the towns thrived. On the south bank, Virginia and Kentucky comparatively slumbered, with few towns and mile after mile of apparent wilderness.

Not coincidentally, the Ohio became an American River Jordan to Southern slaves. Beyond the stream was the promised land, the land where they might achieve their freedom if only they could reach it. There had always been kindhearted souls to help them on the journey; as the industrial revolution sharpened the divide between North and South, the number of such helpers increased. They established a covert network of routes and stopping points they called, in a metaphor apt to the moment, the Underground Railroad.

DANIEL WEBSTER FOUND himself in a predicament. He had seen one political cause sink beneath him: Federalism, which foundered off the New England coast in the years after the War of 1812. He thought he discovered a sturdier ship in the principle of free trade, which he defended against the broadsides of Henry Clay's protectionism. As the last stones were being placed in the walls of the locks of the Erie Canal, Webster delivered one of the best speeches of his life, in rebuttal to Clay, whom he accused of misconceiving, or misrepresenting, the nature of commerce. "Commerce is not a gambling among nations for a stake, to be won by some and lost by others," Webster said. "It has not the tendency necessarily to impoverish one of the parties to it, by which it enriches the other. All parties gain, all parties make profits, all parties grow rich, by the operations of just and liberal commerce." Protectionists obsessed over the concept of the balance of trade, contending that if America bought more from a country than it sold to that country, something was amiss and must be remedied. This was far too simplistic, Webster said. "If the world had but one clime and but one soil, if all men had the same wants and the same means, on the spot of their existence, to gratify those wants—then, indeed, what one obtained from the other by exchange would injure one party in the same degree that it benefitted the other." But this was not the world humans lived in. "We inhabit a various earth. We have reciprocal wants, and reciprocal means for gratifying one another's wants."

Commerce between nations was simply commerce between individuals writ large. "Cannot two individuals make an interchange of commodities which shall prove beneficial to both, or in which the balance of trade shall be in favor of both? If not, the tailor and shoemaker, the farmer and the smith, have hitherto very much misunderstood their own interests." Consider commerce between different regions, Webster asked. "Do we ever hear that because the intercourse between New York and Albany is advantageous to one of those places, it must therefore be ruinous to the other?" Of course not. The same principle applied to nations. Americans sold certain goods to Britain, and purchased other goods from Britain. Both sides benefited.

Yet what about countries that sold to the United

States but did not buy a comparable value of goods **from** the United States? Was that imbalance not injurious? By no means, said Webster. Americans bought much more from Russia than they sold to Russia. But commerce was not mere bilateral trade. "We send our own products, for example, to Cuba or to Brazil, we there exchange them for the sugar and coffee of those countries, and these articles we carry to St. Petersburg and there sell them." Other American cargoes went to Holland or Hamburg, where a similar exchange was made for goods that then went to Russia. "What difference does it make, in sense or reason, whether a cargo of iron be bought at St. Petersburg, by the exchange of a cargo of tobacco, or whether the tobacco has been sold on the way, in a better market, in a port of Holland, the money remitted to England, and the iron paid for by a bill on London?"

The protectionists professed a desire to foster new American industries. Webster spoke on behalf of American industries that already existed. Navigation and commerce were industries fully as legitimate as manufacturing, and they currently employed many thousands of workers. These workers would be sacrificed in the name of the notional manufacturing workers of the protectionists' dreams. The protectionists spoke as though every dollar paid by an American for a foreign item went to foreign producers; rather, much of that dollar paid the wages of American sailors, shipbuilders, dockworkers and the like. "Is not every such article the product of our own labor as truly as if we had manufactured it ourselves?"

The protectionists appealed to American security. Americans must produce what they consumed, the protectionists said, lest they be cut off by foreign rivals. These advocates mistook the nature of American power, Webster said. What was it that caused nations to respect America? It was the power that flowed from American prosperity. The protectionists asked: What nation had attained wide prosperity without encouraging manufacturing? Webster rejoined: "What nation ever reached the like prosperity without promoting foreign trade?" Again, the protectionists dreamed of an uncertain world to come; Webster defended the world as it existed, a world in which the United States was doing very well.

WEBSTER JUDGED THAT he had rarely spoken better. As with the other speeches he thought most highly of, he made sure his remarks on free trade soon circulated in printed form. He wrote out his speech and provided it to newspaper publishers and pamphleteers. Before long, though, he wished he could get every copy back.

The argument about free trade and protection was never about free trade and protection only. It was about politics, about influence, about ambition and retribution. After John Quincy Adams, with Henry Clay's help, snatched the presidency from Andrew Jackson, the Jacksonians scorched the earth around the new administration, denouncing Adams and Clay with every breath and every issue of the newspapers they founded for the purpose. They mobilized at once for the campaign of 1828. The caucus was dead as a vehicle for nominating candidates, with William Crawford's failure in 1824 supplying the death rattle. But no one knew what would replace it, and until something did, nominations fell to whichever groups stepped forward. The Tennessee legislature nominated Andrew Jackson almost before Adams had been inaugurated, ensuring that every act of Adams's tenure would be seen as a part of the next election campaign.

On no issue was this clearer than on the tariff, except that nothing was clear about the tariff. The opposing philosophical camps—the free traders and the protectionists—lost their coherence when tariff schedules began being written. Protectionists sought protection for their constituents and benefactors, not for industries or regions as a whole. Free traders wanted free trade in the articles produced by others, not in those they produced. Beyond this was the political maneuvering in the schedule writing; members of the House and Senate would swap protection for their constituents in exchange for protection for the constituents of other members. Confusing the matter further was the looming presidential election. The Jacksonians wrote schedules for the purpose of making Adams look bad; the Adams men tried to do the same to the Jacksonians. Members would introduce amendments intending to disown them after catching their opponents out. Through the murk and mire it became nearly impossible to discern definite principles in the positions of the opposing sides.

What eventually emerged was the tariff of 1828. Economically this revision of the duty schedules served the purposes of many manufacturers by raising rates on competing imports to as much as 50 percent of the value of the goods. It damaged consumers of those goods, who had to pay protected prices. Because the manufacturers were clustered in New England and some other states of the North, and because those manufacturers had louder voices in the lobbies than Northern consumers did, the tariff drew strong Northern support in the voting in Congress. Southerners felt badly used. As consumers they would pay the high prices, without an offsetting regional benefit to the few Southern manufacturers. There was also the prospect of foreign retaliation: Britain, in particular, might curtail its purchases of Southern cotton in response to the tariff.

Politically the tariff served its purpose of undermining the Adams administration. Tactical voting by members of the Jackson group in Congress, and equivocal statements by Jackson himself, allowed them to position their hero on both sides of the tariff question, as suited their purpose in various states. Adams's only hope of holding the presidency against Jackson in 1828 lay in an alliance of New England with some of the Southern states, but the tariff so plainly favored the former over the latter as to render this axis impossible.

Daniel Webster's political talents were oratorical rather than tactical. He got caught in the eddies of the tariff maneuverings and nearly drowned. His constituents cried for help. An early version of the bill offered insufficient protection to carpet making, declared a carpet maker. The industry faced ruin if the bill weren't changed, and he would be among the victims. "I must stop if the bill now reported is passed in its present form," he told Webster. A group of wool men met at Boston and sent Webster a petition demanding an increase in rates on wool products. "If the said bill should become a law," they predicted, with alarmed specificity, "all the manufactories of coarse woolens in our country, such as baizes, bockings, negro cloths, carpets &c. would be completely ruined."

The demands for protection contradicted Webster's philosophy of free trade. But he was a politician rather than a philosopher, and his philosophy began to weaken. "I fear we are getting into trouble here about the tariff," he wrote to a friend. "The House of Representatives will pass the bill; it will be a poor and inefficient aid to wool and woolens." His turn would come when the bill reached the Senate. "What shall we do with it?" he asked uncertainly.

He received an answer from Abbott Lawrence, a powerful wool man who gave his family name to the mill town of Lawrence, Massachusetts. Friends of wool in the Senate sufficiently amended the bill that Lawrence found it acceptable. "As far as woolens are concerned the bill is very much improved," he wrote to Webster. "New England would reap a great harvest by having the bill adopted as it now is." Lawrence and other New Englanders had worried, during and after the War of 1812, that their region was being eclipsed. The tariff could remedy this injury. "This bill if adopted as amended will keep the South and West in debt to New England the next hundred years."

WHAT ABBOTT LAWRENCE predicted was exactly what John Calhoun feared. Daniel Webster agonized until the end, his free-trade conscience wrestling with his protectionist constituents. "How I shall vote, if the final passage depends on me, nobody knows, and I hardly know myself," Webster told an associate. He felt the eyes of the country upon him. "If you see the **Telegraph** of today, you will see how marked a bird I am." His constituents ultimately won, and his conscience made excuses. "What reconciles me, in some measure, to the bill is that New England will, certainly, on the whole be benefitted by it; and some things which are wrong and bad we may hope to amend hereafter."

It was the sectionalism of the vote that rankled Calhoun. The vice president had nothing against protection per se; unlike Webster, he told himself, **he** hadn't changed his mind from the days when he had endorsed Henry Clay's American

System. Prudent protection of American industry against unfair competition made good sense. But **this** tariff, far from being a shield for the nation, was a sword swung by one section against the others. Calhoun wasn't privy to Abbott Lawrence's prediction to Webster that the South would be in debt to New England for a century, but from his chair as president of the Senate Calhoun heard the chortles of glee of the friends of the Northern manufacturers as they revised the bill to the satisfaction of Lawrence and his manufacturing colleagues.

Calhoun was hardly alone in feeling the South was being put upon. When discussion in the Senate turned to the appropriate title for the bill, John Randolph, with cynicism more accurate than was sometimes his norm, observed, "The bill, if it had its true name, should be called a bill to rob and plunder nearly one half of the Union for the benefit of the residue." Soon after passage the South started calling the new measure the "tariff of abominations."

Calhoun noted that the tariff hit the South at a vulnerable moment. A textile rebound of the early 1820s, after the effects of the 1819 panic wore off, had caused cotton prices to soar, prompting Southern planters to borrow money to bring new lands under cotton cultivation. Planters in other countries did the same, with the result that cotton glutted the market in 1828. Prices fell two-thirds between 1825 and 1828; leveraged planters found themselves over their heads in debt. "Never was there such universal and severe pressure on the whole South, excepting the portion which plants sugar," Calhoun wrote to his brother-in-law. "Our staples hardly return the expense of cultivation, and land and negroes have fallen to the lowest price, and can scarcely be sold at the present depressed rates." The tariff made bad matters much worse. "It is one of the great instruments of our impoverishment, and if persisted in must reduce us to poverty or compel us to an entire change of industry."

Proud Southerners, not least Calhoun, wouldn't stand for such treatment. The North had declared economic war on the South, they said; the South must defend itself. South Carolinians gathered during the summer of 1828 to voice their resistance to Northern tyranny. Many likened the moment to the era of the American Revolution and the tariff to the infamous Stamp Act, another tax measure passed over the objections of South Carolina. At one protest meeting Calhoun offered a toast: "The congress of '76—they taught the world how oppression could be successfully resisted. May the lesson teach rulers that their only safety is in justice and moderation."

The protesters sought a single voice to state their

case. Calhoun came at once to mind, and with the encouragement of the organizers of the protest he set to work. He examined sources old and new, familiar and obscure, general and technical, legal and political. By the time he stopped reading and writing, he had produced a manifesto of thirty-five thousand words.

He didn't publish at once. Calhoun recognized the combustible nature of his subject, and as the election of 1828 drew near, neither he nor other opponents of John Quincy Adams wanted a constitutional crisis to rescue Adams from executive eviction. Calhoun considered another run for the presidency, but such was the resentment among the Jacksonians against Adams that Calhoun could see that 1828 would be Jackson's year. Calhoun hunkered down in the vice presidency, willing to pass from being Adams's number two to being Jackson's if the electors approved.

The electors did approve, and Calhoun eased into a second term. For the presidential candidates, though, the contest was anything but easy. Jackson's advocates howled for Old Hickory, proclaiming to all who would listen that Adams and Henry Clay had stolen the last election and would steal this one if the honest people of the country didn't unite against them. John Eaton, a Jackson intimate and senator from Tennessee, and Sam Houston, a Tennessee congressman and Jackson protégé, formed a committee of correspondence that helped pro-Jackson papers with the writing of editorials and supplied pro-Jackson speakers with prepared remarks.

The Adams side countered with assaults on Jackson's character and accomplishments. Clay's phrase "military chieftain" was revived and recirculated, and it was embellished with allegations of Jackson's wrathfulness toward his soldiers. The Adams men printed and disseminated thousands of "coffin handbills": posters that bore black images of six coffins, one each for soldiers Jackson was said to have executed for wanting to leave his army upon the expiration of their enlistments. The true story was more complicated; their terms had **not** expired and they were therefore deserters, according to the court-martial that had found them guilty. Jackson declined to stay the executions.

The campaign plumbed depths untouched in previous contests. Anonymous Adamsites attacked Jackson's wife, Rachel. The circumstances of their wedding were clouded; Rachel had been married before, but her husband had abandoned her. She met Jackson, and the two fell in love. Word filtered west from Virginia, where her first wedding had taken place, that her husband had filed for divorce. Taking into account the slow pace of news in those days, Rachel and Jackson decided to act as though the divorce had gone through, and married. Only later did they learn that the divorce had **not** gone through and that Rachel was, in the eyes of the law, an adulteress and a bigamist. The irregularity was corrected after the divorce was finally completed; Rachel and Jackson repeated their vows. At the time the couple were young and unknown to the world, and no one in Nashville much cared. Love on the frontier often ran crooked. And the obvious tenderness and devotion Jackson and Rachel showed for each other during the next three decades made questions about the early days of their love seem petty and mean.

Yet the issue came up. It figured in a duel Jackson fought with a man named Charles Dickinson, which escalated from a squabble over a horse race to a deadly encounter at ten paces. Dickinson, firing first, placed a ball beside Jackson's heart, but Jackson, unflinching, leveled his pistol at Dickinson and pulled the trigger. Nothing happened; the cock had been imperfect. The rules of dueling allowed Jackson to recock and fire. He did so remorselessly, and hit Dickinson in the torso. Dickinson was carried from the field bleeding; he died hours later. Jackson survived his wound with the bullet inside him; he never again coughed without reliving the moment.

Jackson's rivals learned from Dickinson's fate to leave Rachel out of their criticism of the general—until Jackson was too famous, and they too numerous, for him to come after each one. In the 1828 campaign they dredged up the old stories and invented new ones. Rachel was an adulteress, a bigamist, a whore. In the ultimate insult to a white woman in the South at that time, she was called a "dirty black wench" by a paper in Henry Clay's Kentucky.

Jackson seethed. "When the midnight assassin strikes you to the heart, murders your family, and robs your dwelling, the heart sickens at the relation of the deed," he told a friend. "But this scene loses all its horrors when compared with the recent slander of a virtuous female propagated by the minions of power for political effect." Jackson understood his enemies' game. "It is evident that it is the last effort of the combined coalition to save themselves and destroy me. They calculated that it would arouse me to some desperate act by which I would fall prostrate before the people." He knew he couldn't strike back, or even answer the libels, without exposing Rachel to further abuse. "For the present my hands are pinioned." But they would not be bound forever. "The day of retribution and vengeance must come, when the guilty will meet their just reward."

AFTER THE LONG and ugly campaign, the election itself was anticlimactic. New England stuck with Adams, who also carried New Jersey and Delaware. Adams and Jackson divided the electoral votes of New York and Maryland. Jackson swept the rest of the country, including the two biggest states, Pennsylvania and Virginia, and everything south of the Potomac and west of the Appalachians. He trounced Adams in the popular vote by a margin of 56 percent to 44 and swamped him among electors by 178 to 83.

Jackson judged his victory less a personal triumph than a vindication of America's rising democracy. The label "Republican" had lost its meaning since the collapse of the Federalists, and Jackson's supporters had started calling themselves Democrats. They were farmers and shopkeepers, mechanics and day laborers, flatboat men and sawyers, butchers and carpenters. Most had modest education, at best. Many were only recently enfranchised. They were strongest in the West and the South. As a group they resented the elites who had controlled the government since the founding. They claimed Andy Jackson—the backcountry orphan, the Indian fighter, the duelist, the scourge of the British and of John Quincy Adams—as their own. They put their hero in the White House, and they delivered Democratic majorities to the Senate and the House. In the name of democracy they prepared to remake the government in the image of the ordinary people of America—in the image of themselves.

Jackson's part in the victory was spoiled almost at once by the greatest tragedy he ever suffered. The trials of the campaign had distressed Rachel tremendously; her health broke down, and in mid-December she suffered a heart attack. After lingering in pain for three days, she died.

Jackson was devastated. He buried her in the garden of the Hermitage, their home near Nashville. A winter rain soaked the ground, and drenched him, as he laid her to rest. He wondered if he could carry on. Rachel had been beside him in war and peace, in winter and summer, in sickness and health. Now he was supposed to go to Washington without her. He didn't know if he could do it. "At the time I least expected it, and could least spare her," he wrote, "she was snatched from me, and I left here a solitary monument of grief, without the least hope of happiness here below."

22

WHILE JACKSON WAS sitting watch by Rachel's bed in Nashville, John Calhoun in Columbia released his tract on the tariff to the world. His name appeared nowhere on the document, which was issued over the signatures of seven members of a select committee of the South Carolina legislature. He didn't acknowledge his authorship, partly because he held to the traditional belief of unsigned editorialists that an argument should stand on its merits rather than on the identity of the author, and partly because it might have been awkward for the vice president of the United States to be seen arguing against an assertion of federal power. Thomas Jefferson, when vice president, had withheld his identity as author of the Kentucky resolutions against the Alien and Sedition Acts, and Calhoun judged that what suited Jefferson suited him.

Calhoun got straight to the point. "The act of Congress of the last session, with the whole system of legislation imposing duties on imports—not for revenue, but for the protection of one branch of industry at the expense of others—is unconstitutional, unequal and oppressive, and calculated to corrupt the public virtue and destroy the liberty of the country," he declared. It was unconstitutional because it went beyond the powers granted to the central government by the Constitution. To be sure, the Constitution gave Congress the authority to establish impost duties. But this authority was given as a taxing power, for revenue, not as a power for protecting the commerce of one region. Indeed a tariff for protection was antithetical to a tariff for revenue, for the protection kept imports out, thereby depriving the government of revenue. The tariff advocates cited precedent as a basis for their law; Calhoun rejected this argument on its face. "Ours is not a government of precedents." Britain had a government of precedents: the common law. America had a government of the Constitution. "The only safe rule is the Constitution itself."

The Constitution had been stretched before, but never in such a blatantly sectional manner, Calhoun said. In this lay the inequality of the tariff. The tariff system subordinated the South to the North. "We are the serfs of the system, out of whose labor is raised not only the money paid into the Treasury but the funds out of which are drawn the rich rewards of the manufacturer and his associates in interest." The tariff let Northern manufacturers raise the price of goods they sold to the South, while the South could secure no comparable advantage for its products. "Our market is the world," Calhoun said. "We have no monopoly in the supply of our products; one half of the globe may produce them." The high prices the South was forced to pay to the North increased its own costs of production, threatening its market share abroad. "Once lost, it may be lost forever," Calhoun said of the South's overseas business. "And lose it we must, if we continue to be constrained, as we now are, on the one hand, by the general competition of the world, to sell **low**; and, on the other, by the Tariff, to buy **high**. We cannot withstand this double action. Our ruin must follow."

The tariff system would transform America into something like Europe; here its corrupting quality became most evident. "No system can be more efficient to rear up a moneyed aristocracy," Calhoun said. "Its tendency is to make the poor poorer and the rich richer." The monopolies would destroy the staple producers of the South, with worse to follow. "After we are exhausted, the contest will be between the capitalists and operatives"—workers—"for into these two classes it must, ultimately, divide society."

What was to be done by South Carolina and the rest of the aggrieved South? The only sure check on the power of the central government was the power of the states, Calhoun said. Jefferson and James Madison had made this argument in the Kentucky and Virginia resolves, and it remained true. "Power can only be restrained by power," Calhoun wrote. Alexander Hamilton had agreed in praising the dual nature of American federalism. "The different governments will control each other," Hamilton had said, and Calhoun concurred.

Calhoun proposed a procedure by which South Carolina could exercise its check. The state should call a convention to weigh the tariff and its effects. "It will belong to the Convention itself to determine, authoritatively, whether the acts of which we complain be unconstitutional; and if so, whether they constitute a violation so deliberate, palpable and dangerous as to justify the interposition of the State to protect its rights. If this question be decided in the affirmative, the Convention will then determine in what manner they ought to be declared null and void within the limits of the State."

Calhoun conceded that the Constitution did not explicitly give states the right to review federal law. Neither did it explicitly give the Supreme Court the right to review federal law. Yet the court **did** review federal law. So should the states. And the states had a constitutional advantage over the court, on account of the Tenth Amendment, which unambiguously reserved to the states and the people those powers not delegated to the central government. "Like other reserved rights," Calhoun said of the states' right of review, "it is to be inferred from the simple fact that it is not delegated."

Calhoun and South Carolina had withheld his protest until after the presidential election. He asserted that the delay reflected no hesitation or lack of conviction. Speaking of and for his fellow South Carolinians, he declared, "They would be unworthy of the name of freemen, of Americans, of Carolinians, if danger, however great, could cause them to shrink from the maintenance of their constitutional rights." Speaking for the committee, Calhoun concluded: "With these views the committee are solemnly of the impression, if the present usurpations and the professed doctrines of the existing system be persevered in, after due forbearance on the part of the State, that it will be her sacred duty to interpose—a duty to herself, to the Union, to the present and to future generations, and to the cause of liberty over the world—to arrest the progress of a usurpation which, if not arrested, must, in its consequences, corrupt the public morals and destroy the liberty of the country."

23

IT WAS AN explosive statement—too explosive, as it turned out, for the South Carolina legislature, which ordered five thousand copies of Calhoun's treatise printed but declined for the moment to adopt it formally. Calhoun hoped it would function as a shot across the bow of the aggrandizers in Washington. Much would depend on the new administration. "We have a dead calm in politics, which will continue until after the arrival of the President elect," he remarked to a South Carolina friend in January 1829. "There has been much idle speculation in relation to the formation of the new cabinet. It is a subject on which General Jackson himself, I take for granted, has not made up his mind, nor will he, if he acts prudently, till he has had an opportunity of seeing the whole ground." On the matter of the tariff in particular, Calhoun detected signs of progress. "I think there is a lowering of tone on the part of the Tariff states, and I am not altogether without hope, if General Jackson takes a correct general view of his position and places a sound man at the head of the Treasury Department, but that something like justice may be done to us." Yet South Carolina and all defenders of states' rights must remain vigilant.

The dead calm gave way to a tempest within weeks. The idea of inaugurating Andrew Jackson sent his supporters into delirium, with thousands deciding to join their champion on his great day. Some came to forestall any last-minute shenanigans by Adams and Henry Clay, whose joint capacity for another corrupt bargain was thought to have no bounds. Some simply wanted to celebrate the coming of age of democracy. Many were Westerners, thrilled to install a neighbor in the White House. Nearly all considered themselves the salt-of-the-earth types Jackson epitomized. More than a few were his former soldiers; on them were lost Clay's warnings about a military man at the head of the government. A sizable portion felt that the political classes in Washington looked down on them; as much as they admired Jackson for his accomplishments, they loved him for the fact that they could look him level in the eye, man to man, and know he'd not take it amiss.

They descended on Washington like an invading army. The national capital had never seen their like. They filled the inns and restaurants; they crowded the sidewalks and spat tobacco juice into the gutters. On the day of the inauguration they converged on the Capitol to witness Jackson's arrival. He entered the Senate chamber and nodded to John Calhoun, presiding. Calhoun administered the oath of office to the new members of the Senate. He had just finished when John Marshall, who would administer the oath to Jackson, entered. The rest of official Washington followed, with members of the House taking seats in the gallery and diplomats and attachés sitting and standing where they could.

On the stroke of noon Calhoun swung his gavel and adjourned the brief indoor session. All proceeded to the eastern portico of the Capitol, where Jackson's partisans awaited his appearance. The moment they saw the gaunt figure topped by the wild white hair, they raised a shout that sounded like a war whoop. Their cheering continued while twenty-four cannons heralded the new commander in chief.

Jackson stood calmly amid the uproar. When the tumult eventually eased, Justice Marshall stepped forward. The hubbub persisted loudly enough that only those in front could hear Marshall's voice and almost none could hear Jackson's. But when Jackson raised to his lips the Bible on which he had sworn, the army of his followers knew the deed was done, and they erupted once more.

Jackson turned to the crowd. His gaze brought them swiftly to silence. His inaugural address was succinct. He cited the free choice of the people as the source of his legitimacy and the fundament of democracy. He pledged to honor the rights of the states and interpret the Constitution strictly. He would pursue peaceful, constructive relations with foreign powers.

"It was grand—it was sublime," wrote Margaret Bayard Smith of the ceremony. "Thousands and thousands of people, without distinction of rank, collected in an immense mass round the Capitol." Mrs. Smith was one of the small group who made Washington their home rather than simply their place of business. She had known Jefferson and she dined with Henry Clay. She was skeptical of Jackson and wary of his followers. But the spectacle of the people claiming the presidency for one of their own caused her to reconsider; perhaps there was something to this idea of democracy after all.

She soon had third thoughts. Upon Jackson's conclusion, the crowd rushed the portico. Jackson shook hands with the first dozen but was compelled to retreat before the crush of the rest. He mounted his white stallion, maneuvered among the masses, and began the procession toward the executive mansion. "Such a cortege as followed him!" wrote Mrs. Smith. "Country men, farmers, gentlemen mounted and dismounted, boys, women and children, black and white. Carriages, wagons and carts all pursuing him to the President's house."

At the mansion the crowd's enthusiasm reached

new heights and its behavior new lows. "What a scene did we witness!" Margaret Smith said. "A rabble, a mob, of boys, negros, women, children, scrambling, fighting, romping. What a pity, what a pity! No arrangements had been made, no police officers placed on duty, and the whole house had been inundated by the rabble mob." Smith arrived too late to see the president, who had been nearly suffocated by well-wishers and been forced to flee to the safety of a nearby hotel. The celebration became a riot. "Cut glass and china to the amount of several thousand dollars had been broken in the struggle to get the refreshments. Punch and other articles had been carried out in tubs and buckets. But had it been in hogsheads it would have been insufficient." The revelers stuffed themselves with cake and ice cream and clamored for more. "Ladies fainted, men were seen with bloody noses, and such a scene of confusion took place as is impossible to describe. Those who got in could not get out by the door again but had to scramble out of windows."

Margaret Smith couldn't decide whether the day augured well or ill. But it certainly augured something new. "It was the People's day, and the People's President, and the People would rule," she said.

THE PEOPLE WOULD rule in the new era of democracy, but **how** they would rule remained to be seen. Advocates of democracy argued that the people knew their interests better than anyone else and that the people therefore were the best judges of government policy. Skeptics of democracy feared the emotionalism of the masses and worried that the people might be led astray through ignorance, shortsightedness or the conniving of small groups who masked self-interest in appeals to patriotism and other popular causes.

The democrats of the hour, the Jacksonians, seemed to have history in their favor. The tide of democracy had been rising for decades; its latest surge had carried democracy's tribune, the hero of New Orleans, into the highest office in the land. The Jacksonians had little reason to think the tide would turn. Nor, for that matter, did the skeptics of democracy. The former prepared for the best, the latter for the worst.

NONE PREPARED FOR a problem that afflicted the Jackson administration from the start. The marriage of John and Floride Calhoun had unfolded without surprises but not without difficulty. She bore one child after another, to a sum of ten. Three died early, leaving painful memories but still a full house at the upcountry plantation they called Fort Hill. The plantation was modest by South Carolina standards, and even by the standards of Floride's family. Without the money she brought to the marriage, Calhoun would have had to devote more of his time to the law, in the manner of Henry Clay and especially Daniel Webster. He built a library, separate from the house, where he did his reading and writing. But often he seemed in his own space, anyway, when he was pondering a point of the Constitution, of policy or of his own path forward.

Floride humored him, without good humor. She had no taste for politics and no tolerance for most of those who practiced it. She kept her distance from Washington, claiming, with cause, that her children needed her more at home than the politicians did at the capital. She eventually sent one of their daughters, Anna Maria—who found public affairs as fascinating as Calhoun did—to stand in for her by her husband's side.

Calhoun, in turn, humored her, as well as he could. She was difficult and opinionated—a combination, he concluded, that ran in her family. He learned to abide her prejudices, saving his energy for battles he thought he might win. A letter to their eldest son, Andrew, captured the resignation he felt toward his spouse. Mother and son had argued; Calhoun thought Andrew had the better case. But he counseled him to accept less than victory. "As to the suspicion and unfounded blame of your mother, you must not only bear them, but forget them," Calhoun said. "With the many good qualities of her mother, she inherits her suspicious and fault-finding temper, which has been the cause of much vexation in the family. I have borne her with patience, because it was my duty to do so, and you must do the same, for the same reason. It has been the only cross of my life."

Floride's opinions seldom intruded on Calhoun's career. A fateful exception occurred at the beginning of Andrew Jackson's presidency. Floride accompanied her husband to Washington for his swearing-in as Jackson's vice president, and immediately conceived a dislike of Margaret Eaton, the wife of John Eaton, Jackson's secretary of war. Peg Eaton was generally thought the most beautiful woman in Washington, and she acted the part. She drew the attention of Washington men and the annoyance of Washington women. She had a history that intensified both responses. As the daughter of a Washington innkeeper, Peg had grown up smiling and flirting with the male guests, who included John Eaton and occasionally Andrew Jackson. Eaton, a widower, flirted back, though Peg was married. Her husband was a young naval officer named John Timberlake. Timberlake's assignments carried him far from Washington for extended periods, leaving Eaton and Peg the opportunity to improve their acquaintance. In 1828, Peg received news that her husband had died. She wasted little time mourning and began seeing Eaton openly. At the end of that year they were engaged; on the first day of 1829 they were wed.

Two months later Jackson was inaugurated and the trouble began. Floride Calhoun, as spouse of the vice president, not to mention a member of the South Carolina aristocracy, was positioned, in the absence of a presidential first lady, to set the social tone in the capital. Tone-setting was deemed by many in Washington to be crucial at this juncture, given the riotous character of the inauguration. Someone must instruct these rowdy Westerners in the protocols of capital life. Someone must keep democracy from descending into anarchy.

Washington looked to Floride Calhoun for cues. Those whom she visited and received would be visited and received by the other women and, with them, their husbands. Floride refused to return a visit from Peg Eaton. She judged that for a woman to carry on so openly while married, to remarry so quickly, affronted the mores on which society rested. Floride didn't consider herself a prig but rather a defender of the family. It perhaps contributed to her opinion that she had grown quite matronly in appearance and manner, while Peg, not many years younger, still looked and acted the coquette. Floride and the other wives of Washington had always wondered, when their husbands traveled to the capital without them, whether the stories told of the political bachelors were true. Peg Eaton suggested that they were, and if she were not rebutted, all the wives would be tarred. Floride took a stand for decency by taking a stand against Peg Eaton.

JOHN CALHOUN APPRECIATED the implications of Floride's decision. Andrew Jackson's sentimental view of women was well known; the two women who had been most important to him—his mother and his wife—he revered as angels. Particularly after the death of Rachel under the weight of slander, he could be expected to take the part of Peg Eaton. It was credibly reported around Washington that John Eaton, a longtime Jackson friend, had sought Jackson's blessing before marrying Peg and had obtained it. Jackson was known to be loyal to a fault. The more a friend of his was attacked, the more ardently he defended him—and his wife.

Calhoun weighed the risks of crossing Old Hickory against those of crossing Floride. He opted for household peace. He accepted Floride's explanation that the fault in the Eaton affair, if any, was not hers. "She said that she considered herself in the light of a stranger in the place," Calhoun later recounted, referring to the capital; "that she knew nothing of Mrs. Eaton, or the truth or falsehood of the imputations on her character; and that she conceived it to be the duty of Mrs. Eaton, if innocent, to open her intercourse with the ladies who resided in the place and who had the best means of forming a correct opinion of her conduct, and not with those who, like herself, had no means of forming a correct judgment."

Calhoun's explanation persuaded no one. Of course a husband would defend his wife. The boycott spread. Other cabinet wives followed Floride's lead and pulled their husbands after them. At first the effects were merely social: awkwardness at receptions and dinners and occasionally on the sidewalks of the capital. But political consequences followed. Washington divided into pro-Peg and anti-Peg camps. Jackson's cabinet became paralyzed as the boycotters refused to attend meetings with the defenders. The affair invaded Jackson's own home when the wife of Andrew Donelson,

Jackson's nephew, surrogate son and private secretary, joined the anti-Peg crowd. Andrew and Emily Donelson lived in the White House with Jackson, helping allay the depression that dogged him after Rachel's death. But when Emily took the side of Floride Calhoun against Peg Eaton, Jackson sent her away. Her husband, forced to choose between his wife and his uncle, chose his wife. Jackson was left alone in the mansion, without family or friend.

Yet the president didn't waver. "Mrs. Eaton is as chaste as those who attempt to slander her," Jackson declared. He would stand by her, and by her husband. "I would sink with honor to my grave before I would abandon my friend."

ONE WHO JOINED Jackson by the side of the Eatons was Martin Van Buren, the secretary of state. Van Buren had been a senator from New York during the tortuous maneuverings that produced the tariff of 1828; he had choreographed the feints and ploys that allowed Jackson to seem a supporter of the tariff in the North and an opponent in the South. Jackson's victory that year owed much to Van Buren, who was rewarded by receiving the state department. Van Buren's cleverness allowed him to play both sides of most streets he traveled, but in the Peg Eaton case he stood squarely with the accused—and beside the president.

As the boycott spread, Van Buren intensified

his efforts on Peg's behalf. He had a weakness for pretty women, and he sincerely sympathized with Peg. Yet he also perceived Peg as a vehicle for ingratiating himself with Jackson. He called on the Eatons personally and made sure to invite them to the receptions he hosted as secretary of state. He defended Peg to foreign diplomats and let them know they must treat her with the dignity due any cabinet spouse.

His approach prospered. "I have found the President affectionate, confidential, and kind to the last degree," Van Buren wrote to a friend. "I am entirely satisfied that there is no degree of good feeling or confidence which he does not entertain for me."

Jackson himself couldn't speak too highly of Van Buren. "I have found him every thing that I could desire him to be, and believe him not only deserving **my** confidence, but the confidence of the nation," the president told John Overton, a Tennessee friend. "Instead of his being selfish and intriguing, as has been represented by some of his opponents, I have ever found him frank, open, candid, and manly. As a counsellor he is able and prudent, republican in his principles and one of the most pleasant men to do business with I ever saw.

"I wish I could say as much for Mr. Calhoun," Jackson continued. "You know the confidence I once had in that gentleman." Calhoun's actions in the Eaton affair caused Jackson to see him in a different light. Calhoun was working at cross-purposes to the administration, the president judged, though Calhoun left the actual obstruction to other hands. "Most of the troubles, vexations and difficulties I have had to encounter since my arrival in this city have been occasioned by his friends." And by his wife, Jackson might have added, had he been less respectful of women as a group.

THE EATON AFFAIR continued as Congress convened in the new year of 1830. The main issue before the legislature was the tariff. John Calhoun's exposition had been disseminated far beyond South Carolina, and many in the capital thought the Carolinians were itching for a fight. The first test of strength came on a matter apparently unrelated to the tariff. Samuel Foot of Connecticut introduced a resolution requesting a review of the process by which federal lands in the West were surveyed and sold. The query might have been a sincere attempt to gather information, but Western representatives bristled at what they took to be an effort by New England to hinder their growth. Thomas Benton of Missouri and others blasted the New Englanders, and they found ready allies among Southern opponents of the tariff, which was similarly attributed to Yankee malevolence.

John Calhoun would have jumped in had he not

been restrained by the Constitution and by Senate practice. As vice president, Calhoun presided over the Senate, hearing every word there spoken. But he was not supposed to speak on matters of substance, and he couldn't vote except to break a tie. The cause of South Carolina fell to Robert Hayne, a veteran of the War of 1812 who had been sent by the South Carolina legislature to the Senate in 1823. Hayne was known for his temper, his sarcasm and his devotion to states' rights. He was not among the first rank of Senate speakers, but in the reaction to Samuel Foot's resolution he stepped forward and during two days defended the honor and practices of his state and region.

Taking Daniel Webster as the spokesman for New England, Hayne imputed to Webster the sins of the Northeast. He scoured Webster's speeches for slights against the South and its institutions and practices. Webster had impugned Southern honor, Hayne said, when, in one address, he had contrasted the prosperity of Ohio with a supposed backwardness in Kentucky and attributed the difference to slavery. Hayne denounced such section-baiting as egregious and partisan. "I thought I could discern the very spirit of the Missouri question," he said. Hayne refused to be lectured to by a senator from Massachusetts. New England acted high and moral on the slave question, but its hands were as dirty as those of any Southern state, and had been so from the beginning. "The profits of the slave trade were not confined to the South," Hayne said. "Southern ships and Southern sailors were not the instruments of bringing slaves to the shores of America, nor did our merchants reap the profits of that 'accursed traffic.'" Northern merchants continued to batten on slavery. "I am thoroughly convinced that, at this time, the states north of the Potomac actually derive greater profits from the labor of our slaves, than we do ourselves." Most Southern trade with the world was conducted through Northern merchants and financial houses; those individuals and firms would be commercial shadows of their current selves if not for Southern slave labor.

The modern South hadn't invented slavery, Hayne remarked. "If slavery, as it now exists in this country, be an evil, we of the present day found it ready made to our hands. Finding our lot cast among a people, whom God had manifestly committed to our care, we did not sit down to speculate on abstract questions of theoretical liberty. We met it as a practical question of obligation and duty." Obligation and duty included accounting for the welfare of the enslaved. "We resolved to make the best of the situation in which Providence had placed us, and to fulfill the high trust which had developed upon us as the owners of slaves, in the only way in which such a trust could be fulfilled, without spreading misery and ruin throughout the land."

Northern abolitionists demanded immediate

freedom for the slaves. Nothing could be more irresponsible, Hayne said. Southerners, who knew slaves better than any Northerners, had discovered generations ago that black slaves were fundamentally different from white men. "We found that we had to deal with a people whose physical, moral, and intellectual habits and character totally disqualified them from the enjoyment of the blessings of freedom." If freed, what would become of the slaves? "We could not send them back to the shores from whence their fathers had been taken; their numbers forbid the thought, even if we did not know that their condition here is infinitely preferable to what it possibly could be among the barren sands and savage tribes of Africa." Hayne asserted that the North had nothing to boast of in its treatment of free blacks, who often huddled in Northern cities. "There does not exist, on the face of the whole earth, a population so poor, so wretched, so vile, so loathsome, so utterly destitute of all the comforts, conveniences, and decencies of life, as the unfortunate blacks of Philadelphia, and New York, and Boston." Liberty to them was a curse, not a blessing.

But neither slavery nor land policy, nor even the tariff, formed the heart of the issue at hand. The crux of the matter was the nature of the Union, Hayne said. Webster and his Northern friends claimed to defend the Union, but what they were really defending was the national government, which they sought to enlarge and consolidate. The Union and the government were two different things, and the distinction was crucial in understanding the true purpose of the Constitution. "It was not to draw power from the States, in order to transfer it to a great national government, but, in the language of the Constitution itself, 'to form a more perfect union,'" Hayne said. How was this to be accomplished? "By 'establishing justice,' 'promoting domestic tranquility,' and 'securing the blessings of liberty to ourselves and our posterity.'" Hayne paused for effect. "This is the true reading of the Constitution," he said.

Hayne hammered Webster for inconsistency, indeed hypocrisy. Webster had ardently opposed tariff protection in 1824, only to reverse course and support it in 1828. Webster claimed to love the Union, but his Federalist friends had been on the verge of secession at the Hartford convention. In fact, Webster's whole program of government aggrandizement was the greatest threat to the Union as it existed under any honest reading of the Constitution.

Who, then, were the true defenders of the Union? "Those who would confine the federal government strictly within the limits prescribed by the Constitution, who would preserve to the states and the people all powers not expressly delegated, who would make this a federal and not a national Union, and who, administering the government in a spirit of equal justice, would make it a blessing and not a curse."

And who were the enemies of the Union? "Those who are in favor of consolidation; who are constantly stealing power from the States and adding strength to the federal government; who, assuming an unwarrantable jurisdiction over the States and the people, undertake to regulate the whole industry and capital of the country."

Hayne disavowed any previous animus toward Webster or New England. "This controversy is not of my seeking," he said. But a South Carolinian did not back down from a fight. "If the gentleman provokes the war, he shall have war. Sir, I will not stop at the border; I will carry the war into the enemy's territory."

HAYNE'S SPEECH PRODUCED a sensation. Charles March was an ally of Webster and an enemy of everything Hayne stood for. But March had to grant that Hayne had done well. "The dashing nature of the attack; the assurance, almost insolence, of its tone; the severity and apparent truth of the accusations; confounded almost every hearer," he recalled. "The immediate impression of the speech was most assuredly disheartening to the cause Mr. Webster upheld." Many others lauded Hayne's effort. "Congratulations from almost every quarter were showered upon the speaker,"

March recorded. "Mr. Benton said, in the full Senate, that much as Col. Hayne had done before to establish his reputation as an orator, a statesman, a patriot and a gallant son of the South, the efforts of that day would eclipse and surpass the whole." The Southern press praised Hayne to the sky. None of the great English orators—Chatham, Burke, Fox—could have done better, the Southern editorialists said.

Yet a few adherents of Hayne's cause weren't convinced he had carried the field. "These gentlemen knew, for they had felt, Mr. Webster's power," March said. "They knew the great resources of his mind, the immense range of his intellect, the fertility of his imagination, his copious and fatal logic, the scathing severity of his sarcasm, and his full and electrifying eloquence." One of the doubters observed, to a Hayne enthusiast who was ready to read last rites over Webster, "He has started the lion. But wait till we hear his roar or feel his claws."

Edward Everett would win renown as an orator the equal of almost any in America; having come to Washington to witness the fight over the tariff, he sought out Webster that evening. "Mr. Webster conversed with me freely and at length upon the subject of the reply, which he felt it necessary to make to Colonel Hayne's speech," Everett recounted. "He regarded that speech as an entirely unprovoked attack upon the Eastern States, which it was scarcely possible for him, as a New England senator, to leave unnoticed. He thought Colonel Hayne's speech, however, much more important in another point of view, that is as an exposition of a system of politics which, in Mr. Webster's opinion, went far to change the form of government from that which was established by the Constitution, into that (if it could be called a government) which existed under the confederation. He expressed his intention of putting that theory to rest for ever, as far as it could be done by an argument in the Senate chamber."

Everett knew Webster well enough to have a basis of emotional comparison. "I never saw him more calm and self-possessed, nor in better spirits," Everett said. "And in fact the dry business tone in which he partly talked and partly read over his points to me, gave me some uneasiness, for fear he was not sufficiently aware how much was expected of him the next day."

26

THAT NEXT DAY—JANUARY 26, 1830—found Washington abuzz in a way it hadn't been for years. Not since the Missouri debate had emotions in Congress been so engaged; not since the War of 1812 had the integrity, even existence, of the Union seemed so imperiled. The personal aspect of the quarrel—face-to-face combat in the political genre the age most revered—made it chillingly delicious. Hayne had issued a challenge; Webster had no choice but to accept it.

The House had scheduled business for that morning, but none was conducted. Members left their chamber to find seats in the Senate. The outer doors opened to visitors at nine, three hours before the scheduled start of the Senate session. Within minutes every spot was filled. Journalists and stenographers elbowed close to where Webster would stand, to take down his words. Printing presses awaited the transcript.

Webster felt the tension of the others but showed

little himself. The weight of expectation lay upon him, but it seemed to concentrate his energies rather than distract or disperse them. He wore a blue coat and a buff vest—the colors of the army of the Revolutionary War—with a white cravat, and his appearance arrested the attention of all in the room. "Time had not thinned nor bleached his hair; it was as dark as the raven's plumage, surmounting his massive brow in ample folds," Charles March recalled. "His eyes, always dark and deep-set, enkindled by some glowing thought, shone from beneath his somber, overhanging brow like lights, in the blackness of night, from a sepulchre."

Webster rose and looked to the chair. "Mr. President," he said, nodding to John Calhoun, and then turned to the rest of the chamber. "When the mariner has been tossed for many days in thick weather, and on an unknown sea, he naturally avails himself of the first pause in the storm, the earliest glance of the sun, to take his latitude, and ascertain how far the elements have driven him from his true course. Let us imitate this prudence, and, before we float farther on the waves of this debate, refer to the point from which we departed, that we may at least be able to conjecture where we now are." He asked for a reading of the Foot resolution. The clerk repeated the query about public lands.

Webster nodded knowingly. "We have thus heard,

sir, what the resolution is, which is actually before us for consideration; and it will readily occur to every one that it is almost the only subject about which something has not been said in the speech, running through two days, by which the Senate has been now entertained by the gentleman from South Carolina. Every topic in the wide range of our public affairs, whether past or present—every thing, general or local, whether belonging to national politics, or party politics, seems to have attracted more or less of the honorable member's attention, save only the resolution before us. He has spoken of every thing but the public lands. They have escaped his notice. To that subject, in all his excursions, he has not paid even the cold respect of a passing glance."

Webster twitted Hayne further. He explained that he hadn't been expecting to be in the Senate when Hayne spoke. "It so happened that it would have been convenient for me to be elsewhere," he said. "The honorable member, however, did not incline to put off the discussion to another day. He had a shot, he said, to return, and he wished to discharge it. That shot, sir, which it was kind thus to inform us was coming, that we might stand out of the way, or prepare ourselves to fall before it, and die with decency, has now been received. Under all advantages, and with expectation awakened by the tone which preceded it, it has been discharged, and has spent its force. It may become me to say no more of its effect, than that, if nobody is found, after all, either killed or wounded by it, it is not the first time, in the history of human affairs, that the vigor and success of the war have not quite come up to the lofty and sounding phrase of the manifesto."

Webster noticed the chuckles of Northern senators but pretended not to. He professed hurt that Hayne had made things so personal by saying that he—Webster—had assailed the South and slavery without cause. There was no basis for such an assertion, Webster said. "I did not utter a single word which any ingenuity could torture into an attack on the slavery of the South. I said, only, that it was highly wise and useful in legislating for the northwestern country, while it was yet a wilderness, to prohibit the introduction of slaves: and added, that I presumed, in the neighboring state of Kentucky, there was no reflecting and intelligent gentleman, who would doubt, that if the same prohibition had been extended, at the same early period, over that commonwealth, her strength and population would, at this day, have been far greater than they are." Smiling slightly, Webster went on, "If these opinions be thought doubtful, they are, nevertheless, I trust, neither extraordinary nor disrespectful."

Webster accounted Hayne and the South too quick to cry meddling in their internal affairs. This suggested a worrisome hypersensitivity; it was also specious. Abolitionists were a fringe element in the North, with no influence on the men who made decisions. "There is not, and never has been, a disposition in the North to interfere with these interests of the South," Webster said. "Such interference has never been supposed to be within the power of government; nor has it been, in any way, attempted. It has always been regarded as a matter of domestic policy, left with the states themselves, and with which the federal government had nothing to do."

Webster observed that Hayne had charged him with contradiction in supporting the tariff of 1828 after previously opposing the tariff. He acknowledged that he had changed his mind, but not so dramatically as South Carolinians had. They now threatened to secede over the tariff, yet little more than a decade earlier they had been in favor. The tariff of 1816 had received the hearty support of South Carolina's votes. "But for those votes, it could not have passed in the form in which it did pass; whereas, if it had depended on Massachusetts votes, it would have been lost."

Such inconsistency, however, had not diminished Webster's respect for South Carolina. "I claim part of the honor, I partake in the pride, of her great names. I claim them for countrymen, one and all. The Laurenses, the Rutledges, the Pinckneys, the Sumpters, the Marions—Americans, all—whose fame is no more to be hemmed in by state lines than their talents and patriotism were capable of being circumscribed within the same narrow limits."

Even so, he couldn't forget his own state. "Mr. President, I shall enter on no encomium upon Massachusetts—she needs none. There she is— behold her, and judge for yourselves. There is her history—the world knows it by heart. The past, at least, is secure. There is Boston, and Concord, and Lexington, and Bunker Hill—and there they will remain forever. The bones of her sons, falling in the great struggle for independence, now lie mingled with the soil of every state, from New England to Georgia; and there they will lie forever. And, sir, where American liberty raised its first voice, and where its youth was nurtured and sustained, there it still lives, in the strength of its manhood, and full of its original spirit."

WEBSTER STOPPED AND looked around the Senate. His halting let the members know the preliminaries were over. He held the silence, then turned to the fundamental purpose for which he spoke. "It is to state, and to defend, what I conceive to be the true principles of the Constitution under which we are here assembled," he said.

He outlined the case Hayne had made for South Carolina. "I understand the honorable gentleman from South Carolina to maintain, that it is a right of the state legislatures to interfere, whenever, in their judgment, this government transcends its constitutional limits, and to arrest the operation of its laws. I understand him to maintain this right, as a right existing **under** the Constitution; not as a right to overthrow it, on the ground of extreme necessity, such as would justify violent revolution. I understand him to maintain an authority, on the part of the states, thus to interfere, for the purpose of correcting the exercise of power by the general government, of checking it, and of compelling it to conform to their opinion of the extent of its powers. I understand him to maintain, that the ultimate power of judging of the constitutional extent of its own authority is not lodged exclusively in the general government, or any branch of it; but that, on the contrary, the states may lawfully decide for themselves, and each state for itself, whether, in a given case, the act of the general government transcends its power. I understand him to insist that if the exigency of the case, in the opinion of any state government, require it, such state government may, by its own sovereign authority, annul an act of the general government which it deems plainly and palpably unconstitutional."

He paused again, now to permit Hayne to object to this characterization of his position. Hayne did not.

Webster then began to dismantle the South Carolinian's argument, point by point. He distinguished between natural rights and constitutional rights. "We, sir, who oppose the Carolina doctrine, do not deny that the people may, if they choose, throw off any government, when it become oppressive and intolerable, and erect a better in its stead. We all know that civil institutions are established for the public benefit, and that when they cease to answer the ends of their existence, they may be changed." This was the **natural** right of revolution. But it was not what Hayne was asserting. Hayne was claiming for the states a **constitutional** right to nullify federal law. "I understand the gentleman to maintain, that, without revolution, without civil commotion, without rebellion, a remedy for supposed abuse and transgression of the powers of the general government lies in a direct appeal to the interference of the state governments."

At this point Hayne did interject, only to agree. He said he argued for the "right of constitutional resistance." In case of a violation of the Constitution by the national government, the states could interpose. And this interposition was constitutional.

"So, sir, I understood the gentleman, and am happy to find that I did not misunderstand him," Webster continued. His tone acquired a sarcastic note. "What he contends for, is, that it is constitutional to interrupt the administration of the

Constitution itself, in the hands of those who are chosen and sworn to administer it, by the direct interference, in form of law, of the states, in virtue of their sovereign capacity."

Webster granted that the people were not bound to obey unconstitutional laws, and that they might disobey them without overturning the government. But he differed with Hayne on who would decide unconstitutionality. This was the crux of the whole argument. "The great question is, whose prerogative is it to decide on the constitutionality or unconstitutionality of the laws?" Hayne contended the prerogative was the states'. Webster asserted that it lay with the federal government, in particular the federal judiciary.

Deciding the question required probing the nature of the national government and the source of its power. "Whose agent is it?" asked Webster. "Is it the creature of the state legislatures, or the creature of the people?" Different answers yielded different conclusions. "If the government of the United States be the agent of the state governments, then they may control it, provided they can agree in the manner of controlling it. If it be the agent of the people, then the people alone can control it, restrain it, modify, or reform it."

Webster took his stand with the people. "It is, sir, the people's Constitution, the people's government; made for the people; made by the people; and answerable to the people." The people of

America had created the national government and made it sovereign. "The people of the United States have declared that this Constitution shall be the supreme law. We must either admit the proposition, or dispute their authority."

Hayne had contended that the states determined constitutionality, and that they did so individually. Webster examined how this must work in practice. "In Carolina, the tariff is a palpable, deliberate usurpation; Carolina, therefore, may **nullify** it, and refuse to pay the duties. In Pennsylvania, it is both clearly constitutional, and highly expedient; and there, the duties are to be paid. And yet we live under a government of uniform laws, and under a Constitution, too, which contains an express provision, as it happens, that all duties shall be equal in all the states! Does not this approach absurdity? If there be no power to settle such questions, independent of either of the states, is not the whole Union a rope of sand? Are we not thrown back again, precisely, upon the old Confederation?" The people had rejected the Confederation by ratifying the Constitution, whose central point was to prevent the states from vetoing measures enacted for the common national good. "The people had had quite enough of that kind of government, under the Confederacy," Webster said.

He asked his listeners to consider how nullification might proceed in practice. He chose the case of the tariff, to which South Carolina so objected. "If we do not repeal it, (as we probably shall not) she will then apply to the case the remedy of her doctrine. She will, we must suppose, pass a law of her legislature, declaring the several acts of Congress, usually called the tariff laws, null and void, so far as they respect South Carolina or the citizens thereof." Up to this point, the fight would be all on paper. But it would soon enter the world of men and arms.

Webster sketched the scenario. "The collector at Charleston is collecting the duties imposed by these tariff laws; he, therefore, must be stopped. The collector will seize the goods if the tariff duties are not paid. The state authorities will undertake their rescue: the marshal, with his posse, will come to the collector's aid, and here the contest begins. The militia of the state will be called out to sustain the nullifying act." Speaking as an aside, Webster again taunted Hayne: "They will march, sir, under a very gallant leader: for I believe the honorable member himself commands the militia of that part of the state."

The militia commander would explain his cause, Webster said. "He will raise the nullifying act on his standard and spread it out as his banner! It will have a preamble, bearing that the tariff laws are palpable, deliberate and dangerous violations of the Constitution!" The militia commander

would march his men to the customhouse.
He would order the collector to cease collecting
the tariff duties.

The collector would weigh the matter. "Here
would ensue a pause, for they say that a certain
stillness precedes the tempest." The collector and
his clerks would have questions for the militia commander. "They would inquire whether it was not
somewhat dangerous to resist a law of the United
States. What would be the nature of their offense,
they would wish to learn, if they, by military force
and array, resisted the execution in Carolina of a
law of the United States, and it should turn out,
after all, that the law **was constitutional**?"

How would Commander Hayne reply? "He
would answer, of course, treason. No lawyer could
give any other answer."

The collectors would ask how he proposed to
defend them. "We are not afraid of bullets, but
treason has a way of taking people off, that we do
not much relish."

The commander would reply, "Look at my floating banner. See there the **nullifying law!**"

"Is it your opinion, gallant commander," they
would say, "that if we should be indicted for
treason, that same floating banner of yours would
make a good plea in bar?"

"South Carolina is a sovereign State," he would
reply.

"That is true. But would the judge admit our plea?"

"These tariff laws are unconstitutional, palpably, deliberately, dangerously."

"That all may be so; but if the tribunals should not happen to be of that opinion, shall we swing for it? We are ready to die for our country, but it is rather an awkward business, this dying without touching the ground! After all, that is a sort of **hemp**-tax, worse than any part of the tariff."

Webster smiled slightly and paused. Then he turned more serious again. He concluded his scenario: "Mr. President, the honorable gentleman would be in a dilemma, like that of another great general. He would have a knot before him, which he could not untie. He must cut it with his sword. He must say to his followers, defend yourselves with your bayonets; and this is war—civil war."

WEBSTER LET THE ominous syllables hang in the air for several seconds. Hayne and the South Carolinians steered clear of this possible consequence of their course, but Webster wanted the Senate to look it in the eye.

Then he sketched another path. Hayne played on fear; Webster asserted hope. "The people have preserved this, their own chosen Constitution, for forty years, and have seen their happiness, prosperity, and renown, grow with its growth, and strengthen with its strength," he said. "It is to that Union we owe our safety at home, and our consideration and dignity abroad. It is to that Union that we are chiefly indebted for whatever makes us most proud of our country." The Union had been forged in the fires of adversity, in the ruined finances and disordered commerce of the decade after the Revolution, and it had turned the nation around. "Under its benign influences, these great interests immediately awoke, as from the dead, and sprang forth with newness of life. Every year of its duration has teemed with fresh proofs of its utility and its blessings; and, although our territory has stretched out wider and wider, and our population spread farther and farther, they have not outrun its protection or its benefits."

The nullifiers complained of the cost of the tariff; they contended that the Union threatened liberty; they said they would choose liberty over the Union. Webster rejoined that the cost was nothing beside the benefits the Union provided, that the Union was liberty's stoutest defense, and that the alternative to the Union was not liberty but chaos. Returning to the question of civil war, he trembled to consider what it might entail. "When my eyes shall be turned to behold, for the last time, the sun in Heaven, may I not see him shining on the broken and dishonored fragments of a once glorious Union; on states dissevered, discordant, belligerent; on a land rent with civil feuds, or drenched, it may be, in fraternal blood!"

No, Webster prayed, not that. Instead: "Let their last feeble and lingering glance, rather behold the gorgeous ensign of the Republic, now known and honored throughout the earth, still full high advanced, its arms and trophies streaming in their original luster, not a stripe erased or polluted, nor a single star obscured—bearing for its motto, no such miserable interrogatory as 'What is all this worth?' Nor those other words of delusion and folly, 'Liberty first, and Union afterwards'—but every where, spread all over in characters of living light, blazing on all its ample folds, as they float over the sea and over the land, and in every wind under the whole Heavens, that other sentiment, dear to every true American heart—'Liberty and Union, now and forever, one and inseparable!' "

THE ROOM FELL hushed when Webster finished. Not a word was uttered; hardly a soul stirred. John Calhoun, in the chair, became disconcerted by the silence and the approbation it implied. He swung the gavel and demanded "Order," though no more orderly place existed within fifty miles.

Nearly all present, even those disagreeing with Webster, were mesmerized. Charles March had watched the Massachusetts delegation while Webster told of their state's glorious part in

American history. "Their feelings were strained to the highest tension," March recounted. "And when the orator, concluding his encomium upon the land of their birth, turned, intentionally or otherwise, his burning eye full upon them—**they shed tears like girls!**" The intensity mounted throughout the chamber as Webster came to his end. "The exulting rush of feeling with which he went through the peroration threw a glow over his countenance, like inspiration. Eye, brow, each feature, every line of the face seemed touched, as with a celestial fire. All gazed as at something more than human. So Moses might have appeared to the awe-struck Israelites as he emerged from the dark clouds and thick smoke of Sinai, his face all radiant with the breath of divinity!" By the time he wrote his memoir, March had witnessed many speeches. But he never saw anything like this. "No one who was not present can understand the excitement of the scene," he said. "No one who was can give an adequate description of it."

Robert Hayne was a proud man, but he wasn't deaf and blind. That night Andrew Jackson held a levee at the executive mansion. Webster and Hayne were both there. Hayne approached Webster, who offered his hand and asked, "How are you this evening, Colonel?"

"None the better for you, sir," said Hayne with a rueful smile.

PART FOUR

A Deep Game

The tariff was only the pretext, and disunion
and a southern confederacy the real object.

—ANDREW JACKSON, 1833

We are growing daily. . . . We want
time only to ensure victory.

—JOHN CALHOUN, 1833

27

JOHN CALHOUN COULDN'T know that
Webster's reply to Hayne would come to be
considered the greatest speech in American
political history. He didn't anticipate that generations of schoolchildren would study it and commit
large parts to memory. But he recognized that
Webster had landed a powerful blow against South
Carolina and the philosophy of states' rights, and
he ached to deliver a riposte.

He felt the constraints of the vice presidency
more than ever. The office had been a promising
post when he first sought it, in 1824. He had recognized that the Republican party was crumbling,
as the four-way contest for the presidency demonstrated. By offering himself for vice president, he
dodged the cross fire and positioned himself to
support, and win the support of, whichever candidate became president. He supposed it would
be Jackson, whose popularity grew by the month.
But when Adams nabbed the prize, Calhoun was

there to lend a hand. He could see that Adams was out of step with the times and likely wouldn't last more than one term. Calhoun could be his successor. When Jackson made plain his determination to avenge his loss to Adams and mounted a campaign for 1828, Calhoun again suppressed his presidential ambitions. There would be no defeating the general and hence nothing gained by trying. He would hold on to the vice presidency, awaiting the next election.

He assumed, as did nearly everyone else, that Jackson would serve only one term. Jackson was not a politician but a soldier; the presidency was not a career ambition but a post-career reward. Anyway he was in poor health, sustained by whiskey, tobacco and gall at his enemies. He should be happy to return to the Hermitage after four years and tend to Rachel's grave.

Calhoun, by contrast, was aging well. He would celebrate his fiftieth birthday in 1832. Gray tinged the auburn in his hair, which he let grow longer than when he was a young man, in keeping with fashion. Swept back, it revealed more of his high, square forehead. His eyes glowed as brightly as ever, with a color that changed according to the light and his mood. He still stood erect; his step was firm. He made an impressive figure, one his compatriots could readily imagine as their president. Or so he thought when he looked at himself in the mirror.

But others too saw presidents in their panes of silvered glass. Henry Clay's ambitions were no secret. Adams's 1828 defeat by Jackson carried Clay into exile with him, but the Kentuckian would certainly be back. And he would return as the foe of Jackson and whoever assumed the Jackson mantle.

Martin Van Buren, another mirror-gazer, believed the mantle should be his. And he had reason to think it would be. Floride Calhoun's campaign against Peg Eaton had proved counterproductive, as even Daniel Webster could see from beyond the Jackson circle. "Mr. Van Buren has evidently, at this moment, quite the lead in influence and importance," Webster wrote to a friend in early 1830. "He controls all the pages on the back stairs, and flatters what seems to be at present the Aaron's serpent among the President's desires, a settled purpose of making out the lady, of whom so much has been said, a person of reputation. It is odd enough, but too evident to be doubted, that the consequence of this dispute in the social and fashionable world is producing great political effects and may very probably determine who shall be successor to the present chief magistrate."

The Eaton affair indeed went far toward determining Jackson's successor, but the succession was delayed. Jackson's words and demeanor initially supported the view that he would serve one term and retire. He lacked the passion for politics that drove the likes of Clay, Calhoun and Webster, and he didn't consider himself a member of the political class. He thought presidents should be restricted to single terms; in his first annual message he advocated amending the Constitution to bar second terms (although he would have made the one term six years long). Yet Jackson discovered what nearly every other president discovered: that his work remained unfinished as his first term ran out. He let it be known that he would serve a second term if the people saw fit to award it to him.

Jackson's change of mind compelled others to reconsider their plans. Calhoun and Van Buren, maneuvering to become his successor, had to decide whether to bide their time for another four years or strike out and challenge him now. Van Buren, holding the inside track, adopted the former course. Calhoun took the latter. The choice wasn't hard. Jackson already blamed Calhoun for Floride's shunning of Peg Eaton, and he increasingly doubted Calhoun's loyalty to the Union amid the South Carolina affront to the tariff.

The rift between the president and the vice president became public at a celebration of Jefferson's birthday in the spring of 1830. Though Jefferson had died—on July 4, 1826, the same day as John Adams, and the fiftieth anniversary of the signing of the Declaration of Independence—and his party had fractured, the remnants of the party still gathered under the portrait of the Sage of Monticello each April 13. Dinner was followed by toasts, with each short speech evincing the beliefs, ambitions, sensibilities or grievances of the toaster. The event this year took place at Washington's Indian Queen Hotel, where proprietor Jesse Brown set places for a hundred guests. Whether all would come was uncertain. The tariff had antagonized the South, and the Webster-Hayne debate had drawn a line between the states' rights men and the Unionists. Yet the pressing question of the hour was the attitude of the president and the vice president toward each other. Jackson's small-government principles were well known; he judged the states better placed in prudence and constitutionality to legislate on most matters. But he was the chief executive of the United States, under oath to protect and defend the Constitution. Calhoun had been an ardent centralizer, yet he had become the principal theorist of South Carolina's opposition to the tariff and to the federal government's authority to enforce it. Calhoun hadn't acknowledged his role in the opposition, but neither did he deny it. Both men would speak this night; all present were keen to hear them.

The toasts unfolded slowly. Jefferson was honored in the first; the Declaration of Independence in the second. Jefferson's epitaph was quoted in the third. The fourth edged slightly into the fray when Jefferson's Kentucky resolves were hailed. Madison's Virginia resolves, the companion pieces in the original nullification set, were praised in the fifth. The rest of the scheduled twenty-four toasts carried the group further into the weeds of states' rights, and deeper into their cups.

The unscheduled toasts were to follow. All heads turned toward Jackson's table. As president he would deliver the first, if he chose to exercise his prerogative. Jackson had never been a public speaker, certainly not of the caliber of Clay, Webster or Calhoun. He let actions do his speaking for him. And no one in the room—no one in the city, no one in the country—had acted with greater determination or result on behalf of the United States. He was carefully groomed, as always, yet those close to him could see the toll the years and his struggles had taken on him. His thin face had grown haggard, his once-firm step was now tentative. His cheeks had hollowed from loss of teeth.

Yet physical decrepitude made his indomitable will the more evident. His voice was not loud when he spoke this evening, but his words rang like rifle shots across the hushed room. "Our Federal Union," Jackson said: "It **must** be preserved."

That was all. The other toasters had rambled through long sentences and into paragraphs. The audience looked and listened to learn whether Jackson would go on. But he said no more. He sat down.

The heads swiveled as one toward Calhoun. The vice president must answer. Until now he had made his case for the states in writing, and semi-anonymously at that. The president had called him out, as plainly as any man had been called out to a duel.

Calhoun couldn't match Jackson's succinctness. Brevity wasn't his style, and his case, in any event, was more complicated than Jackson's uncompromising formula. He had prepared, not knowing just what Jackson would say. He adjusted on the spot. He raised his glass. "The Union . . . ," he said.

For a split second some in the audience thought he had surrendered. But he completed the thought: "The Union—next to our liberty the most dear." He paused, and concluded, "May we all remember that it can only be preserved by respecting the rights of the states and distributing equally the benefit and burden of the Union."

Toasters were supposed to have but one chance to speak. Yet the crowd instinctively turned back toward Jackson. Would the president rejoin?

He would not. Jackson knew better than to debate Calhoun. It would demean the office of the presidency, besides putting him on ground Calhoun trod more confidently. Jackson let his terse imperative stand alone.

DAMNED ONCE BY Jackson for his wife's treatment of Peg Eaton, and a second time for his nullifying philosophy, Calhoun was damned a third time when the president learned that Calhoun's behavior during Jackson's Florida campaign a decade earlier hadn't matched the impression Calhoun gave at the time. Jackson's capture of Pensacola, in excess of his orders but in line with the secret letter he had written to James Monroe, had prompted condemnation by most of Monroe's cabinet. Jackson knew that John Quincy Adams had defended him; he gathered that Calhoun had done so too. But two weeks after the dinner of the dueling toasts, Jackson received a copy of a letter written by William Crawford asserting that such was not the case: Calhoun had condemned him with most of the rest.

"Mr. Calhoun's position in the cabinet was that General Jackson should be punished in some form or reprehended in some form," Crawford recounted. Crawford added that he—Crawford— had been wrongly identified as the chief condemner of Jackson, by none other, he thought, than Calhoun. "An extract of a letter from Washington was published in a Nashville paper, in which it was stated that I had proposed to arrest General Jackson but that he was triumphantly defended by Mr. Calhoun and Mr. Adams. This letter, I always believed, was written by Mr. Calhoun, or by his directions. It had the desired effect. General Jackson became extremely inimical to me, and friendly to Mr. Calhoun."

Jackson sent Calhoun a copy of the Crawford letter. The president's anger was evident beneath the polite language he employed in forwarding it. "Sir, that frankness which, I trust, has always characterized me through life towards those with whom I have been in the habits of friendship induces me to lay before you the enclosed copy," he wrote. "The statements and facts it presents, being so different from what I had heretofore understood to be correct, requires that it should be brought to your consideration. They are very different from your letter to Governor Bibb, of Alabama, of the 13th May, 1818, where you state 'General Jackson is vested with full power to conduct the war in the manner he may judge best,' and different, too, from your letters to me at that time, which breathe throughout a spirit of approbation and friendship, and particularly the one in which you say, 'I have the honor to acknowledge the receipt of your letter of the 20th

ultimo, and to acquaint you with the entire approbation of the President of all the measures you
have adopted to terminate the rupture with the
Indians.'"

Jackson offered Calhoun a chance to explain.
"My object in making this communication is to
announce to you the great surprise which is felt,
and to learn of you whether it be possible that
the information is correct; whether it can be,
under all the circumstances of which you and I
are both informed, that any attempt seriously to
affect me was moved and sustained by you in the
cabinet council, when, as is known to you, I was
but executing the **wishes** of the Government and
clothed with the authority to 'conduct the war in
the manner I might judge best.'"

Jackson likely overstated his surprise at hearing
that Calhoun had not been supportive during
the Florida campaign. Rumors to that effect had
been circulating for years. Yet Jackson initially
had not had other reasons to distrust Calhoun, and
he declined to honor the rumors with his attention. Crawford's letter, if accurate, now provided
evidence Jackson couldn't dismiss. His invitation
to Calhoun to refute the letter threw down a fresh
challenge to the vice president: Disprove it if
you can.

CALHOUN COULDN'T DISPROVE, and so didn't try. Rather, he took the offensive. In terms that echoed John Randolph before the Virginian's duel with Henry Clay, Calhoun refused to answer for actions taken in his official capacity. "I cannot recognize the right on your part to call in question my conduct," he told Jackson. "I acted, on that occasion, in the discharge of a high official duty, and under responsibility to my conscience and my country only." He said he was responding to Jackson purely out of respect for the presidency. He demanded reciprocal respect. "My course, I trust, requires no apology; and if it did, I have too much self respect to make it to any one in a case touching the discharge of my official conduct."

Yet he couldn't leave it at that. Calhoun understood that Jackson wasn't refighting the Florida campaign so much as launching the 1832 election campaign. The court that mattered was not a court-martial but the court of public opinion. And so Calhoun, having just said he wouldn't defend his actions, undertook to do just that. In a series of long and eventually tedious letters, bolstered by the testimony of other parties and witnesses, he explained his position and actions during the time of Jackson's Florida adventure.

———

JACKSON RESPONDED IN words that slammed the door on any chance of reconciliation. "I had a right to believe that you were my sincere friend," he said, "and until now never expected to have occasion to say of you, in the language of Caesar, **Et tu Brute.**"

HENRY CLAY MONITORED the discomfiture of John Calhoun with quiet
satisfaction. Of his congressional peer
group, Calhoun was the one who had worried Clay
the most. Calhoun had been the first to achieve
cabinet rank, as Monroe's secretary of war, and
the first to win national office, as vice president,
twice. Calhoun lacked the rhetorical power of
Daniel Webster and, Clay liked to think, himself.
But he possessed a formidable intellect and, judging by his accomplishments, a knack for political
advancement and survival. To be vice president
under John Quincy Adams and then Andrew
Jackson was no mean feat. Yet Calhoun had finally
been too clever for his own good. Or perhaps he
was too principled. In either case, he was finished,
Clay thought.

Clay had expected to run in 1832 against
Calhoun or Martin Van Buren. But then Jackson
made known he would seek a second term. Clay

considered sitting out, waiting another four years until Jackson must surely retire. But by then he would be almost sixty, nearly as old as Jackson had been on entering office. Jackson appeared ancient these days, staggering from one malady or old wound to another, and though Clay felt fitter than Jackson looked, he didn't want decrepitude to catch him in office. Besides, much could happen in four years. Much was already happening. The splintering of Jefferson's party had created confusion out of which order was slowly re-forming. New ties were being established and new loyalties proclaimed. One group of anti-Jacksonians called themselves National Republicans. Another group gathered under the banner of the Anti-Masonic party. Clay had to act or be left behind.

He chose to act: to challenge Jackson. He had sufficient cause, besides ambition. Jackson was doing his best to block or undermine Clay's American System. Jackson opposed tariff protection. He defended the 1828 tariff solely because it was federal law and he was the nation's chief magistrate. Once the South Carolina nullifiers got the message that they couldn't defeat Old Hickory, he might well side with the many and influential tariff opponents in his party.

Jackson's position on internal improvements, the second pillar of Clay's system, was unrelentingly hostile. And he had announced his opposition in a manner that couldn't have been more insulting to Henry Clay. Kentucky had some of the worst roads in America; barges and steamboats brought goods efficiently to Kentucky's river ports only for the goods to bog down traversing the last muddy miles inland. Clay persuaded Congress to approve federal funding for a road from Maysville, Kentucky, on the Ohio, to Lexington, Clay's hometown. Kentucky cheered the accomplishment and applauded its sponsor.

Jackson vetoed the measure. The president contended that the bill exceeded the constitutional authority of the federal government. Roads and other improvements in the federal territories were one thing, and roads **between** states might sometimes pass muster. But roads **within** states were the responsibility of those states themselves. To tax Massachusetts, which had paid for its own roads, to build roads in Kentucky was beyond anything the framers of the Constitution had intended, Jackson said. And it was beyond anything he would approve.

To Clay's thinking, Jackson's Maysville Road veto was wrongheaded and regressive. For two decades he—Clay—had been making the case that national prosperity required national effort. A thriving national economy depended on robust means of transport, starting with solid roads. Jackson's reasoning would prevent America from ever having such roads in states that lacked the resources of the long-settled East. Of course roads

ran through individual states, but they would be—
or could be—part of a national network. Jackson
was stuck in the eighteenth century, and he would
leave America stuck in the mud.

————————

BUT IT WAS the Bank of the United States, the
third pillar of the American System, that proved
the central battleground between Jackson and
Clay. Clay's support for the bank was public
and of long standing; Jackson's opposition was of
shorter duration but equally well known. "I think
it right to be perfectly frank with you," Jackson
told Nicholas Biddle, the director of the bank. "I
do not think that the power of Congress extends
to charter a bank out of the ten mile square"—the
federal district. "I do not dislike your bank any
more than all banks. But ever since I read the history of the South Sea bubble I have been afraid of
banks."

Jackson's fear of banks as a category gave
Biddle hope, for he thought the president might
be educated. In Jackson's youth banks had been
rare in America; to many Americans of Jackson's
vintage they remained mysterious and therefore threatening. Most people didn't use banks;
they conducted their business affairs in cash. They
didn't borrow; they kept their savings under the
pillow or in tangible assets: a few more acres,

another cow, an extension to the house. When they **did** encounter banks, it was on the banks' terms. Farmers and shopkeepers might accept banknotes in lieu of cash, but the banknotes were only as reliable as the issuing banks. If the banks failed to honor their notes, the holders were out of luck. Ordinary people rarely took on mortgages, but when they did, the interest rates were dictated by the banks. Missed payments resulted in the loss of the mortgaged farms and houses. Meanwhile, bankers were often the wealthiest men in any city or town. They never really worked, that anyone could tell; they never mussed their clothes or calloused their hands. Yet they lived in the biggest houses and drove the finest carriages. It was all a great mystery to ordinary people, and the source of distrust and fear.

Nicholas Biddle spent much of his time attempting to allay the fears of the bank distrusters. He eschewed obvious involvement in politics. "There is no one principle better understood by every officer in the Bank than that he must abstain from politics," Biddle asserted to an associate amid the presidential transition from John Quincy Adams to Jackson. "The course of the Bank is very clear and straight on that point. We believe that the prosperity of the Bank and its usefulness to the country depend on its being entirely free from the control of the officers of the Government, a control fatal to every bank which it ever influenced. In order to preserve that independence it must never connect itself with any administration—and never become a partisan of any set of politicians. In this respect I believe all the officers of the institution have been exemplary. The truth is that with us it is considered that we have no concern in politics. Dean Swift"— Jonathan Swift—"said, you know, that money is neither whig nor tory, and we say with equal truth that the Bank is neither Jackson man nor an Adams man. It is only a bank."

But it was **not** only a bank. If Biddle thought Jackson an innocent in finance, Henry Clay deemed Biddle a child in politics, and he set about tutoring him in the ways of Washington. The bank's twenty-year charter would last until 1836, and although Jackson opposed the bank in principle, he appeared inclined to let the charter run out rather than disrupt the economy by disturbing the bank's current operations. Yet the bank's investors and customers sought reassurance that the institution would last beyond 1836, and some agitated for early renewal of the bank's charter.

Clay initially counseled patience. "It may be assumed as indisputable that the renewal of the charter can never take place, as the Constitution now stands, against the opinion and wishes of the President," he wrote to Biddle in the fall of 1830. "A bill which should be rejected by him for that purpose could never be subsequently passed by the constitutional majority"—the two-thirds necessary for an override of a veto. "There would always be found a sufficient number to defeat such a bill, after its return with the President's objections, among those who are opposed to the Bank on constitutional grounds, those who, without being influenced by constitutional considerations, might be opposed to it upon the score of expediency, and those who would be operated upon by the influence of the Executive."

At this point Jackson had not announced his decision to run again, and Martin Van Buren appeared the likely bearer of the Jackson standard. Clay asserted that Van Buren and his allies sought to make the bank the central issue of the 1832 campaign. "If you apply at the next session of Congress, you will play into the hands of that party," Clay told Biddle. "They will most probably, in the event of such application, postpone the question until another Congress is elected. They will urge the long time that the charter has yet to run; that therefore there is no necessity to act at the next session on the measure; and that public sentiment ought to be allowed to develop itself etc. These and other considerations will induce Congress, always disposed to procrastinate, to put off the question. In the mean time, the public press will be put in motion, every prejudice excited and appeals made to every passion."

Biddle therefore should wait to seek renewal.

"I think the session immediately after the next presidential election would be the most proper time," Clay said. "Then every thing will be fresh; the succeeding presidential election will be too remote to be shaping measures in reference to it; and there will be a disposition to afford the new administration the facilities in our fiscal affairs which the Bank of the United States perhaps alone can render."

BIDDLE TOOK CLAY'S advice, although he professed not to be concerned by the political considerations Clay described. "In respect to General Jackson and Mr. Van Buren," he told a friend, "I have not the slightest fear of either of them, or both of them." He was sure the American people would see the wisdom of support for the bank. "Our country-men are not naturally disposed to cut their own throats to please any body, and I have so perfect a reliance on the spirit and sense of the nation that I think we can defend the institution from much stronger enemies than they"—Jackson and Van Buren—"are. In doing this we must endeavor to reach the understandings of our fellow citizens by the diffusion of correct views of a subject which is much misunderstood."

Biddle aided the diffusion of correctness by a covert campaign of public education. "It is obvious that a great effort will be made to array the influence of the Executive and his party against the Bank," he wrote to one of his lieutenants. "It is not less evident that our most effectual resistance is the dissemination of useful knowledge among the people, and accordingly I am endeavoring to convey to all classes real and positive information in regard to the working of the institution and its beneficial influence on the prosperity of the nation. To do this newspapers must be used, not for their influence, but merely as channels of communication with the people." Biddle had written various articles favorable to the bank and appealing to general readers. "For the insertion of these I will pay either as they appear or in advance. Thus for instance if you will cause the articles I have indicated and others which I may prepare to be inserted in the newspaper in question, I will pay at once to you one thousand dollars." Discretion should be exercised. "There is as you perceive nothing in this communication which I should care to conceal, but as it might be misconstrued, I enclose your letter to me and request that you will have the goodness to return what I have written to you."

The propaganda campaign went forward. It appeared to have good effects in much of the country. Congress seemed to be leaning Biddle's way. But then Jackson revealed that he would seek reelection.

The news spoiled Biddle's plans. Jackson was a

strong favorite to win, no matter who ran against him. Most likely Jackson would still be president when the bank's current charter expired in 1836. If he was, the bank would expire with the charter. Biddle began to think patience no longer a virtue.

HENRY CLAY REACHED the same conclusion. Jackson's decision to run cast the bank's future into grave doubt. If Jackson won, there was no way the bank would survive. Congress, yielding to Jackson's opposition, might refuse to pass a new charter, or the president would veto it.

The only hope for the bank was to press for renewal **before** the election. Clay thought he could shepherd renewal through the legislature. Jackson would probably veto the renewal bill, but then the bank would become an issue in the campaign. And possibly—just possibly—the reaction to a Jackson veto would be sufficient to knock the general off his horse.

Which would be **Clay's** only hope. Jackson looked nearly unbeatable. Clay's one chance was to provoke the president into some intemperate action, one that would unite the various anti-Jackson elements into a single force. Vetoing the bank's recharter could have the desired effect.

Clay didn't show all his cards to Nicholas Biddle. "Have you come to any decision about an application to Congress at this session for the renewal of your charter?" he asked innocently. "The friends of the Bank here, with whom I have conversed, seem to expect the application to be made. The course of the President, in the event of the passage of a bill, seems to be a matter of doubt and speculation. My own belief is that, if **now** called upon he would not negative the bill."

If Clay really believed that, he knew nothing about Andrew Jackson. In fact, he knew a great deal about Jackson, more than he cared to tell Biddle.

DANIEL WEBSTER'S INTEREST in Biddle and the bank was different from Clay's, but not less intense. Webster did legal work for Biddle; that is, Biddle **paid** him for legal work. Webster in reality advised Biddle on politics relating to the bank, and he argued the bank's case in the Senate, in exchange for which Biddle kept him on retainer. The money was important to Webster, as money always was. "I have had an application to be concerned, professionally, against the Bank," he informed Biddle at one point. "I have declined, of course, although I believe my retainer has not been renewed, or **refreshed,** as usual. If it be wished that my relation to the Bank should be continued, it may be well to send me the usual retainer."

Biddle sent the money. Webster, en route from Boston to Washington, stopped in Philadelphia and visited the director at the bank's headquarters. Webster said he would test the ground for renewal. A few days later he reported to Biddle from the capital. "I have seen a great number of persons and conversed with them, among other things, respecting the Bank," Webster said. "The result of all these conversations has been a strong confirmation of the opinion which I expressed at Philadelphia that it **is** expedient for the Bank to apply for the renewal of its charter without delay. I do not meet a gentleman, hardly, of another opinion, and the little incidents and anecdotes that occur and circulate among us all tend to strengthen the impression."

On advice of Clay and Webster, Biddle took the fateful step. At the beginning of 1832 he requested early renewal of the bank's charter.

Webster congratulated him on the decision. "I cannot but think you have done exactly right," he told Biddle. "Whatever may be the event, it seems to me the path of duty is plain." The renewal bill would certainly succeed, at once or eventually. "A failure this session, if there should be one, will not at all diminish the chances of success next session."

Webster pitched in to make the bill succeed. He earned the money Biddle was paying him. "A disordered currency is one of the greatest of political evils," he told the Senate. "It wars against industry, frugality, and economy; and it fosters the evil spirits of extravagance and speculation. Of all the contrivances for cheating the laboring classes of mankind, none has been more effectual than that which deludes them with paper money." The bank was commonly accounted the pet of the rich, but Webster contended that it was really a mainstay of the middling. Without the bank, hardworking men and women would become victims of currency fraud and manipulation. "This is the most effectual of inventions to fertilize the rich man's field by the sweat of the poor man's brow. Ordinary tyranny, oppression, excessive taxation: these bear lightly on the happiness of the mass of the community, compared with fraudulent currencies and the robberies committed by depreciated paper." In the absence of a national bank, merchants and their customers would be thrown back upon state banks, which, sadly, had a dismal record of integrity and solvency. Critics of the bank alleged that it benefited the East at the expense of the West. Webster asserted the opposite. The Western states were the ones most in need of sound currency, which their own banks failed most egregiously to provide. It was fairer to say that Western **banks** sometimes suffered from the existence of the national bank, which prevented their profiteering. But the **people** of the West benefited. "A dollar at St. Louis or Nashville becomes, at once, a dollar in New Hampshire or Maine." Prices equalized across regions, to the advantage of consumers everywhere.

THE FOES OF the bank were at no loss for words. Missouri's Thomas Benton, who acquired the nickname Old Bullion for his opposition to paper money and other artifices of banks, decried the Bank of the United States as unconstitutional, unethical, unprincipled and immoral. "Gentlemen of the South complain of the tariff, and doubtless with much reason," he said. "But the day is at hand when every eye shall see, and every tongue shall confess, that the tariff is not the only, nor the largest, nor the most voracious vampire which sucks at their veins! The Bank of the United States divides that business with the tariff, and, like the stronger brother, takes the largest share to herself. She furnishes her brood of these insatiable suckers. She hangs them on every vein of gold and silver which the South and West exhibit. They gorge to repletion, then vomit their load into the vast receptacles of the Northeast, and gorge again." What, in the day of reckoning, would be the result of this baleful conspiracy? "When that dread day comes, and come it will, and nothing is gained by putting it off, the towns and cities of the South and West, the fairest farms and goodliest mansions, will be set up at auction, to be knocked down to the bank agent, at the mock prices fixed in the compting room of the bank itself. And in these mock sales of towns and cities may be laid the foundations for the titles and estates of our future nobility—Duke of Cincinnati! Earl of Lexington! Marquis of Nashville! Count of St. Louis! Prince of New Orleans!" This specter was what the Senate was to decide upon. "Yes, sir! When the renewed charter is brought in for us to vote upon, I shall consider myself as voting upon a bill for the establishment of **lords and commons** in this America, and for the eventual establishment of a **King**; for when the **lords and commons** are established, the **King** will come of himself!"

Benton's bluster played well in the West and among rank-and-file Jacksonians, who shared the president's suspicions of bankers as a class. But it couldn't keep Henry Clay from marshaling the votes to endorse renewal. The Senate vote was close; the victory in the House more comfortable. Bank critics alleged bribery, which doubtless occurred but probably didn't much exceed the coziness of Webster's arrangement with Biddle. Nor were the opponents' pockets empty, for the state banks, which would benefit from the demise of their national competitor, showed their appreciation by similar means.

THE BANK BILL went to Andrew Jackson. The president knew he was being put to the test. He had distrusted and despised Clay since the Kentuckian accepted John Quincy Adams's offer of the state department. He distrusted and despised him even more now. Jackson hadn't picked this fight; Clay had. And he had done it for political purposes, Jackson judged. Jackson had never backed down from a fight, and he wasn't about to start.

Jackson vetoed the renewal bill, and he sent Congress a stern message explaining why. In the first place, it was unconstitutional. John Marshall and the Supreme Court had declared otherwise, the president acknowledged, but the high court's opinion bound only the lower courts. "The Congress, the executive, and the court must each for itself be guided by its own opinion of the Constitution. Each public officer who takes an oath to support the Constitution swears that he will support it as he understands it, and not as it is understood by others. It is as much the duty of the House of Representatives, of the Senate, and of the president to decide upon the constitutionality of any bill or resolution which may be presented to them for passage or approval as it is of the supreme judges when it may be brought before them for judicial decision. The opinion of the judges has no more authority over Congress than the opinion of Congress has over the judges, and on that point the president is independent of both." Justice Marshall and the Supreme Court might think that the "necessary and proper" clause of the Constitution stretched to cover the charter of a national bank; this president did not.

In time, Jackson's rejection of the authority of the Supreme Court to bind the president would come to seem shocking, almost revolutionary. But the doctrine of judicial review developed slowly, and in Jackson's time it had far to go. His statement defying John Marshall was noteworthy for its boldness, but not for its originality.

Jackson attacked the renewal bill on additional grounds. The bank was bad policy, he said. Its monopoly position enriched its shareholders at the expense of Americans generally. Modest inequalities of wealth were unavoidable and not necessarily injurious to democracy, but great inequalities were a dire threat. The bank aggravated inequality by favoring the already wealthy, who employed its monopoly powers to enrich themselves further. The bank's renewal would compound the problem. "Distinctions in society will always exist under every just government," Jackson said. "Equality of talents, of education, or of wealth can not be produced by human institutions. In the full enjoyment of the gifts of Heaven and the fruits of superior industry, economy and virtue, every man is equally entitled to protection by law; but when the laws undertake to add to these natural and just advantages artificial distinctions, to grant titles, gratuities, and exclusive privileges, to make the rich richer and the potent more powerful, the humble members of society— the farmers, mechanics and laborers—who have neither the time nor the means of securing like favors to themselves, have a right to complain of the injustice of their government. There are no necessary evils in government. Its evils exist only in its abuses. If it would confine itself to equal protection, and, as Heaven does its rains, shower its favors alike on the high and the low, the rich and the poor, it would be an unqualified blessing."

The bank had just the opposite effect. It must be terminated. The renewal bill was vetoed.

DANIEL WEBSTER SAW the veto coming but still professed shock. "A great majority of the people are satisfied with the bank as it is and desirous that it should be continued," he told the Senate. "They wished no change." As evidence Webster cited conversations with constituents, not to mention the favorable vote for the bank in both houses of Congress. But Jackson had cast the people and Congress aside. "The president has undertaken, on his own responsibility, to arrest the measure, by refusing his assent to the bill." Jackson's assertion of unconstitutionality defied reason, logic and the law, and it established tyranny. "If these opinions of the president be maintained, there is an end of all law and all judicial authority. Statutes are but recommendations, judgments no more than opinions. Both are equally destitute of binding force. Such a universal power as is now claimed for him, a power of judging over the laws and over the decisions of the tribunal, is nothing less than pure despotism. If conceded to him, it makes him at once what Louis the Fourteenth proclaimed himself to be when he said, 'I am the state.'"

NICHOLAS BIDDLE BY this time was not surprised by the veto. Neither was he discouraged. "You ask, what is the effect of the veto?" he wrote to Henry Clay. "My impression is that it is working as well as the friends of the Bank and of the country could desire. I have always deplored making the Bank a party question, but since the President will have it so, he must pay the penalty of his own rashness. As to the veto message, I am delighted with it. It has all the fury of a chained panther biting the bars of his cage. It is really a manifesto of anarchy, such as Marat or Robespierre might have issued to the mob of the Faubourg St. Antoine; and my hope is that it will contribute to relieve the country from the dominion of these miserable people."

Biddle thought the veto would benefit Clay. "You are destined to be the instrument of that deliverance," he said, "and at no period of your life has the country ever had a deeper stake in you. I wish you success most cordially, because I believe the institutions of the Union are involved in it."

CLAY WASN'T AS sanguine as Biddle, for he knew the American electorate better. The veto solidified anti-Jackson sentiment in the expected places: the boardrooms of creditors, the offices of large merchants, the editorial desks of newspapers, the clubs of the wealthy and educated. But among the populace as a whole, among the many Americans as suspicious of banks as Jackson was, the veto seemed a defense of the people against the moneyed interests. "It diffuses universal joy among your friends and dismay among your enemies," a delighted John Randolph wrote to Jackson from Virginia, regarding the veto.

Jackson himself exhibited a rare smile. "The veto works well everywhere," he told a close friend. "It has put down the Bank instead of prostrating me."

The veto indeed worked well for Jackson. The Anti-Masons, in the first national nominating convention in American history, chose William Wirt of Maryland, a colleague and sometime rival of Daniel Webster at the Supreme Court bar. The convention idea caught on, and the National Republicans made Henry Clay their champion. A convention of Jacksonians, adopting the name Democrats, nominated Jackson, with Martin Van Buren as his running mate.

In the balloting that autumn, Jackson carried sixteen states and won 219 electoral votes. Clay won six states and 49 electoral votes. Wirt carried one state, and John Floyd, who ran on a nullification platform, carried South Carolina.

Henry Clay's defeat was disappointing to him and those who hoped to stop the Jackson juggernaut, but at least it left him with a party to fall back on. John Calhoun had no such solace. Cast out of the Democrats by Jackson, unwelcome among the National Republicans, Calhoun was a man without a party. Yet he had friends in the South Carolina legislature, which elected him senator. He resigned the vice presidency and entered the upper chamber as an ordinary member rather than the presiding officer.

The timing was crucial, for the nullification struggle between South Carolina and the Jackson administration had reached the point of explosion. In late November 1832 a special convention in South Carolina approved an ordinance of nullification. The measure denounced the tariff of 1828 and a revised version passed in 1832 that left the principle of protection firmly in place. The ordinance declared the two tariff statutes "unauthorized by the constitution of the United States" and therefore "null, void, and no law, nor binding upon this State, its officers or citizens." The ordinance went on to declare unlawful any attempt by officials of South Carolina or the United States to collect the tariffs. Should the government of the United States try to enforce the tariffs, South Carolinians would resist. If the federal Congress passed a law authorizing the use of force against South Carolina, that law would be deemed "inconsistent with the longer continuance of South Carolina in the Union." Should the federal government persist, "the people of this State will henceforth hold themselves absolved from all further obligation to maintain or preserve their political connection with the people of the other States; and will forthwith proceed to organize a separate government, and do all other acts and things which sovereign and independent States may of right do."

WITH THIS STATEMENT the nullifiers took the bit in their teeth and galloped headlong toward secession. And they left Andrew Jackson no choice but to respond, which he did with equal vigor. In early December the president issued a proclamation condemning the South Carolinians' ordinance as being "in direct violation of their duty as citizens of the United States, contrary to the laws of their country, subversive of its Constitution, and having for its object the destruction of the Union." Jackson declared as plainly as he could, "I consider, then, the power to annul a law of the United States, assumed by one State, **incompatible with the existence of the Union, contradicted expressly by the letter of the Constitution, unauthorized by its spirit, inconsistent with every principle on which it was founded, and destructive of the great object for which it was formed.**"

Jackson had been born in South Carolina, and he appealed to those who had been his neighbors to turn from their perilous course. "Fellow-citizens of my native state, let me not only admonish you, as the First Magistrate of our common country, not to incur the penalty of its laws, but use the influence that a father would over his children whom he saw rushing to certain ruin. In that paternal language, with that paternal feeling, let me tell you, my countrymen, that you are deluded by men who are either deceived themselves or wish to deceive you." The nullifiers weren't what they purported to be, nor were South Carolinians what the nullifiers claimed. "They are not champions of liberty, emulating the fame of our Revolutionary fathers, nor are you an oppressed people." The nullifiers spoke as though determination would carry their project through. Once more they misled. "You can not succeed. The laws of the United States must be executed." Jackson concluded with chilling bluntness: "Be not deceived by names. Disunion by armed force is **treason**."

JOHN CALHOUN ROSE in the Senate to answer Jackson. In his nearly four years as Jackson's vice president he had gone from being Jackson's ally and possible heir to his most dangerous foe. The zealotry of the South Carolina fire-eaters thrilled emotionalists in the Palmetto State, but it was the cold logic of Calhoun that would—or would not—bring other states to South Carolina's side. Calhoun blamed Jackson for escalating the tension between South Carolina and the national government. The president spoke as though South Carolina were in arms and eager to fight. Nothing could be further from the truth, Calhoun said. "There is not a shadow of foundation for such a statement. There is not a state in the Union less disposed than South Carolina to put herself in such attitude of hostility." South Carolina had said it would resist aggression, but it was not and would not be the aggressor. The president was trying to intimidate South Carolina. If war came, it would be because the president had initiated it.

"It is obvious that the country has now reached a crisis," Calhoun continued. The wonder was that it had taken so long. "It has often been said that every thing which lives carries in itself the elements of its own destruction. This principle is no less

applicable to political than to physical construc-
tions. The principle of decay is to be found in our
institutions, and unless it can be checked and corrected in its course by the wisdom of the federal
government, its operation will form no exception
to the general course of events." Americans must
choose. "The time has at length come when we
are required to decide whether this shall be a confederacy any longer, or whether it shall give way to
a consolidated government."

Calhoun paused to let his fellow senators reflect
on this issue. For himself, he knew where he stood.
"As I live, I believe that the continuance of any
consolidated government is impossible. It must
inevitably lead to a military despotism." This was
not what South Carolina had agreed to in ratifying the Constitution. "South Carolina sanctioned
no such government. She entered the confederacy
with the understanding that a state, in the last
resort, has a right to judge of the expediency of
resistance to oppression, or secession from the
Union. And for so doing, we are threatened to
have our throats cut, and those of our wives and
children."

Calhoun caught himself. "No, I go too far. I did
not intend to use language so strong. The Chief
Magistrate has not yet recommended so desperate
a remedy."

Yet the country was very close to that. "The
present is a great question, and the liberties of

the American people depend upon the decision of it." Calhoun spoke from the heart, with fiercer feeling than his colleagues had ever seen in him. "I have been, from my earliest life, deeply attached to the Union," he said. "In my early youth I cherished a deep and enthusiastic admiration of this Union. I looked on its progress with rapture and encouraged the most sanguine expectations of its endurance. I still believe that if it can be conformed to the principles of 1798, as they were then construed, it might endure forever. Bring back the government to those principles, and I will be the last to abandon it. And South Carolina will be among its warmest advocates. But depart from these principles and in the course of ten years we shall degenerate into a military despotism. The cry has been raised: 'The Union is in danger.' I know of no other danger than that of military despotism. I will proclaim it on this floor, that this is the greatest danger with which it is menaced, a danger the greatest which any country has to apprehend."

Calhoun caught himself again. He begged pardon of the Senate for the warmth with which he had spoken. "Unbecoming as I know that warmth is, I must throw myself on my country and my countrymen for indulgence. Situated as I am, and feeling as I do, I can not have done otherwise."

———

THE SENATORS WATCHED in amazement. Few had thought Calhoun harbored such intense emotions. But feelings ran high on all sides. Andrew Jackson made plain he would brook no interference with the laws of the country: no nullification and certainly no secession. He ordered his secretary of war, Lewis Cass, to gird an army to march against South Carolina if necessary. "We must be prepared to act with promptness and crush the monster in its cradle," he told Cass. To South Carolinian Joel Poinsett, an opponent of the nullifiers, Jackson declared, "The wickedness, madness, and folly of the leaders and the delusion of their followers in the attempt to destroy themselves and our Union has not its parallel in the history of the world. The Union will be preserved." To John Coffee, a Tennessee friend, he was more adamant still. "The Union must be preserved," Jackson told Coffee. "I will die with the Union."

When a South Carolina congressman asked if the president had any message for the people in his district, Jackson replied, "Yes, I have. Please give my compliments to my friends in your state, and say to them that if a single drop of blood shall be shed there in opposition to the laws of the United States, I will hang the first man I can lay my hand on engaged in such treasonable conduct, upon the first tree I can reach."

H ENRY CLAY WATCHED and listened as the war of words escalated. He yielded nothing to Andrew Jackson in devotion to the Union, but he judged that Jackson's temper and penchant for fighting posed as great a danger to the Union as the threats of the nullifiers. John Calhoun he found harder to read. Clay recalled the days when Calhoun had been his ally; in those times he had seemed the soul of reasonableness. But since the passage of the tariff of 1828 he had been seized by something Clay couldn't put his finger on. It might have been simple ambition, a desire for the same high office Clay had twice contested for. Clay was the last person to ignore ambition as a driver in men who found their way to the banks of the Potomac. But if ambition it was, it took strange forms in Calhoun. The South Carolinian seemed a man possessed—not by evil spirits but by ideas, ideas that wouldn't let him go. It might have been expedience that suggested

the idea that the Constitution created a compact
of American states rather than a government of
the American people, but once seized of the idea,
Calhoun couldn't escape the conclusions to which
it led him.

Yet Calhoun was the one Clay had to work
with. Calhoun held the key to a compromise that
might avert the day of reckoning. Through Robert
Letcher, his fellow Kentuckian, Clay proposed a
meeting with Calhoun. He invited Calhoun to
his private apartment. Calhoun was suspicious
of Clay and initially resisted. Perhaps at Clay's
urging, Letcher related to Calhoun that Andrew
Jackson was about to arrest those he considered
the leaders of the nullification movement, starting
with Calhoun. A treason prosecution could be
expected to follow. Calhoun chose to accept Clay's
invitation.

When Calhoun entered the room, Clay rose,
bowed and offered him a seat. Calhoun stiffly took
it. Robert Letcher tried to ease the atmosphere,
without success. Calhoun looked coldly at Clay,
who looked back almost as grimly. Letcher, acting
as mediator, turned to the subject at hand. The
nation needed a compromise, he said. The beneficiaries of the tariff must give back some of what
they had taken in 1828; the nullifiers must step
away from the brink of secession and war.

Calhoun yielded no ground. He barely spoke.
Clay couldn't get him to open up, even to com-

mence negotiations. After an uncomfortable few minutes the meeting ended. Nothing was agreed to, nothing compromised. A spy at the door, watching Calhoun leave, might have supposed that the crisis was as intractable as ever.

But something had happened. Likely Clay measured the strength of Calhoun's resolve; Calhoun did the same of Clay's. Possibly they recalled particular memories of their former, more cooperative days. Each apparently satisfied himself of the sincerity of the other. Each concluded he could work with the other.

Clay went first. The author of the Missouri Compromise let out that he was going to offer another compromise. Washington took notice, and the Senate was crowded as he took the floor to explain. "When I survey, sir, the whole face of our country," Clay declared, "I behold all around me evidences of the most gratifying prosperity, a prospect which would seem to be without a cloud upon it, were it not that through all parts of the country there exist great dissensions and unhappy distinctions." The dissensions over the tariff, the distinctions between North and South, East and West, threatened America's prosperity and imperiled the country itself. America's elected officials had caused the troubles; it was up to America's elected officials to ease or end them.

The tariff was a principal cause of the troubles, so the tariff must be a large part of the solution, Clay said. This was a striking admission by the father of the American System, of which the protective tariff was a central pillar. More striking still was Clay's warning about the future of the tariff. "The tariff stands in imminent danger," he said. "If it should even be preserved during this session, it must fall at the next session." The South had always opposed the tariff; the West, never more than tepid, had grown cooler of late. The Democrats as a party appeared happy to sink it. Clay lamented the demise of the protective tariff, citing the businesses that had been built on the expectation of its continuance. But statesmen must deal with realities, he said. If the friends of the tariff didn't reduce it slowly, its enemies would erase it at once. Professing to speak as the truest friend of the tariff, Clay offered a bill dictating its gradual reduction. Over nine years, rates would fall from their current protective level to a revenue level—that is, the level at which they would pay for the operations of the government, but no higher.

Protectionists would complain, Clay acknowledged. But they had little basis for doing so. "What was the principle which had always been contended for in this and in the other House?" he asked. "That, after the accumulation of capital and skill, the manufacturers would stand alone, unaided by the government, in competition with the articles from any quarter." American industry was flourishing, and in the years of the tariff drawdown it would flourish even more.

Clay granted that his compromise was imperfect. But what compromise was not? "It has been remarked, and justly remarked, by the great Father of our Country himself, that if the work which is the charter of our liberties, and under which we have so long flourished, had been submitted, article by article, to all the different states composing this Union, the whole would have been rejected; and yet, when the whole was presented together, it was accepted as a whole." If George Washington could be so wise, his heirs could not afford not to be.

Some would say he was capitulating to the secessionists of South Carolina, that legislative compromise under threat of war denied every principle of democracy. Clay deflected the premise. Earlier news reports had indeed led him to believe that South Carolina was already in arms, itching to battle the United States. "But since my arrival here I found that South Carolina does not contemplate force, for it is denied and denounced by that state. She disclaims it and asserts that she is merely making an experiment. The experiment is this: By a course of state legislation, and by a change in her fundamental laws, she is endeavoring, by her civil tribunals, to prevent the general government from carrying the laws of the United States into operation within her limits. That she has professed to be her object. Her appeal is not to arms but to another power; not to the sword but to the law."

Clay didn't say that his informant on this subject was John Calhoun, but word of his meeting with Calhoun had gotten out and his auditors drew the inference. "It seems to me the aspect of South Carolina has changed, or rather, the new light which I have obtained enables me to see her in a different attitude," Clay continued. "South Carolina is doing nothing more, except that she is doing it with more rashness, than some other states have done." Virginia and Kentucky had started down this path in 1798, several states of New England during the War of 1812. None of those states had seceded, and neither would South Carolina. "I say it is utterly impossible that South Carolina ever desired, for a moment, to become a separate and independent state." Yet South Carolina was proud and might be provoked; it must be treated with the respect due every state. "Sir, I repeat, that I think South Carolina has been rash, intemperate, and greatly in the wrong; but I do not want to disgrace her, nor any other member of this Union. No; I do not desire to see the luster of one single star dimmed of that glorious confederacy which constitutes our political sun. Still less do I wish to see it blotted out and its light obliterated forever."

Clay appealed to the goodwill and tolerance of his fellow lawmakers. "Allow me to entreat and implore each individual member of this body to bring into the consideration of this measure, which I have had the honor of proposing, the same love of country which, if I know myself, has actuated me, and the same desire for restoring harmony to the Union which has prompted this effort." Statesmen should put aside party and section and heed only their feelings as Americans. "I should hope that under such feelings, and with such dispositions, we may advantageously proceed to the consideration of this bill and heal, before they are yet bleeding, the wounds of our distracted country."

CLAY'S ABANDONMENT OF the principle of protection caught many in the Senate off guard, but his broader appeal for compromise seemed in keeping with his long-standing preference for the middle path. By contrast, John Calhoun's endorsement of the middle path jolted nearly everyone. Calhoun—a compromiser? It was hard to imagine.

Yet there he was, standing where Clay had stood and saying much the same thing. "He who loves the Union must desire to see this agitating question brought to a termination," Calhoun declared of the troubles provoked by the tariff. "Until it is terminated, we can not expect the restoration of peace or harmony, or a sound condition of things, throughout the country." The Clay proposal made a good start. And the broader Clay approach—of seeking not victory over the other side, but accommodation—made an even better one. "It has been my fate to occupy a position as hostile as any one could, in reference to the protecting policy," Calhoun conceded. "But if it depended on my will, I would not give my vote for the prostration of the manufacturing interest. A very large capital has been invested in manufactures, which have been of great service to the country; and I would never give my vote to suddenly withdraw all those duties by which that capital was sustained in the channel into which it had been directed."

Echoing Clay, Calhoun acknowledged that all compromises were imperfect. There were parts of the Clay bill he would like to see changed. "But I look upon these minor points of difference as points in the settlement of which no difficulty will occur, when gentlemen meet together in that spirit of mutual compromise which, I doubt not, will be brought into their deliberations, without at all yielding the constitutional question as to the right of protection."

Calhoun might have spoken more, and indeed he would speak more. But the gallery erupted in cheers at the gulf that had been crossed by the senators from Kentucky and South Carolina.

The president pro tem pounded his gavel and ordered the gallery cleared, but two members, evidently supporters of compromise, petitioned for a stay of the order. The president pro tem acceded, even as he told the sergeant at arms that another outburst must cause his order to be implemented at once.

DANIEL WEBSTER HAD not been invited to the love fest. Nor did he desire to join it. He congratulated Clay and Calhoun for seeking peace between the sections on the tariff issue. But peace was one thing, and principle another. "There are principles in it to which I do not at present see how I can ever concur," he said of Clay's bill. The Kentucky senator's words tried to reassure protectionists, but his bill would sacrifice them. Consumers in the South might cheer, but the manufacturers in the North, and their employees and suppliers, would suffer. Webster challenged a basic premise of Clay's argument: that the tariff was in sudden, imminent danger. "I know nothing which has happened, within the last six or eight months, changing so materially the prospects of the tariff," he said. In any event, senators should act out of courage, not out of fear. He would stick to his principles, and stand by the tariff.

Webster was just warming up. So, it turned out, was John Calhoun. But when the battle was rejoined, it involved a measure even more controversial than the tariff. Andrew Jackson's warning to South Carolina was followed by an administration request of Congress for explicit authority to employ force in case South Carolina obstructed collection of the tariff in the state. The administration called the measure a "revenue collection bill"; everyone else called it a force bill. And it inflamed South Carolina the more by making explicit the specter of war on South Carolina's soil against South Carolina's people. Several other Southern states were only slightly less alarmed.

Calhoun accused Jackson of double-crossing the South, which had looked to him to solve the tariff problem. Southerners, including South Carolinians, had turned out in great numbers and carried Jackson to victory in the two elections. "But little did the people of Carolina dream that the man whom they were thus striving to elevate to the highest seat of power would prove so utterly false to all their hopes."

The force bill was abhorrent in the unfettered powers it would confer on the executive, Calhoun said. "It puts at the disposal of the president the army and navy, and the entire militia of the country." And to what purpose? "To make war against one of the free and sovereign members of this confederation, which the bill proposes to deal with not as a state but as a collection of banditti or outlaws, thus exhibiting the impious spectacle of this government, the creature of the states, making war against the power to which it owes its existence."

The force bill was egregiously unconstitutional, Calhoun said. "This bill proceeds on the ground that the entire sovereignty of this country belongs to the American people, as forming one great community, and regards the states as mere fractions or counties, and not as an integral part of the Union, having no more right to resist the encroachments of this government than a county has to resist the authority of a state." The bill declared war on South Carolina—indeed, worse than war, for it set an organized force against an unorganized people. "It decrees a massacre of her citizens!" It gave the chief executive powers no man should ever wield. "It authorizes the president, or even his deputies, when they suppose the law to be violated, without the intervention of a court or jury to kill without mercy or discrimination!"

Supporters of the force bill declared that the law must be enforced. "The law must be enforced!" Calhoun repeated scornfully. What they meant was: "The imperial edict must be executed." Sixty years earlier Britain's Lord North had said the tea tax must be enforced, and he had driven the American colonies to rebellion. The president was doing the same to the Southern states.

Backers of the force bill said the Union must be preserved. "And how is it proposed to preserve the Union? By force! Does any man in his senses believe that this beautiful structure, this harmonious aggregate of states produced by the joint consent of all, can be preserved by force?" There was not a chance. "Its very introduction will be certain destruction of this federal Union. No, no; you cannot keep the states united in their constitutional and federal bonds by force. Force may indeed hold the parts together, but such union would be the bond between master and slave, a union of exaction on one side and of unqualified obedience on the other."

Calhoun leveled a warning. "Disguise it as you might, the controversy is one between power and liberty, and I will tell the gentlemen who are opposed to me that strong as might be the love of power on your side, the love of liberty is still stronger on ours." He acknowledged that his side lacked numbers and arms; the odds were fearful against them. Yet this made their duty all the clearer and potentially more rewarding. "To discharge successfully this high duty requires the highest qualities, moral and intellectual, and should we perform it with a zeal and ability in proportion to its magnitude, instead of being mere planters, our section will become distinguished for its patriots and statesmen." Failure to oppose the president would exact a terrible cost. "If we yield to the steady encroachment of power, the severest and most debasing calamity and corruption will overspread the land."

NO APPLAUSE INTERRUPTED John Calhoun this time; none followed his conclusion. In response to Henry Clay's tariff bill he had praised reason and compromise; in reply to Andrew Jackson's force bill he threatened war and the destruction of the Union. His words sobered even his supporters.

Daniel Webster rose at once to rebut him. Webster blamed Calhoun for a mode of address ill befitting a member of Congress. "The gentleman has terminated his speech in a tone of threat and defiance toward this bill, even if it should become a law of the land, altogether unusual in the halls of Congress," Webster said. But the tone was not worse than the argument itself. "He does himself no justice. The cause which he espouses finds no basis in the Constitution, no succor from public sympathy, no cheering from a patriotic community. He has no foothold on which to stand, where he might display the powers of his acknowledged talents. Every thing beneath his feet is hollow and treacherous."

Calhoun couldn't be more wrong about the constitutionality of nullification and secession, Webster said. "The Constitution does not provide for events which must be preceded by its own destruction. Secession, therefore, since it must bring these consequences with it, is revolutionary. And nullification is equally revolutionary." What was revolution? That which overturned or arrested the legitimate authority of government. "This is the precise object of nullification. It attempts to supersede the supreme legislative authority. It arrests the arm of the executive magistrate. It interrupts the exercise of the accustomed judicial power." South Carolina's ordinance of nullification did all these things. Indeed, nullification was worse than revolutionary. "It raises to supreme command four-and-twenty distinct powers"—the twenty-four states—"each professing to be under a general government and yet each setting its laws at defiance at pleasure. Is this not anarchy, as well as revolution?"

The fulcrum of Calhoun's argument was that the Constitution was a compact among states, forming a confederacy or a league rather than a unified nation. Webster examined the Constitution itself for evidence of this. "Does it call itself a compact? Certainly not. It uses the word 'compact' but once, and that is when it declares that states shall enter into no compact. Does it call itself a league, a confederacy, a subsisting treaty between the states? Certainly not. There is not a particle of such language in all its pages."

What was it, then? "It declares itself a constitution." Americans were fully familiar with constitutions, from their experience in the states. "We are at no loss to understand what is meant by the constitution of one of the states, and the constitution of the United States speaks of itself as being an instrument of the same nature."

A compact or a confederation—like that of the Articles of Confederation—acted upon states. But the Constitution acted upon the people as individuals. "This government may punish individuals for treason and all other crimes in the code, when committed against the United States. It has power, also, to tax individuals, in any mode and to any extent, and it possesses the further power of demanding from individuals military service. Nothing, certainly, can more clearly distinguish a government from a confederation of states than the possession of these powers. No closer relations can exist between individuals and any government."

The Constitution granted Congress the power to declare war. Under Calhoun's theory, the states should be able to nullify war declarations as easily as any other congressional acts, Webster said. "Can any thing be more preposterous?" Half the country go to war, and the other half abstain?

"The truth is, Mr. President, and no ingenuity of argument, no subtlety of distinction, can evade it, the people of the United States are one people. They are one in making war, and one in making peace. They are one in regulating commerce, and one in laying duties of impost. The very end and purpose of the Constitution was to make them one people in these particulars, and it has effectually accomplished its object."

The framers had made their purpose patent at the start. "How can any man get over the first words of the Constitution itself?—'We, the people of the United States, do ordain and establish this constitution.' These words must cease to be part of the Constitution, they must be obliterated from the parchment on which they are written, before any human ingenuity or human argument can remove the popular basis on which that Constitution rests and turn the instrument into a mere compact between sovereign states."

The nullifiers railed at the oppressions they claimed to suffer. They protested far too much, Webster said. Americans, including Southerners, had never lived better. "At this very moment, sir, the whole land smiles in peace and rejoices in plenty. A general and a high prosperity pervades the country. And, judging by the common standard, by increases of population and wealth, or judging by the opinions of that portion of her people not embarked in those dangerous and desperate measures, this prosperity overspreads South Carolina herself."

Against this horizon of happiness, the malcontents in South Carolina worked their selfish mischief. "One danger only creates hesitation; one doubt only exists to darken the otherwise unclouded brightness of that aspect which she exhibits to the view and to the admiration of the world." Would the nullifiers wreck the Union? That was the question. America wanted to know; the world wanted to know. "All Europe is, at this moment, beholding us and looking for the issue of this controversy—those who hate free institutions, with malignant hope; those who love them, with deep anxiety and shivering fear."

Senators, and all Americans, must choose sides in this fateful struggle. "For myself, sir, I shun no responsibility justly devolving on me, here or elsewhere, in attempting to maintain the cause," Webster said. "I shall exert every faculty I possess in aiding to prevent the Constitution from being nullified, destroyed or impaired; and even should I see it fail, I will still, with a voice feeble, perhaps, but earnest as ever issued from human lips and with fidelity and zeal which nothing shall extinguish, call on the people to come to its rescue."

The dashing, impetuous Henry Clay mastered the House of Representatives the moment he arrived in 1811.

John Calhoun joined Clay in demanding war against Britain to avenge insults to America and extend the American domain—and advance the careers of those with the boldness to bring the war on.

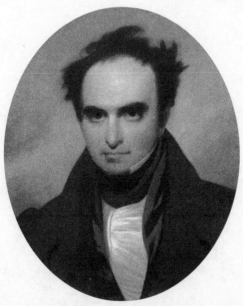

Daniel Webster denounced the war as divisive, deluded and doomed. He put the blame on Clay and Calhoun as he made a case for New England's right to secede from the Union.

The War of 1812 went badly for the United States and hence for Clay and Calhoun. The nadir came in August 1814 when the British raided Washington and burned the Capitol (seen here in the aftermath), the White House and other buildings.

Andrew Jackson's surprise victory at New Orleans in January 1815 saved the United States and the careers of Clay and Calhoun. Webster was left in the lurch.

Virginia congressman John Randolph took pleasure in assaulting Clay with words. The feud turned almost deadly when they escalated to pistols.

Jackson was the popular hero in the dawning age of democracy. He eclipsed Clay and Calhoun and then became their worst enemy. His dying regret was that he hadn't shot Clay and hanged Calhoun.

John Quincy Adams opposed Clay before allying with him. Adams wound up president after the 1824 election, with Clay as secretary of state. Foes of Adams and Clay alleged a "corrupt bargain," and the charge damaged both men. Adams's career never recovered; he had to content himself with being America's conscience.

When Clay needed a refuge from politics, he returned to Ashland, his home near Lexington, Kentucky. But celebrity followed him there, too.

Calhoun's retreat was his South Carolina plantation, Fort Hill, where he constructed the intellectual bridge that carried him from his Unionist youth to his maturity as the arch-advocate of states' rights.

Webster's seaside farm at Marshfield, Massachusetts, tempted him to retire from public life. But the farm ate up all his income from elected office and the law, and he had to keep working.

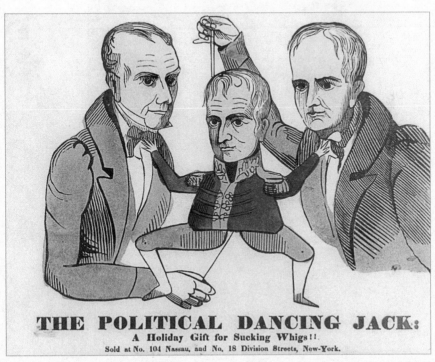

THE POLITICAL DANCING JACK:
A Holiday Gift for Sucking Whigs!!
Sold at No. 104 Nassau, and No. 18 Division Streets, New-York.

Clay's critics lambasted his dominance of the Whig party. In 1840 he and Virginia representative Henry Wise were said to have Whig presidential nominee William Henry Harrison by the puppet strings.

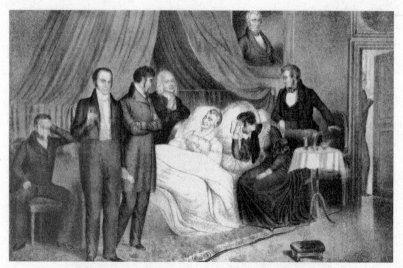

The sudden death of President Harrison in April 1841, barely a month after inauguration, threw the country's politics into confusion. Webster (second from left) had to decide whether to stay on as secretary of state.

Clay hoped his third try at the presidency, in 1844, would be the charm. Democrat James Polk had other ideas, and Clay was frustrated again.

The decades-long contest among the three reached a climax in the debate over Clay's Compromise of 1850. Clay (center, speaking) pleaded for the Union above all. Webster (seated with head in hand) stunned his Massachusetts constituents by joining Clay in conciliating the South. Calhoun (third from right) condemned Clay and Webster for not giving the South enough.

Henry Clay was eulogized as the
model American statesman by fellow
Whig Abraham Lincoln, who prayed
that heaven would send another such
champion in the Union's next trial.

John Calhoun's political heirs
employed his theory of states' rights
and his defense of slavery to justify
secession in 1860 and 1861.

Daniel Webster's constituents posthumously forgave
his compromising and remembered his formula for the
survival of American self-government: "Liberty and Union,
now and forever, one and inseparable!"

THIS TIME THE gallery did erupt. Webster's close brought his listeners to their feet shouting and applauding. The president pro tem glowered at the sergeant at arms, who hustled the offenders out the door.

Yet Webster was the hero of the moment only. The force bill rallied the many opponents of Calhoun and the nullifiers, but in doing so it drove the nullifiers deeper into their trenches. When the bill's Senate supporters compelled a vote, over the objections of the Calhoun cohort, the latter walked out of the chamber in protest. The measure passed on a shrunken tally and in an atmosphere of growing bitterness.

Henry Clay managed to be absent at the time of the vote, not to protest the bill, but to preserve his position as mediator. And he immediately tried to refocus the Senate on the tariff bill. The force bill was Jackson's measure, not Clay's, yet Clay realized that the force bill, besides being unstoppable, could become a crucial adjunct to his tariff bill. The tariff bill applied persuasion to get the nullifiers to reconsider their opposition to federal authority; the force bill threatened coercion should persuasion fail.

Not everyone appreciated Clay's artful approach. Daniel Webster denounced Clay's tariff bill as a surrender to extortion, a capitulation to a willful minority, a perversion of constitutional principles of republican self-rule. The existing tariff had won the requisite majorities in Congress; its beneficiaries were under no obligation to apologize for what they had accomplished fairly and honorably, Webster told the Senate. South Carolinians were unhappy with the status quo; Americans at large would be unhappy with the proposed change. "If this bill should become a law, there will be an action on the part of the people at the next session to overthrow it," Webster predicted. "It will not be all requiem and lullaby when this bill shall be passed. On the contrary, there will be discord and discontent." Webster had nothing against South Carolina. "I would do as much to satisfy South Carolina as any man." But he couldn't swallow Clay's scheme. "My constituents will excuse me for surrendering their interests, but they will not forgive me for a violation of the Constitution."

BEFORE WEBSTER'S LISTENERS could respond, before they even realized he had finished, Henry Clay was on his feet. Clay knew Webster's power, and knew he had to counter it at once. "I have long, with pleasure and pride, cooperated in the public service with the senator from Massachusetts, and I have found him faithful, enlightened and patriotic," Clay declared. "I have not a particle of doubt as to the pure and elevated motives which actuate him." But in rejecting the tariff revision, Webster was recklessly shortsighted. "Let us not deceive ourselves. Now is the time to adjust the question in a manner satisfactory to both parties. Put it off until the next session and the alternative may and probably then would be a speedy and ruinous reduction of the tariff or a civil war with the entire South." The revision offered hope. "The bill before us strongly recommends itself by its equality and impartiality. It favors no one interest, and no one state, by an unjust sacrifice of others. It deals equally by all." Was it imperfect? Undoubtedly. But it could be fixed later. Clay took a page from America's founding. "Let us, on this occasion of compromise, pursue the example of our fathers who, under the influence of the same spirit, in the adoption of the Constitution of the United States, determined to ratify it, and go for amendments afterward."

The Senate's approval of the force bill made tariff revision more crucial than ever, Clay said. The two measures together, and only together, held the key to resolving the current crisis. "The first will satisfy all who love order and law and disapprove the inadmissible doctrine of nullification. The last will soothe those who love peace and concord, harmony and union. One demonstrates the power and the disposition to vindicate the authority and supremacy of the laws of the Union; the other offers that which, if it be accepted in the fraternal spirit in which it is tendered, will supersede the necessity of the employment of all force." Webster and those who joined him in opposition to the tariff bill saw only half the picture. "The difference between the friends and the foes of the compromise under consideration is that they would, in the enforcing act, send forth alone a flaming sword; we would send that out also, but along with it the olive branch, as a messenger of peace. They cry out, the law! the law! the law! Power! power! power! We, too, reverence the law and bow to the supremacy of its obligation; but we are in favor of the law executed in mildness and of power tempered with mercy. They, as we think, would hazard a civil commotion, beginning in South Carolina and extending God only knows where. While we would vindicate the authority of the federal government, we are for peace, if possible, union and liberty. We want no war; above all, no civil war, no family strife. We want to see no sacked cities, no desolated fields, no smoking ruins, no streams of American blood, shed by American arms."

Clay closed on a personal note. Some critics of the compromise read ambition into his sponsorship of the bargain. He was looking to the 1836 presidential election, they declared. Clay shook his head in weariness at their failure to understand his motives. His ambitions for higher office were spent, he said. His only ambition was to retire in peace. "Pass this bill, tranquilize the country, restore confidence and affection in the Union, and I am willing to go home to Ashland and renounce public service forever."

THE DEBATE CONTINUED, filling a month of the Senate's calendar. Daniel Webster parried Henry Clay and again rebutted John Calhoun; Calhoun answered Webster; Clay riposted both. The teamwork was complicated, with Clay and Calhoun partnering against Webster on the tariff bill, and Clay and Webster allying against Calhoun on the force bill.

Progress toward a resolution came slowly. The two bills moved through the Senate and the House at different paces. The Senate, having passed the force bill, inched toward a vote on the tariff. The House bogged down in a debate over a competing tariff bill sponsored by Gulian Verplanck of New York, with the force bill yet to be considered.

Clay still didn't like Jackson's force bill yet continued to judge it unstoppable. And this judgment made him work harder than ever for his compromise tariff. The force bill would increase the risk of civil war by playing into the hands of the hot-heads in South Carolina, but a compromise tariff would give heart to moderates there, allowing the state to step back from nullification without losing face.

Clay was a senator, yet he remembered the ways of the House. At a critical moment he enlisted his House friend Robert Letcher to offer Clay's Senate tariff bill as a substitute for the Verplanck bill. The maneuver caught the House opponents of tariff compromise off guard, and Clay's measure sailed through.

The victory in the House added momentum to Clay's tariff bill in the Senate, which approved it on March 1, 1833. On the same day the House, freed from its tariff tangle, adopted the force bill.

Clay was elated and relieved. "Yesterday was perhaps the most important Congressional day that ever occurred," he wrote to James Barbour on March 2. "I shall get some curses," he acknowledged. "But more blessings. I am content if they neutralize each other."

In South Carolina they just about did. The new tariff caused the nullifiers to rescind the ordinance of nullification. But lest the world think they were yielding anything, they passed an ordinance nullifying Jackson's Force Act. The move was belligerent but largely symbolic. The crisis ended.

———

IT DID SO just in time for Andrew Jackson's second inaugural address. Jackson joined the compromise chorus. While reiterating the duty of all states and citizens to abide by laws passed by Congress, he praised the principle of states' rights. The key was balance. The Union must be preserved, but the government of the Union must honor the prerogatives of the states.

In private Jackson was ambivalent about what had been accomplished. "I have had a laborious task here, but nullification is dead," he wrote to an old friend. "Its actors and exciters will only be remembered by the people to be execrated for their wicked designs to sever and destroy the only good government on the globe, and that prosperity and happiness we enjoy over every other portion of the world. Haman's gallows ought to be the fate of all such ambitious men who would involve their country in civil war and all the evils in its train, that they might reign and ride on its whirlwinds and direct the storm."

Yet Jackson worried that nullification would rise again, in a more virulent form on a more divisive topic. "The tariff was only the pretext, and disunion and a southern confederacy the real object," Jackson said. "The next pretext will be the negro, or slavery, question."

———

IF JACKSON HAD read John Calhoun's correspondence, he would have been even more convinced that nullification would be back—and more certain that Calhoun, the ringleader of the nullifiers, must be hanged one day. To Calhoun the purpose of the compromise of 1833 was to buy time. "A year would make an immense difference in our position," he wrote amid the crisis to a South Carolina associate. "We are growing daily. Our cause would be better understood, our strength increased, and the temper of the South and the other sections better ascertained. To take issue now would be to play into the hands of the administration, while to delay the issue would derange all of their calculations. I feel confident; we want time only to ensure victory."

The compromise delivered the time. And the struggle to achieve it convinced Calhoun that he had been right about the intentions of the administration and the North. "All that I see and hear satisfies me that the spirit of liberty is dead in the North, and but confirms the truth of the principles for which I have contended under so many difficulties," he told a friend. "It is of the very genius of a consolidated government to elevate one portion of the community while it corrupts the other. That form of government is now established by law under the bloody act"—the Force Act— "and unless there should be a complete reaction, a reaction which shall repeal that atrocious act and completely reform the government, we must expect and prepare to sink under corruption and despotism. Of such reaction and reform, there is not the least hope but from the South and through the agency of state rights."

The South must follow the lead of South Carolina, Calhoun said. "The oppressed states must act on the principle systematically that no unconstitutional act shall be enforced within their respective limits. There is no other remedy. We have commenced the system, and as it regards the tariff, the most difficult of all acts to resist, with encouraging success."

The tariff was but the start. The Union, as defined by the South's oppressors, had been grievously wounded. "Nullification has dealt the fatal blow." And it would deliver more. Calhoun accounted South Carolina's rejection of the Force Act a portent of things to come. "It will never be enforced in this state. Other states may live under its reign, but Carolina is resolved to live only under that of the Constitution. There shall be at least one free state."

PART FIVE

Temptations of Empire

I certainly am not willing to involve this
country in a foreign war for the object of
acquiring Texas. . . . I think it far more wise and
important to compose and harmonize the present
confederacy, as it now exists, than to introduce a
new element of discord and distraction into it.

—HENRY CLAY, 1844

35

Harriet Martineau arrived in Washington in the aftermath of the nullification crisis. She didn't think much of the city or its inhabitants. "Washington is no place for persons of domestic tastes," she wrote. "Persons who love dissipation, persons who love to watch the game of politics, and those who make a study of strong minds under strong excitements, like a season at Washington; but it is dreary to those whose pursuits and affections are domestic. I spent five weeks there and was heartily glad when it was over."

Martineau was an English writer who visited the United States to see if the extravagant things she had heard about America's system of popular government were true. She had the advantage over Alexis de Tocqueville, a Frenchman whose visit and purposes overlapped hers, of being English, which lowered the language barrier between her and the objects of her study; of being a non-aristocrat, which rendered America's emerging democratic culture less foreign to her own sensibilities; and of being a woman, which made her seem harmless to most of those she encountered.

She sailed from Liverpool in August 1834. Steamboats now plied the rivers and coastal waters of Europe and North America, but sailing ships still carried passengers across the ocean. Martineau's seven-week journey was longer than most, due to unfavorable winds, yet it was otherwise ordinary. The voyage gave her time to get to know the other cabin passengers—that is, the first-class travelers who had accommodations to themselves. Some of these were merchants who commuted back and forth across the ocean. She and the other cabin passengers had little contact with the larger number of men, women and children in steerage, who were not allowed free run of the deck and lived communally below.

She sojourned in New York City before heading up the Hudson to Albany and then west via the Erie Canal to Buffalo and then Niagara Falls, the single must-see stop on every European's tour of America. She turned south to Philadelphia, which she found charming, and Washington, which she did not.

"The approach to the city is striking to all strangers from its oddness," she wrote. "I saw the dome of the Capitol from a considerable distance, at the end of a straight road; but though I was prepared by the descriptions of preceding travellers, I was taken by surprise on finding myself beneath the splendid building, so sordid are the enclosures and houses on its very verge. We wound round its base, and entered Pennsylvania Avenue, the only one of the grand avenues, intended to centre in the Capitol, which has been built up with any completeness." The boardinghouse where Martineau stayed, with some traveling companions, was on Pennsylvania Avenue, a short walk from the Capitol and a mile from the White House. The British legation was nearby, as were the residences of various cabinet secretaries.

Apart from the government buildings, Washington seemed a frontier village. "The city is unlike any other that ever was seen—straggling out hither and thither—with a small house or two, a quarter of a mile from any other; so that in making calls 'in the city,' we had to cross ditches and stiles, and walk alternately on grass and pavements, and strike across a field to reach a street."

Washington's weather flummoxed one accustomed to England's predictability. "The weather was so strange, sometimes so cold that the only way I could get any comfort was by stretching on the sofa drawn before the fire, up to the very fender (on which days every person who went in and out of the house was sure to leave the front door wide open); then the next morning, perhaps, if we went out muffled in furs, we had to turn back and exchange our wraps for a light shawl."

The people of Washington were all that made the city worth seeing, Martineau concluded. "Foreign ambassadors; the American government; members of Congress, from Clay and Webster down to Davy Crockett, Benton from Missouri, and Cuthbert, with the freshest Irish brogue, from Georgia; flippant young belles; 'pious' wives dutifully attending their husbands and groaning over the frivolities of the place; grave judges; saucy travellers; pert newspaper reporters; melancholy Indian chiefs; and timid New England ladies trembling on the vortex—all this was wholly unlike any thing that is to be seen in any other city in the world, for all these are mixed up together in daily intercourse, like the higher circle of a little village, and there is nothing else. You have this or nothing; you pass your days among these people or you spend them alone."

Martineau learned to distinguish among the members of Congress by their region. She was drawn to the Southerners, despite being adamantly opposed to slavery. "The Southerners appear to the most advantage, and the New Englanders to the least: the ease and frank courtesy of the gentry of the South (with an occasional touch of arrogance, however), contrasting favourably with the cautious, somewhat **gauche,** and too deferential air of the members from the North. One fancies one can tell a New England member in the open air by his deprecatory walk. He seems to bear in mind perpetually that he cannot fight a duel, while other people can. The odd mortals that wander in from the Western border cannot be described as a class, for no one is like anybody else. One has a neck like a crane, making an interval of inches between stock and chin. Another wears no cravat, apparently because there is no room for one. A third has his lank black hair parted accurately down the middle and disposed in bands in front, so that he is taken for a woman when only the head is seen in a crowd. A fourth puts an arm round the neck of a neighbor on either side as he stands, seeming afraid of his tall wire-hung frame dropping to pieces if he tries to stand alone. A fifth makes something between a bow and a curtsey to every body who comes near, and proses with a knowing air—all having shrewd faces and being probably very fit for the business they come upon."

Martineau discovered a quirk in the American Constitution through conversations with a senator who shared meals at the boardinghouse with her. "The senator happened, from a peculiar set of circumstances, to be an idle man just now," she recorded. The Senate was in session, but he had nothing to do. "This gentleman's peculiar and not very agreeable position arose out of the troublesome question of Instructions to Representatives.

Senators are chosen for a term of six years, one third of the body going out every two years, the term being made thus long in order to ensure some stability of policy in the Senate. If the government of the state from which the senator is sent"—that is, the legislature that chose the senator—"changes its politics during his term, he may be annoyed by instructions to vote contrary to his principles, and, if he refuses, by a call to resign, on the ground of his representing the opinions of the minority." Martineau's companion had experienced such a turnaround and call to resign. In this new age of democracy, he had taken his case to the people of his state. He ran for governor, without resigning his Senate seat. He lost. "No course then remained but resigning, which he did immediately, when his Senate term was within half a session of its close." The former senator was closing out his affairs in Washington when he met Martineau. He would soon head home.

MARTINEAU'S QUARTERS ATTRACTED the most powerful men in Congress, who spent evenings at the fireside. The celebrated trio of Henry Clay, Daniel Webster and John Calhoun were pointed out to her, and she paid particular attention. "Mr. Clay, sitting upright on the sofa, with his snuff-box ever in his hand, would discourse for many an hour, in his even, soft, deliberate tone, on any one of the great subjects of American policy which we might happen to start, always amazing us with the moderation of estimate and speech which so impetuous a nature has been able to obtain," she wrote. "Mr. Webster, leaning back at his ease, telling stories, cracking jokes, shaking the sofa with burst after burst of laughter, or smoothly discoursing to the perfect felicity of the logical part of one's constitution, would illuminate an evening."

Martineau found less to admire in the third member of the trio. "Mr. Calhoun, the cast-iron man, who looks as if he had never been born and never could be extinguished, would come in sometimes to keep our understandings upon a painful stretch for a short while, and leave us to take to pieces close, rapid, theoretical, illustrated talk, and see what we could make of it. We found it usually more worth retaining as a curiosity than as either very just or useful. His speech abounds in figures, truly illustrative, if that which they illustrate were but true also. But his theories of government (almost the only subject on which his thoughts are employed), the squarest and compactest theories that ever were made, are composed out of limited elements, and are not therefore likely to stand service very well."

Martineau wished Calhoun had devoted his talents to policies more to her liking. "It is at first extremely interesting to hear Mr. Calhoun talk, and there is a never-failing evidence of power in all he says and does, which commands intellectual reverence. But the admiration is too soon turned into regret—into absolute melancholy. It is impossible to resist the conviction that all this force can be at best but useless, and is but too likely to be very mischievous. His mind has long lost all power of communicating with any other. I know no man who lives in such utter intellectual solitude. He meets men and harangues them by the fireside as in the Senate; he is wrought, like a piece of machinery, set a-going vehemently by a weight, and stops while you answer. He either passes by what you say, or twists it into a suitability with what is in his head, and begins to lecture again."

Her acquaintance with the three senators inspired Martineau to visit their place of business. "The American Senate is a most imposing assemblage," she recorded. "When I first entered it, I thought I never saw a finer set of heads than the forty-six before my eyes—two only being absent, and the Union then consisting of twenty-four states. Mr. Calhoun's countenance first fixed my attention: the splendid eye; the straight forehead surmounted by a load of stiff, upright, dark hair; the stern brow; the inflexible mouth. It is one of the most remarkable heads in the country. Next him sat his colleague, Mr. Preston, in singular contrast: stout in person, with a round, ruddy, good-humoured face, large blue eyes, and wig,

orange today, brown yesterday, and golden tomorrow. Near them sat Colonel Benton, a temporary
people's man, remarkable chiefly for his pompos-
ity. He sat swelling amidst his piles of papers and
books, looking like a being designed by nature
to be a good-humoured barber or innkeeper, but
forced by fate to make himself into a mock-heroic
senator. Opposite sat the transcendent Webster,
with his square forehead and cavernous eyes; and
behind him sat the homely Clay, with the face
and figure of a farmer, but something of the air of
a divine, from his hair being combed straight back
from the temples."

Martineau couldn't get over the variety. "All these
and many others were striking, and for nothing
more than for their total unlikeness to each other.
No English person who has not travelled over half
the world can form an idea of such differences
among men forming one assembly for the same
purposes and speaking the same language. Some
were descended from Dutch farmers, some from
French Huguenots, some from Scotch Puritans,
some from English cavaliers, some from Irish
chieftains. They were brought together out of law
courts, sugar fields, merchants' stores, mountain
farms, forests and prairies. The stamp of originality was impressed on every one, and inspired a
deep, involuntary respect. I have seen no assembly
of chosen men, and no company of the high-
born, invested with the antique dignities of an

antique realm, half so imposing to the imagination as this collection of stout-souled, full-grown, original men, brought together on the ground of their supposed sufficiency to work out the will of their diverse constituencies."

She got to know her favorites better. "Mr. Webster owes his rise to the institutions under which he lives—institutions which open the race to the swift and the battle to the strong; but there is little in him that is congenial with them. He is aristocratic in his tastes and habits, and but little republican simplicity is to be recognized in him. Neither his private conversation nor his public transactions usually convey an impression that he is in earnest. When he is so, his power is majestic, irresistible; but his ambition for office and for the good opinion of those who surround him is seen too often in alternation with his love of ease and luxury to allow of his being confided in as he is admired. If it had been otherwise, if his moral had equaled his intellectual supremacy, if his aims had been as single as his reason is unclouded, he would long ago have carried all before him and been the virtual monarch of the United States. But to have expected this would have been unreasonable. The very best men of any society are rarely or never to be found among its eminent statesmen; and it is not fair to look for them in offices which, in the present condition of human affairs, would yield to such no other choice than of speedy failure or protracted martyrdom."

She knew Webster's reputation as an orator. She noted what made him effective. "Mr. Webster speaks seldom in the Senate. When he does, it is generally on some constitutional question, where his reasoning powers and knowledge are brought into play, and where his authority is considered so high that he has the glorious satisfaction of knowing that he is listened to as an oracle by an assemblage of the first men in the country. Previous to such an exercise, he may be seen leaning back in his chair, not, as usual, biting the top of his pen, or twirling his thumbs, or bursting into sudden and transient laughter at Colonel Benton's oratorical absurdities, but absent and thoughtful, making notes and seeing nothing that is before his eyes. When he rises, his voice is moderate and his manner quiet, with the slightest possible mixture of embarrassment; his right hand rests upon his desk and the left hangs by his side. Before his first head is finished, however, his voice has risen so as to fill the chamber and ring again, and he has fallen into his favorite attitude, with his left hand under his coat-tail and the right in full action. At this moment, the eye rests upon him as upon one under the true inspiration of seeing the invisible and grasping the impalpable. When the vision has passed away, the change is astonishing. He sits at his desk, writing letters or dreaming, so that he does not always discover when the Senate is going to a division. Some one of his party has not seldom to jog his elbow and tell him that his vote is wanted."

Henry Clay was quite different. "His appearance is plain in the extreme, being that of a mere west-country farmer," Martineau wrote. "He is tall and thin, with a weather-beaten complexion, small grey eyes, which convey an idea of something more than his well-known sagacity—even of slyness. It is only after much intercourse that Mr. Clay's personal appearance can be discovered to do him any justice at all. All attempts to take his likeness have been in vain, though upwards of thirty portraits of him, by different artists, were in existence when I was in America. No one has succeeded in catching the subtle expression of placid kindness, mingled with astuteness, which becomes visible to the eyes of those who are in daily intercourse with him. His mode of talking, deliberate and somewhat formal, including sometimes a grave humour, and sometimes a gentle sentiment, very touching from the lips of a sagacious man of ambition, has but one fault: its obvious adaptation to the supposed state of mind of the person to whom it is addressed. Mr. Clay is a man of an irritable and impetuous nature, over which he has attained a truly noble mastery. His moderation is now his most striking characteristic, obtained, no doubt, at the cost of prodigious self-denial, on his own part, and on that of his friends, of some of the ease, naturalness and self-forgetfulness of his manners and discourse. But his conversation is rich in information and full charged with the spirit of justice and kindliness, rising, on occasion, to a moving magnanimity. By chances, of some of which he was totally unaware, I became acquainted with several acts of his life, political and private, which prove that his moderation is not the mere diffusion of oil upon the waves, but the true stilling of the storm of passion and selfishness."

Martineau heard that Clay was going to speak against the Jackson administration's Indian policy. Congress had approved the Indian Removal Act, compelling relocation of the Eastern tribes to the West, but the lawmakers still wanted to hear what Clay had to say. The House suspended proceedings, with members abandoning their chamber for the aisles of the Senate. The gallery was jammed, with visitors hanging over the balustrade. The substance of the speech was largely lost on Martineau, but not its effects. "I never saw so deep a moral impression produced by a speech," she recounted. "The chief characteristic of his eloquence is its earnestness. Every tone of his voice, every fibre of his frame bears testimony to this. His attitudes are, from the beginning to the close, very graceful. His first sentences are homely, and given with a little hesitation and repetition, and with an agitation shown by a frequent putting on and taking off of spectacles, and a trembling of the hands among the documents on the desk. Then, as the speaker becomes possessed with his subject, the agitation changes its character, but does not subside. His utterance is still deliberate, but his voice becomes deliciously winning. Its higher tones disappointed me at first, but the lower ones, trembling with emotion, swelling and falling with the earnestness of the speaker, are very moving, and his whole manner becomes irresistibly persuasive. I saw tears, of which I am sure he was wholly unconscious, falling upon his papers, as he vividly described the woes and injuries of the aborigines. I saw Webster draw his hand across his eyes."

36

ANDREW JACKSON WAS not impressed by Henry Clay's eloquence or by anything else about the Kentucky senator. The president acknowledged Clay's help in defusing the nullification crisis, but he ascribed it to opportunism rather than principle. He took a similar view of Clay's part in the fight over the charter of the Bank of the United States. Jackson found it nearly impossible to believe that anyone who differed with him on an important matter could be sincere, let alone correct. Clay was despicable and corrupt, and that was that.

The fight over the bank persisted into Jackson's second term. Clay and Nicholas Biddle hoped to salvage something from the fiasco they had created, perhaps a reprieve from the execution scheduled for 1836. If the bank could somehow outlast Jackson, they judged, it might win another life. Jackson, for his part, imputing such designs to his enemies, determined to strike first and deliver the coup de grâce.

It could be done quite simply. The lifeblood of the bank was the deposits it held from the United States government. If those deposits were removed and placed in state banks, the national bank would quickly expire. Opinions differed on who had the authority to remove the deposits: the president, the secretary of the treasury, or Congress? Jackson, however, had no doubt; the authority was his, and he intended to use it. He broached the idea to his cabinet and found little support. His treasury secretary, William Duane, was flatly opposed. Jackson thereupon fired Duane, replacing him with Roger Taney, the attorney general, and ignored the remaining skeptics. He plunged ahead.

Nicholas Biddle wasn't surprised, nor was he alarmed. He had sensed it would come to this: a test of strength between Jackson and himself. He thought he had the advantage. "In half an hour, I can remove all the constitutional scruples in the District of Columbia," he told an associate. It was simply a matter of distributing bribes: "Half a dozen presidencies"—of branch banks—"a dozen cashierships, fifty clerkships, a hundred directorships to worthy friends who have no character and no money." Against enticements like these, Jackson stood no chance.

Complementing Biddle's bribery was the bank's

financial leverage. When Jackson announced the removal of the deposits, Biddle ordered his lieutenants to launch a counteroffensive. The bank and its branches recalled outstanding loans, stopped making new ones, and generally starved the economy of the cash it required to operate. Biddle explained the measures as a prudent hedge against the uncertainty produced by the president's decision, and he wasn't lying. But no less was he attempting to show that the country couldn't survive without the bank. Jackson might think the country could, but he was wrong. Biddle would prove it.

HENRY CLAY WAS appalled, though not surprised, at Jackson's unprecedented move. Clay proposed that the Senate officially censure the president for arrogating to himself "the exercise of a power over the treasury of the United States not granted to him by the Constitution and the laws, and dangerous to the liberties of the people." Clay no longer called Jackson a military chieftain; the general's arrogance had gone far beyond that. "We are in the midst of a revolution, hitherto bloodless, but rapidly tending towards a total change of the pure republican character of the government, and to the concentration of all power in the hands of one man," he said. The president had seized the financial assets of the nation. "Where now is the public treasury? Who can tell? It is certainly without a local habitation, if it has a name. Where is the money of the people of the United States? Floating about on treasury drafts or checks, to the amount of millions, placed in the hands of tottering banks to enable them to pay their own just debts instead of being applied to the service of the people. These checks are scattered to the winds by the secretary of the treasury."

The assault on the finances was a symptom of a larger lust for power, Clay asserted. "Why does the executive think of nothing but itself? It is I! It is I! It is I!, that is meant!" The bank heist was of a piece with Jackson's unprecedented use of the veto. "The question is no longer what laws will Congress pass, but what will the executive not veto?" The arrogance of the deposits' removal should send chills through every lover of republican self-rule. "The premonitory symptoms of despotism are upon us; and if Congress do not apply an instantaneous and effective remedy, the fatal collapse will soon come on, and we shall die—ignobly die—base, mean and abject slaves, the scorn and contempt of mankind, unpitied, unwept, unmourned!"

Clay's speech had drawn another large crowd to the Senate chamber, and his final words were followed by loud and sustained applause. Martin Van Buren, presiding, embarrassed by the enthusiasm against the administration, banged his gavel and ordered the galleries cleared.

John Calhoun joined Clay in vehement opposition to Jackson's move. Calhoun reminded the Senate that he and his fellow Carolinians had warned of Jackson's dictatorial tendencies, predicting that what Jackson sought to do to South Carolina he would do to the rest of the country soon enough. The time had come. Caesar had plundered the Roman treasury en route to subverting the Roman republic; Jackson and his henchmen were doing the same to the American republic, only on the sly. "They have entered the treasury, not sword in hand, as public plunderers, but with the false keys of sophistry, as pilferers, under the silence of midnight," Calhoun said. Caesar had cynically boasted that with money he would get men, and with men money. Jackson's strategy was much the same. "With money we will get partisans, with partisans votes, and with votes money, is the maxim of our public pilferers." Calhoun suggested that Americans should appreciate the group, or party, many of them had recently assailed as nullifiers and secessionists. "That party is the determined, the fixed and sworn enemy to usurpation, come from what quarter and under what form it may, whether from the executive upon the other departments of this government, or from this government on the sovereignty and rights of the States."

———

THOMAS BENTON SAW things in a markedly different light. The Missouri senator, Jackson partisan and distruster of all banks thrilled at the president's brave stroke. "I felt an emotion of the moral sublime at beholding such an instance of civic heroism," Benton recalled afterward. "Here was a president, not bred up in the political profession, taking a great step upon his own responsibility from which many of his advisers shrunk, and magnanimously, in the act itself releasing all from the peril that he encountered, and boldly taking the whole upon himself. I say peril, for if the bank should conquer, there was an end to the political prospects of every public man concurring in the removal. He believed the act to be necessary, and believing that, he did the act, leaving the consequences to God and the country."

Benton skeptically monitored the reaction of the bank and its allies. "From the moment of the removal of the deposits, it was seen that the plan of the Bank of the United States was to force their return, and with it a renewal of its charter, by operating on the business of the country and the alarms of the people," he explained. Ergo Biddle's squeeze on credit. "This pressure was made to fall upon the business community, especially upon large establishments employing a great many operatives, so as to throw as many laboring people as possible out of employment." A campaign was set afoot to amplify the cries of the injured. "The first step in this policy was to get up distress meetings—a thing easily done—and then to have these meetings properly officered and conducted." The meetings were held in every state and most congressional districts. "Men who had voted for Jackson, but now renounced him, were procured for president, vice-presidents, secretaries, and orators; distress orations were delivered; and after sufficient exercise in that way, a memorial and a set of resolves, prepared for the occasion, were presented and adopted." The memorials were relayed to Washington not by the mails but by special delegations got up for the purpose. The memorials were presented to the Senate and the House by the members for the states and districts. "Every morning, for three months, the presentation of these memorials, with speeches to enforce them, was the occupation of each house, all the memorials bearing the impress of the same mint, and the orations generally cast after the same pattern," Benton recounted. "These harangues generally gave, in the first place, some topographical or historical notice of the county or town from which it came—sometimes with a hint of its revolutionary services—then a description of the felicity which it enjoyed while the bank had the deposits, then the ruin which came upon it, at their loss; winding up usually with a great quantity of indignation against the man whose illegal and cruel conduct had occasioned such destruction upon their business."

Henry Clay presented a memorial from Lexington that fit the pattern Benton described. "If there was any spot in the Union likely to be exempt from the calamities that had afflicted the others, it would be the region about Lexington and its immediate neighborhood," Clay asserted on his constituents' behalf. "Nowhere, to no other country, has Providence been more bountiful in its gifts. A country so rich and fertile that it yielded in fair and good seasons from sixty to seventy bushels of corn to the acre. It was a most beautiful country—all the land in it, not in a state of cultivation, was in parks"—natural meadows—"filled with flocks and herds, fattening on its luxuriant grass. But in what country, in what climate, the most favored by Heaven, can happiness and prosperity exist against bad government, against misrule, and against rash and ill-advised experiment?" Clay remarked that hemp, the region's staple, had fallen in price by a fifth since the president's unlawful action; corn was comparably depressed. Hogs and cattle could not be sold at any price. "We are not a complaining people," Clay said of his fellow Kentuckians. "We think not so much of distress. Give us our laws, guarantee to us our Constitution, and we will be content with almost any form of government."

Daniel Webster delivered a similar memorial from Lynn, Massachusetts. "It is a beautiful town, situated upon the sea, is highly industrious, and has been hitherto prosperous and flourishing," Webster said. Lynn's chief business was the manufacture of shoes; of the town's eight thousand inhabitants, three thousand worked in the shoe mills. They had been prosperous but were no longer. "A most serious change has taken place. They find their usual employments suddenly arrested, from the same cause which has smitten other parts of the country, with like effects." They knew whom to blame. "Their memorial is short," Webster said. "It complains of the illegal removal of the deposits, of the attack on the bank, and of the effect of these measures on their business."

Clay, rising again, urged the administration to relieve the suffering of the country. "In twenty-four hours, the executive branch could adopt a measure which would afford an efficacious and substantial remedy, and re-establish confidence," he said. He looked at Van Buren in the Senate chair. He gave the vice president a message to convey to Jackson. "Tell him, without exaggeration, but in the language of truth and sincerity, the actual condition of his bleeding country. Tell him it is nearly ruined and undone by the measures which he has been induced to put in operation. Tell him that his experiment is operating on the nation like the philosopher's experiment upon a convulsed animal, in an exhausted receiver, and that it must expire, in agony, if he does not pause, give it free and sound circulation, and suffer the energies of the people to be revived and restored. . . . Tell him of the tears of helpless widows, no longer able to earn their bread, and of unclad and unfed orphans. . . . Entreat him to pause and to reflect that there is a point beyond which human endurance cannot go, and let him not drive this brave, generous and patriotic people to madness and despair."

Thomas Benton observed Clay's impassioned performance and Van Buren's reaction. "The Vice President maintained the utmost decorum of countenance, looking respectfully and even innocently at the speaker all the while, as if treasuring up every word he said to be faithfully repeated to the President," Benton recounted. "After it was over, and the Vice President had called some senator to the chair, he went up to Mr. Clay and asked him for a pinch of his fine maccoboy snuff, as he often did, and having received it, walked away."

VAN BUREN'S SNUB of Clay was much cooler than Jackson's response to the Kentucky senator. Jackson had concluded that the financial crisis was the cynical work of Clay and Nicholas Biddle, and he interpreted it as personal challenge. "The Bank, Mr. Van Buren, is trying to kill me," he told the vice president. **"But I will kill it!"** Jackson took note of the memorials delivered to Congress and of some sent straight to himself. He refused to reconsider his course. "Were all the worshippers of the golden calf to memorialise me and request a restoration of the deposits," he told Van Buren. "I would cut my right hand from my body before I would do such an act."

Jackson judged the panic grossly exaggerated. "There is no real general distress," he asserted privately. "It is only with those who live by borrowing, trade on loans, and the gamblers in stocks." The country would be better off without them. "It would be a god send to society if all such were put down."

He did his part. A delegation of business types from Baltimore came to the White House. Their leader politely handed Jackson a petition asking relief from the distress. "Relief!" thundered Jackson. "Come not to me! Go to the monster! Did not Nicholas Biddle come here, sir, and on his oath swear before a committee that with six millions in his vaults he could meet the wants of the whole people? And now, when he has wrung more than ten millions from the people, he sends you to me for **relief**! It is folly, sir, to talk to Andrew Jackson. The government will not bow to the monster."

But the people were suffering, the delegation's leader declared.

"The people!" shouted Jackson. "Talk to Andrew Jackson about the people? The people, sir, are with me. I have undergone much peril for the liberties of this people." It was the bank that was punishing the people, and Jackson would punish the bank. "Andrew Jackson yet lives to put his foot upon the head of the monster and crush him to the dust."

The people were suffering, the delegation said again. Surely the president could reconsider.

Never, said Jackson. "I would rather undergo the tortures of ten Spanish inquisitions than that the deposits should be restored or the monster be rechartered."

Jackson blamed Biddle for the implementation of the distress, but he held Henry Clay responsible for giving the banker ideas. The president watched Clay from the distance of the White House and took pleasure in his impotence on the bank question. "The storm in Congress is still raging, Clay reckless and as full of fury as a drunken man in a brothel," he remarked. He himself would stand his ground. "This mammoth of power and corruption must die. The power it possesses would destroy our government in a few years. It is a power that never ought to have existed. Its present course now convinces all honest men that it never ought, and must be put down at the end of its charter. I have it chained. The **monster must perish.**"

37

THE MONSTER DID perish. Most ordinary Americans couldn't have elaborated the theoretical arguments for and against a central bank, but they perceived that Jackson was fighting their battle against the aristocrats of finance, and in the 1834 midterm elections they rewarded Jackson's Democrats and punished Clay's Whigs, as the anti-Jackson alliance of National Republicans and some Anti-Masons had started calling itself. The financial crisis eased as the state banks that received the federal deposits resumed the lending that Nicholas Biddle had curtailed. Biddle's shrunken bank prepared for its 1836 demise.

John Quincy Adams didn't care about the bank any longer, though as president he had dealt amicably with Biddle. For Adams the only thing that mattered was slavery. Every president before Adams had retired from politics upon handing the office to his successor. Adams did too, briefly. And he might have remained retired had slavery not nagged at his republican conscience. But the more he thought about it, and the more he observed the growing pretensions of Southern slaveholders as they involved western territories, the more he felt compelled to return to the public lists. He ran for Congress from the twelfth district of Massachusetts and won.

He had initially considered the connection between slavery and territorial expansion at the time of the Missouri Compromise. The legislation composing the package had been approved by Congress and sent to James Monroe for signature or veto. Monroe was inclined to accept, but he put the matter to his cabinet, asking particularly whether the Constitution allowed Congress and the president to bar slavery from federal territories, in this case the upper portion of the Louisiana Purchase. Adams went further than other members of the cabinet, saying that Congress could bar any new **state** from permitting slavery. And the sooner America was rid of slavery, the better. "The Declaration of Independence not only asserts the natural equality of all men, and their inalienable right to liberty, but that the only just powers of government are derived from the consent of the governed," he said. "A power for one part of the people to make slaves of the other can never be derived from consent, and is, therefore, not a just power." Monroe and the other Southerners present, including the secretary of war, John Calhoun, disagreed, but civilly.

"After this meeting," Adams recorded in his diary, "I walked home with Calhoun, who said that the principles which I had avowed were just and noble, but that in the Southern country, whenever they were mentioned, they were always understood as applying only to white men. Domestic labor was confined to the blacks, and such was the prejudice that if he, who was the most popular man in his district, were to keep a white servant in his house, his character and reputation would be irretrievably ruined."

"I said that this confounding of the ideas of servitude and labor was one of the bad effects of slavery," Adams wrote.

Calhoun answered that Adams was quite mistaken. "He thought it attended with many excellent consequences. It did not apply to all kinds of labor—not, for example, to farming. He himself had often held the plough; so had his father. Manufacturing and mechanical labor was not degrading. It was only manual labor—the proper work of slaves. No white person could descend to that. And it was the best guarantee of equality among the whites. It produced an unvarying level among them. It not only did not excite, but did not even admit of inequalities by which one white man could dominate over another."

Adams disagreed. "I told Calhoun I could not

see things in the same light." And as he later reflected on the day's discussion, he realized how thoroughly he disagreed with nearly everything Calhoun and the other Southerners said by way of defense of slavery. "It is, in truth, all perverted sentiment—mistaking labor for slavery, and dominion for freedom. The discussion of this Missouri question has betrayed the secret of their souls. In the abstract, they admit that slavery is an evil, they disclaim all participation in the intro-duction of it, and cast it all upon the shoulders of our old Grandam Britain. But when probed to the quick upon it, they show at the bottom of their souls pride and vainglory in their condition of masterdom. They fancy themselves more gen-erous and noble-hearted than the plain freemen who labor for subsistence. They look down upon the simplicity of a Yankee's manners, because he has no habit of overbearing like theirs and can-not treat negroes like dogs. It is among the evils of slavery that it taints the very sources of moral principle. It establishes false estimates of virtue and vice; for what can be more false and heartless than this doctrine which makes the first and holi-est rights of humanity to depend upon the color of the skin? It perverts human reason, and reduces man endowed with logical powers to maintain that slavery is sanctioned by the Christian reli-gion, that slaves are happy and contented in their condition, that between master and slave there are ties of mutual attachment and affection, that the virtues of the master are refined and exalted by the degradation of the slave; while at the same they vent execrations upon the slave-trade, curse Britain for having given them slaves, burn at the stake negroes convicted of crimes for the terror of the example, and write in agonies of fear at the very mention of human rights as applicable to men of color."

Adams had never pondered slavery at such length, and the experience made him fear for the future of the republic. "The impression produced upon my mind by the progress of this discussion is that the bargain between freedom and slavery contained in the Constitution of the United States is morally and politically vicious, inconsistent with the principles upon which alone our Revolution can be justified; cruel and oppressive, by riveting the chains of slavery, by pledging the faith of freedom to maintain and perpetuate the tyranny of the master; and grossly unequal and impolitic, by admitting that slaves are at once enemies to be kept in subjection, property to be secured or restored to their owners, and persons not to be represented themselves, but for whom their masters are privileged with nearly a double share of representation. The consequence has been that this slave representation has governed the Union."

Attachment to the South and its slave owners had brought the rest of the Union nothing but grief,

Adams judged. "It would be no difficult matter to prove, by reviewing the history of the Union under this Constitution, that almost everything which has contributed to the honor and welfare of the nation has been accomplished in despite of them or forced upon them, and that everything unpropitious and dishonorable, including the blunders and follies of their adversaries, may be traced to them. I have favored this Missouri compromise, believing it to be all that could be effected under the present Constitution, and from an extreme unwillingness to put the Union at hazard."

But he might have been wrong. "Perhaps it would have been a wiser as well as a bolder course to have persisted in the restriction upon Missouri till it should have terminated in a convention of the states to revise and amend the Constitution. This would have produced a new Union of thirteen or fourteen states unpolluted with slavery, with a great and glorious object to effect, namely that of rallying to their standard the other states by the universal emancipation of their slaves. If the Union must be dissolved, slavery is precisely the question upon which it ought to break."

YET THE UNION wasn't ready to break, and not over slavery. The crack-up of the Republican party and the emergence of democracy, with its attendant turmoil, kept Americans too busy during the decade after the resolution of the Missouri question to take on slavery directly. But an event occurred in the summer of 1831 that riveted the attention of the country, terrified Southern slaveholders, and thrust the peculiar institution back onto center stage of American politics. A Virginia slave named Nat Turner led a band of several dozen slaves and free blacks on a murderous spree in Southampton County that claimed the lives of some sixty white men, women and children. Turner, a charismatic figure possessed by a mystical vision, hoped to inspire other slaves in that black-majority region of Virginia to rise up against their masters. Yet the white militia responded more quickly, and in a bloody reprisal captured or killed hundreds of slaves and free blacks, including many who had nothing to do with Turner or his rebellion. Turner escaped capture for two months but was finally found, tried, convicted and hanged.

The uprising sent shudders through Virginia and the broader South. Virginians concluded that something was drastically wrong with the state's policy toward slaves and slavery, and something had to be done about it. But different groups in the state proposed competing solutions. Quakers predictably called for abolition, but even many people less prompted by religion concluded that slavery was a rotten institution Virginia would be better rid of, eventually if not at once. The calls for emancipation were often accompanied by plans for colonizing the freed slaves in Africa. Most slaveholders contended that emancipation was a terrible idea; they held that the answer to the Turner rebellion was not less slavery but more of it—that is, more stringent restrictions on what slaves could do. Nat Turner was well educated for a slave; his education, the restrictionists said, was what had put ideas in his head and allowed him to communicate them to others. Education should henceforth be denied slaves. Slaves had often been allowed to gather outside the view of whites, and it was outside white view that Turner's conspiracy had been hatched; slaves therefore must be more carefully monitored. Other groups asserted that the presence of free blacks encouraged slaves to aspire to a freedom they didn't deserve and shouldn't have. Free blacks should be driven from the state, and manumission made more difficult.

The debate lasted weeks, spilling from the legislature into the larger Virginia community. Quite possibly the advocates of emancipation had a numerical advantage in the state; they also had the endorsement of influential papers like the **Richmond Enquirer**. But the slaveholders and the other opponents had greater weight in the legislature, and in the end the Select Committee on the Colored Population reaffirmed the status quo by declaring, "It is inexpedient for the present to make any legislative enactments for the abolition of slavery."

The inexpedience persisted, and deepened. In short order a strong trend in the opposite direction took hold: toward the proposed curbs on education of slaves, manumission and the rights of free blacks.

NOR DID THE new restrictions apply only to blacks. The Virginia debate had been open and free, but before long the promotion of abolitionist ideas became effectively forbidden in the South. It wasn't lost on the defenders of slavery that the first issue of William Lloyd Garrison's stridently abolitionist newspaper **The Liberator** was published in Boston just months before the Turner rebellion. Garrison's opening editorial explained that he had previously promoted gradual abolition but had decided it was morally wrong and politically counterproductive. "I will be as harsh as truth and as uncompromising as justice," he promised. "On this subject, I do not wish to think or speak or write with moderation. No! no! Tell a man whose house is on fire to give a moderate alarm; tell him to moderately rescue his wife from the hand of the ravisher; tell the mother to gradually extricate her babe from the fire into which it has fallen; but urge me not to use moderation in a cause like the present. I am in earnest—I will not equivocate—I will not excuse—I will not retreat a single inch—AND I WILL BE HEARD."

To Southern conservatives, the writings of
Garrison and other abolitionists were incendiary.
Read and repeated by the likes of Nat Turner, they
made killers out of contented slaves. They threatened the property rights of slaveholders and the
stability of Southern society. They promoted race
war and possibly, when the South took measures
to defend itself, civil war. Not least of all, they
fostered a moral smugness in the North about
the South, a demonization of the God-fearing
white men and women to whose care the black
slaves of the region had been entrusted. The
nineteenth-century South hadn't invented slavery,
its defenders repeated again and again in the years
after the Turner rebellion. The institution was an
inheritance. Like other inheritances it came with
responsibilities, and the responsibility of the current generation was not to deny the inheritance
but to administer it as humanely as possible.

38

SAM HOUSTON COULD have become the next Andrew Jackson—Young Hickory to Old Hickory—if not for a marriage gone badly wrong. As a soldier in Jackson's army, Houston had won the general's esteem for conspicuous bravery; as a congressman from Tennessee, he helped direct Jackson's campaign for president; as governor of Tennessee at the time of Jackson's inauguration, he showed a political flair that endeared him to the same people who had voted for Jackson. But his recent marriage to a woman half his age blew up just weeks after the wedding, and the humiliated Houston spun out of control. He resigned his governorship and vanished into the West. Periodic reports from Arkansas Territory, where he lived among the Indians, indicated that he spent much of the next two years on an epic bender, drowning his heartbreak. The Indians called him Big Drunk, and people who had known him in better times, including Jackson, wondered if he would ever recover. Finally he resurfaced, with a plan for regaining his honor and the respect of Jackson, whom he considered a second father. He would travel quietly to Texas, which Jackson had been trying to purchase from Mexico, and rouse American expatriates there to rebellion. Once freed from Mexico's grip, Texas would apply for admission to the United States. Jackson would get the territory he wanted and would welcome back his prodigal son. Houston would be a hero and either the first governor of American Texas or one of its first senators.

Houston's project commenced according to plan. Mexico's president and commanding general, Antonio López de Santa Anna, alarmed at the unruliness of the Americans who poured into Texas in defiance of Mexican immigration laws, launched a crackdown that enabled the Americans to wrap themselves in the mantle of 1776 and claim spiritual kinship to the Americans who rose in rebellion against George III. A Texas declaration of independence echoed Thomas Jefferson's version, and after a bloody setback at the Alamo, the Texans won a decisive victory at San Jacinto, where Sam Houston accepted the surrender of Santa Anna.

But the second phase of the project—the annexation of Texas to the United States—got stuck. Texans practiced slavery, and American opponents of slavery, including John Quincy Adams, objected to the addition of its vast territory, large enough for multiple states, to slavery's existing realm in the South. Adams's Massachusetts constituents mostly agreed with him that slavery was a blight on America's honor and republican conscience. They sent him petition after petition imploring Congress to keep Texas out of the Union. Adams duly presented the petitions to the House, adding his own opposition.

Adams thought the entire Texas affair dubious in the extreme. He knew of the close relationship between Houston and Andrew Jackson, and he suspected Jackson of abetting the Texas rebellion. When Jackson's 1836 annual message congratulated the Texans on achieving independence, Adams excoriated the president's "very lame account of the wanton disregard of the rights of nations in the invasion of the Mexican territories." Adams proposed resolutions calling on the president to hand over documents bearing on the Texas matter. The resolutions failed to gain a majority, but Adams commenced his own investigation. A defector from the Jackson side shared intelligence the defector said demonstrated the chicanery of Jackson toward Mexico and Texas. "It is so," Adams agreed in his diary, "and proves that Jackson's bold and dashing character was nevertheless capable of double-dealing worthy of Ferdinand the Catholic or of Tiberius Caesar. All the proceedings relating to Texas and Mexico have been in the same style."

Adams's protests got little attention. "Wind and tide are against me on this subject," he remarked. But he had never required public approbation to do what he deemed right, and he pressed on. He tested the patience of the leadership in the House, which allowed him to speak on Texas but only intermittently. The result was a disjointed series of one-hour addresses that spanned three weeks during the summer of 1838. Adams adduced various reasons why Texas should not be annexed, starting with the lies and warmongering of the president and his aides. "The conduct of the executive administration of this government toward Mexico was marked by duplicity and hostility—by hostility to the extent of a deliberate design of plunging us into a war with that power, for the purpose of dismembering her territories and annexing a large portion of them to this Union," he said. Adams challenged the power of Congress to authorize annexation of a foreign republic. Nothing like this had ever been attempted, he noted, and nothing in the Constitution authorized it.

But the most compelling reason Texas should be kept out of the Union was that annexation would spread the evil empire of bondage. After Adams had cited instance after instance of the barbarity of slavery, Francis Pickens of South Carolina complained that Adams, a Yankee, had no knowledge of slavery in practice. Adams retorted that Pickens, a slaveholder, was the one who lacked

knowledge. "He knows nothing of the real operation of the system," Adams said. "I do not in the
least doubt that he is, himself, a kind and indulgent
master; so, I doubt not, are all the gentlemen who
represent his state on this floor. They know not
the horrors that belong to the system." Pickens
didn't associate with the worst of the slaveholding
class. "He does not know the cruel, the tyrannical,
the hard-hearted master. He does not know the
profligate villain who procreates children from his
slaves and then sells his own children as slaves. He
does not know the crushing and destruction of all
the tenderest and holiest ties of nature which that
system produces, but which I have seen, with my
own eyes, in this city of Washington."

Adams gave an example: "Twelve months have
not passed since a woman in this District was taken
with her four infant children and separated from
her husband, who was a free man, to be sent away,
I know not where. That woman, in a dungeon in
Alexandria, **killed with her own hand two of her
children**, and attempted to kill the others." This
was what slavery did to human beings, Adams said,
and this was why its expansion must be halted.

———

ADAMS AND OTHER critics of slavery became
such a thorn in the side of the Democratic majority,
and the petitions, memorials and remonstrances

they brought from antislavery groups such an obstruction to legislation on other topics, that the House adopted a gag rule regarding antislavery petitions. Such petitions would be tabled without discussion or consideration.

Adams protested the gag rule as unconstitutional and immoral. The First Amendment guaranteed the right of petition, he pointed out. And by silencing antislavery petitioners, the gag rule kept the House from confronting the overriding moral issue of the age. Adams refused to obey the rule, finding one means and then another to introduce the petitions.

A group of Southern congressmen proposed to censure Adams. One of the first of several measures drafted for the purpose resolved: "That John Quincy Adams, a member from the State of Massachusetts, by his attempts to introduce into this House a petition from slaves, for the abolition of slavery in the District of Columbia, committed an outrage on the rights and feelings of a large portion of the people of this Union; a flagrant contempt of the dignity of this House; and, by extending to slaves a privilege only belonging to freemen, directly invites the slave population to insurrection; and that the said member be forthwith called to the bar of the House, to be censured by the Speaker."

Adams deflected this thrust by pointing out that he had not in fact introduced a petition from slaves for the abolition of slavery in the District of Columbia, worthy though that end was. He had merely inquired whether a petition from slaves, as opposed to petitions from voters, fell under the gag rule.

The Southerners answered the question with another censure resolution: "That the right of petition does not belong to the slaves of this Union, and that no petition from them can be presented to this House, without derogating from the rights of the slaveholding states and endangering the integrity of the Union." The resolution added: "That any member who shall hereafter present any such petition to the House ought to be considered as regardless of the feelings of the House, the rights of the South, and an enemy to the Union."

Adams couldn't contain his disgust. "Regardless of the feelings of the House!" he sneered. "What have the feelings of the House to do with the free agency of a member in the discharge of his duty? One of the most sacred duties of a member is to present the petitions committed to his charge, a duty which he cannot refuse or neglect to perform, without violating his oath to support the Constitution of the United States.

"Regardless of the rights of the South!" he continued, his temper rising. "What are the rights of the South? **What is the South?**" The South consisted of masters, nearly all white; of slaves, entirely black; and of other persons of both races. But it was only the rights of the first group that were being considered by the authors of the gag rule. "The rights of the South, then, here mean the rights of the masters of slaves, which, to describe them by an inoffensive word, I will call the rights of **mastery**." Adams acknowledged that these rights were recognized implicitly by the Constitution. "But they are rights incompatible with the inalienable rights of all mankind, as set forth in the Declaration of Independence; incompatible with the fundamental principles of the constitutions of all the free states of the Union.

"An enemy to the Union!" he went on. "For presenting a petition! An enemy to the Union!" Adams shook his head in wonder that the South was reaching so far, trampling the Constitution and invoking the specter of treason as employed by tyrants. The gag rule was wholly unprecedented. "Since the existence of the Constitution of the United States, there has never before been an example of an attempt in the House of Representatives to punish one of its members for words spoken by him in the performance of his duty." And it was another sign that slavery had corrupted the essence of republicanism. "Slavery has already had too deep and too baleful an influence upon the affairs and upon the history of this Union. It can never operate but as a slow poison to the morals of any community infected with it. Ours is infected with it to the vitals."

A member from Virginia had objected to Adams's effort to introduce a petition from some colored women of Fredericksburg. "The gentleman went further," Adams said, "and made the objection that I had presented a petition from women of infamous character—prostitutes, I think he called them."

The member interrupted: "It was not so. When the gentleman presented that petition, which I knew came from mulattoes in a slave state, I meant to confine my objection to petitions of mulattoes or free negroes in the Southern states. I meant to rescue the ladies of Fredericksburg from the stigma of having signed such a petition. Sir, no lady in Fredericksburg would sign such a petition."

Adams almost snarled: "With respect to the question what female is entitled to the character of a lady, I should be sorry to enter into a discussion here." Yet he denied having used the word in question. "When I have presented these petitions, I have usually said they were from **women,** and that, to my heart, is a dearer appellation than **ladies.**" Adams was mistaken in this case; he had in fact written the phrase "ladies of Fredericksburg" on the petition. But he wasn't going to let his opponent off the hook. "The gentleman from Virginia says he knows these women, and that they are infamous. **How** does the gentleman know it?"

Laughter rippled through the House.

The member defended himself. "I did not say

that I knew the women personally," he explained. "I knew from others that the character of one of them was notoriously bad."

"I am glad the gentleman now says he does not know these women, for if he had not disclaimed that knowledge, I might have asked **who** it was that made these women infamous, whether it was those of their own color or their masters," Adams rejoined. "I have understood that there are those among the colored population of slaveholding states who bear the image of their masters."

The House erupted again, but this time in Southern anger. Adams was unfazed. A member from South Carolina had observed that a lawmaker in his state who proposed abolition was subject to grand jury indictment. Adams sneered again. "Did the gentleman think he could frighten me from my purpose by his threat of a grand jury? If that was his object, let me tell him, **he mistook his man**. I am not to be frightened from the discharge of a duty by the indignation of the gentleman from South Carolina, nor by all the grand juries in the universe."

39

PERHAPS HE SHAMED them. Perhaps they decided that the best way to shut him up was to stop provoking him. At any rate, the censure resolutions against Adams all failed to win majorities, though the gag rule remained in force. Yet Adams's outspoken opposition to slavery had another effect, one less favorable to his cause. It, and the swelling chorus of criticism by abolition- ists, caused the defenders of slavery to mount a moral counterattack. Leading the charge, unsur- prisingly, was John Calhoun.

Calhoun addressed the Senate at almost the same moment Adams was ridiculing the House. As proud and self-assured as he had ever appeared, Calhoun rejected the idea that the South had anything to apologize for about slavery, and he urged his fellow slaveholders to rally in their own defense. "I do not belong to the school which holds that aggression is to be met by concession," he declared. "Mine is the opposite creed, which teaches that encroachments must be met at the beginning." The Senate was debating a gag rule of its own; should it refuse to accept antislavery petitions? Calhoun thought it definitely should. To allow a questioning of the moral and constitutional basis of slavery would open the South to further and endless attack. "In this case in particular, I hold concession or compromise to be fatal. If we concede an inch, concession would follow concession—compromise would follow compromise, until our ranks would be so broken that effectual resistance would be impossible."

Calhoun noted that at the time of the debate over Andrew Jackson's force bill, he had predicted that the centralizing philosophy that motivated the measure would prompt Northern abolitionists to try to get the central government to suppress slavery. "A large portion of the Northern states believed slavery to be a sin, and would consider it as an obligation of conscience to abolish it if they should feel themselves in any degree responsible for its continuance," Calhoun said. "I then predicted that it would commence as it has with this fanatical portion of society, and that they would begin their operations on the ignorant, the weak, the young, and the thoughtless, and gradually extend upwards till they would become strong enough to obtain political control." That had been but four years ago. "And all this is already in a course of regular fulfillment."

Things would get worse. "They who imagine that the spirit now abroad in the North will die away of itself without a shock or convulsion have formed a very inadequate conception of its real character. It will continue to rise and spread, unless prompt and efficient measures to stay its progress be adopted." It had seized schools, pulpits and much of the Northern press. Reasonable men and women in the North did not yet buy what the abolitionists were selling. But this would change. "In the course of a few years they will be succeeded by those who will have been taught to hate the people and institutions of nearly one-half of this Union, with a hatred more deadly than one hostile nation ever entertained towards another."

The result would be the rending of the Union. "By the necessary course of events, if left to themselves, we must become, finally, two people. It is impossible under the deadly hatred which must spring up between the two great nations, if the present causes are permitted to operate unchecked, that we should continue under the same political system. The conflicting elements would burst the Union asunder, powerful as are the links which hold it together."

Calhoun stated the matter as starkly as he could. "Abolition and the Union cannot coexist." He spoke as a friend of the Union, he said, and it was for the sake of the Union that he made his declaration. The South could not remain in the Union if the central government allowed the abolitionists to spread a doctrine that undermined the Southern way of life. "We of the South will not, cannot, surrender our institutions. To maintain the existing relations between the two races, inhabiting that section of the Union, is indispensable to the peace and happiness of both. It cannot be subverted without drenching the country in blood, and extirpating one or the other of the races. Be it good or bad, it has grown up with our society and institutions, and is so interwoven with them that to destroy it would be to destroy us as a people."

Calhoun shifted from politics to morality, and in doing so set down a marker that transformed the debate over slavery. "Let me not be understood as admitting, even by implication, that the existing relations between the two races in the slaveholding states is an evil," he said. "Far otherwise; I hold it to be a good, as it has thus far proved itself to be to both, and will continue to prove so if not disturbed by the fell spirit of abolition. I appeal to facts. Never before has the black race of Central Africa, from the dawn of history to the present day, attained a condition so civilized and so improved, not only physically, but morally and intellectually. In the meantime, the white or European race"—in the South—"has not degenerated. It has kept pace with its brethren in other sections of the Union where slavery does not exist. It is odious to make comparison; but I appeal to all sides whether the

South is not equal in virtue, intelligence, patriotism, courage, disinterestedness, and all the high
qualities which adorn our nature."

Lest listeners mistake his point, Calhoun reiterated: "In the present state of civilization, where
two races of different origin and distinguished
by color and other physical differences, as well as
intellectual, are brought together, the relation now
existing in the slaveholding states between the two
is, instead of an evil, a good—a positive good."

WITH THIS SENTENCE, Calhoun added to the
lexicon of slavery a phrase that became a battle cry
of the South. Since independence, slavery had typically been treated as something evil—a necessary
evil, perhaps, in those states that allowed slavery,
but evil still. Calhoun understood that such a characterization yielded the moral high ground to the
abolitionists; slaveholders would be at a constant
disadvantage. By asserting instead that slavery was
a "positive good," he claimed moral parity for the
South. The North was no better than the South;
slaveholders had nothing to apologize for.

In fact, Calhoun claimed more than parity.
"There never has yet existed a wealthy and civilized
society in which one portion of the community
did not, in point of fact, live on the labor of the
other," he said. This had been true in ancient
times; it was true at present. And the American

system, which allowed slavery, was more humane than the systems of Europe, which did not. "In few countries is so much left to the share of the laborer, and so little exacted from him, or is more kind attention paid to him in sickness or infirmities of age," Calhoun said. "Compare his condition with the tenants of the poor houses in the more civilized portions of Europe—look at the sick, and the old and infirm slave, on one hand, in the midst of his family and friends, under the kind superintending care of his master and mistress, and compare it with the forlorn and wretched condition of the pauper in the poor house."

Slavery, moreover, enhanced the stability of society. "Here I fearlessly assert that the existing relation between the two races in the South, against which these blind fanatics"—the abolitionists—"are waging war, forms the most solid and durable foundation on which to rear free and stable political institutions. It is useless to disguise the fact. There is and always has been, in an advanced stage of wealth and civilization, a conflict between labor and capital. The condition of society in the South exempts us from the disorders and dangers resulting from this conflict, which explains why it is that the political condition of the slaveholding states has been so much more stable and quiet than that of the North."

The abolitionists would destroy the stability of the South without improving the material lot of those they professed to care about. This was why Southerners must make the case for the morality of their system. "If we do not defend ourselves, none will defend us; if we yield we will be more and more pressed as we recede; and if we submit we will be trampled underfoot. Be assured that emancipation itself would not satisfy these fanatics; that gained, the next step would be to raise the negroes to a social and political equality with the whites; and that being effected, we would soon find the present condition of the two races reversed. They and their Northern allies would be the masters, and we the slaves."

40

ANDREW JACKSON'S PARTING gift to Martin Van Buren was the White House. The New Yorker coasted to victory in the 1836 election on the residual popularity of the hero of New Orleans. The opposition Whigs did themselves no favors by adopting the novel strategy of putting four separate candidates before the voters, hoping to garner enough electors from the different parts of the country to deny Van Buren a majority and then to defeat him when the contest went to the House of Representatives. Daniel Webster was the New England candidate of the Whigs, but he carried only his home state of Massachusetts. Ohio's William Henry Harrison, the frontier general from the War of 1812, ran strongest among the Whigs, winning seven states. But the Whig total fell short of Van Buren's fifteen states and 170 electoral votes, and the vice president became president. The Whigs learned that divide-and-conquer didn't work when their own party was the one divided.

Van Buren's prize was soon spoiled by a delayed effect of Jackson's war on the Bank of the United States. State banks, flush with the deposits Jackson took from the national bank, had expanded credit rapidly, inflating a speculative bubble in Western lands. Jackson before leaving office felt obliged to restrain the speculation and issued an order—the "specie circular"—requiring that federal lands be paid for in gold or silver. The land bubble burst, and a panic seized the nation's finances in 1837. When the trouble spread to the larger economy during the next several months, millions suffered from foreclosures, layoffs and evictions. Voters turned against Van Buren and the Democrats, giving Whigs reason to believe that 1840 could be their year to elect a president.

HENRY CLAY TOOK the lead in the early going. His loss to Jackson in 1832 was a distant memory, and he had spent much of the time since then trying to unify the Whigs. Daniel Webster had shown he was a regional candidate at best, and William Harrison's military record hadn't exactly carried voters away. Clay was hopeful, if cautious. "My friends are very sanguine about my election to the next presidency, and with reason, if I am to credit the information which daily reaches me," he wrote to his son James in early 1838. "But I strive to prevent my feelings being too much enlisted in the subject." He avoided contentious topics like Texas. "I do not think that the question of annexation is one that ought to be considered or entertained at all, during the existence of war between Mexico and Texas," he told his New York friend Peter Porter. Mexico had not yet acknowledged its loss of Texas, and it occasionally conducted military raids into what it deemed its renegade province. "I would not for a moment consent to involve this country in war to acquire that country," Clay continued. "Nor, if its independence were acknowledged by Mexico, and peace were established between them, would I concur in incorporating Texas in this confederacy, against the decided wishes of a large portion of it"—of America. "I think it is better to harmonize what we have than to introduce a new element of discord into our political partnership, against the consent of existing members of the concern."

His caution paid off. "If I am to judge from information which daily, almost hourly, reaches me, there is **every where** an irresistible current setting in towards me," Clay wrote to his son Henry in March 1838. "I believe that if the election were to come on in sixty days I should be elected by acclamation." Yet he realized that the election was **not** sixty days away. "The election is nigh three years off, great changes may take place, I may die, and therefore we should look to the future with all the uncertainty which hangs over it."

John Calhoun's deepening sectionalism and his radical defense of the morality of slavery had largely eliminated the South Carolinian from serious contention for the presidency, but Clay sought to isolate him further, lest he inhibit the pro-Clay groundswell. Clay lashed Calhoun for embracing in Van Buren policies he had opposed in Jackson, starting with an endorsement of the Democratic administration's preference for state banks over a national bank. "I handled Mr. Calhoun without gloves," Clay boasted to Nicholas Biddle. To a claim by Calhoun that nullification had overthrown the protective tariff and ended the crisis of 1833, Clay responded with scorn. "Nullification, Mr. President, overthrew the protective policy?!" he declared mockingly in the Senate. "No, sir! The compromise was not extorted by the terror of nullification. . . . It was a compassionate concession to the imprudence and impotency of nullification! The danger from nullification itself excited no more apprehension than would be felt by seeing a regiment of a thousand boys, of five or six years of age, decorated in brilliant uniforms, with their gaudy plumes and tiny muskets, marching up to assault a corps of 50,000 grenadiers, six feet high."

When Calhoun responded with a blistering counterattack, Clay congratulated himself on a job

well done. "I believe in private life he is irreproach-
able," he said of Calhoun to an associate. "But I
believe he will die a traitor or a madman. His
whole aim, and the tendency of all his exertions of
late, is to sow the seeds of dissension between the
different parts of the Union, and thus to prepare
the way for its dissolution. His little clique, distinguished more by activity and paradoxes than by
numbers, is now busily endeavoring to propagate
the notion that all the operations of the federal
government, from the commencement, have been
ruinous to the South, and aggrandizing to the
North. This, although 40 years of the 48 during
which the government has existed, have Southern
men directed the course of public affairs!"

Clay turned his attention to Daniel Webster. In
letters and conversations, including conversations
with Webster, Clay said that the Massachusetts
senator should eliminate himself from presidential
consideration lest the Whigs be as divided at the
next election as they had been at the last. Webster
resisted. "I yesterday had a long interview and
conversation with Mr. W.," Clay reported to an
ally in June 1838. "It was conducted throughout
and terminated amicably; but he will do nothing at present in regard to withdrawing from the
contest. I think he will ultimately be forced by his
friends to adopt that course, but if he does he will
embrace it slowly and sullenly. I shall avoid every
thing on my part which might tend to produce

a breach." In another letter, Clay wrote, "The administration party is, beyond all doubt, prostrated. Nothing can continue it in power but the division among the Whigs as to their candidate for the presidency. **Our** division is now **their** only remaining strength. The people appear to be likely to remove that obstacle, by concentrating on one individual. Much, however, remains to be done." And most of that could be done by Webster. "If Mr. W. were to retire (and I think his retirement would add strength to the cause and to his own high pretensions) all other difficulties would speedily vanish."

When Webster continued to refuse to withdraw, Clay broadened his campaign. He treated Webster kindly in the Senate, not wishing to break Whig ranks in public. But he worked on Webster's backers in private. "The partiality for Mr. W., and the admiration of his abilities, in your quarter are quite natural," he wrote to a New England friend, who was a friend of Webster as well. "The same admiration extends everywhere. It is nevertheless perfectly manifest that he cannot be elected president at the next election. If I were withdrawn, Harrison would sweep every thing before him. I think then it is best for Mr. W. to retire from a position which, whilst it exhibits us divided and thereby encourages our opponents and discourages our friends, can lead to no issue favorable to himself. It is best for **him** and best for the common cause. It would be regarded as a measure of great magnanimity, and his praises would be generally sounded. It could not fail to redound to his benefit hereafter." And it would solve the party's problem—and Clay's. "The feelings at the North, now stifled, would burst forth, and General H.'s friends would perceive the utter hopelessness of his remaining in the field. In six months from Mr. W.'s retirement, the whole matter would be finally settled."

AN UNEXPECTED EVENT in September 1838 dealt Clay's plans a blow. The Whig slate in Maine elections lost to the Democrats. State and local elections in those days were the closest thing to public opinion polls, and members of Clay's party searched their souls to discover where they had failed. The Boston **Atlas,** a Whig paper, opined that the party needed to promote a popular hero, a Jackson-like character who could bring out the masses. The only Whig hopeful who approximated Jackson was Harrison. Clay had been tested at the polls in 1832 and been found wanting. Webster in 1836 had done even worse. "There remains, then, only General Harrison," the paper declared.

Clay rejected the diagnosis and the prescription. He denied any responsibility for the Whig defeat in Maine. He thought the **Atlas** editor had an agenda he wasn't sharing. "I am mortified, shocked, disgusted with the course of some men," Clay said. "I had hoped for better things of them." He suspected Webster of spurring the paper—published in Webster's hometown—to this gambit. Without explicitly accusing Webster of guiding the editor's hand, Clay cast strong aspersion. "Putting all circumstances together," he remarked to a friend, "without an explicit disavowal from him, the conviction will be irresistible that his views and wishes have not been overlooked."

WEBSTER KEPT MUM, and Clay became convinced he had connived in the editorial. Yet the heart of Clay's problem was not what Webster did or didn't do; it was what he himself wouldn't or couldn't do about the most controversial issue of the day. Even while he worked to get Webster to drop out of the race, Clay received a letter from Lewis Tappan, a New York merchant converted to abolitionism. "An opportunity exists for you to render a service to your country and to mankind such as you have never known," Tappan said. Henry Clay should come out for emancipation. Tappan granted that there would be political risks for Clay. But the rewards to his reputation and to his place in the hearts of his compatriots would more than offset his losses. "To be **the man** who, at this junction, would nobly stand forth as the champion of human rights would be a greater honor than any of our countrymen has yet attained. If I mistake not, his contemporaries in his own country would acknowledge the wisdom of his course—certainly the wise and good in all lands would name him with gratitude—and success would attend his efforts. What is the reputation of a Jefferson, or Madison, or Franklin compared with the reputation such a man would acquire?"

Clay didn't respond at once. He realized that what he said would alienate either New England or the South, and possibly both. He needed to choose his words with care. "I hope that you will believe that my omission to answer earlier your last favor has not proceeded from any intention to treat you with the slightest disrespect," he finally wrote, a month after receiving Tappan's letter. "The subject of your letter is one on which we unfortunately differ in opinion, and ascribing to you the same good motives which I claim for myself, I apprehend that there is no prospect of reconciling our conflicting opinions. I most conscientiously believe that the Northern agitation of the question of abolition is productive of no good. I believe it injurious to the unfortunate black race and hazardous to the harmony, peace and union of the whites. I am sure that you can not view the matter in the same light. But with our opposite sentiments, it has not appeared to me profitable to enter upon a discussion, for which indeed I have no time, and which is not likely to lead to any useful result."

Clay told another abolitionist, James Birney, that the abolitionists were making emancipation more difficult. He cited his own state, Kentucky, which had pondered a convention to consider phased emancipation. The convention never happened. "It is my clear conviction that a decision against a convention was mainly produced by agitation of the question of abolition at the North," Clay wrote. "I will not say that without that agitation this state was ripe for gradual emancipation, but it was rapidly advancing toward that point. We are thrown back fifty years."

Clay hoped that his middle position—between radical opponents of slavery like Tappan and Birney and radical apologists for slavery like John Calhoun—would suit the majority of Americans who similarly eschewed extremes. But that majority didn't find itself under the scrutiny Clay did, and didn't suffer the simultaneous attacks he endured. "The abolitionists are denouncing me as a slaveholder, and slaveholders as an abolitionist," he remarked wryly to a friend.

THIS MIDDLE POSITION might win him the nomination. Then again, it might not. Nearly everyone in the Whig party acknowledged Clay's talents and experience; most felt gratitude for the compromises he had secured on the Union's behalf. But the longer the economic hard times in the country lasted, and the more likely a Whig victory in the next election appeared, the more the party leaders determined to get behind the least controversial candidate. William Harrison had served in Congress from Ohio and been territorial governor of Indiana, but he had avoided the major controversies of the era and was shrewd enough to rest on the laurels of his military service.

Clay observed the trend yet tried to explain it away. The Anti-Masonic party met in November 1838 and nominated Harrison for president and Webster for vice president. The decision didn't commit the Whigs in any way, but its logic reflected thinking like that of the Whig leaders. Clay waved it off. "The nomination has fallen still born," he wrote dismissively. "It will work directly in the opposite way from that which was intended. Prudence alone suppresses the public expression of the indignation which it has excited in the Whigs." Even so, Clay was candid enough to acknowledge that things weren't going as he had planned. "Our cause is surrounded by embarrassments," he said of the Whigs. "These are chiefly to be traced to our divisions which constitute our weakness, as they do the hopes of our adversaries."

H E DECIDED HE might as well be hanged for a sheep as for a lamb. With his tactical maneuvers failing, Henry Clay determined to speak his conscience. A petition to have Congress end slavery in the District of Columbia prompted reflection on the phenomenon of abolitionism. Clay identified three groups of abolitionists. The first comprised Quakers and other religious groups that had always opposed slavery. These philanthropic abolitionists were a threat to no one, because they opposed violence even more than they opposed slavery, and they confined themselves to reasoned persuasion. Clay's second group consisted of individuals who were affronted by the gag rule and who allied with the abolitionists for the purpose of vindicating the First Amendment. These operational abolitionists were no threat either, because they were more interested in freedom of speech and petition than in freedom for slaves.

It was the third group that caused all the trouble. "The third class are the real ultra-abolitionists, who are resolved to persevere in the pursuit of their object at all hazards, and without regard to any consequences, however calamitous they may be," Clay told the Senate. The radical abolitionists were a grave threat to American constitutionalism and the rule of law. "With them the rights of property are nothing; the deficiency of the powers of the general government is nothing; the acknowledged and incontestable powers of the states are nothing; civil war, a dissolution of the Union, and the overthrow of a government in which are concentrated the fondest hopes of the civilized world, are nothing. A single idea has taken possession of their minds, and onward they pursue it, overlooking all barriers, reckless and regardless of all consequences."

The radical abolitionists were currently demanding an end to slavery in the federal district, and also in the federal territory of Florida. They wanted to bar interstate commerce in slaves, and they insisted that Congress admit no more slave states. They presented these aims as modest and quite within the constitutional powers of Congress. But they had a larger agenda, Clay said. "Their purpose is abolition, universal abolition—peaceably if it can, forcibly if it must be." The legal approach they avowed was not the only or most important part of their campaign. "Another, and much more lamentable one, is that which this class is endeavoring to employ, of arraying one portion against another portion of the Union. With that view, in all their leading prints and publications, the alleged horrors of slavery are depicted in the most glowing and exaggerated colors, to excite the imaginations and stimulate the rage of the people in the free states, against the people in the slave states. The slaveholder is held up and represented as the most atrocious of human beings. Advertisements of fugitive slaves and of slaves to be sold are carefully collected and blazoned forth, to infuse a spirit of detestation and hatred against one entire and the largest section of the Union."

Clay recounted some history. In the early days of the republic, he said, the founders had feared two dangers to the Union. One was the Allegheny Mountains, which divided the waters running east from those running west. That danger had been allayed by the construction of roads across the mountains, by the Erie and other canals, and by the development of the steamboat. The second threat was slavery. "It was this which created the greatest obstacle, and the most anxious solicitude, in the deliberations of the convention that adopted the general Constitution," Clay said. The framers concluded to keep their distance. "The convention wisely left to the several states the power over the institution of slavery, as a power not necessary to the plan of union which it devised, and as one with which the general government could not be invested without planting the seeds of certain destruction." Clay paused for effect. "There let it remain undisturbed by any unhallowed hand."

But it was **not** remaining undisturbed, and Clay feared the result. Suppose the abolitionists succeeded in uniting the inhabitants of the free states against those of the slave states. "Union on the one side will beget union on the other," Clay said. "And this process of reciprocal consolidation will be attended with all the violent prejudices, embittered passions, and implacable animosities, which ever degraded or deformed human nature. A virtual dissolution of the Union will have taken place, while the forms of its existence remain. The most valuable element of union, mutual kindness, the feelings of sympathy, the fraternal bonds, which now happily unite us, will have been extinguished for ever. One section will stand in menacing and hostile array against the other. The collision of opinion will be quickly followed by the clash of arms."

What would this civil war look like? "Abolitionists themselves would shrink back in dismay and horror at the contemplation of desolated fields, conflagrated cities, murdered inhabitants and the overthrow of the fairest fabric of human government that ever rose to animate the hopes of civilized man." Nor should the abolitionists flatter themselves that victory in such a war would be assured. "All history and experience proves the hazard and uncertainty of war. And we are admonished by Holy Writ, that the race is not to the swift, nor the battle to the strong."

Even if they triumphed, whom would they have conquered? "A foreign foe, one who had insulted our flag, invaded our shores and laid our country waste? No, sir; no, sir. It would be a conquest without laurels, without glory; a self, a suicidal conquest; a conquest of brothers over brothers, achieved by one over another portion of the descendants of common ancestors who, nobly pledging their lives, their fortunes, and their sacred honor, had fought and bled, side by side, in many a hard battle on land and ocean, severed our country from the British crown, and established our national independence."

The radical abolitionists dreamed of a world that didn't exist; statesmen had to deal with the world that did. "If the question were an original question, whether, there being no slaves within the country, we should introduce them, and incorporate them into our society, that would be a totally different question." Slavery was a bane, a corrupter of democratic values. But slavery existed in America, Clay observed, and it couldn't be wished away. "The slaves are here. No practical scheme for their removal or separation from us has been yet devised or proposed; and the true inquiry is what is best to be done with them."

The abolitionists had not made life better for the slaves, the objects of their asserted sympathy. By the alarm they had raised in the South, they had made the life of slaves worse. "They have thrown back for half a century the prospect of any species of emancipation of the African race, gradual or immediate," Clay said. "They have increased the rigors of legislation against slaves in most, if not all, of the slave states."

The abolitionists acted as though the world could be remade overnight. It could not, Clay said. Emancipation would come, but it would take time. And it would come most swiftly under the auspices of the Union. The abolitionists might soothe their consciences by demanding immediate emancipation, but they did no practical good and risked great harm, to the slaves no less than to the country at large. Clay asked Americans to remember what they had to lose. "Was ever a people before so blessed as we are, if true to ourselves? Did ever any other nation contain within its bosom so many elements of prosperity, of greatness and of glory? Our only real danger lies ahead, conspicuous, elevated and visible." The abolitionists brought the danger closer.

CLAY'S ATTACK ON the abolitionists reflected his honest belief about the threat they posed to the Union and the welfare of all its people. Clay was never less than sincere in speaking about the Union. But he simultaneously could hope that his anti-abolitionist stance would win him votes in the South.

The question was whether it would cost him heavily in the North. He had reason to believe it would not, because the abolitionists were as deeply suspect in many Northern communities as they were in the South. At first he thought the speech had hit the mark he intended. "I expected it would enrage the Ultras more than ever against me, and I have not been disappointed," he wrote to a friend. But among broader groups it seemed to prosper. "Its reception at the North has far exceeded my most sanguine expectations." Clay assumed a favorable response in other regions. "I hope it will do good everywhere." He congratulated himself on a statement of conscience that paid political dividends. "From all quarters, the most gratifying intelligence is received as to my future prospects."

He spoke too soon. The Whigs were still struggling to coalesce. Born in opposition to Jackson, they had yet to develop a national leadership that could answer such basic questions as when the party's nominating convention would be held. Clay argued for an early convention, in order that the party pull together behind its nominee. William Harrison sought delay, judging that men in the public eye like Clay would make enemies by the positions they would have to take on the controversial issues of the day. The sidelines had suited Andrew Jackson in his quest for the presidency, and they suited Harrison. Yet it was less Harrison's preference than the overall confusion among the Whigs that caused the convention to keep being pushed back. And with each month's delay, the mood in the party shifted further toward Harrison.

Clay could feel the shift. He sensed it in planted rumors that he had decided to drop out of the race. He denied the rumors even while realizing that his response added to the doubt they intentionally sowed. Erstwhile supporters began to defect. "Your friends in this state with whom I have conversed—and no man ever had more ardent ones—are looking with painful anxiety to the determination of the Whig national convention in the selection of the candidate," an Indiana ally reported. "If they thought your success probable, they would not hesitate in warmly soliciting your name to be placed before them as their candidate. But they can not bear the idea of seeing you placed in a doubtful and desperate contest at this time." Clay had often emphasized the need for party unity. The call was echoed back to him. "The opinion of your friends here, so far as I have been able to learn it, is that you and the party have much to gain and nothing to lose by your indicating in such terms as your own good sense may suggest your willingness or desire that Gen. Harrison may be the nominee of the convention."

Clay reluctantly accepted the inevitable. "I have no wish to be the candidate if there be any other Whig more acceptable to the greater number than myself," he replied to the Indianan, with the understanding that the message would be repeated.

This was all the Harrison forces needed to hear. Many paid honor to Clay for his leadership in Congress while reiterating their argument that that very leadership had made him unelectable. Peter Porter, Clay's New York ally, reported the result from the Whig convention, finally held in Harrisburg, Pennsylvania. "General Harrison is nominated," Porter wrote to Clay, "and what is most extraordinary, by a body of men three fourths of whom, as well as their constituents, if their own open declarations are to be credited, are decidedly of the opinion that you ought to be the president of the United States in preference to any other individual!" Porter offered solace along with an explanation. "If I looked alone to your personal comfort or, I think I may add, to your future fame, I should be glad with all my heart that General Harrison is nominated, for we know that you have some bitter political enemies who would surely do all in their power to thwart you. And the scale of the party is so nearly balanced that a small diversion from our ranks would turn it. And if you were to be defeated you would be placed in a most unpleasant predicament—whereas now, whatever may be the result, you will by your magnanimous course have secured the eternal admiration of the country."

Clay did take the magnanimous course. No sooner had the news of the convention's decision reached Washington than he endorsed it and the nominee. "If I have friends," he told a gathering of Whigs, "friends connected with me by the ties of blood, by my regard of common friendship, if I have any one that loves me, I assure them that they cannot do me a better service than to follow my example and vote heartily, as I shall, for the nomination which has been made." Clay's audience cheered. Clay continued, "We have not been contending for Henry Clay, for William Henry Harrison, for Daniel Webster, or for Winfield Scott"—another general favored by some. "No! We have been contending for principles! Not men, but principles, are our rules of action." The party must and would unite against the ills that afflicted the country. "William Henry Harrison and John Tyler"—the Virginian nominated for vice president—"are the medicine which will cure us."

JOHN QUINCY ADAMS thought it would take a great deal more than Whig medicine to cure what ailed America. Adams had never reconciled himself to the habits of democracy, and his pessimism about popular politics increased with his advancing years. The campaign of 1840 seemed evidence that America had lost its mind. "The whole country throughout the Union is in a state of agitation upon the approaching Presidential election such as was never before witnessed," he wrote in his diary that summer. "Not a week has passed within the last four months without a convocation of thousands of people to hear inflammatory harangues against Martin Van Buren and his administration, by Henry Clay, Daniel Webster, and all the principal opposition orators in or out of Congress." Adams received invitations to the campaign events, but declined them as too partisan for his taste. The events proceeded without him. "One of these assemblies was held yesterday by a public dinner given to Caleb Cushing by some of his constituents at Newburyport, and a ball in the evening by him to them. I was invited also there, but did not attend. Mr. Webster and Mr. Saltonstall were there, and a stump-speech scaffold, and, it is said, a procession of six thousand people or more, and a dinner of eighteen hundred. Here is a revolution in the habits and manners of the people. Where will it end? These are party movements, and must in the natural progress of things become antagonistical. These meetings cannot be multiplied in numbers and frequency without resulting in yet deeper tragedies. Their manifest tendency is to civil war."

The tumultuous politicking continued into the autumn. "This practice of itinerant speech-making has suddenly broken forth in this country to a fearful extent," Adams recorded. "Electioneering for the presidency has spread its contagion to the president himself, to his now only competitor, to his immediate predecessor, to one at least of his cabinet councilors, the secretary of war, to the ex-candidates Henry Clay and Daniel Webster, and to many of the most distinguished members of both houses of Congress. Immense assemblages of the people are held—of twenty, thirty, fifty thousand souls—where the first orators of the nation address the multitude, not one in ten of whom can hear them, on the most exciting topics of the day. As yet, the parties call and hold these meetings separately, and seldom interfere with each other. But at the Baltimore convention last May"—where the Democrats renominated Van Buren—"one of the marshals of the procession, a respectable mechanic of the city, was killed by an attempt of individuals of the opposite party to break it up. At a meeting a few days since, on Long Island, Mr. Webster, in a speech of two hours and a half, observed that there was to be held a meeting of the opposite party—another great meeting— at the same place the next day; and he gave what was equivalent to a challenge to Silas Wright and all the administration leaders to meet him on the stump." Adams saw nothing good ahead. "The tendency of all this, undoubtedly, is to the corruption of the popular elections, both by violence and fraud."

The hoopla and uproar eventually produced a win for Harrison. "Mutual gratulation at the downfall of the Jackson–Van Buren administration is the universal theme of conversation," Adams wrote in the aftermath. "One can scarcely imagine the degree of detestation in which they are both held." Yet he saw little reason for optimism. "No one knows what is to come. In four years from this time the successor may be equally detested."

The democracy inaugurated by Andrew Jackson was still working its damage on the American republic, Adams judged. "Jackson's administration commenced with fairer prospects and an easier career before him than had ever before been presented to any president of the United States. His personal popularity, founded exclusively upon the battle of New Orleans, drove him through his double term, and enabled him to palm upon this nation the sycophant who declared it glory enough to have served under such a chief for his successor." What had Jackson and Van Buren accomplished? What remained of democracy's grand promises? Nothing at all. "Their edifice has crumbled into ruin by the mere force of gravity and the wretchedness of their cement." What would follow? "No halcyon days. One set of unsound principles for another; one man in leading-strings for another. Harrison comes in upon a hurricane; God grant he may not go out upon a wreck!"

43

WHAT ADAMS DECRIED as a hurricane was in fact the new model of American politics. In the age of democracy, voters expected to be wooed and entertained, feted and fed. Candidates had to display a common touch. Americans in the republican age of George Washington were willing to defer to their leaders; in the democratic age of Andrew Jackson they expected their leaders to defer to **them.** Harrison was no commoner, but he let himself be portrayed as such, and his "log cabin and hard cider" campaign—so dubbed for the falsified place of his birth and the beverage he pretended to favor—established a standard that became a permanent feature of the political landscape.

The campaign left Harrison weary. Yet the four months between the election and the inauguration allowed him time to recuperate. This was no small matter, in that Harrison, at sixty-eight, was the oldest person yet to assume the presidency (a dis-

tinction he would retain until the inauguration of
Ronald Reagan almost a century and a half later).
Feeling hale by early March 1841, Harrison gave
the longest inaugural address in American history
(a record he still holds), despite lacking a hat and
coat amid a nasty late-winter storm. He then
proceeded to greet the guests while still wet and
shivering. He shrugged off urgings to change into
dry clothes, saying he had endured far worse as a
frontier soldier. But he had been younger then. He
fell ill and never recovered, dying of pneumonia,
fever or some combination of the two a month
after taking the oath.

Henry Clay and Daniel Webster had only just
made their peace with yielding to Harrison as
leader of the Whigs; to find themselves in the
shadow of John Tyler was more than they could
bear. Harrison's was the first death of a sitting
president, and the status of Tyler wasn't immediately clear. The Constitution declared that upon
the death of the president the powers and duties
of the office should "devolve on" the vice president,
but it didn't say that the vice president would actually **become** president. None of the Whigs had
intended that Tyler be president, and many were
unwilling to acknowledge that he now was. They
referred to him as the vice president still, or as the
acting president. But Tyler immediately realized
what they soon discovered: that the presidential
powers, however acquired, make their wielder

the president, whatever he is called. Tyler acted as president and in doing so became president.

But he also became a man without a party. Tyler had never been more than an opportunistic Whig; his pro-slavery, states' rights views put him closer to many Southern Democrats than to most Whigs. Whig leaders like Henry Clay and Daniel Webster had accepted such latitudinarianism in a vice presidential candidate, for it broadened the Whig ticket and helped carry Harrison to victory. But they didn't want it in a president, least of all one who bore the brand of the Whig party.

Webster tactfully let Tyler know that he was expected to conform to Whig principles. William Harrison, before his death, had tried to mend fences with Clay and Webster by offering them positions in the cabinet. Clay declined but Webster accepted the state department. As senior member of the administration, Webster became Harrison's confidant. Harrison let Webster preview his inaugural address and offer suggestions for stylistic improvement. Webster took the draft and labored over Harrison's lugubrious prose and frequent references to ancient history. At the end of a long day he returned to the house where he was lodging. His landlady said he looked tired and upset. "I hope nothing has gone wrong," she said. "I really hope nothing has happened." Webster smiled wearily. "You would think that something had happened if you knew what I have done," he said. "I have killed **seventeen Roman consuls** as dead as smelts, every one of them."

At Tyler's first cabinet meeting as president, convened the day after Harrison died, Webster rose to address the new chief executive. "Mr. President," he said, "I suppose you intend to carry out the ideas and customs of your predecessor, and this administration, inaugurated by President Harrison, will continue in the same line of policy under which it has begun."

Tyler nodded vaguely, unsure where Webster was going.

Webster went on, "Mr. President, it was our custom in the cabinet meetings of the deceased president that the president should preside over them. All measures whatever relating to the administration were obliged to be brought before the cabinet, and their settlement was decided by the majority, each member of the cabinet and the president having but one vote."

Tyler looked at Webster and around at the others. He stood up, signaling to Webster to sit. "I beg your pardon, gentlemen," he said firmly. "I am very glad to have in my cabinet such able statesmen as you have proved yourselves to be. And I shall be pleased to avail myself of your counsel and advice. But I can never consent to being dictated to as to what I shall or shall not do. I, as president, shall be responsible for my administration. I hope to have your hearty cooperation in carrying out its measures. So long as you see fit to do this, I shall be glad to have you with me. When you think otherwise, your resignations will be accepted."

RELATIONS BETWEEN TYLER and the cabinet grew tenser from there. Nor did things go well between the new president and the Whig leadership in Congress. Henry Clay had expected to guide William Harrison's administration toward a revival of the American System, including a reincarnation of the Bank of the United States. Harrison took offense at Clay's presumption, in particular at a suggestion that Harrison summon a special session of Congress, for which Clay had drafted a proclamation. Harrison didn't like this one bit. "You are too impetuous," he wrote to Clay. The senator acted as though he spoke for all the Whigs, Harrison said. In fact he did not. "Much as I would rely upon your judgment, there are others whom I must consult and in many cases to determine adversely to your suggestions."

Clay professed to be hurt. "I was mortified by the suggestion you made to me on Saturday, that I had been represented as dictating to you or to the new administration," he responded. "Mortified, because it is unfounded in fact, and because there is danger of the fears that I intimated to you at Frankfort"—where Harrison and Clay had met en route to Washington—"of my enemies poisoning your mind towards me." Clay reminded Harrison that he had sought no office for himself in the administration. He had asked none for any friend. His diffidence had cost him. "A thousand times have my feelings been wounded by communicating to those who have applied to me that I am obliged to abstain inflexibly from all interference in official appointments."

Clay and Harrison reached an accommodation, and the special session was called. Then Harrison died, and Tyler began asserting his independence. He didn't cancel the call for a special session, but he threw cold water on the purpose for which the session had been called. "As to a Bank, I design to be perfectly frank with you," he told Clay. "I would not have it urged prematurely. The public mind is still in a state of great disquietude in regard to it." The Democrats would raise a ruckus against a new bank. Tyler refused to commit himself one way or the other. "I have no intention to submit any thing to Congress on this subject to be acted on, but shall leave it to its own action, and in the end shall resolve my doubts by the character of the measure proposed."

Clay could only read this message as a threat to veto a bank bill, and he wondered if Tyler hid a Jacksonian streak. Nevertheless, taking the new president at his word, Clay ushered a bank bill through Congress. He shaped the bill to Tyler's suggestions on points of form and minor substance, and he interpreted the president's participation in the process as support for the measure. Members of Tyler's administration, including Daniel Webster, detected other signs of approval for the bank. And so when the bank bill passed Congress and Tyler abruptly vetoed it, the negative took the capital by surprise.

Clay resented the veto deeply. He thought it misguided as policy, in that the country needed a national bank more than ever. He judged it bad precedent, for continuing the Jacksonian practice of vetoing whatever the president didn't like. He deemed it a usurpation by an unelected chief executive. And he took it as an insult to the Whig party and the principles for which the party stood.

Clay responded to the veto by doing something America had never seen. The Senate leader of the president's party publicly chastised that president. Clay asserted that Tyler had not accorded the legislative branch the respect it was due. "He has not reciprocated the friendly spirit of concession and compromise which animated Congress in the provisions of this bill," he said. A remarkable change had come over the new president in a short time. Clay recalled reading Tyler's first message after Harrison's death. "It was emphatically a Whig address from beginning to end. Every inch of it was Whig and was patriotic." Clay had entertained hopes for good relations with the chief executive. "I reflected with pleasure that I should find at the head of the executive branch a personal and political friend, whom I had long and intimately known and highly esteemed." But the veto revealed a president who wouldn't bend his stiff neck to serve the good of the country. Clay imagined what the father of the most recent Bank of the United States, a man whom Tyler should have respected as a fellow Virginian, would have done in this situation. "If it were possible to disinter the venerated remains of James Madison, reanimate his perishing form, and place him once more in that chair of state which he so adorned, what would have been his course?" Clay asked. "He would have said that human controversy in regard to a single question"—the bank question—"should not be perpetual, and ought to have a termination." Clay noted that the national bank had won the approval of several Congresses, the Supreme Court, and all but one president. Tyler should heed history. "Human infallibility has not been granted by God, and the chances of error are much greater on the side of one man than on that of the majority of a whole people and their successive legislatures during a long period of time."

Clay reminded the Senate—as if it needed reminding—that Tyler lacked the authority of an elected president. "The people did not foresee the contingency which has happened. They voted for him as Vice President. They did not, therefore, scrutinize his opinions with the care which they probably ought to have done, and would have done, if they could have looked into futurity." If the Whigs at Harrisburg, and then the people of the United States, had known what was to happen, they would not have chosen Tyler. "He would not have received a solitary vote in the nominating convention, nor one solitary electoral vote in any state of the Union." Clay did not declare a break with Tyler, yet. But he warned that it was coming. And it would be the president's doing. "It will not be my fault if our amicable relations should unhappily cease."

44

THE CLASH BETWEEN Henry Clay and John Tyler threw Washington into confusion. "The papers will inform you of the extraordinary state of things here," Clay told an ally. "The Whigs present the image of a body with its head cut off. Yet that body is powerful, united and indivisible. We have lost a few, but very few, by desertion. The residue are stronger from that fact. In what all this state of things will end, it is difficult to conjecture. The president, I apprehend, will leave us; it is more doubtful where he will go. We have made some sacrifices, may make more, to retain him; but the seeds of mutual distrust are, I fear, so extensively sown that it will be difficult to reunite and harmonize us all again." Congress had done its part, passing the measures Clay had sought. "If the president had been cordially with us, what a glorious summer this of 1841 would be!"

The summer ended far from gloriously. Clay crafted a modified version of the bank bill and once more brought Congress along. He meanwhile warned Tyler against a second veto, which would amount to apostasy from the Whigs and an embrace of the Democrats. "I do not pretend to know what may be his feelings, but I am sure that were I in his situation, and the possibility of such an act of treachery were affirmed of me, the reproach would fill my heart in its inmost recesses with horror and loathing," Clay told the Senate. He avowed disbelief that Tyler would actually commit such a heinous crime. "The soil of Virginia is too pure to produce traitors. Small indeed is the number of those who have proved false to their principles and to their party. I knew the father of the president, Judge Tyler of the general court of Virginia, and a purer patriot or more honest man never breathed the breath of life." Like father, like son, Clay hoped. "I am one of those who hold to the safety which flows from honest ancestors and the purity of blood." Surely such a heritage would keep the president true. "No, gentlemen, the president never will disgrace himself, disgrace his blood, disgrace his state, disgrace his country, disgrace his children, by abandoning his party," Clay said. "Never, never. If it were among the possibilities of human turpitude to perpetuate an act like that, I cannot conceive on what principle or for what reason the president could rush upon a deed so atrocious, and deliver himself over to infamy so indelible." Clay shook his head and furrowed his brow at the mere thought. "No, gentlemen, no. Never will the president of the United States be guilty of such a crime."

DANIEL WEBSTER WATCHED the storm develop from inside the Tyler cabinet. "I am with the president a good deal," Webster wrote to his wife. "He seems quite kind, but is evidently much agitated." Webster owed little more to Tyler than Clay did, but Webster thought the Whig party and the country would suffer from a breach between the president and the party's leader in Congress. He worked quietly for a compromise. He wrote a letter to a confidant, intending that the letter be published without his name attached. And so it was. The letter urged the two sides to make peace. "While one says he is of Paul, and another that he is of Apollos, not only does time run by, leaving nothing done, but a wily and reckless adversary"—the Democratic party—"is heading in upon our ranks and is very likely to be able to thwart every thing. Union, decision and energy are all indispensable. But UNION is first. If we will but unite, we can form decisive purposes and summon up our energies." Tyler and Clay must come to some understanding on the bank bill. "There is but one path out of this labyrinth," the anonymous Webster wrote. "There is but one remedy for the urgent necessities of the country, but one hope of the salvation of the Whig party—it is **union,** immediate UNION. Let us try such a bank as we can agree upon and can establish."

Webster also mediated directly between Tyler and Clay, conveying to the latter what the former considered essential in a bank bill. Yet he did so with discretion. **"I have done or said nothing as from you by your authority, or implicating you in the slightest degree,"** Webster told Tyler. **"If any measure pass, you will be perfectly free to exercise your constitutional power wholly uncommitted."**

He found the middle excruciating. "I try to keep cool, and to keep up courage," he wrote to a friend. "The agony will soon be over. We are on the very point of deciding whether the Whig party and the president shall remain together." He wished people would calm down. "I am tired to death of the folly of friends."

Webster's associates in the cabinet observed his discomfiture. "I called to see Mr. Webster and had a long conversation with him," wrote Thomas Ewing, the treasury secretary, in his diary. "He expressed great anxiety about the condition of things and seemed to anticipate a dissolution of the cabinet. He said he could not sleep well of nights for thinking of it—said if he were rich he would not mind it personally, but that he felt great unwillingness at his age to return to the bar. We agreed that the situation at the head of a department here was enviable, if the president had intellect and was in harmony with his cabinet and all supported by a good majority in the two houses." But when these conditions did not apply, as at present, the job lost much of its appeal.

THE STORM BURST in early September. Congress passed the second bank bill, and Tyler vetoed it. Tyler's cabinet responded by resigning en masse, except for Webster. The Whigs in Congress gathered to condemn Tyler and ended by casting him out of the party. "The conduct of the president has occasioned bitter mortification and deep regret," the Whig caucus declared. "Those who brought the president into power can be no longer, in any manner or degree, justly held responsible or blamed for the administration of the executive branch of the government."

Nothing like this had ever happened before. No president had ever been excommunicated by his party. Astonishment suffused the capital.

The casting out of Tyler made Daniel Webster's position even more uncomfortable. He still liked being secretary of state, and he thought he could do good work in that position. Yet siding with the excommunicant put his own future with the Whigs in peril. Webster's rivalry with Henry Clay had kept within the bounds of party regularity, but sticking with Tyler might cause it to burst into the open. Webster wasn't sure he could survive an explicit test of strength.

He decided to remain for a limited period and a specific purpose, a purpose close to the heart of a New England lawyer. For decades the boundary between the United States and British Canada in the vicinity of northern Maine had been in dispute. The matter grew more pressing with the entry of loggers into the area, and in the late 1830s local authorities on both sides of the border huffed and postured and occasionally arrested interlopers from the other side. Things escalated when a British military force entered and occupied a part of the disputed region. The government of Maine responded by calling out the militia and appealing to Congress, which voted ten million dollars toward the defense of American honor and American soil. President Martin Van Buren dispatched General Winfield Scott to Maine. The "Aroostook war," named for the controverted region, ended in a truce before any shots had been fired, but it left the underlying dispute unresolved. Webster hoped to be the one, on the American side, to resolve it.

His British counterpart, Alexander Baring, was a principal in Baring Brothers bank, one of London's most powerful financial firms. For his service to Britain and the Tory party he was elevated to the peerage as Lord Ashburton, and as Ashburton he came to the United States in early 1842 to settle the border question.

Webster found Ashburton congenial. "His personal demeanor makes friends," Webster wrote to Edward Everett, at this point the American minister to Britain. "We all think he has come with an honest and sincere intent of removing all causes of jealousy, disquietude or difference between the two countries."

The talks went smoothly and, for discussions of this sort, quickly. In four months Webster and Ashburton resolved the border question and additional matters besides. A rebellion in Canada had prompted British officials to seize an American ship engaged by the rebels; in the seizure an American was killed. Authorities in New York state subsequently arrested one of those responsible for the seizure. The British asserted that as an agent of the British government he could not be tried in an American court. He was tried nonetheless, and acquitted, but the question of whose law governed what territory persisted. Similar questions vexed navigation on the Great Lakes and other waters shared by the United States and Canada. A separate boundary issue, resulting from vague language in an earlier treaty, left the border west of Lake Superior uncertain. Finally, Britain wanted the United States to cooperate in suppressing the Atlantic slave trade.

The result of the discussions was the Webster-Ashburton Treaty, signed in August 1842. The treaty resolved the border issues and specified terms of law enforcement and extradition. Webster refused to grant Britain the right to search American vessels on the high seas for slaves, but he approved a provision committing the U.S. navy to assist in patrols off the coast of Africa.

Webster and Ashburton parted as the best of friends. "I must at last run away, or rather sail away, without seeing you," Ashburton wrote to Webster as he left America. "This is provoking, but I cannot help it. I had indeed little to say, but it is, notwithstanding, a mortification to me to leave these shores without first shaking your hand. The pain would be greater if I did not confidently hope to see you in the old world." He invited Webster to visit him in England. Yet Webster must make haste. "My taper is burning away fast." Ashburton closed, "Adieu, my dear Mr. Webster. Let me hear from you if you have leisure, but above all let me see you if you can."

SOLOMON NORTHUP ARRIVED in Washington at the moment of William Henry Harrison's funeral. Northup was a black man, free from birth, who lived with his wife and three children in Saratoga Springs, New York. The town was a summer vacation spot for residents of New York and the surrounding region; Northup worked various jobs connected to the hospitality trade. During winter the opportunities dwindled, and he took whatever employment he could find. He built railroads and canal boats; he sawed wood and drove wagons; he played fiddle for weddings and other celebrations.

His fiddle attracted the attention of two visitors, who introduced themselves as Merrill Brown and Abram Hamilton. They said they had connections with a circus based in Washington, D.C., to which they were about to return. They staged small exhibitions while they traveled, and they needed a musician. Would he join them as far as New

York City? He would receive one dollar per day, plus three dollars for each night's show; his travel expenses would be covered as well. With nothing better at hand, Northup accepted the bargain. He didn't think to write to his wife, who had traveled to another town to serve as a cook during a session of the circuit court there. One of the children was with her, and the two others were with an aunt; he didn't inform them, either. He expected to be back before any of them knew he had gone.

The three men journeyed by carriage to Albany and on to New York. The nightly shows drew disappointing crowds and so were suspended. Brown and Hamilton said it was better if they continued directly to Washington. They asked Northup to go with them. They promised him a regular job at higher pay than he could make in Saratoga. He had never been to Washington, and he assented.

As a precaution, they said, he should secure papers proving he was a free man. They would be entering slave territory, and one could never be too careful. Northup took their advice, even while wondering if the precaution was necessary. "I thought at the time, I must confess, that the papers were scarcely worth the cost of obtaining them," he wrote afterward. But Brown and Hamilton seemed to have done this kind of thing before, so he took their word for it. "Paying the officer two dollars, I placed the papers in my pocket and started with my two friends to the hotel."

They traveled to Baltimore by stagecoach and from Baltimore to Washington by train. They arrived the night before the funeral of Harrison and were lucky to find rooms at Gadsby's Hotel on Pennsylvania Avenue. Brown and Hamilton paid Northup forty-three dollars, which was more than they owed him but which they ascribed to his willingness to take the circus job on short notice. They warned him to be very careful with the money and with himself, because Washington was full of characters with no compunctions about preying on those new to town. "I was certainly much pre-possessed in their favor," Northup recalled. "I gave them my confidence without reserve and would freely have trusted them to almost any extent." They suggested he stay off the streets at night, when trouble was most likely; he went straight to his room and locked the door.

The next day brought the capital's first funeral of a president. "The roar of cannon and the tolling of bells filled the air, while many houses were shrouded with crape, and the streets were black with people," Northup recounted. "As the day advanced, the procession made its appearance, coming slowly through the Avenue"—Pennsylvania Avenue—"carriage after carriage, in long succession, while thousands upon thousands followed on foot, all moving to the sound of melancholy music."

Northup stuck close to Brown and Hamilton

amid the crowds. "We stood together as the funeral pomp passed by. I remember distinctly how the window glass would break and rattle to the ground after each report of the cannon they were firing in the burial ground. We went to the Capitol and walked a long time about the grounds. In the afternoon, they strolled towards the President's House, all the time keeping me near to them and pointing out various places of interest." Northup wondered why they hadn't seen the circus, but with much to distract him, he didn't raise the question with his companions.

Presently they entered a saloon, to toast the departed president. Brown and Hamilton ordered liquor, and all three drank up. They visited a second saloon and drank another round. Northup felt more confident of his friends than ever. Late in the afternoon, after yet another round, he began feeling ill. "My head commenced aching—a dull, heavy pain, inexpressibly disagreeable," he recalled. "At the supper table, I was without appetite; the sight and flavor of food was nauseous." Brown and Hamilton helped him back to their hotel and expressed hope he would feel better in the morning.

Northup's distress only intensified. "The pain in my head continued to increase until it became almost unbearable. In a short time I became thirsty. My lips were parched. I could think of nothing but water—of lakes and flowing rivers, of brooks where I had stooped to drink, and of the dripping bucket, rising with its cool and overflowing nectar from the bottom of the well." Unable to sleep, he stumbled through the hotel, hoping to find a source of water. He entered the basement kitchen, where a slave woman fetched him a glass of water, and then a second. The relief was temporary; by the time he had staggered back to his room, the thirst caused him greater agony than ever.

He drifted into a state between sleep and delirium. He sensed people in his room. They told him through his daze he needed to see a doctor. They helped him pull on his boots and guided him down a hallway, through an alley and onto the street. He could detect a light glimmering in a window. They seemed to walk toward it. He thought it must be the doctor's house.

The next thing he knew he was lying alone, in darkness and in chains. He had no idea where he was or how long he had been there. His hands were cuffed and his ankles fettered to an iron ring in the stone floor. His coat and hat were missing, and with them his money and the papers attesting his freedom. He spoke, then shouted, but no answer came back. Gradually he reasoned his way to the conclusion that he had been robbed and kidnapped. But why? By whom? "There must have been some misapprehension, some unfortunate mistake," he recalled thinking. "It could not be that a free citizen of New York, who had wronged no man nor violated any law, should be dealt with thus inhumanly."

No one came for him. No one answered his calls for help. The longer he lay there, alone and chained, with the effect of the drug he had been given wearing off, the more he realized his position was no accident. His new friends had not been friends at all. "It was a desolate thought, indeed. I felt there was no trust or mercy in unfeeling man and, commending myself to the God of the oppressed, bowed my head upon my fettered hands and wept most bitterly."

DAY BROKE, AS Solomon Northup inferred from the crowing of roosters and the rumble of carriage wheels on the street outside and above his dungeon cell. But no light entered until a key clattered in the door lock, the door groaned back on rusty hinges, and two men entered. The dominant figure of the two was James Birch, as Northup later discovered, a slave dealer infamous even among those who didn't denounce slavery itself.

"Boy, how do you feel now?" Birch inquired.

Northup said he was ill. He demanded to know why he was there and why in chains.

Birch replied that he was his slave and was about to be shipped to New Orleans.

Northup protested that he was not a slave. He was a free man and a resident of Saratoga, New

York. He had a wife and children, also free. He had been falsely imprisoned. He demanded to be released.

Birch swore at Northup and said he was a slave, from Georgia.

Northup protested that he was no man's slave. Birch must unchain him and let him go.

Birch refused, most angrily. "He flew into a towering passion," Northup recounted. "With blasphemous oaths, he called me a black liar, a runaway from Georgia, and every other profane and vulgar epithet that the most indecent fancy could conceive." Birch told the other man, named Radburn, to get the paddle and the cat-o'-nine-tails. Radburn left the room and soon returned, bearing a flat-sawn board not quite two feet long and a whip of unraveled rope, with each of the strands tied into a knot at the end. Birch and Radburn roughly stripped Northup bare and laid him over the bench, with Radburn holding him down. Birch beat him with the paddle a dozen times. He paused and asked Northup if he still thought he was a free man. Northup said he was. The beating resumed. Again the question; the same response. More blows. Birch switched to the whip. "This was far more painful than the other," Northup remembered.

In time he could not respond at all to Birch's question. Birch lashed him several more times. Finally he ceased. Cursing again, he told Northup that if he ever again said he was a free man or that he had been kidnapped, he would receive even worse punishment. He and Radburn left.

For a few days Northup saw only Radburn, who brought him water and food, the latter consisting of bread and fried pork. Radburn, clearly Birch's subordinate and less violent than his superior, spoke to him in the tones of a counselor, saying he would be wise to heed Birch's warning. If he wanted to survive, he should never again talk about being free and having been kidnapped.

Eventually Northup was allowed out of his cell into an enclosed yard. It had a wall of brick, perhaps ten feet high, and a shed roof along the wall. The center of the yard was open to the sky. Northup later saw the yard from the outside. "The building to which the yard was attached was two stories high, fronting on one of the public streets of Washington," he observed. "Its outside presented only the appearance of a quiet private residence. A stranger looking at it would never have dreamed of its execrable uses. Strange as it may seem, within plain sight of this same house, looking down from its commanding height upon it, was the Capitol. The voices of patriotic representatives boasting of freedom and equality, and the rattling of the poor slave's chains, almost commingled. A slave pen within the very shadow of the Capitol!"

———

THE SLAVE POPULATION of the United States at the time of the 1840 census was nearly 2.5 million, out of a total population of 17 million. Virginia had the largest number of slaves, with South Carolina second and North Carolina, Georgia and Alabama roughly tied for third. Yet Virginia's slave population was smaller than it had been in the immediately previous census, and those of the Carolinas were essentially stable, while the slave populations of the states of the Gulf Coast were increasing dramatically. The cotton industry was growing rapidly there and with it the demand for slave labor.

This fact of agricultural economics made America's founders look shortsighted or cynical. The bargains the fathers of American republicanism talked themselves into over slavery were premised on the idea that slavery was a dying model of labor mobilization. The soils of Virginia and the Carolinas were exhausted by generations of tobacco culture, and long-staple cotton, which was easier on the soil than tobacco, grew well only near the coast. Already slavery had become economically unattractive in most of the North, where legislatures were acknowledging reality and giving the institution a decent burial. Slavery was expected to die of its own inflexible weight in the South, too. George Washington, Thomas Jefferson and other slaveholders uneasy with their own and their region's complicity in bondage assumed that time would solve the remaining slave problem peacefully.

But a Connecticut tinkerer and a Tennessee soldier proved them wrong. Eli Whitney invented an engine for efficiently removing seeds from short-staple cotton, which flourished more widely than the long-staple variety. Whitney's cotton gin dismantled the single biggest barrier to the transformation of cotton cloth from a luxury product purchased by the few to a staple of the wardrobes of the many. The potential market for cotton expanded enormously.

The Tennessee soldier was Andrew Jackson, whose battles with Indians before, during and after the War of 1812 opened huge tracts of the Gulf Plain to settlement by cotton entrepreneurs. These were the planters who required the slaves whose numbers swelled so fast in the 1820s and after.

Part of the demand for slaves in Alabama, Mississippi, Louisiana, Missouri and Arkansas was met by procreation among slaves the new planters took with them, but the larger growth was the result of the importation of slaves from states of the Atlantic coast. Plantations in Virginia and Maryland had difficulty competing with plantations of the Deep South, where land was cheaper and more fertile. Had field crops been the only export of those Eastern plantations, many would have failed commercially. And had those plantations failed, their owners and others in their states might have lost interest in slavery. But the plantations exported something else—slaves—and so remained viable.

The demand for slaves was insatiable. It drove prices to record levels, until slaves became the most valuable asset of Southern planters, more valuable than the planters' land. Slaves served as collateral for loans, so that planters who might have considered freeing their slaves couldn't do so until their creditors were paid. Because many planters ran regular debts, often to Northern banks, the silent underwriters of slavery, emancipation was out of their hands and largely out of the question. Writ large, emancipation was out of the question for most of the Southern states; it would have been the ruin of their economies.

The rising demand had other ramifications. It made slaveholders in the Eastern states not merely indifferent to the possibility of resuming the importation of slaves from Africa, but downright opposed. If slaveholders had been as convinced of the positive effects of slavery on the slaves as John Calhoun professed to be, they might have clamored to extend its benefits to Africans not yet enslaved. But they didn't. Instead they became protectionists, much like the protectionist manufacturers they criticized, and for the same reason. Protection—in this case not simply a tariff on imported slaves but a ban—pushed prices higher than they would have been in an open market. Slave owners in the Gulf states would have been happy to revive the overseas slave trade, but they were outweighed politically by the slave owners of the East.

Meanwhile the economics of the internal slave trade made access to new markets—that is, new slave territories and states—essential. In time the Gulf states would become saturated with slaves, and prices for slaves would start to fall. But new markets—in Texas, in territory taken from Mexico directly, in the West Indies perhaps—could keep demand and prices high. The political debate over the extension of slavery was typically couched in terms of regional balance, with the South insisting that it not be marginalized in Congress. New Northern states must be offset by new Southern states. But beneath the politics was the basic economics of supply and demand. Slavery in Mississippi made slavery in Virginia profitable today; slavery in Texas would make it profitable tomorrow.

The rising value of slaves meanwhile drove the criminal activities to which Solomon Northup fell victim. A healthy young man could fetch more than a thousand dollars at sale, and though Northup, in his early thirties, was older than the slaves who typically brought the highest prices, his experience and skills—including his musical talent—offset his age. The profit motive inspired slave dealers and their agents to range as far as New York and New England to find unsuspecting blacks like Northup, whom they would lure close enough that they might be kidnapped, transported to New Orleans and sold to the planters of the Deep South.

THE SLAVE PEN in which Solomon Northup was confined was owned by William Williams. It was often called the Yellow House, for the color it showed to the street. Nearby was a similar facility, Robey's Tavern, operated by Washington Robey in conjunction with the slave-trading firm of Joseph W. Neal and Company. The two structures were, as Northup remarked, within sight of the Capitol, and although the slaves confined in them could not hear the voices of Henry Clay, John Calhoun, Daniel Webster and the others debating their fate, the senators and representatives **could** hear the melancholy rattle of the chains of slaves as they shuffled in coffles to and from the Yellow House, Robey's Tavern and wharves on the Potomac.

Northup took his place in such a coffle and was marched to the river. He thought of crying out that he was a free man, but James Birch and his whip were always close by. He realized that even if he managed to utter a few words before being beaten silent, the words of Birch, a white man, would weigh more with the authorities in the city. He reasoned that greater hope of escape lay in acting submissively, biding his time and watching for the moment when Birch's attention flagged.

He was trooped aboard a steamboat that dropped down the Potomac. He and the other slaves in his coffle were shoved into the hold, to find such places to sit or lie as they could among the crates and barrels there. The ship's bell tolled as they steamed past Mount Vernon and the grave of George Washington. "Birch, no doubt, with uncovered head, bowed reverently before the sacred ashes of the man who devoted his illustrious life to the liberty of his country," Northup remarked later, with bitter irony.

At Aquia Creek the steamboat stopped and Birch and his slaves debarked. They boarded a stage for Fredericksburg. Birch was in good spirits. Three of the slaves were children; Birch bought them gingerbread at a roadside tavern. He encouraged Northup to appear less glum. "He told me to hold my head up and look smart," Northup recalled. "That I might, perhaps, get a good master if I behaved myself."

At Fredericksburg they switched from the stagecoach to a train for Richmond. At the Virginia capital they were marched to a slave pen similar to the Yellow House in Washington, but larger. The owner, William Goodwin, apparently did regular business with Birch, and he greeted Birch warmly.

He examined the slaves Birch had brought, including Northup. "Boy, where did you come from?" he asked Northup.

"From New York," Northup replied, without thinking.

"New York! Hell, what have you been doing up there?"

Northup noticed Birch's face turning livid. Catching himself, he mumbled that he had simply been traveling there. Goodwin didn't pursue the matter, but Birch shortly spat in Northup's ear that if he ever said another word about New York, it would be his last. "I will kill you," Birch said. "You may rely on that."

Richmond was the gathering spot for slave cargoes bound for New Orleans. Once a sufficient number of slaves had been collected, Northup was driven with the coffle aboard a sailing vessel, the **Orleans**. This was the last he saw of James Birch until years later, under very different circumstances. Birch returned to Washington to do to other unfortunates what he had done to Northup.

The **Orleans** sailed down the James River to the Chesapeake Bay and thence to Norfolk. The ship took on more slaves and set to sea. The shackles were removed from the slaves and they were allowed onto deck. But their relative comfort didn't last, for a storm struck terror into many and made nearly all wretchedly sick, with their vomit rendering their close quarters odious and filthy. Still worse was smallpox that appeared among the slaves and carried some of them off. Northup contracted the disease, though its symptoms didn't surface until after the ship had reached its destination.

At New Orleans, Northup was taken in hand by Theophilus Freeman, partner to James Birch. Where Birch was the procurer of slaves, Freeman was the distributor. He ordered Northup and the fifty other slaves in his pen to wash and groom themselves. They were given fresh clothes and instructed to look as presentable and attractive as possible. They largely obliged. Freeman's aim was profit; theirs was to be purchased by a wealthy, genteel master who would treat them better than a struggling planter desperate to wring the last ounce of effort from them.

For Northup, Freeman initially asked a price of fifteen hundred dollars. But after Northup became ill with smallpox, nearly died, and emerged from the experience with the facial scars characteristic of the disease, Freeman let him go for one thousand dollars. The purchaser was William Ford, who had a plantation on the Red River in north-western Louisiana.

Ford seemed a decent man, a good Christian, to Northup. He spoke in a kindly fashion and treated his slaves well, although he evinced no doubt of the morality of slavery as an institution. "He was a model master," Northup allowed, "walking uprightly, according to the light of his understanding, and fortunate was the slave who came into his possession. Were all men such as he, slavery would be deprived of more than half its bitterness."

Northup was tempted to tell his story to Ford. But he couldn't be sure Ford was everything he appeared to be. Ford had spent a thousand dollars on him, and even a good master would be loath to lose that. The slave system didn't brook contradiction, and the contradiction it brooked least of all was the claim that a slave was in fact a free man. "I knew well enough the slightest knowledge of my real character would consign me at once to the remoter depths of slavery," Northup recalled. "I was too costly a chattel to be lost, and was well aware that I would be taken farther on, into some by-place, over the Texas border, perhaps, and sold; that I would be disposed of as the thief disposes of his stolen horse, if my right to freedom was even whispered. So I resolved to lock the secret closely in my heart—never to utter one word or syllable as to who or what I was—trusting in Providence and my own shrewdness for deliverance."

JOHN CALHOUN STILL had ambitions, though he couldn't say just what they were. The presidency had been a long shot since his embrace of nullification against Andrew Jackson, and his emergence as the chief apologist for slavery lengthened the odds still more. His estrangement from the two parties left him without the allies political advance typically required.

The death of William Harrison and the accession of John Tyler reopened the door a tad. Tyler was a Whig in name only; he might look with favor to other men lacking strong party ties. Yet the proud Calhoun would take no position less than the secretaryship of state, and Tyler wasn't about to ask for the resignation of Daniel Webster, the only cabinet member who had stuck by him. As long as Webster wanted his job, he could keep it. But Webster decided, after the Senate confirmed his treaty with Ashburton, to step down.

Even then Tyler passed over Calhoun, preferring

Abel Upshur, the secretary of the navy and, like Tyler, a Virginian. Calhoun might bring talent to the administration, but he would also bring enemies, and Tyler, with foes enough already, didn't want to add to their ranks. Upshur, like Tyler, was an advocate of Texas annexation, and as secretary of state he labored to bring the Lone Star republic into the Union. He engaged in quiet diplomacy with envoys from Texas to craft a treaty of annexation and, with Tyler's approval and support, lobbied senators to secure ratification. John Tyler Jr., the president's son and sometime assistant, recalled how Upshur won over Thomas Benton by giving his son-in-law, army officer John C. Frémont, command of an expedition of Western exploration. "Senator Benton could be flattered as easily as any man who ever entered the United States Senate chamber," the younger Tyler said. "He had consented to espouse the cause of annexation, and it was thought that the treaty was altogether arranged."

Just then, however, a terrible accident occurred. President Tyler and four hundred Washington luminaries were taking an inspection cruise on a recent addition to the American fleet, the steam-driven warship **Princeton**. Among the guests were David Gardiner, a wealthy and well-connected New York lawyer, and his daughter Julia, to whom the widowed Tyler was paying court. The vessel carried the biggest gun ever mounted on a ship until then, a monster affectionately called the Peacemaker. Commander Robert Stockton was proud of the ship and its armament, and he wished to demonstrate the awe the craft could inspire in potential enemies. He ordered the Peacemaker fired. Two mighty blasts nearly deafened the guests and gave notice to all within ten miles that the United States could bring fearsome power to bear in war. As their hearing slowly returned, the guests sat down to luncheon on the deck. Tyler led the group in a toast to the ship, its captain and its powerful gun.

Some while later, as the ship churned by Mount Vernon, Commander Stockton ordered the crew to reload the gun for a salute to George Washington. The guests were scattered around the deck and below when Stockton himself pulled the lanyard to ignite the charge. Perhaps he had instructed the primers to pack a little extra powder into the gun, to intensify the impression made earlier. Perhaps they did so on their own. Maybe they miscalculated. But this time as the charge ignited, it burst the barrel of the gun, sending flames, searing heat and deadly shrapnel out the side. Abel Upshur and several others, including David Gardiner, were killed instantly. Tyler had been below deck and was coming up the ladder when the explosion occurred; he escaped death by a few seconds. Julia Gardiner swooned when she learned her father had been killed; Tyler took her in his arms and carried her away from the scene of death and destruction. Until now she had been skeptical about Tyler, who was old enough to be her father. But the loss of her own father, and the president's decisive action in the aftermath, won her over. They were married within months.

THE PRINCETON TRAGEDY threatened to undo Abel Upshur's work on Texas. Tyler had to decide on a replacement. He was still considering the matter when Henry Wise, a Virginia Whig who had stood by the president, intervened. "He was a man of great ability, but the very devil as an adviser," John Tyler Jr. said of Wise. "On the day of Upshur's death, without any consultation with my father, he went to McDuffie, the leading senator from South Carolina, and instructed him to write to John C. Calhoun to come at President Tyler's request and accept the portfolio of State."

The next day Wise went to the White House to tell Tyler what he had done. "President Tyler was thunderstruck," Tyler Jr. said. "He gripped his chair with all his force. It was all he could do to resist telling Wise to begone from him forever. Before saying a word he got up and walked across the floor, and then came back in front of Mr. Wise, and, looking him sternly in the eye, said, 'Mr. Wise, you certainly have not done this thing!' Mr. Wise quailed, but said nothing. Father then walked to the other side of the room again, and, returning, exclaimed emphatically, 'Mr. Wise, you cannot have done this thing!' And, as Mr. Wise still said nothing, he exclaimed in rage, 'Wise, have you done this thing?'"

Wise said he had.

"It was all my father could do to keep from telling him to go away and never to come into his sight," Tyler's son continued. "But Wise was his chief friend in Congress, and he did not dare to break with him. As it was, it was years before he felt well towards him, and he never really forgave him. But the letter had been sent, and it could not be withdrawn. Calhoun was appointed."

The result was just as Tyler feared. Abel Upshur's careful work was undone. "Tom Benton raged around like a great bull," Tyler Jr. said. Benton hated Calhoun as much as Andrew Jackson did. "Calhoun's name had the effect of the red rag flaunted in his face. When the treaty came up he howled against it, and defeated it by calling it a Calhoun conspiracy."

"CONSPIRACY" WAS A strong word but not inapt. Calhoun sought Texas, yet something more than Texas; he sought international recognition of the moral righteousness and permanent legitimacy of slavery. And maybe—just maybe—a last chance at the presidency.

Calhoun's instrument was his pen, and his agent was Richard Pakenham, the British minister in Washington. Pakenham had held the post for nearly a decade and had conducted himself as a model diplomat, representing Britain vigorously to the United States government while keeping clear of the divisive issues of American politics. Calhoun, however, insisted on drawing Pakenham in. The new secretary of state wrote a letter to Pakenham excoriating the minister for what Calhoun characterized as British tampering with American slavery. Pakenham's sin? Declaring that Britain looked forward to the eventual end of slavery around the world and was doing what it could to achieve this end. Calhoun granted that Britain was free to adopt whatever policy it chose for its own dominions. "But when she goes beyond, and avows it as her settled policy, and the object of her constant exertions, to abolish it throughout the world, she makes it the duty of all other countries whose safety or prosperity may be endangered by her policy to adopt such measures as they may deem necessary for their protection."

Britain's policy was particularly troubling as it applied to Texas, Calhoun asserted. The British were urging the Texans to abolish slavery in exchange for British support of Texas against Mexico. This took unfair advantage of Texas, and it posed a threat to the United States. "The consummation of the avowed object of her wishes in reference to Texas would be followed by hostile feelings and relations between that country and the United States, which could not fail to place her under the influence and control of Great Britain." The United States had, within the memory of its older citizens, fought two wars against Britain. The American government would never allow Britain to plant itself on America's southwestern border.

Calhoun thereupon broke the news to Pakenham of the American treaty with Texas, which heretofore had not been publicly announced. "This step has been taken as the most effectual, if not the only, means of guarding against the threatened danger and securing their permanent peace and welfare." The treaty would be submitted to the Senate for ratification forthwith.

To this point Calhoun's letter must have struck Pakenham as extreme. The British minister was aware the Americans and the Texans had been negotiating, and he couldn't have been surprised that they had reached terms. But for the treaty to be cast as a response to British aggression was outrageous.

Yet what followed was downright bizarre. Calhoun launched into a defense of slavery as an institution for the uplift of Africans. He quoted statistics purporting to show that the incidence of insanity and serious disability was far higher among free Negroes in the Northern states than among slaves in the South. Massachusetts, the home of the American abolitionist movement, was among the worst offenders. "By the latest authentic accounts, there was one out of every twenty-one of the black population in jails or houses of correction, and one out of every thirteen was either deaf and dumb, blind, idiot, insane, or in prison." America's slaves, by contrast, were prospering. "The condition of the African race throughout all the states where the ancient relation between the two races has been retained enjoys a degree of health and comfort which may well compare with that of the laboring population of any country in Christendom; and it may be added that in no other condition, or in any other age or country, has the negro race ever attained so high an elevation in morals, intelligence or civilization." British officials should take note before they meddled in America's affairs. Should Britain succeed in abolitionizing the United States, it would have much to answer for. "So far from being wise or humane, she would involve in the greatest calamity the whole country, and especially the race which it is the avowed object of her exertions to benefit."

IT DIDN'T TAKE long for Pakenham to realize he was only incidentally the audience for Calhoun's effusion. His guess was confirmed when the gist of Calhoun's nominally confidential letter began circulating in Washington. The letter established Calhoun as the defender of America against Britain, as well as of slavery and the South against all foes. Calhoun's appointment to be secretary of state had served as a step in his possible rehabilitation as a national figure. The secretary of state stood second only to the president in dignity and prestige. Calhoun had now exploited this position to take on Britain, America's historic foe. The greatest threat to slavery and the South heretofore had been the abolitionists of the North. Calhoun's attacks on them pleased Southern slaveholders but did nothing for his national reputation. Attacking Britain was another matter. Andrew Jackson had reached the White House on the strength of his record against Britain. What had worked for Jackson might work for John Calhoun.

BUT IT DIDN'T work for Texas. Calhoun's Pakenham letter torpedoed the Texas negotiations. Abel Upshur had kept the matter quiet in hope the treaty might slip through the Senate. He deliberately downplayed the role of slavery in Texas, trying to make annexation seem a real estate deal, like the Louisiana Purchase. His success had been reflected in the willingness of Thomas Benton to abide the bargain.

Calhoun's emphasis on slavery in the Texas matter, and his unprovoked attack on Britain, guaranteed the full attention of the country. Calhoun's action enraged Benton, as Calhoun knew it would. It doomed the Texas treaty in the Senate, where a two-thirds majority was required. Calhoun knew it would do that, too. But he knew something else: that a man could be elected president with much less than two-thirds of the nation's vote.

HENRY CLAY, TOO, had his eye on the White House, again. Clay had made the most of his break with John Tyler. The schism unnerved many of the Whigs, and Clay felt obliged to buck them up. The Whig caucus gathered for a last time before its members went home at the end of the special session. "I distinctly recollect that night; it was dark and rainy," Oliver Hampton Smith, a senator from Indiana, recounted. "Every thing around us looked like the weather and the night, dark and gloomy. Our hopes had been blasted; President Tyler had deceived us; our triumphant victory had been turned into ashes in our mouths; we were about to part, with no cheering prospects." The members drowned their sorrows in booze.

And then their leader took charge. "The tall and majestic form of Henry Clay was seen rising in the west end of the room," Smith recollected. "All eyes were upon him; he wore a bewitching smile upon his countenance. He addressed the Chair in a voice that indicated at once that he was not about delivering a dolorous address, adding to our gloomy feelings." Clay declared, "Mr. Chairman, this is a dark night. There is no moon, and the little stars are slumbering in their beds, behind the dark canopy that is spread over the heavens. This is not the first time that the heavenly lights have been obscured, and the world kept in temporary darkness. Is this emblematic of our party? It may be so; but not of our principles. We senators will soon pass away, but our principles will live while our glorious Union shall exist. Let our hearts be cheerful. Let our minds look through the temporary clouds that overspread the heavens, and see the sun there, as in midday, shining upon our principles, fixed above like planets in the firmament. They may be obscured for a time by the cry of the demagogue, by the political treason of those we have cherished in our bosoms—but they must and will prevail in the end."

Clay gazed around the room. "My friends, we have done our duty," he said. "We have maintained the true policy of the government. Our policy has been arrested by an executive that we brought into power. Arnold escaped to England after his treason was detected. Andre was executed. Tyler is on his way to the Democratic camp. They may give him lodgings in some outhouse, but they never will trust him. He will stand here, like Arnold in England, a monument of his own perfidy and disgrace."

He turned to Chairman Nathan Dixon, who was known for his hands-off policy in caucus meetings, which allowed the members to go at one another hammer and tongs. "Night after night we have looked upon your good-natured, gentlemanly countenance," Clay said, his eye now twinkling. "We have seen with high gratification the very able and impartial manner in which you have discharged your duty, and especially the manner in which you have, by a single look, kept order at our meetings; the most excited, the most boisterous, has been quieted at once and brought into lamb-like docility." The caucus members chuckled, recalling full well that nothing like order and certainly no lamb-like docility had characterized the meetings. "Could you have been seen while presiding, by the whole civilized world," Clay continued, struggling to keep a straight face, "Europe, Asia, Africa and Oceanica would have raised a united voice in your praise."

Turning back to the group, Clay concluded, "Gentlemen, one and all, permit me to bid you an affectionate farewell!"

The room erupted in laughter and applause. The rain outside continued, but the glumness in the room had lifted.

Chairman Dixon, however, insisted on the last word. "I have heard with infinite delight the remarks of the senator from Kentucky, and more especially those he has been pleased to address directly to myself, so just and so true," he said. He nodded gravely, to underscore his seriousness. The gathered members quieted down. Dixon held them in silence. "The senator from Kentucky, at one time during his address, looked as if he was not in full earnest," he went on. "But when you are as well acquainted with the senator as I am, you will give him full credit for sincerity for any remarks he may make before ten o'clock at night. After that there may be some doubts."

The gathered lawmakers checked their watches, raised their glasses, and roared again.

CLAY RESIGNED HIS Senate seat in the spring of 1842 to rest, to tend to the affairs of Ashland and what remained of his law practice, and to ponder a final run at the presidency. He understood that in politics as in some other walks of life, familiarity can breed contempt. He guessed that the country might appreciate him more if he stepped off the stage for a time.

The strategy worked. Long before the regular campaigning in the 1844 election began, Clay was the only Whig anyone spoke of for the presidency. Henry Clay Clubs appeared in cities and towns across the country; members sung their favorite's praises, endorsed his policies, and strove for his election. Twenty years he had sought the presidency; now he felt it surely within his grasp.

One thing alone might cause a stumble: Texas. Clay avoided the issue as much as possible. On a tour of the South in the first months of 1844 he talked about every subject **but** Texas. He initially averred a disinclination to discuss politics at all, saying his tour was simply a response to invitations from Southern friends to visit their fair states and cities. "A long cherished object of my heart is accomplished," he told an audience in Raleigh. "I am at your capital and in the midst of you. I have looked forward to this, my first visit to North Carolina, with anxious wishes and with high expectations of great gratification." His hopes had been more than fulfilled. "I did not expect to witness such an outpouring. I did not expect to see the whole state congregated together. But here it is!" He wouldn't intrude on the good feeling by venturing into politics. "I have come with objects exclusively social and friendly. I have come upon no political errand. I have not come as a propagandist. I seek to change no man's opinion, to shake no man's allegiance to his party."

Yet people had asked his views on various public matters. He would be impolite not to answer. He would make it short. "I am a Whig, warmly attached to the party which bears that respected name, from a thorough persuasion that its principles and policy are best calculated to secure the happiness and prosperity of our common country," he said. He explained his party's policies. He and the Whigs favored tariff protection for American industries. Protection strengthened the entire country, building up its industries, including the textile industry, the principal purchaser of Southern cotton. Clay had tracked changing sentiments in the South; he realized the region was less opposed to protection than it had been a decade earlier. Even so, he stressed that differences on this and other issues should be resolved by compromise rather than confrontation. "Extremes, fellow citizens, are ever wrong. Truth and justice, sound policy and wisdom always abide in the middle ground, always are to be found in the **juste milieu**. Ultraism is ever baneful and, if followed, never fails to lead to fatal consequences." He advocated a national bank and a national currency. States were sufficient for many things, but not for the nation's currency. "The several states can no more supply a national currency than they can provide armies and navies for the national defense." As he did at every opportunity, Clay emphasized the need for Americans to resist the siren call of separatism. "This Union will not, must not, shall not be dissolved."

On the subject of slavery and abolition, Clay said nothing new. He simply reminded his listeners of what he had already said. "My opinion was fully expressed in the Senate of the United States a

few years ago, and the expression of it was one of
the assigned causes of my not receiving the nomination as a candidate for the presidency." Clay's
audience knew that his excoriation of the abolitionists had prompted the Whigs to nominate
the uncontroversial Harrison. They wondered if
he had softened his stand. He made clear he had
not. He wouldn't change a word of what he
had said. He still judged the abolitionists a curse.
If this view cost him the nomination again, he
could live with that.

He intended to leave Texas alone. He might
have succeeded if John Calhoun hadn't forced
the issue. Days before Calhoun's Pakenham letter
became the talk of Washington, Clay remarked to
a friend, "I have found a degree of indifference
or opposition to the measure of annexation which
quite surprised me." In an open letter written from
Raleigh, Clay explained that he had not previously
spoken on the Texas question because he saw no
benefit from injecting that vexing topic into the
current political discussion. But the news that
the administration had signed a treaty of annexation made a comment imperative. Clay noted, in
his Raleigh letter, that Mexico still claimed Texas
and had recurrently tried to enforce its claim.
"Under these circumstances, if the government
of the United States were to acquire Texas, it
would acquire along with it all the encumbrances
which Texas is under, and among them the actual

or suspended war between Mexico and Texas." Prudence dictated that America keep its distance. "I certainly am not willing to involve this country in a foreign war for the object of acquiring Texas." Yet even if Mexico consented to American annexation of Texas, Clay said, he would not support it. It would aggravate the already raw feelings between North and South. "I think it far more wise and important to compose and harmonize the present confederacy, as it now exists, than to introduce a new element of discord and distraction into it." Annexation, moreover, would do grave harm to America's reputation. "It would be to proclaim to the world an insatiable and unquenchable thirst for foreign conquest or acquisition of territory. For if today Texas would be acquired to strengthen one part of the confederacy, tomorrow Canada may be required to add strength to another."

THE INITIAL RESPONSE to his Raleigh letter on Texas pleased Clay. He discounted flutters in Washington as part of the nervousness that afflicted the political classes there. "I feel perfectly confident in the ground which I have taken," he declared to a friend. "I entertain no fears from the promulgation of my opinion. Public sentiment is every where sounder than at Washington."

But public sentiment shifted during the spring and early summer of 1844. Its prime mover was

Andrew Jackson. From his home outside Nashville, Jackson had followed the fortunes of Texas and of Sam Houston, the wayward protégé who had led Texas to independence and become president of the Texas republic. Houston favored the annexation of Texas to the United States but had grown frustrated by the refusal of the United States to take Texas in. He finally wrote a letter to Jackson explaining that if America continued to spurn Texas, Texas must make other arrangements. "My venerated friend, you will perceive that Texas is presented to the United States as a bride adorned for her espousal," Houston said. "But if, now so confident of the union, she should be rejected, her mortification would be indescribable." Texas would look elsewhere for aid. "She would seek some other friend."

Houston knew that Jackson understood that the other friend was Britain. Houston also knew that Jackson abhorred Britain as much as ever, and that Jackson would move heaven and earth to keep Britain from gaining a foothold in Texas. Jackson responded as Houston supposed he would: he demanded that the Democratic party make annexation its first priority. Martin Van Buren, Jackson's other protégé, had been the favorite to win the Democratic nomination for president, but Van Buren was waffling on Texas, not wishing to alienate Northerners. When Van Buren declined to declare for annexation, Jackson abruptly withdrew his support and threw it behind dark horse James K. Polk, a former governor of Tennessee. Jackson's endorsement carried Polk to the Democratic nomination and set him on a platform that belligerently endorsed annexation.

Henry Clay had expected to run against Van Buren. The emergence of Polk compelled him to recalibrate his stance on Texas. "Personally I could have no objection to the annexation of Texas," he wrote in an open letter on July 1. Readers of his Raleigh statement scratched their heads, for that document had given the distinct impression that he opposed annexation. "But I certainly would be unwilling to see the existing Union dissolved or seriously jeoparded for the sake of acquiring Texas," he continued, placing his objection on policy grounds rather than personal preference. "If any one desires to know the leading and paramount object of my public life, the preservation of this Union will furnish him the key."

By the end of July he had moved a bit more. "Far from having any personal objection to the annexation of Texas, I should be glad to see it, without dishonor—without war, with the common consent of the Union, and upon just and fair terms," he said. This still left annexation a stretch, in that Mexico continued to threaten war, and many Northerners remained opposed. Clay tried to separate Texas from the broader slavery issue. "I do not think that the subject of slavery ought to affect the question, one way or the other. Whether Texas be independent, or incorporated in the United States, I do not believe it will prolong or shorten the duration of that institution. It is destined to become extinct, at some distant day, in my opinion, by the operation of the inevitable laws of population." Under these circumstances, annexation might not be so bad after all. "It would be unwise to refuse a permanent acquisition, which will exist as long as the globe remains, on account of a temporary institution." Again he cited his touchstone: "I should be governed by the paramount duty of preserving this Union entire and in harmony."

As before, Clay found himself in the exposed middle. Polk's expansionist platform united the Democrats by including a demand for the Oregon country to balance the demand for Texas. The former would make free states, the latter slave. The Whigs nominated Clay but lacked a comparably galvanizing platform. "My position is very singular," Clay wrote in early September. "Whilst at the South I am represented as a liberty man, at the North I am decried as an ultra supporter of slavery, when in fact I am neither one nor the other."

He tried to return the debate to less divisive ground. He talked up a national bank and a tariff with something for everyone. But he couldn't escape Texas. Clay parried charges of having shifted his position. "Could I say less?" he asked a friend. "Can it be expected that I should put myself in opposition to the concurrent will of the whole nation, if such should be its will?" Unconvincingly he added, "I think any one who will take a fair and candid view of all my letters together must be satisfied with their import and perfectly convinced of their entire consistency."

He strove to hearten his supporters. "The prospects of the Whig cause are very encouraging," he wrote on September 19. But unflagging energy must be the rule. "Our opponents are every where making the most strenuous exertions and they ought to be met by countervailing efforts."

Straws in the political wind showed a trend toward Polk, yet Clay continued to battle. "The great contest, fraught with such important consequences to our country, will now soon be decided," he wrote to John Quincy Adams in the last week of October. "The elections of the current year have been remarkable for the closeness of the majorities which determined them. Still, if I am to judge of the final result by the information which I have received, the Whigs will succeed by a large electoral majority."

———

IT WAS NOT to be. The Oregon plank of the Democratic platform appealed to voters in the westernmost states of the North, which were already sending settlers to the Willamette Valley, while Polk's Texas demand guaranteed the support of the lower South. Clay's middle position on slavery cost him votes in New York and Michigan, where he ended up losing by a few thousand votes each. Had these states tipped his way, they would have sufficed, with his victories in the upper South, mid-Atlantic and New England, to put him in the White House. Instead it was Polk, the newcomer to national politics, who won the office for which Clay had been so long striving.

He couldn't conceal his disappointment. "The sad result of the contest is now known," he wrote to William Seward, a New York Whig. "We are only left to deplore that so good a cause, sustained by so many good men, has been defeated." The Whigs had struggled mightily, and they had lost. "As for myself, it would be folly to deny that I feel the severity of the blow most intensely." His career's goal, which had been so close, was suddenly beyond reach, probably forever. "My duty now is that of resignation and submission, cherishing the hope that some others more fortunate than myself may yet arise to accomplish that which I have not been allowed to effect."

PART SIX

The Fatal Compromise

Secession! Peaceable secession! Sir, your eyes and mine are never destined to see that miracle. The dismemberment of this vast country without convulsion! The breaking up of the fountains of the great deep without ruffling the surface! Who is so foolish—I beg everybody's pardon—as to expect to see any such thing?

—DANIEL WEBSTER, 1850

PHILIP HONE HAD been mayor of New York during the 1820s, but he became more famous for the friends he made and the diary he kept, in which he told of his friends' faults and foibles, among many other things. Yet he found little to fault in Daniel Webster, who seemed to him the model of the American statesman. Even so, it was the domestic life of Webster that Hone found especially appealing.

He visited Webster at his home in Massachusetts. Webster's first wife, Grace, had died after twenty years of their marriage, leaving him three children. He married again, to Caroline, and shortly purchased a farm near Marshfield, thirty miles southeast of Boston. Webster fell in love with the place, borrowing money to improve and expand the property. Marshfield became a personal haven from his professional cares; visitors found him more relaxed there than in Washington and no less proud of what he accomplished on his saltwater farm than of what he achieved in politics or law.

"Our reception by the noble master of the mansion and his amiable, kind and ladylike wife was everything that heart could wish," Hone recorded in his diary in the summer of 1845. "At one moment instructive and eloquent, he delights his guests with the charms of his conversation; then, full of life and glee as a boy escaped from school, he sings snatches of songs, tells entertaining stories, and makes bad puns." A hearty dinner was followed by blissful slumber in a breeze off the sea. "After breakfast Mr. Webster drove Draper"—another guest—"and me over his extensive grounds down to the beach, where his boats were ready for a fishing excursion, which is one of his greatest enjoyments. Here was this wonderful man, on whose lips unsurpassed eloquence has so often hung, whose pen has directed the most important negotiations, and whose influence has governed Senates, in a loose coat and trousers, with a most picturesque slouched hat, which a Mexican bandit might have coveted, directing his people—whose obedience grows out of affection, and who are governed by the force of kindness—regulating the apparatus, examining the bait, and helping to hoist the sails and hold on to the main sheet." The wind was brisk and the waves were boisterous. The bouncing was more than Hone could manage. "I don't wish it made too public, sir," he told Webster, "nor would I have it put in the newspapers; but I am sick! sick!" Webster smiled weakly. "My case exactly," he said. "I have tried to keep this unusual circumstance a secret; but it won't do, and we must go ashore."

The next day, after Hone visited the historic sites around nearby Plymouth, the tour of Marshfield manor continued. "Farmer Webster showed us his capacious barns, in which many a ton of good Puritan hay is just now being condemned to the rack; fields of oats supporting their heavy heads upon slender but healthy limbs; cattle combining the advantages of foreign and domestic blood; cows whose sleek sides bear the comfortable signs of milk, butter and cheese; every vegetable from the diminutive bean up to the unwieldy pumpkin; while the broad sea lay before him, containing a certain harvest of piscatory enjoyments."

A second sail proved more productive than the first. "The wind was favorable, the weather fine, and all things propitious. Casting anchor five or six miles from land, we went to work, and the result of our labour was the capture of twenty-six cod and twenty-two haddock, weighing more than three hundred pounds. I had never had such sport and never saw such spoils, and the sail home in our beautiful yacht was delightful. We returned to a late dinner, of which our fish formed an important part, and the cool wine, taken under the shade of the noble lime trees in front of the house, to which the agreeable conversation of our noble host gave a zest of the richest character, closed a day to which there was no alloy but the recollection that it was the last we had to spend at Marshfield."

WEBSTER ENJOYED MARSHFIELD more than any of his guests did, and the pleasure he found there made it hard for him to leave. It was never harder than in the mid-1840s. Henry Clay's coup against John Tyler had left Webster hanging, and though some of his fellow Whigs forgave him for remaining in the state department to negotiate the British treaty, many took offense that he didn't resign immediately thereafter. Webster had no devious plan in remaining; he was not a devious planner in anything he did. Nor did he remain for long. But his continued association with Tyler allowed Clay's supporters to question his loyalty to the Whig party. Lest possibility persist of his derailing Clay's 1844 nomination, a pro-Clay paper in Louisville published a story that Webster had sexually assaulted the wife of one of the clerks in the state department. Webster categorically denied the offense, for which no evidence was adduced, and the paper was compelled to retract the allegation. Yet the episode allowed the gossip-prone to recirculate stories of Webster's amours. Such stories were a staple of Washington life, and they attached at times to Henry Clay and many

others, as well as Webster. By themselves the stories rarely disqualified a man from office. James
Buchanan would be elected president despite a
common belief among his Washington contemporaries that he was homosexual. Yet a candidate
weakened on other grounds could find the gossip
debilitating.

Amid the snarking, Webster pondered retirement, a definitive retreat to Marshfield. But his
creditors wouldn't let him. Marshfield didn't pay
his debts; instead it increased them. And for all
the disappointment and discomfiture politics
sometimes occasioned, he couldn't deny the allure
power and celebrity held for him. Finally, and
not least important, he still had work to do. The
Union and the Constitution needed defending,
and he couldn't think of anyone more capable
than himself.

Webster had opposed the annexation of Texas
since before Texas asked for it, and he continued
to oppose it. He disliked the precedent annexation would set. "I have always wished that this
country should exhibit to the nations of this earth
the example of a great, rich and powerful republic
which is not possessed by the spirit of aggrandizement," he explained. He joined Henry Clay in
fearing that annexation would trigger war with
Mexico. And he questioned the constitutionality
of annexation. He asserted that the constitutional
bargain allowing the original slave states their

excess representation—from counting three-fifths of slaves toward apportioning the House of Representatives—didn't and shouldn't apply to new slave states. "I never could, and never can, persuade myself to be in favor of the admission of other states into the Union as slave states, with the inequalities which were allowed and accorded by the Constitution to the slave-holding states then in existence. I do not think that the free states ever expected, or could expect, that they would be called on to admit more slave states, having the unequal advantages arising from the mode of apportioning representation under the existing Constitution."

Webster might have been right about the attitudes that existed when the Constitution was adopted. But he was behind times since then, for the free states had repeatedly acquiesced in the creation of new slave states, which entered the Union with the same representational advantage the original slave states enjoyed. Representatives of the free states had sometimes complained, but not in sufficient numbers to keep the slave South from expanding.

WEBSTER WAS BEHIND times in another regard. The election of James Polk had essentially guaranteed the annexation of Texas. It meanwhile put the final nail in the coffin of John Calhoun's diminished hopes for the presidency. Calhoun's Texas play for the presidency had foundered upon the emergence of Polk, who cornered the market on the annexationist vote. It had been a long shot anyway; Calhoun was too identified with nullification and its evil stepsister, secession, to appeal outside the Deep South. When the Democrats united behind Polk, Calhoun saw his last chance for the presidency vanish.

But he still might claim credit for Texas. Polk's election gave crucial momentum to the Texas cause, prompting lame duck John Tyler to press for annexation before leaving office. The arithmetic of the Constitution precluded another treaty attempt, so Tyler and Calhoun chose the route of a joint resolution of the Senate and the House. The advantage of a joint resolution was that it required simple majorities in the two chambers, rather than the two-thirds of the Senate needed for treaty approval.

The **dis**advantage of a joint resolution was that no one knew whether it was constitutional. The United States had never annexed an independent country, and certainly not one including many thousands of slaves. The Constitution was silent on the subject. Yet the Constitution had been silent on the purchase of territory from a foreign power, and even a strict constructionist like

Thomas Jefferson had found sufficient authority for the acquisition of Louisiana. Surely the Constitution could brook the admission of Texas.

This was what Daniel Webster disputed, too late. The joint resolution on Texas first came up in early 1845; it was approved by Congress just days before Tyler's term expired. The Texans then had to ratify annexation and write a constitution that passed congressional muster. The process took several months, during which Webster resumed his seat in the Senate. He arrived in time to register his opposition and that of those who sent him. He realized that the bargain had already been struck and was probably irrevocable. But he had to speak out nonetheless. "I agree with the unanimous opinion of the legislature of Massachusetts," he told the Senate. "I agree with the great mass of her people. I reaffirm what I have said and written during the last eight years, at various times, against this annexation. I here record my own dissent and opposition, and I here express and place on record, also, the dissent and protest of the state of Massachusetts."

The Senate ignored Webster and Massachusetts and gave its final approval to annexation. The House did likewise, and in December 1845 Texas became the twenty-eighth state of the Union.

FOUR MONTHS LATER James Polk made prophets of Henry Clay and Daniel Webster by commencing a war with Mexico.

Polk's war was a land grab wrapped in self-defense. Texas entered the Union with its southern boundary in dispute. The United States claimed the Rio Grande as the border; Mexico claimed the Rio Nueces, more than a hundred miles to the north. Mexico nominally claimed the rest of Texas as well, never having acknowledged the loss of its rebellious province. But though it responded to the American annexation of Texas by severing relations with the United States, it took no military action to challenge the new regime on its northern frontier.

This frustrated Polk. The president's expansionist appetite grew with the eating; not content with depriving Mexico of Texas, Polk coveted California as well. He attempted to purchase California, but the Mexican government rebuffed him. Polk then sought a pretext for declaring war on Mexico. He sent troops to the disputed strip between the rivers, hoping to goad the Mexicans to attack. Weeks went by and the Mexicans refused to take the bait. Polk, more vexed than ever, prepared a war message for Congress, in which he blamed the Mexicans for insults and injuries against American honor and interests. It was a flimsy document, as Polk himself recognized, but he was determined to have California and its Pacific harbors, by whatever means necessary. Then, just as he was about to transmit his message to Congress, he received news that Mexican troops had finally engaged the Americans. "After reiterated menaces, Mexico has passed the boundary of the United States, has invaded our territory and shed American blood upon the American soil," Polk told Congress. "War exists, and notwithstanding all our efforts to avoid it, exists by the act of Mexico itself." For emphasis the president added, "The two nations are now at war."

JOHN CALHOUN BEGGED to differ. Polk wanted Congress simply to endorse his assertion that war existed and give him authority to prosecute it. Calhoun wasn't going to be stampeded into anything. "The question now submitted to us is one of the gravest character, and the importance of the consequences which may result from it we cannot now determine," he told the Senate. "The president has announced that there is war; but according to my interpretation, there is no war according to the sense of our Constitution." Calhoun didn't challenge Polk's account of the attack on American forces. Nor did he question Polk's authority to resist and repel such attacks. But he distinguished hostilities from war. "It is **our** sacred duty to make war," he told his fellow senators, "and it is for **us** to determine whether war shall be declared. If we have declared war, a state of war exists, and not till then."

Calhoun succeeded in slowing the rush to war, but not by much. Congress debated the president's request, with most of the negative comments coming from the Whigs. Some asked whether Polk had done all he could to avoid armed conflict; their strong implication was that he had not. A few went so far as to charge Polk with provoking the war. "This war was begun by the president," Garrett Davis, a Kentucky Whig, told the House. Some inquired whether the Mexican attack, if it indeed had occurred as the president said, had been authorized by the Mexican government. Still others rejected Polk's assertion that the soil on which the blood had been shed was American. Some said flatly that it was Mexican; others remarked that ownership was still in dispute.

But Polk knew the American political mind better than the dissenters did. He understood that the shedding of American blood—under whatever circumstances—created an irresistible impulse toward war. A negative vote could be characterized as an unpatriotic vote, and no lawmaker lightly risked that. The few surviving former Federalists remembered how their party had wrecked on its opposition to the War of 1812. In the end scarcely a dozen Whigs refused the president's request. John Calhoun haughtily abstained.

DANIEL WEBSTER DODGED. His conscience and his constituents opposed the war, but as one of those Federalist refugees, he recalled how the winds of war could blow popular sentiment in unexpected directions. When the vote was taken, he was not in the Senate chamber.

Yet he reserved the right to complain. So did other Whigs and even some Democrats, including David Wilmot of Pennsylvania, who amid House discussions of a war-funding bill proposed an attachment stipulating that slavery be barred from any territory taken from Mexico in the war. The Wilmot proviso passed the House but fell short in the Senate; it was reintroduced and again passed the House, and again failed in the Senate. The proviso became a lightning rod between the anti-slavery and the pro-slavery elements in Congress and between North and South. The opponents of slavery decried the ability of Southern obstructionists in the Senate to negate the will of a growing majority in the country; the defenders of slavery pointed to the proviso as the latest recrudescence of the tyrannical moralism of the abolitionist North.

Daniel Webster hadn't abandoned hopes for the White House. He had watched John Calhoun disqualify himself by his extreme sectionalism, and he had seen Henry Clay get caught in the sectional cross fire. Of the threesome who entered Congress almost together nearly four decades earlier, only Webster still had a chance at the presidency. James Polk had pledged, before his election, that he would serve but one term if elected; unless he reneged, the 1848 race would be wide open. After Clay's failure in 1844 and subsequent retreat to Ashland, Webster became the leading figure in the Whig party and the favorite to win the party's nomination.

But he had to walk a narrow path. He couldn't oppose an important antislavery measure like the Wilmot proviso without antagonizing his Massachusetts supporters and most Northern Whigs and contradicting his own antislavery statements. But he couldn't support the Wilmot measure without alienating Southern Whigs.

He tried to change the subject. "Sir, we are in the midst of a war, not waged at home in defense of our soil, but waged a thousand miles off, and in the heart of the territories of another government," he declared after American troops had invaded Mexico proper. "Of that war no one yet sees the end, and no one counts the cost. It is not denied that this war is now prosecuted for the acquisition of territory; at least, if any deny it, others admit it, and all know it to be true." Webster decried the aggression and supported an amendment forbidding **all** taking of territory from Mexico. "We want no extension of territory," he said. "We want no accession of new states. The country is already large enough." This position suited most of Massachusetts and many Northern Whigs. It also allowed Webster to rise above the debate over whether territories taken from Mexico should be slave or free.

But the no-acquisition amendment failed. The expansionist mood was too powerful, and even many Northerners were willing to chance the spread of slavery if necessary to enlarge the national domain. More than a few recalled Henry Clay's reasoning regarding Texas: that slavery was temporary, while the national domain was permanent.

Webster blamed Northern Democrats for the failure of the amendment. "It has been voted down by the Northern Democracy," he said. "If this Northern Democracy had supported this amendment, it would have prevailed, and we should then have had no new territory at all, and of course no new slave territory; no new states at all, and of course no new slave states."

Yet wherever the blame lay, Webster was left to vote for or against the Wilmot proviso. He couldn't vote against it; his constituents would have been outraged. But a vote in favor might rile the South and cost him the Whig nomination for president.

He voted in favor and hoped no one would notice.

I T WASN'T AN impossible hope. There was much to distract the country. Wars make heroes, which helps explain their enduring appeal. The war with Mexico made two heroes. Zachary Taylor came first, as the general of American forces at the initial battles on the Rio Grande and then as victor over Mexico's Santa Anna at Buena Vista. The Buena Vista victory gave American newspapers a great story and caused Taylor, in the tradition that ran from George Washington through Andrew Jackson to William Henry Harrison, to be spoken of as a candidate for president in 1848. James Polk took notice of Taylor's celebrity and also of his politics, which tended Whiggish. Though Polk himself would not be running in 1848, he disliked leaving the credit to a Whig for a war he and his fellow Democrats had started. So he maneuvered to deflect glory away from Taylor and toward Winfield Scott, to whom he gave command of an invasion of central Mexico. Scott succeeded even better than Taylor, capturing Veracruz, defeating Santa Anna at Cerro Gordo, and then taking Mexico City. This didn't solve Polk's political problem, in that Scott was also a Whig, but it raised the possibility of a split among the opposition.

Daniel Webster hoped the division of fame between the generals would work in **his** favor. Scott's occupation of Mexico City prompted peace talks. Nicholas Trist of the state department represented the American government; a special commission spoke for Mexico. Polk's minimal demand was California and New Mexico, with an American payment to Mexico to cast a cloak of purchase over the military seizure. The Mexican negotiators were loath to sign away half their country, and they stalled for time. Polk, to increase the pressure on them, asked Congress for more money and troops, presumably to expand the American hold on Mexico. He told Trist to break off negotiations and return to Washington.

Trist refused. Reasoning that he knew better than Polk what the balance of politics and military force in Mexico would bear, he continued the negotiations and concluded a treaty transferring California and New Mexico to the United States in exchange for fifteen million dollars. The treaty didn't mention Texas by name, but in accepting the Rio Grande as the border between the United States and Mexico, the Mexican government conceded the loss of that province as well.

Polk pondered whether to reject the unauthorized treaty and insist on more. Some in his party, espousing the doctrine of "manifest destiny," which claimed divine sanction for American expansion, wanted to annex all of Mexico. But voters were growing tired of the war; volunteers were itching to get home and resume their lives. And Polk wasn't eager to give Scott or Taylor a chance to become still more famous. So he grudgingly sent the treaty to the Senate.

BY THIS POINT it was Whig orthodoxy that Polk had manufactured the border incident that had triggered the war. A first-term Whig congressman from Illinois offered a series of resolutions demanding that the president show the precise spot where the American blood had been shed and prove that it was indeed American soil. Abraham Lincoln's "spot resolutions" didn't win a majority, but they contributed to what became a formal censure of Polk by the Whig-led House for unnecessarily and unconstitutionally starting the war.

Daniel Webster endorsed the censure, and he said the American people did too. "I hold that to be the most recent and authentic expression of the will and opinion of the majority of the people of the United States," he told the Senate. Webster accused Polk of intending conquest all along. "This war was waged for the object of creating new states on the southern frontier of the United States, out of Mexican territory," he said. He mocked manifest destiny as self-serving political hokum. "When 'manifest destiny' shall be unrolled, all these strong panegyrics, wherever they may light, made beforehand, laid up in pigeonholes, studied, framed, emblazoned and embossed, will all come out; and then there will be found to be somebody in the United States whose merits have been strangely overlooked, marked out by Providence, a kind of miracle, while all will wonder that nobody ever thought of him before as a fit, and the only fit, man to be at the head of this great republic!"

Statesmen, as opposed to demagogues, had to treat the hard reality of expansion, Webster said. He left the question of slavery aside, focusing on more basic issues of constitutional representation. The agreement that had brought Texas into the Union allowed that state—the largest by far of all the states—to be divided into as many as five smaller states. New Mexico and California, if annexed, would push the total of new states to seven. They would elect fourteen senators, as many as all of New England sent to Washington. Yet the total population of the new regions was less than that of Vermont. The original allocation of two senators per state had been a bargain of necessity, to persuade the small states to swap the Articles of Confederation for the Constitution. But it had always compromised the principle of equal representation. Webster didn't propose to undo the initial bargain, yet he saw no reason to extend it unnecessarily. And this was precisely what the president wanted to do. "I see a course adopted which is likely to turn the Constitution of the land into a deformed monster, into a curse rather than a blessing; in fact a frame of an unequal government, not founded on popular representation, not founded on equality, but on the grossest inequality." Webster feared the worst. "I think this process will go on, or that there is danger that it will go on, until this Union shall fall to pieces. I resist it, today and always!"

He resisted in vain. Thirteen other senators joined Webster in refusing assent to the Mexican treaty, but thirty-eight voted in favor, and the treaty was approved.

51

JOHN QUINCY ADAMS never learned that the war had ended. "A mournful and agitating event occurred in the House of Representatives yesterday," a reporter covering Congress wrote in the last week of February 1848. "Just after the yeas and nays were taken on a question, and the speaker had risen to put another question to the house, a sudden cry was heard on the left of the chair: 'Mr. Adams is dying!'"

Everyone looked toward the place where the former president was accustomed to sit. Adams had not been in good health; his attacks on slavery and its minions had grown rarer and weaker. Yet he continued to vote his conscience, which increasingly was the conscience of New England and the North on slavery. He could have retired; many of his colleagues, especially from the South, wished he would. But that conscience kept him at his post, watchful lest the slave power seize more than it already possessed.

"We beheld the venerable man in the act of falling over the left arm of his chair, while his right arm was extended, grasping his desk for support," the reporter continued. "He would have dropped upon the floor had he not been caught in the arms of the member sitting next him. A great sensation was created in the house, members from all quarters rushing from their seats and gathering round the fallen statesman, who was immediately lifted into the area in front of the clerk's table." The speaker asked for a motion to adjourn, which was offered and accepted, and the business of the House halted. A sofa was brought in from the hallway and Adams gently laid upon it. The sofa was carried out of the chamber to the rotunda, where the air was fresher. But the sofa was soon surrounded by congressmen and senators, the latter having left their own chamber on learning of Adams's distress. A representative who was also a physician tried to push the crowd back; this failing, he directed that the sofa be carried to the door leading from the rotunda to the east portico. The door was opened and the breeze allowed to blow onto Adams's face. But the winter air was cold and damp and threatened to chill the patient. The sofa was carried back into the Capitol and placed in the suite of the speaker of the House. The doors of the suite were closed and guarded to keep well-wishers and onlookers at a distance. This proved necessary, for as the word of Adams's condition spread across Washington, people hurried to the Capitol to catch sight of the city's foremost living monument.

Adams stirred slightly. Those closest to him caught what proved to be his final words. "This is the last of earth," he said. "I am content."

He fell silent. He lay insensible on the sofa in the speaker's room, unable to recognize his wife, Louisa, when she arrived, or anyone else. Doctors debated whether to move him. But the end seemed nigh, and the conclusion was easily reached that the stubborn statesman would have wanted to die on duty, in the building where he had fought his most worthy battles. He held on through one night, and then a day and another night. On February 23, his indomitable spirit finally let go.

52

I F COMMUNICATIONS HAD been faster in 1815, there never would have been a Battle of New Orleans. If they had been faster in 1848, the negotiations to end the war between the United States and Mexico might have taken a very different turn. Neither Nicholas Trist nor his Mexican counterparts knew, in ironing out the last details of the treaty, that three weeks earlier a discovery had been made in California that dramatically increased the value of that province. A carpenter named James Marshall, digging a channel for a sawmill on the American River above what would become Sacramento, stumbled across a gold nugget. Further investigation revealed that the area was littered with gold, which could be gathered from streambeds with ease and in large quantities.

But the news didn't arrive in Mexico City before the treaty was signed, and it didn't reach Washington until after the Senate ratified the pact.

Indeed, though rumors drifted east during the summer of 1848, it wasn't until months later that the rumors were sufficiently confirmed for James Polk to proclaim the discovery, in his December annual message.

By then the gold rush was on. America's peculiar laws regarding natural resources meant that whoever first laid hands on the gold in California got to keep it. The laws didn't distinguish between American citizens and foreigners; as a result, California almost overnight became the most cosmopolitan place on earth. Gold seekers poured north from Mexico, followed by Peruvians and Chileans. Hawaiians, Australians and Chinese churned the Pacific en route east to the goldfields. Countries and communities that bordered on the Atlantic Ocean were slower to react than those of the Pacific basin, being much farther away, especially as the ship sailed, but small armies of Europeans eventually joined the ranks of the argonauts, as the gold hunters called themselves.

Americans were the largest contingent, leaving every state for the goldfields. Some traveled by sailing ship around Cape Horn. Others took sailing craft or steamers to Panama; crossed the isthmus on foot, burro and dugout canoe; and sailed or steamed up the coast of Central America and Mexico to California. Still others—the greatest number—ventured overland. From jumping-off points on the Missouri River they struck out across the Great Plains, the Rocky Mountains, the Great Basin and the Sierra Nevada to the goldfields.

It was the swiftest mass migration in American history, one of the most rapid in world history. What had been a sparsely populated land was suddenly teeming with forty, sixty, eighty thousand souls, and more arriving constantly. Most cared little for politics, so obsessed were they with making their fortunes. But they discovered they couldn't manage without government. Ad hoc committees lacked the authority to adjudicate competing claims to mining properties; vigilante groups punished wrongdoing haphazardly. In September 1849 a few dozen of the most civically minded gathered in Monterey to craft a constitution for a state of California. No one in Washington had given them permission; no one in Washington even knew what they were about. They themselves were often at a loss. What were the boundaries of the state they proposed? They couldn't say. Should they model their state government on existing state governments, or create something new? They split the difference.

Certain things they agreed on without much debate. California must have a government at once. Life, liberty and property were precarious without it. Most had come to California as sojourners, intending to make their fortunes and return whence they had come. But many found

California more appealing than their homes and decided to stay. Yet they couldn't stay safely— and they couldn't bring out their wives and children—without the security of a government. Without government, California would remain a mining camp. With government, it would become a place where decent people could live and thrive.

They also agreed that California would be a free state. Some Southern gold hunters brought slaves, who toiled beside them in the goldfields. But the experience reinforced the message of the terrain and the climate: that California could not support the plantation agriculture that made slavery profitable in the South. The constitution the Monterey convention drafted declared straightforwardly, "Neither slavery nor involuntary servitude, unless for the punishment of crimes, shall ever be tolerated in this state."

The constitution was submitted to the people of California, who ratified it in November 1849. It was then dispatched to Washington, carrying the hopes and prayers of California's new inhabitants that it be approved by Congress and they rescued from the legal limbo in which they would languish until it was.

HAD HENRY CLAY been fifty years younger, he might have joined the rush to California. His relocation to Kentucky in the 1790s had been part of the same westward sweep that had just reached the Pacific; he had sought opportunity in Lexington in the same way the gold hunters sought opportunity in the Sierra Nevada. And he had found his way into politics much as the framers of the California constitution had done. He could easily see himself—a younger self, that is—joining the Monterey convention and speaking out against slavery in the new state. More and more he wished the founders of the American republic had taken the bold step of ending slavery, if not at once then gradually, as the importation of slaves had been ended. More and more he feared that slavery was the rock that would break the Union. If only one could go back in time, to when the rock wasn't smack in the middle of the stream of America's history, the river could have been channeled around it. He applauded the Californians for doing what Americans should have done; he imagined being one of them.

But it was merely imagining. He was old, weeks from his seventy-third birthday. He was sick. He had a cough that wouldn't go away. He had seen consumption slowly claim contemporaries; it would claim him before long. Anyway, he couldn't start over. Neither could America. Slavery existed; the rock loomed large and sinister amid the stream. While the young men in California dug their gold, the old men in the East had the task of keeping the republic from crashing against the rock.

Clay hadn't expected to be part of the effort. After his defeat by James Polk he had returned to Ashland to live out his life tending to private matters. His model was Thomas Jefferson in retirement at Monticello. He corresponded; he improved the property and the livestock; he greeted the men and women who came to his door almost every day. No visit to Lexington was considered complete unless it included a call on the great statesman in his home at the edge of town.

He didn't mind the visitors much. They flattered his ego. They listened to his stories and laughed at his jokes. They filled the house with human voices. When they left, the house was very quiet. The footfalls of the children had long since ceased. Their memory brought deep sadness. Lucretia had given him eleven children; death had taken seven of them. Their six daughters all were gone, claimed as infants, girls or young women. The sons had fared better, with four of the five growing into young men. But the eldest son, Theodore, had demons that wouldn't let him go; at a loss for his sake and theirs, Clay and Lucretia had placed him in a mental hospital, where he remained. One heartbreak was still fresh. Henry junior, the son to whom the father was closest, had been a brilliant student at West Point and, after fulfilling his obligation to the army, had launched a promising career in law and politics. When the war with Mexico began, he raised a regiment of Kentucky volunteers and joined the force of Zachary Taylor. He had served gallantly in the invasion of northern Mexico, but he had been killed at Buena Vista.

Henry Clay had opposed the war. He distrusted James Polk and the purposes for which the war was fought. He knew that disposing of any territory taken from Mexico would require reopening the debate over slavery. He wasn't sure the country could survive it. But he had **not** known that the costs of the war would be so personal and painful. He had hoped that the sons left to him and Lucretia would outlive their parents; he had hoped to be spared yet another reprise of that most excruciating task of a parent, the burying of a child. Fate had decreed otherwise.

He had meant to leave public affairs to the

younger generation. He had done his part; let them take up the task. But the death of his son made him reconsider. In his old work he might find solace. And he might give meaning to Henry's death. Henry had died beneath the flag of the Union. His father sensed that the Union was in greater danger than ever. He could make a final effort to save it. He wasn't sure his health could stand it. But what his son had given, he could give too, if it came to that.

HE LET HIS friends in Kentucky know he was willing to serve once more. The legislature made him senator again, and he followed the familiar route to Washington. New faces occupied the old seats; of his generation of lawmakers only John Calhoun, Daniel Webster and a few others remained. Yet the newcomers deferred to him; in the crisis that faced the country, well-wishers to the Union hoped Henry Clay could summon his magic one last time and prevent the states from flying apart.

It wouldn't be easy. The man of the middle found the middle ground narrower and more precarious than ever. Much of the North had long distrusted him as a slaveholder and a critic of the abolitionists. Many in the South thought him increasingly unreliable. Even as the rush to California was commencing, Clay had reiterated his support for gradual emancipation. Kentucky had called a convention to amend its constitution; Clay worked to write an end to slavery into the state's charter. "I am aware that there are respectable persons who believe that slavery is a blessing— that the institution ought to exist in every well organized society, and that it is even favorable to the preservation of liberty," he declared in a letter for publication. "Happily, the number who entertain these extravagant opinions is not very great." The apologists' argument failed on its own terms, Clay said. "If slavery be fraught with these alleged benefits, the principle on which it is maintained would require that one portion of the white race should be reduced to bondage to serve another portion of the same race when black subjects of slavery could not be obtained." In Africa, blacks would be justified in enslaving whites. The apologists asserted blacks' intellectual inferiority as justification for their enslavement. Clay countered that this principle would allow one white nation to enslave another white nation it considered less intelligent or educated. The principle would apply to individuals, too. "The wisest man in the world would have a right to make slaves of all the rest of mankind!" And even if the claim of white superiority were true, the appropriate response was kindness, not oppression. "We ought to fulfill all the obligations and duties which it imposes; and these would require us not to subjugate or deal unjustly by our fellow men, who are less blessed than we are, but to instruct, to improve and to enlighten them." Clay recommended a program of gradual emancipation linked to colonization of the freed slaves in Africa. The latter condition was a nod to reality; Clay understood how strongly slaveholders and many non-slaveholding whites objected to the proximity of free blacks, and he judged that blacks, slave or free, would never get a fair shake in Kentucky or the larger South.

Clay's recommendation failed. And it branded him an enemy of slavery in the eyes of much of the South. Clay understood this. But it was what he believed. He knew that there were others in the South who believed the same thing. He hoped to give them heart, and perhaps a voice. He hoped Northerners would realize slavery needn't be forever. The South could evolve toward freedom, if given time.

TIME WAS WHAT Clay aimed for when he rose to address the Senate in January 1850. Word that the old conjurer was going to speak had rippled across the city; again the galleries filled early. The chamber fell silent; all strained to hear.

"Mr. President, I hold in my hand a series of resolutions which I desire to submit to the consideration of this body," Clay said. "Taken together, in combination, they propose an amicable arrangement of all questions in controversy between the free and the slave states growing out of the subject of slavery."

Clay's listeners nodded and exchanged looks. This was the Clay of yore. A bargain was to be struck.

He proceeded slowly, displaying little emotion. His first resolution called for the admission of California as a state "without the imposition by Congress of any restriction in respect to the exclusion or introduction of slavery." Clay's phrasing was innocuous: Congress would leave the matter of slavery to the Californians. But the meaning was unmistakable: California would enter the Union as the free state the Californians had already declared it to be.

Clay's second resolution proposed that one or more territorial governments be established for the rest of the territory taken from Mexico, generally referred to as New Mexico. Declaring it "inexpedient" for Congress to legislate either for or against slavery in this territory, this resolution proposed that the territorial governments be established "without the adoption of any restriction or condition on the subject of slavery."

Clay's third and fourth resolutions came as a pair. The third would define the boundary between Texas and New Mexico, granting to the latter some land claimed by the former; the fourth would compensate Texas by transferring the preannexation public debt of Texas to the United States.

The fifth and sixth resolutions were likewise a pair. The fifth, again employing the term "inexpedient," would leave slavery in the District of Columbia alone; the sixth would terminate the slave **trade** in the federal district.

The seventh and eighth resolutions dealt with the transport of slaves across state lines. The seventh addressed a long-standing grievance of the South against the North for obstructing the return of fugitive slaves. "More effectual provision ought to be made by law, according to the requirement of the Constitution, for the restitution and delivery of persons bound to service or labor in any state who may escape into any other state or territory," Clay's seventh resolution asserted. The eighth, and last, resolution disavowed congressional authority over the trade in slaves between slave states; that trade would be for those states to work out.

Clay paused to catch his breath. The days when he could effortlessly speak for hours were past. He said he would explain his resolutions in due course. On this day he would make but a few additional comments. He supposed some Northerners would feel he was asking too much of them. By this time every Northern legislature had endorsed the Wilmot proviso forbidding slavery in the Mexican cession; his second resolution frustrated that proviso. And several Northern states had enacted personal liberty laws that made more difficult the capture of fugitive slaves; his seventh resolution would undercut these laws.

Clay asked Northerners to consider that slavery meant different things to residents of the different parts of the country. "With you, gentlemen senators of the free states, what is it? An abstraction, a sentiment—a sentiment, if you please of humanity and philanthropy; a noble sentiment, when directed rightly, with no sinister or party purposes; an atrocious sentiment, a detestable sentiment, or rather the abuse of it, when directed to the accomplishment of unworthy purposes." But a sentiment still. To the South, by contrast, slavery was a living institution of economic necessity and social order. Northerners seeking restrictions on slavery or its entire abolition asked nothing of themselves, but a great deal of others. "On your side it is a sentiment without sacrifice, a sentiment without danger, sentiment without hazard, without peril, without loss." On the other side? "There is a vast and incalculable amount of property to be sacrificed, and to be sacrificed not by your sharing in the common burdens but exclusive of you. And this is not all. The social intercourse, habit, safety, property, life, everything, is at hazard in a greater or less degree in the slave states."

No longer emotionless, Clay likened the fight over slavery to a house in flames. "Listen, sir, to the rafters and beams which fall in succession, and the flames ascending higher and higher as they tumble down," he said. "Behold those women and children who are flying from the calamitous scene, and with their shrieks and lamentations imploring the aid of high heaven." But the fire threatened one section primarily, Clay said. "Whose wives and children are they? Yours in the free states? No. You are looking on in safety and security, whilst the conflagration which I have described is raging in the slave states, and produced not intentionally by you, but produced from the inevitable tendency of the measures which you have adopted, and which others have carried far beyond what you have wished."

Clay apologized for saying more than he had intended. But he had one last thing to relate, something that struck him as so timely it seemed almost mystical. A man had visited his room that morning, without knowing what he—Clay—was going to say in the Senate several hours later. The man reached into his pocket and pulled out a small piece of wood, which Clay now held in his hand. "It is a fragment of the coffin of Washington, a fragment of that coffin in which now repose in silence, in sleep and speechless, all the earthly remains of the venerated Father of his Country," Clay said. "Was it portentous that it should have been thus presented to me? Was it a sad presage of what might happen to that fabric which Washington's virtue, patriotism and valor established? No, sir, no. It was a warning voice, coming from the grave to the Congress now in session to beware, to pause, to reflect before they lend themselves to any purposes which shall destroy that Union which was cemented by his exertions and example."

CLAY REQUESTED THAT his colleagues refrain from comment on his package until they had a chance to weigh and balance its parts. In an earlier day and a different place, when he had been speaker of the House, he had been able to enforce such reticence. But the Senate brooked no constraints on freedom of speech, and Clay hadn't sat down before Thomas Rusk of Texas bellowed that Clay aimed to deprive his state of half its territory and that he, Rusk, would never tolerate the theft. Jefferson Davis of Mississippi objected to surrendering California to the abolitionists. "I here assert that never will I take less than the Missouri compromise line extended to the Pacific Ocean, with the specific recognition of the right to hold slaves in the territory below that line," Davis declared.

Clay had hoped to work the cloakrooms and corridors to enlist support for his compromise package, but the uproar that followed the mere unveiling of his resolutions persuaded him to mount a preemptive public defense. Over two days—February 5 and 6—he gave the speech of his life, the speech on which hung everything he had worked for since entering Congress four decades earlier. His consistent goal had been to hold the Union together. Until now he had succeeded. But if he failed at this point, all his previous work would be for nothing.

"Never on any former occasion have I risen under feelings of such deep solicitude," he began. "I have witnessed many periods of great anxiety, of peril, and of danger even to the country. But I have never before risen to address any assembly so oppressed, so appalled, so anxious." He might have blamed sectionalism, but he started with partisanship. "If I were to mention, to trace to their original source, the cause of all our present dangers and difficulties, I should ascribe them to the violence and intemperance of party spirit," he said. "Parties, in their endeavors to obtain the one the ascendancy over the other, catch at every passing and floating plank in order to add strength and power to themselves." Party spirit inflamed passion, which in turn aggravated partisanship. "It is passion, passion—party, party," Clay said. "That is all I dread in the adjustment of the great questions which unhappily at this time divide our distracted country."

To calm the passion and quell the partisanship

had been his purpose in crafting his compromise, Clay said. Three principles had guided him. One was comprehensiveness: to resolve all the problems slavery raised for the sections and the country. "It seemed to me to be doing very little if we settled one question and left other disturbing questions unadjusted. It seemed to me to be doing but little if we stopped one leak only in the ship of state and left other leaks capable of producing danger, if not destruction, to the vessel." The second principle was respect for fundamental beliefs. Clay said he asked neither side to surrender any core tenet; the accommodations he urged left basic principles intact. Clay's third principle was reciprocation. Each side had to give something—"not of principle, not of principle at all," Clay said, "but of feeling, of opinion in relation to the matters in controversy between them." Mutual forbearance was critical to success.

Clay considered his eight resolutions in the order he had given them. To Southerners who complained that the admission of free California violated the spirit of the Missouri Compromise, he replied it did no such thing. The Missouri Compromise had not guaranteed slavery south of the 36° 30′ line; it merely **allowed** slavery in territories there, while forbidding it in territories north of the line. The assumption was always that new states formed from the territories would determine their own positions on slavery as they

entered the Union. Slavery was being barred from
California not by Congress but by the people
of California themselves. Moreover, the vote in the
constitutional convention in Monterey had been
unanimous, with more than a dozen delegates
from slaveholding states voting against slavery in
California. California was doing what every other
state had a right to do. If Virginia tomorrow voted
to abolish slavery, neither Congress nor the other
states could prevent its doing so. For that matter, if
Ohio or another state created from the territory of
the old Northwest, from which slavery had been
barred by the Northwest Ordinance of 1787, voted
tomorrow **in favor** of slavery, Congress and the
other states would be equally impotent to prevent
the action. On the issue of slavery, the states were
sovereign. Clay's broader point was that the admission of California as a free state was no concession
to the North; it was merely an acknowledgment
of the inherent right of states to chart their own
destinies.

Clay's second resolution, not to decide for or
against slavery in New Mexico, had indeed provoked Northern backers of the Wilmot proviso,
as he had anticipated. They wasted their breath,
he said. Slavery was barred from New Mexico by
a higher law than any that Congress could craft:
the law of nature. Every report from New Mexico
revealed that it was even more unsuited to slavery
than California, whose unfitness for slavery the

slaveholders there had themselves acknowledged. "You have got what is worth more than a thousand Wilmot provisos," Clay told the Northerners. "You have nature on your side." To the Southerners who sought a statement affirming the role of slavery in the new lands of the West, he said they were wasting their breath, too. "If nature has pronounced the doom of slavery in these territories—if she has declared, by her immutable laws, that slavery cannot and shall not be introduced there— whom can you reproach but nature and nature's God? Congress you cannot."

Clay's third and fourth resolutions, involving the borders of Texas and the assumption of its debt, engaged no broad principles of national interest. Some Northerners, and some Southerners too, queried the appropriateness of the assumption of a state's debts by the national government. Clay pointed out that Texas had incurred its debts at a time when, as a republic, it controlled its import duties. On annexation to the United States, it surrendered those duties to the federal government. Justice suggested compensating Texas, which was what Clay proposed to do.

Clay's fifth and sixth resolutions, preserving slavery in the District of Columbia but ending the slave trade there, were touchy in theory but relatively uncontroversial in practice, which was why he had worded them the way he had. Even abolitionists considered the practice of slavery in the district, where most slaves were household servants, workers in shops or assistants in offices, innocuous compared with the gang slavery of cotton, rice and tobacco plantations. As to the slave **trade** in the district, it was such a small part of the overall commerce in slaves that even zealous advocates of slavery saw little reason to defend it. The slave markets in Maryland and especially in the Virginia towns across the Potomac gave the traffickers all the scope and space they required.

Yet Clay, by characterizing as "inexpedient" the termination of slavery in the district, implicitly granted Congress the authority to abolish slavery there if notions of expedience changed. Southerners were decreasingly willing to concede that Congress had the authority to abolish slavery anywhere—not in the states, certainly; not in the federal territories; and not in the federal district. Clay summoned his skills as a lawyer and a statesman to defend his position. Clay the lawyer read the Constitution and observed that it granted Congress the power "to exercise exclusive legislation in all cases whatsoever" in the federal district. This certainly included slavery. But Clay the statesman refrained from wielding the conferred power in a way as to offend the South unnecessarily.

Of Clay's seventh and eight resolutions, on the return of fugitive slaves and the traffic in slaves between slave states, the latter was easily dealt with, because it left the status quo in place. Abolitionists had formerly sought to apply the leverage of the commerce clause of the Constitution against this domestic trade, but the thrust of their efforts had moved on to the larger agenda of killing slavery itself.

The seventh resolution, on the fugitive slaves, was quite different, for it involved issues deeply held by both sides. Southerners furiously believed that the North was flouting the Constitution by harboring fugitives, against the explicit language of Article IV, which required that a person bound to service or labor in one state and having fled to another be "delivered up on claim of the party to whom such service or labor may be due." Northerners who opposed the return of slaves sometimes tried to explain away the fugitive slave clause, but mostly they appealed to higher laws of liberty and justice. Neither side would yield without a fight.

Clay took the part of the South. And he did so with deliberate vigor. "This clause in the Constitution is not amongst the enumerated powers granted to Congress, where, if it had been placed, it might have been argued that Congress alone can legislate and carry it into effect," he said. "It is one of the general powers, or one of the general rights secured by this constitution or instrument, and it addresses itself to all who are bound by the Constitution of the United States." Antislavery sheriffs and judges in free states had sometimes asserted that the clause did not bind them, because they were not federal officers. Clay said they were wrong and remiss. Antislavery individuals, too, acted as though the Constitution didn't constrain them. They were equally misguided, he said. "All state officers are required by the Constitution to take an oath to support it, and all men who love their country, and are obedient to its laws, are bound to assist in the execution of those laws." The personal liberty laws of the free states had to yield.

Clay professed hope that the free states would recognize their error and bring their laws and practices into conformance with the Constitution, and thereby restore comity between the sections. But Congress must act in any event. "Whether they do it or not, it is our duty to do it. It is our duty to make the laws more effective; and I will go with the furthest senator from the South in this body to make penal laws, to impose the heaviest sanctions upon the recovery of fugitive slaves and the restoration of them to their owners."

Clay was well into his second day of speaking on his compromise package, and he seemed prepared to go on to a third. A fellow senator, worried about Clay's strength, moved to adjourn until the morrow. Clay waved his hand and said he was almost done. "I begin to see land. I shall pretty soon arrive at the end."

He prayed that a spirit of forbearance and

compromise would infuse the discussions of his resolutions. He said others might improve on what he had offered. But the spirit was the thing, and it could carry the country through the present crisis, as it had carried the country through crises past. "Adopt these or similar measures and I venture to predict that, instead of the distractions and anxieties which now prevail, we shall have peace and quiet for thirty years hereafter, such as followed the disposition of the same exciting and unhappy subject after the Missouri compromise," Clay said. In thirty years, he supposed, the changes that had rendered slavery unprofitable in the North would do the same in the South, and the problem would resolve itself.

A lack of forbearance, an unwillingness to compromise, an insistence on an immediate trial of principles, would lead to ruin, he said. Speaking to the North, Clay pleaded that the South not be pushed to the wall, lest it secede and the Union be destroyed. Liberty, for which the Northern abolitionists expressed such concern, would be dealt a mortal blow, for the Union was liberty's surest protector. Speaking to the South, Clay warned against secession. Secession would aggravate the very problems against which the South currently complained. If the Ohio River became the boundary not between states but between countries, fugitive slaves would never be returned. Grievances of the South against the North that were now adjudicated in courts of law or the chambers of politics would be resolved on the field of battle.

Clay wished his listeners to be in no doubt as to the results of secession. "War and the dissolution of the Union are identical and inseparable," he said. Even supposing the Northern states didn't forcibly resist Southern secession, war would come, and soon. "If possibly we were to separate by mutual agreement and by a given line, in less than sixty days after such an agreement had been executed, war would break out," Clay said. "Yes, sir, sixty days. In **less** time than sixty days, I believe, our slaves from Kentucky would be fleeing over in numbers to the other side of the river, would be pursued by their owners, and the excitable and ardent spirits who would engage in the pursuit would be restrained by no sense of the rights which appertain to the independence of the other side of the river, supposing it, then, to be the line of separation. They would pursue their slaves; they would be repelled, and war would break out. In less than sixty days, war would be blazing forth in every part of this now happy and peaceable land."

But in fact the North would never agree to separation, Clay said. Look only at the Mississippi Valley. "My life upon it, sir; that vast population that has already concentrated, and will concentrate, upon the headwaters and tributaries of the

Mississippi will never consent that the mouth of that river shall be held subject to the power of any foreign state whatever."

Clay asserted as strongly as he could that there was no right of secession. "The Constitution of the thirteen states was made not merely for the generation which then existed but for posterity—undefined, unlimited, permanent and perpetual." He likened the Union to a marriage. Marriages had their troubles; the Union had its troubles. But good marriages lasted, and so could the Union. "Let us say what man and wife say to each other: We have mutual faults; nothing in the form of human beings can be perfect; let us, then, be kind to each other, forbearing, conceding; let us live in happiness and peace."

The alternative was almost too horrible to contemplate. "Dissolution of the Union and war are identical and inseparable," Clay repeated. "Such a war, too, as that would be, following the dissolution of the Union! Sir, we may search the pages of history, and none so furious, so bloody, so implacable, so exterminating, from the wars of Greece down, including those of the Commonwealth of England, and the revolution of France—none, none of them raged with such violence, or was ever conducted with such bloodshed and enormities as will that war which shall follow that disastrous event—if that ever happens—of dissolution."

Clay cast his gaze across the Senate chamber. "I

conjure gentlemen, whether from the South or the North, by all they hold dear in this world, by all their love of liberty, by all their veneration for their ancestors, by all their regard for posterity, by all their gratitude to Him who has bestowed upon them such unnumbered blessings, by all the duties which they owe to mankind and all the duties they owe to themselves; by all these considerations I implore them to pause, solemnly to pause, at the edge of the precipice, before the fearful and disastrous leap is taken into the yawning abyss below, which will inevitably lead to certain and irretrievable destruction."

He shook his head. "And finally, Mr. President, I implore, as the best blessing which Heaven can bestow upon me upon earth, that if the direful and sad event of the dissolution of the Union shall happen, I may not survive to behold the sad and heart-rending spectacle."

55

JOHN CALHOUN WAS not moved by Clay's appeal to love of the Union. He was unimpressed by Clay's siding with the South on the fugitive slaves. Clay called for compromise; Calhoun wanted nothing to do with compromise. Clay hinted at mortality in his conclusion; Calhoun felt mortality in his bones. And in his lungs, in the consumption that had carried him to death's very door. In earlier times he would have leaped to his feet to challenge his Kentucky rival. But these days he often could hardly stand. A winter cold complicated his condition. He hoped to regain sufficient strength and breath to deliver his rebuttal to Clay, but a week passed, and then another, with no improvement. Finally he conceded that he might never be hale enough to battle his old foe as he desired, as the crisis demanded.

He dragged himself to the Senate in early March. His appearance surprised many, gratifying some and disappointing others. He was recognized by the chair, and he addressed the body in a voice that was a reedy remnant of that in which he had formerly held forth. "As much indisposed as I have been, Mr. President and senators, I have felt it my duty to express to you my sentiments upon the great question which has agitated the country and occupied your attention," he said. "I had hoped that it would have been in my power during the last week to have delivered my views in relation to this all-engrossing subject, but I was prevented from doing so by being attacked by a cold which is at this time so prevalent, and which has retarded the recovery of my strength."

The senators listened carefully. Most knew that something far worse than a cold was stealing his voice. Many guessed they might be hearing and seeing the cast-iron man for the last time.

"Acting under the advice of my friends, and apprehending that it might not be in my power to deliver my sentiments before the termination of the debate, I have reduced to writing what I intended to say," Calhoun continued, in little more than a whisper. "And without further remark, I will ask the favor of my friend, the senator behind me, to read it."

James Mason of Virginia stepped forward. "It affords me great pleasure to comply with the request of the honorable senator," he said. Conspicuously displaying the sheaf of papers containing Calhoun's words, Mason began.

"I have, senators, believed from the first that the agitation of the subject of slavery would, if not prevented by some timely and effective measure, end in disunion," Calhoun said, through Mason. "Entertaining this opinion, I have, on all proper occasions, endeavored to call the attention of each of the two great parties which divide the country to adopt some measure to prevent so great a disaster, but without success. The agitation has been permitted to proceed, with almost no attempt to resist it, until it has reached a period where it can no longer be denied or disguised that the Union is in danger. You have thus had forced upon you the greatest and the gravest question that can ever come under your consideration: How can the Union be preserved?"

Answering the question required assessing the cause of the danger, Calhoun continued, through Mason. A doctor couldn't cure a patient without knowing the cause of the illness; neither could statesmen save the Union without understanding the source of its dissensions. To Calhoun the answer was straightforward: "The immediate cause is the almost universal discontent which pervades all the states composing the Southern section of the Union." The discontent wasn't new. "It commenced with the agitation of the slavery question, and has been increasing ever since." What was the nature of the discontent? "It will be found in the belief of the Southern states, as prevalent as the discontent itself, that they cannot remain, as things are now, consistently with honor and safety, in the Union."

The basis of this belief was a fundamental shift in the balance of power in the country. "The equilibrium between the two sections"—North and South—"in the government, as it stood when the Constitution was ratified and the government put in action, has been destroyed," Calhoun said. "At that time there was nearly a perfect equilibrium between the two, which afforded ample means to each to protect itself against the aggression of the other; but, as it now stands, one section has the exclusive power of controlling the government, which leaves the other without any adequate means of protecting itself against its encroachment and oppression."

The South would have had no grounds for complaint at this transformation, Calhoun said, had it been the work solely of time and the faster growth of the Northern population. "But such was not the fact. It was caused by the legislation of this government." Slavery had been excluded from federal territories, starting with the Northwest Ordinance of 1787, continuing through the Missouri Compromise of 1820, and including, most recently, a decision to bar slavery from the Oregon Territory. Meanwhile the tax policy of the government—to wit, the protective tariff—

had favored the North, drawing more immigrants there than the South received. Aggravating all this was the steady accretion of power in Washington, as the federal government claimed for itself powers once reserved to the states. Andrew Jackson epitomized this trend when he threatened war against South Carolina over the tariff, but he was hardly alone.

"The result of the whole of these causes combined is that the North has acquired a decided ascendancy over every department of this government, and through it a control over all the powers of the system," Calhoun said. "A single section, governed by the will of the numerical majority, has now, in fact, the control of the government and the entire powers of the system. What was once a constitutional, federal republic is now converted, in reality, into one as absolute as that of the autocrat of Russia and as despotic in its tendency as any absolute government that ever existed."

The Northern despotism might be endured, Calhoun said, if there were no existential questions that divided North and South. But such was not the case. "There is a question of vital importance to the Southern section, in reference to which the views and feelings of the two sections are as opposite and hostile as they can possibly be." That question, of course, was slavery. Every part of the North was, to one degree or another, antagonistic to slavery. Some Northerners deemed slavery a sin, others a crime, still others a blot on the American character. Yet all felt obliged to work against it.

The South viewed slavery, and the existing relation between the races, quite differently. "The Southern section regards the relation as one which cannot be destroyed without subjecting the two races to the greatest calamity and the section to poverty, desolation and wretchedness; and accordingly they feel bound by every consideration of interest and safety to defend it."

The peril to the South, and therefore to the Union, came from the increasing influence in the North of radical abolitionism. "What is to stop this agitation before the great and final object at which it aims, the abolition of slavery in the states, is consummated?" asked Calhoun. Nothing currently enforced in law or politics, he answered. "Is it then not certain that if something decisive is not now done to arrest it, the South will be forced to choose between abolition and secession?"

Henry Clay wept for the Union; Calhoun couldn't take him seriously. "The cry of 'Union, Union, the glorious Union!' can no more prevent disunion than the cry of 'Health, health, glorious health!' on the part of the physician can save a patient lying dangerously ill," Calhoun said. "Besides, this cry of Union comes commonly from those whom we cannot believe to be sincere. It usually comes from our assailants. But we cannot believe them to be sincere, for if they loved the Union they would necessarily be devoted to the Constitution. It made the Union, and to destroy the Constitution would be to destroy the Union."

Calhoun identified the injuries the North had done the Constitution. One was the regular and egregious violation of the fugitive slave clause by the Northern states. "I cite this, not that it is the only instance, for there are many others, but because the violation in this particular is too notorious and palpable to be denied." Another was the endless agitation of the slavery question by abolitionists who didn't disguise their intention to terminate slavery in the Southern states. This aim was patently unconstitutional, as even most Northern senators and representatives acknowledged. But those Northern senators and representatives were too cowardly to call the abolitionists out.

Henry Clay, of course, **had** called the abolitionists out, but his current transgressions outweighed the good he had done on that score. Clay had summoned the ghost of George Washington on behalf of his proposed compromise. The Father of His Country would have had nothing to do with such a monstrosity, Calhoun declared. He would have stood with his fellow Southerners on behalf of the Constitution. "He was one of us, a slaveholder and a planter. We have studied his history and find nothing in it to justify submission to wrong. On the contrary, his great fame rests on the solid foundation that, while he was careful to avoid doing wrong to others, he was prompt and decided in repelling wrong." Southerners had profited by his example.

They would continue to do so, Calhoun said. "Nor can we find anything in his history to deter us from seceding from the Union, should it fail to fulfill the objects for which it was instituted, by being permanently and hopelessly converted into the means of oppressing instead of protecting us. On the contrary, we find much in his example to encourage us, should we be forced to the extremity of deciding between submission and disunion." After all, what was the American Revolution if not secession? "There existed then, as well as now, a union—that between parent country and her then colonies." For generations the British union had nurtured and protected the colonies. George Washington had flourished and prospered in this union. By all evidence he was devoted and attached to it. "But his devotion was a rational one. He was attached to it not as an end but as a means to an end. When it failed to fulfill its end and, instead of affording protection, was converted into a means of oppressing the colonies, he did not hesitate to draw his sword and head the great movement by which that union was forever severed and the independence of these states established. This was the great and crowning glory of his life, which has spread his fame over the whole globe and will transmit it to the latest posterity."

Henry Clay had presented a plan to save the Union. It would do no such thing, Calhoun asserted. He declined to answer Clay item by item, perhaps because his strength was failing. And there was little for him to gainsay in most of Clay's proposals. But the starting point of Clay's package—admission of California under the free-state constitution drafted by its inhabitants—was utterly unacceptable, Calhoun said. The Californians had no authority to legislate for that region. If the Californians had gone into Mexican territory as adventurers and proceeded to effect a revolution against Mexican authority, then, Calhoun granted, they would have had the right to draft their own constitution and laws. But this was not how things had happened. "It was the United States who conquered California and finally acquired it by treaty. The sovereignty, of course, is vested in them"—the United States— "and not in the individuals who have attempted to form a constitution and a state, without their consent." Congress, consequently, was the only body with the authority to create a government for California.

What should be done with California? "Remand her back to the territorial condition," Calhoun said. Congress had done something similar when Tennessee had acted prematurely in writing a constitution. All had turned out well in that case, and all would turn out well in this case.

If Clay's plan would not save the Union, what would? Calhoun agreed with Clay that piecemeal efforts would never work. A comprehensive settlement was required. But where Clay called for compromise, Calhoun demanded justice. "The South asks for justice, simple justice, and less she ought not to take. She has no compromise to offer but the Constitution."

And the Constitution, as Calhoun now interpreted it, demanded a measure so extreme as to blast any hope of compromise to pieces. Taking dead aim at Henry Clay, Calhoun blamed the Missouri Compromise for leading the country astray and placing the South in jeopardy. By negating the rights of the South in the upper part of Louisiana, Clay's 1820 compromise had put the country on the course that led to the current crisis. Any comprehensive settlement must start with rectification of this old injury. The Missouri Compromise must be repealed. "Such a settlement would go to the root of the evil and remove all cause of discontent by satisfying the South she could remain honorably and safely in the Union, and thereby restore the harmony and fraternal feelings between the sections which existed anterior to the Missouri agitation."

Could this be done? Calhoun said yes. But it had to be done by the North, the stronger party. "The North has only to will it to accomplish it, to do justice by conceding to the South an equal right in the acquired territory."

Meanwhile the North must agree to enforce the fugitive slave clause of the Constitution. And Northern leaders must compel an end to the agitation of the abolitionists.

Would the North agree? "It is for her to answer," Calhoun declared. "But I will say, she cannot refuse if she has half the love of the Union which she professes to have, or without justly exposing herself to the charge that her love of power and aggrandizement is far greater than her love of the Union. At all events, the responsibility of saving the Union rests on the North and not the South."

The South needed to know—the country and the world needed to know—the North's intentions on the issues dividing the nation. "If you, who represent the stronger portion, cannot agree to settle them on the broad principle of justice and duty, say so; and let the states we both represent agree to separate and part in peace. If you are unwilling we should part in peace, tell us so, and we shall know what to do, when you reduce the question to submission or resistance. If you remain silent, you will compel us to infer by your acts what you intend."

Calhoun drew to an end. "I have now, senators,

done my duty in expressing my opinions fully, freely and candidly on this solemn occasion. In doing so, I have been governed by the motives which have governed me in all the stages of the agitation of the slavery question since its commencement. I have exerted myself, during the whole period, to arrest it, with the intention of saving the Union, if it could be done; and, if it could not, to save the section where it has pleased Providence to cast my lot, and which I sincerely believe has justice and the Constitution on its side."

56

It was Daniel Webster's turn, as his colleagues understood. Webster had never faced a more daunting task. John Calhoun's stunning demands—starting with repeal of the Missouri Compromise and apparently including the suspension of the First Amendment rights of abolitionists—threw profound doubt on the prospects of a compromise. Indeed, many in Washington concluded that the South Carolinian had already chosen secession. His conditions were simply an effort to shift the blame for the Union's demise to the North. Daniel Webster had given great speeches in the past, but if the Union would be saved, he would have to outdo himself.

He wasn't ready to reply to Calhoun at once. "As soon as may be, perhaps Wednesday or Thursday next"—this was Monday—"I shall be very glad to have an opportunity to address the Senate," he told the members.

Robert Winthrop was Massachusetts's other

senator, a Whig like Webster. He had been in Boston and arrived back in Washington on March 6. "The evening of my return, I pulled Mr. Webster's doorbell, thinking he might be glad to see some one fresh from Boston before making his speech the next day," Winthrop recorded in his diary. "His servant said he was very busy, but added that he knew he would see **me,** and insisted upon showing me up to his study. I found him in the last agonies of preparation, and in the act of dictating passages to his son Fletcher. I apologized for disturbing him and was making off, when he called out, 'What say our friends in Boston?'"

Winthrop replied that he didn't think Boston would insist on the Wilmot proviso. This was somewhat surprising, because the proposed ban on slavery in territory taken from Mexico had received a great deal of support in New England.

Webster nodded, pleased. "I have not told a human being what I am going to say tomorrow," he said. "But as you are here at the last moment, I will say to you that I don't mean to have anything to do with the proviso."

Webster revealed no more to Winthrop, and when he rose to speak on March 7, the Senate had little idea what he would say. The senators supposed they had heard Henry Clay's finest speech ever, a few weeks before; they had heard John Calhoun's likely **final** speech, just days ago. At least the equal was expected of Webster. America's preeminent orator would address America's gravest crisis; the air in the chamber sizzled with anticipation.

An additional element piqued the collective interest. Webster, alone of the three, might yet be America's president. The shadows grew longer over Clay and Calhoun; as they did, the shade they cast upon the path of Webster diminished. A Whig general, Zachary Taylor, sat in the White House; he might be succeeded by a Whig senator, the one on whom every eye in the upper house now focused.

"Mr. President, I wish to speak today not as a Massachusetts man, nor as a Northern man, but as an American, and a member of the Senate of the United States," Webster commenced. "We live in the midst of strong agitations and are surrounded by very considerable dangers to our institutions of government. The imprisoned winds are let loose. The East, the West, the North and the stormy South all combine to throw the whole ocean into commotion, to toss its billows to the skies and to disclose its profoundest depths." Precisely because he could still be considered for president, Webster disclaimed personal ambition. He said he thought of the public interest only. "I have a part to act, not for my own security or safety, for I am looking out for no fragment upon which to float away from the wreck, if wreck there must be, but for the good of the whole, and the preservation of the whole; and there is that which will keep me to my duty during this struggle, whether the sun and stars shall appear, or shall not appear, for many days." He let the image linger for a moment. Then to his point: "I speak today for the Union. Hear me for my cause."

He rehearsed the events that had delivered the new territories of the West to the Union. He recounted the gold discovery and the sudden peopling of California. He described how the Californians, desperate for some government to provide order and stability, had convened to draft a constitution, and how their convention had chosen to bar slavery from California, with the sixteen delegates from slave states joining the others in the unanimous vote.

Here Webster was interrupted by the noise of new people trying to squeeze into the already packed chamber. Vice President Millard Fillmore, in the Senate chair, ordered the sergeant at arms to restore order and to allow no more visitors to enter. The doors were forcibly closed, but the hubbub beyond the doors only increased.

Webster raised his voice and carried on. He observed that slavery was an ancient institution, as old as humanity itself. The Greeks and Romans had practiced it; the Hebrew Bible allowed it; the Christian gospel accepted it. Of late, divisions had arisen among sects of Christians in America, with some Northern denominations condemning slavery as violating the spirit of Christianity if not the quoted words of Jesus, and Southern denominations defending it on religious, historical and practical grounds. Webster conceded the sincerity and conscientiousness of both the Northern and the Southern groups; such was human nature and the complicated issue of slavery. He wished others would share his tolerance. Those who didn't had caused much of the anguish that afflicted America at present. "They deal with morals as with mathematics, and they think what is right may be distinguished from what is wrong with the precision of an algebraic equation. They have, therefore, none too much charity toward others who differ with them. They are apt, too, to think that nothing is good but what is perfect, and that there are no compromises or modifications to be made in submission to difference of opinion or in deference to other men's judgment."

Webster didn't have to identify these perfectionists, but all knew of whom he spoke. He urged the abolitionists to heed the words of Saint Paul: "We are not to do evil that good may come." He reminded them of the slow pace of moral progress. "The doctrines and the miracles of Jesus Christ have, in eighteen hundred years, converted only a small portion of the human race." Even among the converted, great vices—including vices in the affairs of state—persisted. "Thus wars are waged, and unjust wars."

Webster noted that at the time of the writing of

the Constitution, the North and the South saw slavery in much the same light. "Both parts of the country held it equally an evil, a moral and political evil." The greater objection to it was as a political evil. It undermined republican values and contradicted the egalitarian message of the Declaration of Independence. Strikingly, the condemnations of slavery came more frequently and more stridently from the South than from the North. "The North was not so much excited against it as the South," said Webster. "The reason is, I suppose, because there was much less at the North; and the people did not see, or think they saw, the evils so prominently as they were seen, or thought to be seen, at the South."

The framers of the Constitution had been willing to tolerate slavery because they deemed it a dying institution. They gave its end an assist by allowing a ban on the import of slaves after twenty years. "They thought that slavery could not be continued in the country if the importation of slaves were made to cease," Webster said. He reminded the Senate that the words "slave" and "slavery" appeared nowhere in the Constitution. This was the idea of James Madison, a slaveholder besides being the chief author of the document. "He said that he did not wish to see it recognized by the Constitution of the United States of America that there could be property in men." Webster remarked that at the same time that the Constitutional Convention was meeting in Philadelphia, the Confederation Congress was meeting in New York. And in the very month when the former was projecting a ban on the importation of slaves, the latter was imposing a ban, via the Northwest Ordinance, on the introduction of slaves into the Ohio country. "And so far as we can now learn, there was a perfect concurrence of opinion between these respective bodies." Both saw slavery as a blight; both looked and worked toward its end.

To this point in his remarks Webster had not mentioned John Calhoun by name or directly addressed his arguments. He didn't see Calhoun among the crowd in the Senate chamber when he said, "An honorable member whose health does not allow him to be here today—"

"He is here," interrupted a senator sitting near Calhoun, who himself said nothing.

"I am very happy to hear that he is," said Webster, without missing a beat. "May he long be in health and the enjoyment of it to serve his country." He resumed his thought, that Calhoun had cited the Northwest Ordinance as the first of the depredations of the North against the South. This was quite wrong, Webster said. "It was done with the entire and unanimous concurrence of the whole South. Why, there it stands! The vote of every state in the Union was unanimous in favor of the ordinance."

The unanimity didn't last. "Soon a change began at the North and the South, and a severance of opinion showed itself—the North growing much more warm and strong against slavery, and the South growing much more warm and strong in its support." Webster didn't assign blame in this. "I impute to the South no particularly selfish view, in the change which has come over her. I impute to her certainly no dishonest view. All that has happened has been natural. It has followed those causes which always influence the human mind and operate upon it." Chief among the causes was the unexpected expansion of cotton cultivation. "It was the cotton interest that gave a new desire to promote slavery, to spread it and to use its labor," Webster said. "The age of cotton became a golden age for our Southern brethren. It gratified their desire for improvement and cultivation, at the same time that it excited it. The desire grew by what it fed upon, and there soon came to be an eagerness for other territory—a new area or areas for the cultivation of the cotton crop; and measures leading to this result were brought about somewhat rapidly, one after another, under the lead of Southern men at the head of the government, they having a majority in both branches, to accomplish their ends."

Webster again contradicted Calhoun, citing Calhoun's assertion that the North had dominated the national government all along. "If that be true, sir, the North has acted either very liberally and kindly, or very weakly," Webster said, "for they never exercised that majority five times in the history of the government. Never." Calhoun had things just backward. It was the South that had dominated. "No man acquainted with the history of the country can deny that the general lead in the politics of the country, for three-fourths of the period that has elapsed since the adoption of the Constitution, has been a Southern lead." The South, acting through the national government, had repeatedly secured the admission of new slave states: nine since the ratification of the Constitution, with Texas likely to spawn more.

The annexation of Texas particularly showed the ability of the South to have its way. And it demonstrated that the North did not oppose the South as Calhoun had claimed. Texas—"this immense territory over which a bird can not fly in a week"—might still become five states, and Northern votes had made it possible. "New England, with some of her votes, supported this measure. Three-fourth of the votes of liberty-loving Connecticut went for it in the other house, and one-half here. There was one vote for it in Maine." Massachusetts, that hotbed of abolition, had provided a vote. Representatives and senators from other Northern states added their support, to the sum of fifty free-state votes in the House for annexation and thirteen in the Senate.

Without these votes, annexation would not have occurred.

Webster again cited Calhoun, this time in the South Carolinian's capacity as secretary of state, the office he held in the period leading to Texas annexation. Calhoun's correspondence with the American chargé d'affaires in Texas had been published. "The secretary had the boldness and candor to avow in that correspondence that the great object sought by the annexation of Texas was to strengthen the slave interest of the South," Webster said.

Calhoun broke in. "Will the honorable senator permit me to interrupt him for a moment?" he said.

"Certainly," Webster replied.

"I did not put it on the ground assumed by the senator," Calhoun said. "I put it upon this ground: that Great Britain had announced to this country, in so many words, that her object was to abolish slavery in Texas, and through Texas to accomplish the abolishment of slavery in the United States and the world. The ground I put it on was that it would make an exposed frontier, and if Great Britain succeeded in her object, it would be impossible that that frontier could be secured against the aggression of the abolitionists; and that this government was bound, under the guarantees of the Constitution, to protect us against such a state of things."

Webster yielded nothing. "That comes, I suppose, sir, to exactly the same thing. It was that Texas must be obtained for the security of the slave interest in the South." Yet he credited Calhoun with forthrightness. "The honorable member did avow this object himself, openly, boldly and manfully. He did not disguise his conduct or his motives."

"Never, never," said Calhoun.

"What he means he is very apt to say," Webster continued.

"Always, always," said Calhoun.

"And I honor him for it," Webster declared.

He turned to the other territories acquired from Mexico, and here echoed Henry Clay. "As to California and New Mexico, I hold slavery to be excluded from those territories by a law even superior to that which admits and sanctions it in Texas. I mean the law of nature, of physical geography, the law of the formation of the earth. That law settles forever, with a strength beyond all terms of human enactment, that slavery cannot exist in California or New Mexico." Webster granted that personal servants could be taken to California; nothing of climate or geology prevented this. He understood that a form of peonage had existed under Spanish and Mexican rule. But the kind of slavery practiced in the plantation South—"slaves in gross, of the colored race, transferable by sale and delivery like other property"—was impossible. So it would forever be, regardless of what the Congress of the United States declared.

For this reason, congressional declarations on slavery there were idle. The Californians had already acknowledged the reality of nature; their decision should stand. As for New Mexico, Congress should keep silent. It might pass a law creating a territorial government for New Mexico, but in such a law it should say nothing about slavery. "I would not take pains to reaffirm an ordinance of nature nor to reenact the will of God," Webster said. "And I would put in no Wilmot proviso for the purpose of a taunt or a reproach. I would put into it no evidence of the votes of a superior power, to wound the pride—even whether a just pride, a rational pride or an irrational pride—to wound the pride of the gentlemen who belong to the Southern states."

A STIR SUDDENLY rippled through Webster's audience. The senator from Massachusetts had defied the legislature that had sent him to Washington! He had contradicted his own earlier vote for the Wilmot proviso. He had broken ranks with the North and with most of the Whig party. Members and visitors looked at one another wonderingly. Only Robert Winthrop wasn't surprised.

Webster ignored the fuss. He turned to the question of fugitive slaves. On this he agreed with

Calhoun, and with Clay. He **dis**agreed—again—with the people in his own state and, by much evidence, most of the people in the North. "It is my judgment that the South is right," he said of the complaints about the obstructions thrown in the path of the slave catchers. "And the North is wrong."

The gasps in the Senate chamber were audible now. Members stared at Webster, then back at one another.

Webster observed the commotion but once more gave no sign. In his addresses he sometimes spoke like a prophet or a preacher; now he spoke like a lawyer. Article IV of the Constitution stated a clear obligation, he said. "Every member of every northern legislature is bound, by oath, like every other officer in the country, to support the Constitution of the United States; and this article of the Constitution, which says to these states they shall deliver up fugitives from service, is as binding in honor and conscience as any other article. No man fulfills his duty in any legislature who sets himself up to find excuses, evasions, escapes from this constitutional obligation."

Webster offered that he had long thought that the obligation to return the slaves lay with the states individually. "That is my judgment. I have always entertained that opinion, and I entertain it now." But the Supreme Court had ruled, some years earlier, that Congress might intervene if the states did not do their part. Webster wasn't sure this was a wise opinion. Yet it was the law. "As it now stands, the business of seeing that these fugitives are delivered up resides in the power of Congress." Webster intended to assist in the exercise of that power. "My friend at the head of the judiciary committee has a bill on the subject, now before the Senate, with some amendments, which I propose to support, with all its provisions, to the fullest extent."

More gasps. Daniel Webster had joined the slave catchers! Could it be?

He continued, unmoved. "I desire to call the attention of all sober-minded men, of all conscientious men, in the North, of all men who are not carried away by any fanatical idea or by any false idea whatever, to their constitutional obligations. I put it to all these sober and sound minds at the North, as a question of morals and a question of conscience: What right have they, in all their legislative capacity, or any other, to endeavor to get round this Constitution, to embarrass the free exercise of the rights secured by the Constitution, to the persons whose slaves escape from them? None at all—none at all. Neither in the forum of conscience, nor before the face of the Constitution, are they justified, in my opinion."

Behind the opposition to the return of slaves were the abolitionist societies. "I do not think them useful," Webster said. "I think their operations for the last twenty years have produced nothing good or valuable." He didn't impugn the motives of the members of the societies. "I know thousands of them are honest and good men, perfectly well-meaning men. They have excited feelings; they think they must do something for the cause of liberty; and in their sphere of action they do not see what else they can do than to contribute to an abolition press or an abolition society or to pay an abolition lecturer." These were understandable sentiments. "But I am not blind to the consequences. I cannot but see what mischiefs their interference with the South has produced. And is it not plain to every man?" Webster reminded the Senate that in the early 1830s the legislature of Virginia had held an open and searching debate on slavery. All sides of the question were aired. Not much later the abolitionist societies began their campaign of vilification. "They created great agitation in the North against Southern slavery. Well, what was the result? The bonds of the slaves were bound more firmly than before; their rivets were more strongly fastened. Public opinion, which in Virginia had begun to be exhibited against slavery and was opening out for the discussion of the question, drew back and shut itself up in its castle."

Webster conceded that the South had grievances against the North, just as the North had grievances against the South. But while these grievances must be acknowledged, they should not be encouraged. And under no circumstances should they be employed to justify disunion. Here Webster took dead aim at Calhoun. "I should much prefer to have heard from every member on this floor declarations of opinion that this Union should never be dissolved, than the declaration of opinion that in any case, under the pressure of circumstances, such a dissolution was possible. I hear with pain and anguish and distress the word secession, especially when it falls from the lips of those who are eminently patriotic and known to the country, and known all over the world, for their political services."

Webster's tone assumed the pain and anguish he described. "Secession! Peaceable secession! Sir, your eyes and mine are never destined to see that miracle. The dismemberment of this vast country without convulsion! The breaking up of the fountains of the great deep without ruffling the surface! Who is so foolish—I beg everybody's pardon—as to expect to see any such thing?"

"Peaceable secession!" Webster repeated. "Peaceable secession! The concurrent agreement of all the members of this great republic to separate! A voluntary separation, with alimony on one side and on the other. Why, what would be the result? Where is the line to be drawn? What states are to secede? What is to remain American? What am I to be—an American no longer? Where is the flag of the republic to remain? Where is the eagle still to tower? Or is he to cower? And shrink and fall to the ground?" The fathers of the current generation would rebuke those who let the Union crumble. Their children and grandchildren would point the finger of blame.

Webster caught his breath and calmed his voice. He refused to end on a grim note. "Instead of speaking of the possibility or utility of secession, instead of dwelling in these caverns of darkness, instead of groping with those ideas so full of all that is horrid and horrible, let us come out into the light of day. Let us enjoy the fresh air of liberty and Union." The country had reached a turning point. "Never did there devolve on any generation of men higher trusts than now devolve upon us for the preservation of this Constitution and the harmony and peace of all who are destined to live under it." The Union was a wondrous thing. "No monarchical throne presses these states together; no iron chain of despotic power encircles them. They live and stand upon a government popular in its form, representative in its character, founded upon principles of equality and calculated, we hope, to last forever."

Webster promised to do his part to preserve this inheritance from the founders. He urged the other senators to do theirs.

DANIEL WEBSTER'S SPEECH stunned the Senate and outraged New England. A defense of slaveholders' interests was expected of John Calhoun and even Henry Clay, but a defense of those interests by Daniel Webster? It was too much to bear. Webster's supporters in Massachusetts were appalled; one of Webster's staunchest backers was reported to have required a week of bed rest to recover. The Massachusetts legislature felt betrayed; a Whig leader there who had been proud to call Webster a friend and a model declared, "We are now on the opposite sides of the moral universe." Poet John Greenleaf Whittier set his disappointment to verses that Massachusetts congressman Horace Mann read to the House of Representatives: "Of all we loved and honored, naught / Save power remains,— / A fallen angel's pride of thought, / Still strong in chains. / All else is gone; from those great eyes / The soul has fled; / When faith is lost, when honor dies / The man is dead." Ralph Waldo Emerson spat on one to whom he had looked for leadership. "Liberty! Liberty! Pho!" said Emerson. "Let Mr. Webster for decency's sake shut his lips once and forever on this word. The word **liberty** in the mouth of Mr. Webster sounds like the word **love** in the mouth of a courtezan." The normally meditative Emerson couldn't contain himself; he went on, "Tell him that he who was their pride in the woods and mountains of New England is now their mortification; that they never name him; they have taken his picture from the wall and torn it—dropped the pieces in the gutter; they have taken his book of speeches from the shelf and put it in the stove."

Some who had humorously suggested that Webster had sold his soul to the devil in exchange for his other-worldly powers of address now declared, with stony seriousness, that he had bartered it a second time, to win the presidency. Why else would he have given up his principles, his constituents, his friends and admirers? Southern Whigs applauded the pragmatism and broad-mindedness of Webster's speech, and the endorsement was read in the North as corroboration of the presidential-ambition theory. New England's Whigs, Webster's natural base, mobilized to deny him the ultimate prize. Faneuil Hall in Boston hosted an anti-Webster protest more vitriolic than many of the antislavery protests common in the Massachusetts capital. John Calhoun was portrayed as honorable compared with Webster; at least Calhoun didn't stab his supporters in the back.

WHETHER WEBSTER'S ENDORSEMENT of Henry Clay's compromise did the Clay package any good was difficult to tell for several weeks, during which time the attention of Congress and the country was wrenched in another direction. After his long battle with lung disease, John Calhoun died on March 31.

Clay acknowledged a worthy foe. "He is gone!" he told the Senate. "No more shall we witness from yonder seat the flashes of that keen and penetrating eye of his, darting through this chamber. No more shall we behold that torrent of clear, concise, compact logic poured out from his lips, which, if it did not always carry conviction to our judgment, commanded our great admiration. Those eyes and those lips are closed forever!"

Clay recalled his first encounters with Calhoun, at the time of the War of 1812. "Of all the Congresses with which I have had any acquaintance since my entry into the service of the federal government, in none, in my humble opinion, has been assembled such a galaxy of eminent and able men as were in the House of Representatives of that Congress which declared the war, and in that immediately following the peace. And amongst that splendid assemblage none shone more bright and brilliant than the star which is now set." Then and for years after, Clay said, he and Calhoun had stood shoulder to shoulder on policy foreign and domestic, and even when domestic issues had drawn them apart, they still shared a vision of America's importance to the world. In all things, Calhoun was a statesman to admire. "He possessed an elevated genius of the highest order," Clay said. "In felicity of generalization of the subjects of which his mind treated, I have seen him surpassed by no one. And the charm and captivating influence of his colloquial powers have been felt by all who have conversed with him. I was his senior, Mr. President, in years—in nothing else. According to the course of nature, I ought to have preceded him. It has been decreed otherwise; but I know that I shall linger here only a short time and shall soon follow him."

Clay adduced a lesson. "How brief, how short is the period of human existence allotted even to the youngest amongst us!" he said. "Sir, ought we not to profit by the contemplation of this melancholy occasion? Ought we not to draw from it the conclusion how unwise it is to indulge in the acerbity of unbridled debate? How unwise to yield ourselves to the sway of the animosities of party feeling?" Clay didn't pretend to agree with Calhoun on the central issues confronting the nation at this moment. But he hoped to emulate Calhoun in devotion to duty. "I trust we shall all be instructed by the eminent virtues and merits of his exalted character, and be taught, by his bright example, to fulfill our great public duties by the lights of our own judgment and the dictates of our own consciences, as he did, according to his honest and best conceptions of those duties, faithfully and to the last."

Daniel Webster echoed Clay. "I have not, in public nor in private life, known a more assiduous person in the discharge of his appropriate duties," Webster said of Calhoun. "I have known no man who wasted less of his life in what is called recreation, or employed less of it in pursuits not connected with the immediate discharge of his duty. He seemed to have no recreation but the pleasure of conversation with his friends. Out of the chambers of Congress, he was either devoting himself to the acquisition of knowledge pertaining to the immediate subject of the duty before him, or else he was indulging in those social interviews in which he so much delighted."

Calhoun's eloquence was of the first order, Webster said. "It grew out of the qualities of his mind. It was plain, strong, terse, condensed, concise; sometimes impassioned—still always severe. Rejecting ornament, not often seeking far for illustration, his power consisted in the plainness of his propositions, in the closeness of his logic, and in the earnestness and energy of his manner." Calhoun was the model of the gentleman and statesman. "No man was more respectful to others; no man carried himself with greater decorum, no man with superior dignity." His accomplishments made him a man for the ages. "He has lived long enough, he has done enough, and he has done it so well, so successfully, so honorably, as to connect himself for all time with the records of his country." Webster concluded, "He is now a historical character. Those of us who have known him here will find that he has left upon our minds and our hearts a strong and lasting impression of his person, his character and his public performances, which, while we live, will never be obliterated."

CALHOUN'S DEATH DEPRIVED the opposition to Clay's compromise of its most powerful voice. A second death removed another foe. Zachary Taylor didn't like Clay's package, and he didn't like Clay. Taylor's record as a soldier had won him nomination by the Whig party in 1848 and election by the American people, and he harbored the soldier's skepticism of career politicians. He fancied himself the leader of the Whig party and objected to Clay's failure to defer to him on party matters. He had his own ideas about dealing with the California question, preferring to admit California as a free state without reference to the other issues that roiled sectional politics. He felt upstaged by Clay's comprehensive approach.

But Taylor took abruptly ill in the summer of 1850. A sweltering Independence Day ceremony was followed by severe gastrointestinal distress. Some friends and physicians blamed the cherries and iced milk he consumed at the ceremony's end; others suggested one of the fevers that afflicted Washington during hot weather. Taylor suffered for several days before dying of what the doctors called cholera morbus, a vague term that merely summarized his symptoms. The nation was shocked; Old Rough and Ready had seemed hale and strong.

Taylor's death left Clay as the unchallenged head of the Whig party, and it rendered his compromise package the only viable solution to the California crisis. At the suggestion of Henry Foote, a Democrat from Mississippi, Clay had agreed to roll his several resolutions into a single bill, but the omnibus approach had stalled as opponents of one part of the big bill linked arms with opponents of other parts to subvert the whole thing. Taylor's death, and his replacement by Millard Fillmore, a Clay ally, essentially eliminated the chance of a presidential veto at the end of the legislative process and gave supporters of the compromise new energy.

They needed all the energy they could muster—more energy than Clay himself could sustain. The summer's heat drove him from the capital to the seacoast at Newport. An ambitious first-term Democrat from Illinois, Stephen A. Douglas, quietly took charge of the several parts of the compromise and found separate majorities for each. By the time Clay returned at the end of August, the grand compromise he had laid out in January awaited little more than the president's signature, which Fillmore duly furnished. The deal was done.

Washington sighed with relief. No one thought the Compromise of 1850, as it was soon dubbed, had spiked sectionalism forever. But Henry Clay understood that forever was a concept foreign to politics. The compromise had bought years, perhaps even a decade or two. The South would not secede during that time; civil war would not rend the country. In politics such an outcome was as much as any statesman could ask. Clay, suddenly feeling the full weight of his seventy-three years, celebrated the passage of the compromise in comparative silence. He left to Daniel Webster to summarize the meaning of the achievement. "We have gone through the most important crisis which has occurred since the foundation of the government," Webster said. "Whatever party may prevail hereafter, the Union stands firm. Faction, disunion and the love of mischief are put under, at least for the present, and I hope for a long time."

58

SOLOMON NORTHUP KNEW nothing of the fight for Henry Clay's compromise. Northup knew very little beyond his shrunken existence as a slave. So long as he was the property of William Ford, his life was not unbearable. "I think of him with affection," Northup recalled of Ford, "and had my family been with me, could have borne his gentle servitude, without murmuring, all my days." But fate, operating through the cash nexus of the Louisiana economy, had other plans. Ford had guaranteed a note held by his brother, and when the brother failed to pay, the creditors came after Ford. He had to sell some slaves to make the debt good, and Solomon Northup, without a family that Ford knew of, which would suffer as a result of his departure, was one he chose. Northup's purchaser was a carpenter named John Tibeats. Tibeats couldn't pay the full price, leaving him on the hook to Ford for four hundred dollars. But Northup became his slave.

Tibeats was a very different master from Ford. He drove Northup relentlessly. "From earliest dawn until late at night, I was not allowed to be a moment idle," Northup remembered. He did his best, but Tibeats was never satisfied. "He was continually cursing and complaining. He never spoke to me a kind word. I was his faithful slave, and earned him large wages every day, and yet I went to my cabin nightly loaded with abuse and stinging epithets."

And worse. Tibeats employed a whip against Northup to spur greater effort and to assert his authority. Northup knew the danger of resisting the whip, but one day, when they were constructing a building on a property owned by William Ford, he refused to submit. He had done nothing to warrant the lash, and he told Tibeats so. This angered Tibeats, who vowed to teach him not to answer back. He ordered Northup to strip for punishment.

"I will **not**," Northup said.

Enraged, Tibeats leaped upon Northup, seized him by the throat with one hand and raised the whip to beat him with the other. Northup defended himself and wrestled Tibeats to the ground, pinning him to the earth with his foot. He tore the whip from Tibeats's hand and began beating him with its wooden stock. "I cannot tell how many times I struck him," Northup recounted. "Blow after blow fell fast and heavy upon his wriggling form. At length he screamed—cried murder—and at last the blasphemous tyrant called on God for mercy. But he who had never shown mercy did not receive it. The stiff stock of the whip warped round his cringing body until my right arm ached."

The overseer of the property where Tibeats and Northup were working, a man named Chapin, heard the commotion and came running. Chapin, like his boss William Ford, was a kind-hearted man, and he judged Tibeats a disgrace to Southern manhood. Chapin let Northup explain himself. Then Chapin and Tibeats consulted privately, and Tibeats rode away in a black mood.

Northup was tempted to run, but Chapin told him to stay. He did so, and an hour later Tibeats returned with two other men. The three approached Northup with whips and ropes. Outnumbered, he didn't resist. They bound him and put a noose around his neck. They were about to hang him from a tree branch when Chapin reappeared, with a pistol in either hand. He called Tibeats a scoundrel who had deserved the beating Northup had given him. Beyond that, he reminded Tibeats that William Ford was owed four hundred dollars on Northup. Chapin, as Ford's agent, was not going to see the collateral on that debt—Northup—destroyed. There would be no hanging.

Chapin's intervention saved Northup, but it didn't solve Northup's Tibeats problem. Tibeats lay in wait for a time when Chapin would be absent. The time came, and Tibeats, conjuring a reason for anger at Northup, seized a hatchet and approached him with murder in his eyes. "It was a moment of life or death," Northup recalled. "The sharp, bright blade of the hatchet glittered in the sun. In another instant it would be buried in my brain."

Northup again fought back. He grabbed the hatchet arm and kicked Tibeats in the groin, causing him to double over and drop the hatchet. Northup seized the hatchet and weighed using it on Tibeats. But he wasn't ready to become a murderer, and he tossed the hatchet away.

Tibeats took up a heavy stick and assaulted Northup again. Once more Northup parried the attack and disarmed his attacker.

Angrier than ever, Tibeats reached for an ax lying near. But Northup got his hands about Tibeats's throat. As Tibeats continued to fight, Northup tightened his grip. The choke hold took effect. "He became pliant and unstrung," Northup recounted. "His face, that had been white with passion, was now black from suffocation. Those small serpent eyes that spat with such venom were now full of horror—two great white orbs starting from their sockets."

Still not ready to murder, Northup gave Tibeats's throat a final squeeze and let him go. This time he had no choice but to run, and off he went. He escaped drowning in the bayous that crisscrossed

the region; he dodged alligators and water mocca-
sins; he distanced the dogs Tibeats put on his trail.
But after several hours he realized the futility of it
all. He was a thousand miles from home and hundreds of miles from free soil. An unaccompanied
black man in the slave South was instantly suspect;
any white man could seize him as a runaway and
expect a reward. He lacked survival skills and even
the simplest tools. He would be caught sooner or
later; better to turn himself in.

He found his way to William Ford's plantation
and threw himself on the mercy of his erstwhile
owner. Ford sheltered him and talked Tibeats
into selling him, arguing that Tibeats would kill
Northup if Northup didn't kill him first. Tibeats
assented, and Northup found himself with a new
master.

EDWIN EPPS WASN'T much improvement over
Tibeats. "When sober, he was silent, reserved and
cunning," Northup recalled. But he was very often
not sober. "When 'in his cups,' Master Epps was
a roistering, blustering, noisy fellow, whose chief
delight was in dancing with his 'niggers' or lash-
ing them about the yard with his long whip, just
for the pleasure of hearing them screech and scream
as the great welts were planted on their backs."

Epps had been an overseer before acquiring
property and becoming a planter himself. He

remained a hard taskmaster, compelling his slaves to toil from first light to last, regardless of weather, season or compromised health. Cotton was his main crop, and during harvest the slaves were required to meet rigorous quotas, averaging two hundred pounds per picker per day, or be whipped for their failure.

Northup never mastered the art of picking. His hands could pull tunes from a fiddle, but they fumbled over the fluffy bolls. Epps whipped him again and again, to no avail. Finally Epps gave up and set Northup to other work.

"Ten years I toiled for that man without reward," Northup recalled. "Ten years of my incessant labor has contributed to increase the bulk of his possessions. Ten years I was compelled to address him with downcast eyes and uncovered head, in the attitude and language of a slave."

Yet they were ten years in which he never stopped pondering how he might regain his freedom. His experience with James Birch had convinced him of the folly of proclaiming his true identity so long as he remained in the sealed world of the South. But he continually looked for cracks in the wall that separated his present from his past. On board the **Orleans** during his passage south, he had met a sympathetic sailor, an Englishman who had lived in Massachusetts. Northup told the fellow his story, and the sailor helped him write a letter addressed to Henry Northup, a white man of the family that had once owned Solomon's father. Northup explained his circumstances and asked for help. The sailor said he would post the letter at New Orleans. For more than a decade Northup didn't know whether the letter had reached its destination.

During that time he had no other opportunity. An apparent chance fell through when a man Northup sounded out on sending a letter to friends in New York betrayed his confidence, forcing Northup to swear the man was lying. Finally, though, he met a Canadian named Bass, a journeyman carpenter. Bass was outspoken in his criticism of slavery, and he habitually engaged Epps in debates on the subject. Had he been an American, especially a Yankee, his opinions might not have been tolerated. But because he was a foreigner, and because he seemed slightly daft, Epps and the neighbors let him talk.

Northup overheard and cautiously cultivated him. In time he told Bass his story. Bass said he would help him regain his freedom. He asked Northup for the names of friends in New York who could testify to his having been a free man. He wrote letters on Northup's behalf. Both hoped for the best.

Months passed with no answer. Solomon Northup began to fear that the letters had gone astray or that his friends, assuming they were still alive, had not seen fit to pursue his case. He concluded he would never regain his freedom.

More months passed. And then, in January 1853, Henry Northup appeared at Epps's plantation. Northup was astonished and overcome. "As my eyes rested on his countenance, a world of images thronged my brain," he recalled. "All the scenes and associations of childhood and youth, all the friends of other and happier days appeared and disappeared, flitting and floating like dissolving shadows before the vision of my imagination." He saw his wife and children, his father and mother. Finally he focused on the man before him. "**Henry B. Northup!** Thank God—thank God!"

Confirming Northup's deliverance required satisfying several conditions. In theory Southern law decried trafficking of the sort that had led to Northup's captivity, for it lent credence to the complaints of the abolitionists against the slave system. In practice Southern authorities threw hurdles in the path of those who would do what Henry Northup was attempting. But Henry Northup knew what he was about. He had consulted lawyers and men with experience of Southern ways. He had taken care not to give Epps forewarning of his arrival, lest Epps cause Northup to disappear. In fact, simply finding Northup had been difficult, for during his whole time in the South he had been known as Platt.

But when Northup, with affidavits carried by Henry Northup, proved his true identity, his shackles fell away. With Henry Northup he boarded a steamboat on the Red River for New Orleans. He saw the slave pen from which he had been purchased by William Ford. Another boat bore them to Virginia. At Richmond, Northup showed Henry the slave pen he had inhabited there.

In Washington, Northup identified the Yellow House and swore out a criminal complaint against James Birch, who was still engaged in his nefarious business. Birch was arrested and brought before a magistrate. But he hadn't survived in the slave trade without acquiring a few tricks. He produced witnesses who swore that he had come by Northup honestly, or at least innocently. Two men had approached him saying they had a Georgia slave for sale, on behalf of a master who had fallen on hard times. If there was any deception, Birch and the witnesses said, the fault was theirs, not his. The court allowed the testimony of Birch and the witnesses, but it refused to hear Northup's. As a black man, his testimony was inadmissible in the District of Columbia. The case against Birch was dismissed.

Finally Northup reached home. His wife and children had known he was in bondage, for his letter from the **Orleans** had reached them. But it gave insufficient information for them to mount a search, which was beyond their unaided means anyway. The long silence that followed made them fear he had died. The children had grown. One daughter was married, with a child of her own, named for the boy's missing grandfather. Northup's son had been saving money to purchase his father's freedom, should he ever learn where Northup was. His wife had continued to hope, even as the basis for hope dwindled.

Twelve years of his life had been lost—but not lost entirely, for he was persuaded to tell his story, and when it was published, **Twelve Years a Slave: Narrative of Solomon Northup, a Citizen of New-York, Kidnapped in Washington City in 1841, and Rescued in 1853, from a Cotton Plantation near the Red River, in Louisiana** became a compelling contribution to the case the abolitionists were making against the slave system of the South.

59

SOLOMON NORTHUP'S STORY confirmed what Henry Clay had long been saying about the corrupting effects of slavery. Yet by bolstering the arguments of the abolitionists, it undermined Clay's Compromise of 1850. The Fugitive Slave Act, the part of the compromise embodying Clay's proposal to strengthen the constitutional guarantee of the return of escaped slaves, shifted the burden of proof from slave hunters to alleged escapees, and it compelled the cooperation of Northern sheriffs, judges and private individuals in the capture of the fugitives. Many Northerners found themselves caught between conscience and the law, and resented being placed in such a predicament. The teeth of the new law were beginning to bite seriously when Solomon Northup's story became known. Northup's experience demonstrated how badly justice had failed under the older system; the miscarriages of justice threatened to be far worse under the new system.

Many Southerners meanwhile resented the compromise for the same reasons John Calhoun had opposed it. The admission of free California tipped the balance in Congress, perhaps forever, to the North. Southern zealots increasingly rejected **any** restraints on slavery in territory acquired by the collective effort of the nation; California's admission came as a slap in their face. Calhoun's death, amid his fight against the compromise, made him a martyr to the Southern cause, and though calls for immediate secession eased in the wake of the compromise, the ideology of eventual secession grew stronger than ever. Calhoun continued the struggle posthumously, through the publication of two political tracts describing how his concept of states' rights and sectional balance might function in practice. Few people, even in the South, actually read **A Disquisition on Government** or **A Discourse on the Constitution and Government of the United States,** yet the documents enhanced Calhoun's reputation as the deep thinker of Dixie and the stalwart of states' rights.

Henry Clay had devoted his career to the middle ground of compromise, but the ironic effect of the Compromise of 1850 was to cut away much of what remained of that threatened region. This was hardly Clay's fault; without the compromise the middle ground might have disappeared entirely and at once. Yet rather than calming North and South, Clay's compromise agitated them further.

Each side had something new and specific to blame the other for, and each held Henry Clay accountable. The Kentuckian's reputation among moderates remained strong, but the moderates were increasingly shouted down by the radicals. The death of Calhoun left leadership in South Carolina to the fire-eaters, who found emulators in other Southern states. Some denounced even Calhoun's lip service to devotion to the Union; their states' rights sensibilities on hair trigger, they vowed secession at the first opportunity. The perceived apostasy of Daniel Webster had a similar effect in Massachusetts and the North, where abolitionism grew stronger and more militant than ever. William Lloyd Garrison captivated an antislavery rally near Boston by burning a copy of the Fugitive Slave Act, a copy of a court order requiring local enforcement, and finally a copy of the Constitution, which he denounced as "a covenant with death and an agreement with hell." As the audience cheered and the flames consumed the Union's charter, Garrison declared, "So perish all compromises with tyranny!"

HENRY CLAY WATCHED the anger intensify, helpless at last to prevent it. The compromise effort had worn him down; it was all he could do to answer the roll call in the Senate, let alone guide the upper house to new legislation. Yet he refused to despair. And when his voice gave out, he turned to writing to defend the compromise and the principles on which it was based. Three hundred New Yorkers asked Clay to visit their city and hearten moderates there. He replied that his failing health precluded travel, but he appended an upbeat report of the general acceptance of the compromise, notwithstanding the protests of what he deemed a relative few. He recounted history and cited statistics showing how well the Union established by the Constitution had served the American people. "Such are the gratifying results which have been obtained under the auspices of that Union, which some rash men, prompted by ambition, passion and fury, would seek to dissolve and subvert!" he said. "To revolt against such a government, for any thing which has passed, would be so atrocious, and characterized by such extreme folly and madness, that we may search in vain for an example of it in human annals." He appealed to America's native good sense. "Let us enjoy the proud consolation afforded by the conviction that a vast majority of the people of the United States, true to their forefathers, true to themselves, and true to their posterity, are firmly and immovably attached to this Union; that they see in it a safe and sure, if not the sole, guaranty of liberty, of internal peace, of prosperity, and of national happiness and greatness."

This affirmation proved his valedictory. He

retreated to his room at Washington's National Hotel and rarely emerged. The consumption claimed more and more of his lung capacity; his respiration grew thinner and more labored. In June 1852 he breathed his last.

ONLY DANIEL WEBSTER remained of the trio who had commanded the attention of the country for four decades. In idle moments he dreamed that the Whigs might turn to him in 1852, but minds better grounded in the demands of democratic politics understood that a brilliant orator was no match for a victorious general in appeal to a broad public. Winfield Scott was their man. Millard Fillmore meanwhile invited Webster to reprise his role as secretary of state. Webster reckoned that the diplomatic post would remove him from the line of political fire of his still-livid constituents, and he accepted.

His second stint at the state department was cut short. In May 1852, while on a home visit to Marshfield, he suffered a severe blow to the head and injuries to internal organs when his carriage overturned. He continued working for several months, but he never regained his strength. He died in October.

———

THE DEATHS OF Calhoun, Clay and Webster appeared less uncannily timed than the same-day deaths of Jefferson and Adams on the fiftieth anniversary of the Declaration of Independence. Nothing could match that earlier coincidence. But if the passing of the two founders in 1826 had symbolized the end of the first generation of America's nationhood, the demise of the three senators amid the controversy surrounding the Compromise of 1850 marked the end of the second. The founders had won freedom for America and created the Union of the states; their heirs had confirmed freedom and guided the Union through four decades of crisis. Neither group felt that its task was complete; American self-government was always a work in progress. Jefferson had shuddered at what the fight over the Missouri Compromise portended; Clay, Calhoun and Webster understood that the Compromise of 1850 might purchase time but guaranteed no final resolution of the struggle between the sections.

In their deaths the country honored the three as it had not always done in their lives. Henry Clay became the first American to lie in state in the Capitol; his funeral train took the long way to Lexington, looping north to Philadelphia and New York before turning west. Hundreds of thousands of mourners lined the route and paid their respects as the black-veiled car rolled by. When

Clay's will was read, Americans learned that he had acted individually as he had urged his state and wished the South to act, by providing for gradual emancipation of his slaves. Children born to Clay slaves would be freed at adulthood and assisted to emigrate to Liberia, the West African colony for freed American slaves.

The honors accorded John Calhoun were fittingly sectional. His remains were carried to Richmond; thousands journeyed to the Virginia capitol to pay their respects. Another train took him to Charleston, where thousands more viewed the casket in the city hall. He was interred in a churchyard not far from the harbor.

Daniel Webster, having died in his home, was buried there and required no transport. But half of Massachusetts, it seemed, clogged the railways and roads to Marshfield to acknowledge their debt to the state's most famous adopted son. Faneuil Hall forgave him; curtains covered the windows as a silent throng summoned the voice and spirit that had moved so many in earlier days.

AMERICANS FELT GREAT loss in the aftermath of the three deaths, but the nation required several years to determine just what the loss entailed. The Whig party fell to pieces, deprived of the leadership of Clay and Webster. A successor coalition, taking the name of Jefferson's party, organized

Northern Whigs and free-soil Democrats into a new Republican party, which was explicitly anti-slavery and effectively anti-Southern. The ghost of Henry Clay shook his head in sorrow, while John Calhoun's specter nodded grimly at this fulfillment of his prophecy of escalation against the South.

The sectional contest took a bloody turn after Stephen Douglas pushed a bill through Congress repealing the Missouri Compromise, the more swiftly to settle Kansas and Nebraska. John Calhoun's shade again nodded, this time in approval. Slaveholders poured into Kansas from neighboring Missouri; antislavery activists rushed to counter them. The result was an irregular war between zealots of the two sides. Among the antislavery militants was the charismatically monomaniacal John Brown, who led a band of followers in a brutal murder of several pro-slavery settlers.

While Kansas bled, the federal courts heard a case involving a slave named Dred Scott. The eventual verdict by the Supreme Court confirmed John Calhoun's judgment that slaveholders could not be barred from taking their slaves into the federal territories. The Missouri Compromise had been unconstitutional all along.

The South celebrated; many in the North despaired. But the South was the side despairing after John Brown and a larger band of antislavery militants staged a raid on the federal arsenal at

Harpers Ferry, Virginia, with the aim of inciting a slave rebellion. The mission failed; the rebellion never materialized. Brown was captured, tried and executed. Yet in much of the North he was treated as a martyr, one who did what other abolitionists simply talked about. The South was aghast: a murderer made into a saint? Never had the gulf between North and South yawned wider.

Within weeks of the tenth anniversary of the Compromise of 1850, Abraham Lincoln was elected president on a Republican ticket and a Republican platform. Lincoln received not a single electoral vote from a Southern state. Southerners interpreted the outcome as proof that the federal government was irretrievably in hostile hands. South Carolina finally made good on John Calhoun's repeated threats to secede. Six other slave states followed. When Lincoln resisted secession and attempted to resupply Fort Sumter in Charleston's harbor, the Civil War began—within rifle shot of Calhoun's grave.

In battling the legacy of Calhoun, Lincoln looked to Henry Clay and Daniel Webster. Lincoln had been born in Kentucky while Clay was launching his career; he took notes on Clay's climb to national prominence as he himself calculated how to advance in the political world. Lincoln called Clay "my beau-ideal of a statesman, the man for whom I fought all my humble life." When Lincoln learned, in Springfield, Illinois, that Clay had died, he organized a memorial for his hero and insisted on giving the eulogy. "Mr. Clay's predominant sentiment, from first to last, was a deep devotion to the cause of human liberty, a strong sympathy with the oppressed everywhere and an ardent wish for their elevation," Lincoln said. To be sure, Clay had countenanced slavery. "Mr. Clay was the owner of slaves. Cast into life where slavery was already widely spread and deeply seated, he did not perceive, as I think no wise man has perceived, how it could be at **once** eradicated, without producing a greater evil, even to the cause of human liberty itself." Yet Clay's tolerance was nothing more than a temporary nod to reality. "He was ever, on principle and in feeling, opposed to slavery." Lincoln accepted Clay's pragmatic belief that progress came in steps. And he endorsed unreservedly Clay's central conviction that the Union was the prerequisite of all that America had done and could do on behalf of liberty.

Lincoln didn't know, as he concluded his eulogy for Clay, how aptly his prayer for Clay would become a prayer for himself. "Henry Clay is dead," Lincoln said. "His long and eventful life is closed. Our country is prosperous and powerful. But could it have been quite all it has been, and is, and is to be, without Henry Clay? Such a man the times have demanded, and such, in the providence of God, was given us. But he is gone. Let us strive to deserve, as far as mortals may, the continued care of divine providence, trusting that in future emergencies He will not fail to provide us the instruments of safety and security."

Where Henry Clay furnished Lincoln the philosophy of democratic politics, Daniel Webster gave him the words. The young Lincoln had thrilled to read Webster's reply to Robert Hayne, and he put much of it to memory. When Lincoln as president made his own contribution to the American canon, he edited Webster's formulation of democracy—"the people's government; made for the people; made by the people; and answerable to the people"—into "government of the people, by the people, and for the people." And when, in the same Gettysburg address, Lincoln tied the fate of liberty, by then including freedom for the slaves, to that of the Union, he echoed Webster's ringing affirmation: "Liberty and Union, now and forever, one and inseparable!"

The equation of liberty and the Union was the central article of faith of Webster and Clay, and of Lincoln. It was what separated them from John Calhoun, who perceived liberty—for the states, and specifically for slaveholders in the Southern states—as increasingly threatened by the Union. Liberty and Union, said Clay and Webster. Liberty **or** Union, said Calhoun.

This was what the struggle came down to during the lives of the three. And it was the heart of the struggle they bequeathed to the next generation of

Americans. Lincoln and the Union army, at great cost, assured the triumph of Clay and Webster over Calhoun and the Confederacy.

Yet the struggle persisted. Slavery was its most salient aspect at the midpoint of the nineteenth century, but the contest between the states and the national government had hinged on other issues at other times: freedom of speech in 1798, war powers in 1814, the tariff in 1833. So it wasn't surprising that the struggle outlived slavery. Clay and Webster, with Lincoln's help, won the argument that the Union must be unbroken, but Calhoun's insistence on the need for balance between the states and the nation found adherents on matters that ranged, during the next several generations, from civil rights and business regulation to school funding and the environment.

The struggle originated with the founders. It continued with their heirs. It is with us still.

Acknowledgments

The author's first thanks go to the scholars who devoted decades to gathering, transcribing, annotating and publishing the often far-flung papers of the main figures of my story. The leaders of the teams are identified in the Sources description below, but there were very many more. Without their work, mine would not have been possible.

Kris Puopolo at Doubleday has been a wonderful editor, as always. Dan Meyer makes the trains run on time. Bill Thomas's skeptical eye at the beginning sharpens the end product. Ingrid Sterner edits copy with a light but sure touch.

My colleagues and students at the University of Texas at Austin have asked questions, answered questions and heard more about Clay, Calhoun and Webster than they probably cared to.

My partners in the Monday morning seminar—Greg Curtis, Steve Harrigan and Larry Wright—have been their typical amusing, insightful selves.

Sources

Henry Clay, John Calhoun and Daniel Webster were sufficiently celebrated in their day that people flocked to hear them speak; those who lacked the proximity or pull to get into the Capitol contented themselves purchasing printed versions of the speeches, often readied for sale within days of the delivery. Periodically the speeches were collected and published in book form. As time passed, new editions supplanted the old ones and often included correspondence. Eventually, long after the deaths of the three, each became the subject of a sustained, scholarly editing project that gathered, annotated and published a comprehensive and authoritative collection of speeches, correspondence and other papers.

For Henry Clay, the definitive collection is **The Papers of Henry Clay,** edited by James F. Hopkins and Mary W. M. Hargreaves, 11 vols. (University of Kentucky Press, 1959–92). For John Calhoun, it is **The Papers of John C. Calhoun,** edited by

Robert L. Meriwether et al., 28 vols. (University of South Carolina Press, 1959–2003). And for Daniel Webster, it is **The Papers of Daniel Webster,** edited by Charles M. Wiltse and Harold D. Moser, 14 vols. (University Press of New England for Dartmouth College, 1974–89). These collections form the primary-source backbone of the present work. Occasionally letters and speeches are drawn from other collections; these are identified in the notes.

Much as Congress was taking shape during the four decades of service of the three men, so were the legislature's record-keeping practices. Addresses and remarks by members were reported sketchily at first, then more fully, in a series of published sets. The **Annals of Congress** covered the early years of Clay, Webster and Calhoun; it was followed by the **Register of Debates** and then the **Congressional Globe** (and ultimately by the **Congressional Record**). The editing in the collections was occasionally haphazard; for the present book, errors have been corrected without comment. Sometimes speeches were recorded indirectly ("Mr. Calhoun said that the senator from Kentucky was grievously mistaken"); these have been rendered directly (Calhoun said, "The senator from Kentucky is grievously mistaken").

The best source for presidential speeches and messages is **The Public Papers of the Presidents,** compiled by the online American Presidency Project.

Published memoirs and secondary sources are identified in full in the notes. A few secondary works deserve special mention: Charles M. Wiltse, **John C. Calhoun,** 3 vols. (1944–51); Irving H. Bartlett, **Daniel Webster** (1978) and **John C. Calhoun** (1993); Merrill D. Peterson, **The Great Triumvirate: Webster, Clay and Calhoun** (1987); and Robert V. Remini, **Henry Clay** (1991) and **Daniel Webster** (1997).

Notes

CHAPTER 1

13 "No troops could behave worse": George Robert Gleig, **A Narrative of the Campaigns of the British Army at Washington, Baltimore and New Orleans** (1821), 125–32.

21 "All America acknowledges": "To the Electors of Fayette County," Clay writing as "Scaevola" in the **Kentucky Gazette** (Lexington), April 16, 1798, in **Papers of Clay**, 1:6.

23 "Each gentleman will take": **Lexington Reporter**, Jan. 26, 1809, in A. C. Quisenberry, **The Life and Times of Hon. Humphrey Marshall** (1892), 102.

24 "My damned pistol snapped": Clay to James Clark, Jan. 19, 1809, in **Papers of Clay**, 1:400.

24 "We deem it justice": **Lexington Reporter**, Jan. 26, 1809, in Quisenberry, **Life and Times of Hon. Humphrey Marshall**, 102.

25 "Worthy Friend!": James Johnson to Clay, Jan. 28, 1809, in **Papers of Clay**, 1:401.

26 "You have heard": Clay defense in **Frankfort Western World,** Dec. 18, 1806, in **Papers of Clay,** 1:259.

26 "It seems that we have been much mistaken": Clay to Hart, Feb. 1, 1807, in **Papers of Clay,** 1:273.

28 "The real cause": Clay speech, Dec. 31, 1811, in **Papers of Clay,** 1:608–9.

29 "All hope of honorable": Unsigned Clay essay in **National Intelligencer,** April 14, 1812, in **Papers of Clay,** 1:645–48.

CHAPTER 2

31 "At the North": James Parton, **Famous Americans of Recent Times** (1871), 120.

32 "We have now reached": Theodore Dwight, **Oration Delivered at New-Haven on the 7th of July, a.d. 1801** (1801), 29.

32 "far removed": Calhoun to Andrew Pickens Jr., Jan. 21, 1803, in **Papers of Calhoun,** 1:7.

33 "When on our coasts": "Resolutions on the Chesapeake-Leopard Affair," Aug. 3, 1807, in **Papers of Calhoun,** 1:34–37.

35 "I know not how": Calhoun to Mrs. Colhoun, Sept. 13, 1810, in **Papers of Calhoun,** 1:56.

35 "I rejoice, my dearest": Calhoun to Floride Colhoun, Sept. 28, 1810, in **Papers of Calhoun,** 1:57–58.

36 "a desolating war": "Report on Relations with Britain," Nov. 29, 1811, in **Papers of Clay,** 1:63–69.

CHAPTER 3

38 "A tall, gawky-looking": E. S. Thomas, **Reminiscences of the Last Sixty-Five Years** (1840), 1:56.

39 "Go, sir, and ask": Parton, **Famous Americans of Recent Times**, 195.

40 "Johnny, all this land": Hugh A. Garland, **The Life of John Randolph of Roanoke** (1851), 1:18.

41 "I passed the night": Parton, **Famous Americans of Recent Times**, 181–82.

41 "I want not a single negro": Ibid., 192.

43 "like the sun setting": Ibid., 194.

46 "Soon or late": **Annals of Congress**, 12th Cong., 1st sess., cols. 441–51.

CHAPTER 4

48 "War, in this country": **Annals of Congress**, 12th Cong., 1st sess., cols. 476–83.

49 "With this evidence": Madison annual message to Congress, Nov. 5, 1811, in **Public Papers of the Presidents**.

50 "The conduct of her government": Madison special message to Congress, June 1, 1812, in **Public Papers of the Presidents**.

51 "If long forbearance": Committee of Foreign Relations, House of Representatives, **Report, or Manifesto of the Causes and Reasons of War with Great Britain** (1812), June 3, 1812, 3–17.

CHAPTER 5

53 "I do not remember": Autobiographical notes, circa 1829, in **Papers of Webster: Correspondence**, 1:6–8

55 "When he had built": Ibid., 5–18.

58 "The first and greatest": Webster to Samuel Bradley, June 30, 1803, in **Papers of Webster: Correspondence**, 1:45.

58 "I never heard": Webster to Ezekiel Webster, May 5, 1804, in **Papers of Webster: Correspondence**, 1:54.

59 "Money is scarce": Webster to Ezekiel Webster, n.d. (May 25, 1805), in **Papers of Webster: Correspondence**, 1:71.

59 "This was equal": Autobiographical notes, circa 1829, in **Papers of Webster: Correspondence**, 1:19–21.

62 "I am so particularly pushed": Webster to Ezekiel Webster, Nov. 27, 1810, in **Papers of Webster: Correspondence**, 1:120.

62 "After counting up": Webster to Ezekiel Webster, Sept. 14, 1811, in **Papers of Webster: Correspondence**, 1:125.

63 "We regard commerce": Webster, Rockingham Memorial, Aug. 5, 1812, in **Papers of Webster: Speeches and Formal Writings**, 1:6–17.

67 "**Curse this Government!**": George Herbert to Webster, April 28, 1813, in **Papers of Webster: Correspondence**, 1:135–36.

67 "It has not the wealth": Webster to Samuel

Bradley, May 28, 1813, in **Papers of Webster: Correspondence,** 1:141.

68 "I went yesterday": Webster to Edward Cutts, May 26, 1813, in **Papers of Webster: Correspondence,** 1:139.

68 "Speaker Clay made": Webster to Moody Kent, June 12, 1813, in **Papers of Webster: Correspondence,** 1:148–49.

68 "Public business seems": Webster to Jedediah Morse, June 28, 1813, in **Papers of Webster: Correspondence,** 1:154.

CHAPTER 6

70 "The militia of Kentucky": Clay remarks, in **Annals of Congress,** 11th Cong., 2nd sess., col. 580.

72 "Party spirit is more violent": Calhoun to James McBride, June 23, 1813, in **Papers of Calhoun,** 1:177–78.

73 "When it is simply": Calhoun speech, Jan. 15, 1814, in **Papers of Calhoun,** 1:189–200.

74 "It is the war": Calhoun speech, Oct. 25, 1814, in **Papers of Calhoun,** 1:255–59.

CHAPTER 7

75 "It continues to go": Webster speech, in **Annals of Congress,** 13th Cong., 3rd sess., cols. 461–62.

76 "We are here": Webster to Ezekiel Webster,

Nov. 29, 1814, in **Papers of Webster: Correspondence,** 1:177.

78 "It is an attempt": Webster speech, Dec. 9, 1814, in **Papers of Webster: Speeches and Formal Writings,** 1:20–31.

81 "We hear that the British": Webster to Ezekiel Webster, Jan. 9, 1815, in **Papers of Webster: Correspondence,** 1:179.

81 "The present state": Webster to William Rowland (probably), Jan. 11, 1815, in **Papers of Webster: Correspondence,** 1:181.

CHAPTER 8

85 "From the General": Gleig, **Narrative of the Campaigns of the British Army,** 266–67, 278–79, 283–84, 310, 320–21, 324, 328–31, 336.

CHAPTER 9

95 "Mr. Madison is wholly unfit": Clay to Caesar Rodney, Dec. 29, 1812, in **Papers of Clay,** 1:750.

97 "We were prepared": Clay to Monroe, Aug. 18, 1814, in **Papers of Clay,** 1:963–69.

98 "Mr. Adams in a very bad": James Gallatin diary, July 15, Aug. 10 and Oct. 29, 1814, in **The Diary of James Gallatin,** ed. Count Gallatin (1916 ed.), 27–32.

98 "We had been three hours": Adams to Louisa Catherine Adams, Dec. 16, 1814, in **Writings**

of John Quincy Adams, ed. Worthington Chauncey Ford (1915), 5:237.

99 "I dined again": Adams diary, July 8, 1814, in **Memoirs of John Quincy Adams,** ed. Charles Francis Adams (1874), 2:656.

99 "The terms of this instrument": Clay to Monroe, Dec. 25, 1814, in **Papers of Clay,** 1:1007.

101 "France was annihilated": Clay speech in House, Jan. 29, 1816, in **Papers of Clay,** 2:141–48.

CHAPTER 10

104 "The Constitution, it is true": Clay speech, June 3, 1816, in **Papers of Clay,** 2:201–4.

107 "What was the object": Clay speech, March 7, 1818, in **Papers of Clay,** 2:451–63.

111 "A new epoch": Clay speech, April 26, 1820, in **Papers of Clay,** 2:826–45.

CHAPTER 11

118 "I have settled my purpose": Webster to Ezekiel Webster, March 26, 1816, in **Papers of Webster: Correspondence,** 1:196.

122 "I was told": Goodrich quoted in Rufus Choate eulogy of Webster in **New Englander** 11 (1853): 631–32.

126 "The grant of powers": Webster argument in **McCulloch v. the State of Maryland,** in **The Writings and Speeches of Daniel Webster,** national ed. (1903), 15:263–67.

129 "The power to tax": Marshall for the court, 17 U.S. 431 (1819).

CHAPTER 12

134 "The Missouri subject": Clay to John Crittenden, Jan. 29, 1820, in **Papers of Clay**, 2:769.

134 "It is a most unhappy question": Clay to Adam Beatty, Jan. 20, 1820, in **Papers of Clay**, 2:766.

134 "I think the Constitution": Clay to Jonathan Russell, Jan. 29, 1820, in **Papers of Clay**, 2:771.

135 "Everyone felt the electricity": **Kentucky Reporter**, March 1, 1820, quoted in Merrill D. Peterson, **The Great Triumvirate: Webster, Clay and Calhoun** (1987), 62.

138 "The settlement of the Missouri": Clay to Henry Brackenridge, March 7, 1820, in **Papers of Clay**, 2:789.

140 "I had for a long time": Jefferson to John Holmes, April 22, 1820, Jefferson Papers, Library of Congress.

CHAPTER 13

142 "The years 1819 and '20": Thomas Hart Benton, **Thirty Years' View** (1854), 1:5–6.

143 "The subscribers have associated": Advertisement in **Kentucky Reporter**, Aug. 23, 1820, in **Papers of Clay**, 2:886.

144 "The information which you have": Clay to

Langdon Cheves, Oct. 30, 1820, in **Papers of Clay,** 2:896.

147 "This Missouri storm": Clay to Caesar Rodney, Feb. 16, 1821, in **Papers of Clay,** 3:42.

147 "Put off the question!": **Kentucky Reporter,** Feb. 19, 1821, in **Papers of Clay,** 3:21n.

148 "About him was gathered": William Henry Sparks, **The Memories of Fifty Years** (1872 ed.), 231–32.

150 "No human being": Clay to Langdon Cheves, March 5, 1821, in **Papers of Clay,** 3:58–59.

CHAPTER 14

157 "This done, it puts all opposition": Jackson to Monroe, Jan. 6, 1818, in **Correspondence of Andrew Jackson,** ed. John Spencer Bassett (1927), 2:345–46.

158 "I was sick in bed": Monroe to Calhoun, May 19, 1830, in **Niles' Register,** March 5, 1831, 23. Also **Papers of Calhoun,** 11:165.

158 "In accordance with the advice": Jackson, "Exposition," in Benton, **Thirty Years' View,** 1:170, 179.

160 "Mr. Calhoun is extremely": Adams diary, July 13, 15, 20 and 21, 1818, in **Memoirs,** 4:107–15.

CHAPTER 15

166 "This is the characteristic difference": Clay speech, Jan. 14, 1824, in **Papers of Clay,** 3:576.

166 "Two classes of politicians": Clay speech, March 30–31, 1824, in **Papers of Clay,** 3:683–727.

168 "My friends are perfectly": Clay to Peter Porter, Jan. 31, 1824, in **Papers of Clay,** 3:628–29.

169 "Be assured that the Crawford": Clay to Peter Porter, Jan. 31, 1824, in **Papers of Clay,** 3:629–30.

169 "The contemplated meeting": Clay to Peter Porter, Feb. 15, 1824, in **Papers of Clay,** 3:640–41.

170 "You may rely upon it": Clay to Francis Brooke, Feb. 23, 1824, in **Papers of Clay,** 3:655.

170 "Mr. Crawford cannot": Clay to Francis Brooke, Feb. 26, 1824, in **Papers of Clay,** 3:662.

171 "Mr. Calhoun will be dropt": Clay to Peter Porter, Feb. 19, 1824, in **Papers of Clay,** 3:653.

CHAPTER 16

172 "The organization of newspaper support": Adams diary, Aug. 23, 1822, in **Memoirs,** 6:56–57.

173 "This feud has become": Adams diary, Oct. 5, 1822, in **Memoirs,** 6:76–77.

174 "Calhoun stimulates the panic": Adams diary, Nov. 13, 1823, in **Memoirs,** 6:185.

174 "who in all his movements": Adams diary, Nov. 15, 1823, in **Memoirs,** 6:187.

174 "the professions of friendship": Adams diary, Feb. 4, 1824, in **Memoirs,** 6:244.

176 "Clay's conduct has always": Adams diary, June 20, 1822, in **Memoirs,** 6:26.

176 "Clay's conduct throughout": Adams diary, Aug. 3, 1822, in **Memoirs,** 6:49.

177 "Nor is there anything": Adams diary, April 22, 1824, in **Memoirs,** 6:303.

178 "Letcher wished to know": Adams diary, Dec. 17, 1824, in **Memoirs,** 6:447.

178 "The object appeared": Adams diary, Dec. 23, 1824, in **Memoirs,** 6:452.

179 "I told him I would": Adams diary, Jan. 1, 1825, in **Memoirs,** 6:457.

179 "Mr. Clay came at six": Adams diary, Jan. 9, 1825, in **Memoirs,** 6:464–65.

180 He left the remaining half: Manuscript Adams diary, Jan. 9, 1825, Massachusetts Historical Society.

181 "Thirty one members": Clay to Porter, Dec. 26, 1824, in **Papers of Clay,** 3:904–5.

181 "What, I should ask": Clay to George McClure, Dec. 28, 1824, in **Papers of Clay,** 3:906.

182 "My position in relation": Clay to Blair, Jan. 8, 1825, in **Papers of Clay,** 4:9–10.

183 "While I respect General Jackson": Porter to Clay, Jan. 14, 1825, in **Papers of Clay,** 4:17–18.

CHAPTER 17

185 "I am a deserter": Clay to Blair, Jan. 29, 1825, in **Papers of Clay,** 4:47.

186 "As a friend of liberty": Clay to Brooke, Jan. 28, 1825, in **Papers of Clay,** 4:45–46.

186 "I am well aware": Jackson to Samuel Swartout, Feb. 23, 1825, reprinted from the **New York National Advocate** in **Niles' Weekly Register**, March 12, 1825, 20–21.

187 "Dear sir: I take up my pen": Letter in **Columbian Observer**, Jan. 25, 1825, reprinted in **Niles' Weekly Register**, Feb. 5, 1825, 350.

188 "I believe it to be": Clay card, Jan. 30, 1825, from **Washington Daily National Intelligencer**, Jan. 31, 1825, in **Papers of Clay**, 4:48.

189 "George Kremer holds himself": Kremer card, Feb. 3, 1825, from **Daily National Intelligencer**, Feb. 3, 1825, in **Papers of Clay**, 4:52.

190 "The batteries of some": Clay to Brooke, Feb. 4, 1825, in **Papers of Clay**, 4:55–56.

191 "May the blessing of God": Adams diary, Feb. 9, 1825, in **Memoirs**, 6:501.

191 "The 'long agony'": Clay to Brooke, Feb. 10, 1825, in **Papers of Clay**, 4:62.

192 "I have seen the abuse": Crittenden to Clay, Feb. 15, 1825, in **Papers of Clay**, 4:67–68.

192 "That if Mr. Clay": Adams diary, Feb. 11, 1825, in **Memoirs**, 6:506–7.

194 "On the one hand": Clay to Brooke, Feb. 18, 1825, in **Papers of Clay**, 4:73.

195 "The **Judas** of the West": Jackson to William Lewis, Feb. 14, 1825, in **Correspondence of Andrew Jackson**, ed. John Spencer Bassett (1926–35), 3:276.

CHAPTER 18

197 "Wherever the standard": **An Address Delivered at the Request of the Committee of Arrangements for Celebrating the Anniversary of Independence at the City of Washington on the Fourth of July 1821** (1821), 32.

198 "It would be more candid": Adams diary, Nov. 7, 1823, in **Memoirs,** 6:179.

199 "The American continents": Monroe annual message, Dec. 2, 1823, in **Public Papers of the Presidents.**

201 "After twenty-six hours' exertion": Randolph speech, March 30, 1826, in **Register of Debates,** 19th Cong., 1st sess., 401.

202 "Your unprovoked attack": Clay to Randolph, March 31, 1826, in **Papers of Clay,** 5:208.

202 "Colonel Tattnall of Georgia": Randolph to Clay, April 1, 1836, in **Papers of Clay,** 5:211–12.

203 "I heard it all": Benton, **Thirty Years' View,** 1:73.

204 "The night before the duel": Hamilton letter to **Columbus (Ga.) Enquirer,** March 4, 1844, in **Niles' Weekly Register,** March 23, 1844, 53.

205 "The family were in the parlor": Benton, **Thirty Years' View,** 1:74.

205 "I shall never forget": Hamilton letter in **Niles' Weekly Register,** March 23, 1844, 53.

207 "The moment came for me": Benton, **Thirty Years' View,** 1:76–77.

CHAPTER 19

209 "Such was the enthusiasm": William L. Stone, "Narrative of the Festivities Observed in Honor of the Completion of the Grand Erie Canal," published as an appendix to Cadwallader D. Colden, **Memoir Prepared at the Request of the Committee of the Common Council of the City of New York and Presented to the Mayor at the Celebration of the Completion of the New York Canals** (1825), 299–326.

CHAPTER 20

217 "Commerce is not a gambling": Webster speech, April 1–2, 1824, in **Papers of Webster: Speeches and Formal Writings**, 1:135–48.

223 "I must stop": Patrick Jackson to Webster, Feb. 11, 1828, in **Papers of Webster: Correspondence**, 2:293–94.

223 "If the said bill": William Tileston and James Robbins to Webster, Feb. 18, 1828, in **Papers of Webster: Correspondence**, 2:300.

223 "I fear we are getting": Webster to Joseph Sprague, April 13, 1828, in **Papers of Webster: Correspondence**, 2:330.

224 "As far as woolens": Lawrence to Webster, May 7, 1828, in **Papers of Webster: Correspondence**, 2:342–43.

CHAPTER 21

225 "How I shall vote": Webster to James Paige, May 12, 1828, in **Papers of Webster: Correspondence,** 2:345.

226 "The bill, if it had its true name": Randolph remarks, April 23, 1828, in **Register of Debates,** 20th Cong., 1st sess., 2472.

227 "Never was there such": Calhoun to James Colhoun, May 4, 1828, in **Papers of Calhoun,** 10:382.

227 "The congress of '76": Calhoun toast, in **Niles' Weekly Register,** Sept. 20, 1828, 62.

231 "dirty black wench": **Frankfort Commentator,** in H. W. Brands, **Andrew Jackson** (2005), 401.

231 "When the midnight assassin": Brands, **Andrew Jackson,** 401.

231 "At the time I least expected it": Ibid., 405.

CHAPTER 22

233 "The act of Congress": Calhoun, "South Carolina Exposition and Protest," Dec. 1828, in **The Works of John C. Calhoun,** ed. Richard C. Crallé (1870), 6:2–57.

CHAPTER 23

239 "We have a dead calm": Calhoun to Patrick Noble, Jan. 10, 1829, in **Papers of Calhoun,** 10:550.

242 "It was grand": Margaret Bayard Smith, **The First Forty Years of Washington Society,** ed. Gaillard Hunt (1906), 290–96.

CHAPTER 24

246 "As to the suspicion": Charles M. Wiltse, **John C. Calhoun: Nullifier** (1949), 164.

249 "She said that she considered": Calhoun reply to John Eaton, from **Pendleton Messenger,** n.d., in **Niles' Register,** Nov. 5, 1831.

250 "Mrs. Eaton is as chaste": Jackson to John McLemore, April 26, 1829, in **The Papers of Andrew Jackson,** ed. Daniel Feller et al. (2007), 7:184.

250 "I would sink with honor": Jackson to John McLemore, May 3, 1829, in **Papers of Jackson,** 7:200–201.

251 "I have found the President": Van Buren to Jesse Hoyt, April 13, 1829, in John Robert Irelan, **History of the Life, Administration and Times of Martin Van Buren** (1887), 134.

251 "I have found him": Jackson to Overton, Dec. 31, 1829, in **Correspondence of Jackson,** 108–9.

CHAPTER 25

254 "I thought I could discern": Hayne speech, Jan. 21 and 25, 1830, in **Speech of Mr. Hayne, of South Carolina, on Mr. Foot's Resolution** (1830), 3–32.

259 "The dashing nature": Charles W. March, **Reminiscences of Congress** (1850), 123–24.

259 "Mr. Webster conversed": Everett quoted in ibid., 125–26.

CHAPTER 26

262 "Time had not thinned": March, **Reminiscences,** 143.

262 "When the mariner": Webster speech, Jan. 26, 1830, in **Papers of Webster: Speeches and Formal Writings,** 1:287–348.

276 "Their feelings were strained": March, **Reminiscences,** 142–51.

CHAPTER 27

281 "Mr. Van Buren has evidently": Webster to Warren Dutton, Jan. 15, 1830, in **The Private Correspondence of Daniel Webster,** ed. Fletcher Webster (1857), 1:483–84.

284 "Our Federal Union": Andrew Jackson toast, April 13, 1830, in Richard R. Stenberg, "The Jefferson Birthday Dinner, 1830," **Journal of Southern History** 4, no. 3 (1938): 341.

285 "The Union—next to our liberty": Calhoun toast, April 13, 1830, in **Papers of Calhoun,** 11:148.

286 "Mr. Calhoun's position": Crawford to John Forsyth, April 30, 1830, in **Correspondence Between Gen. Andrew Jackson and John C.**

Calhoun, President and Vice-President of the
U. States, on the Subject of the Course of
the Latter in the Deliberations of the Cabinet
of Mr. Monroe on the Occurrences in the
Seminole War (1831), 9.

287 "Sir, that frankness": Jackson to Calhoun,
May 13, 1830, in **Correspondence Between
Jackson and Calhoun**, 8.

289 "I cannot recognize": Calhoun to Jackson,
May 29, 1830, in **Correspondence Between
Jackson and Calhoun**, 10.

290 "I had a right to believe": Jackson to Calhoun,
May 30, 1830, in **Correspondence Between
Jackson and Calhoun**, 22–23.

CHAPTER 28

294 "I think it right": Memorandum by Nicholas
Biddle, n.d. (between Oct. 1829 and Jan. 1830),
in **The Correspondence of Nicholas Biddle
Dealing with National Affairs, 1807–1844**, ed.
Reginald C. McGrane (1919), 93.

295 "There is no one principle": Biddle to Samuel
Smith, Dec. 29, 1828, in **Correspondence of
Biddle**, 62–63.

296 "It may be assumed": Clay to Biddle, Sept. 11,
1830, in **Papers of Clay**, 8:263–64.

298 "In respect to General Jackson": Biddle to Mr.
Robinson, Dec. 20, 1830, in **Correspondence of
Biddle**, 122.

298 "It is obvious": Biddle to William Lawrence,

Feb. 8, 1831, in **Correspondence of Biddle,** 123–24.

300 "Have you come": Clay to Biddle, Dec. 15, 1831, in **Papers of Clay,** 8:432–33.

301 "I have had an application": Webster to Biddle, Dec. 21, 1833, in **Papers of Webster: Correspondence,** 3:289.

302 "I have seen": Webster to Biddle, Dec. 18, 1831, in **Papers of Webster: Correspondence,** 3:139.

302 "I cannot but think": Webster to Biddle, Jan. 8, 1832, in **Papers of Webster: Correspondence,** 3:141.

302 "A disordered currency": Webster speech, May 25, 1832, in **Register of Debates: Senate,** 22nd Cong., 1st sess., 956–64.

304 "Gentlemen of the South": Benton speech to Senate, Jan. 20, 1832, in **Register of Debates: Senate,** 22nd Cong., 1st sess., 141.

CHAPTER 29

306 "The Congress, the executive": Jackson veto message, July 10, 1832, in **Public Papers of the Presidents.**

308 "A great majority": Webster speech, July 11, 1832, in **Register of Debates: Senate,** 22nd Cong., 1st sess., 1224, 1233.

309 "You ask, what is the effect": Biddle to Clay, Aug. 1, 1832, in **Correspondence of Biddle,** 196.

310 "It diffuses universal joy": Randolph to Jackson,

July 15, 1832, in **Correspondence of Jackson,** 4:462.

311 "The veto works well": Jackson to William Lewis, Aug. 18, 1832, in **Correspondence of Jackson,** 4:467.

CHAPTER 30

313 "unauthorized by the constitution": South Carolina Ordinance of Nullification, Nov. 24, 1832, in **Niles' Weekly Register,** Dec. 1, 1832.

313 "in direct violation": Jackson proclamation, Dec. 10, 1832, in **Public Papers of the Presidents.**

315 "There is not a shadow": Calhoun speech, in **Register of Debates: Senate,** 22nd Cong., 2nd sess., 100–103.

318 "We must be prepared": Jackson to Cass, Dec. 17, 1832, in **Correspondence of Jackson,** 4:502–3.

318 "The wickedness, madness, and folly": Jackson to Poinsett, Dec. 9, 1832, in **Correspondence of Jackson,** 4:498.

318 "The Union must be preserved": Jackson to Coffee, Dec. 14, 1832, in **Correspondence of Jackson,** 4:499–500.

318 "Yes, I have": William Lewis quoting Jackson in James Parton, **Life of Andrew Jackson** (1861), 3:284–85.

CHAPTER 31

320 When Calhoun entered the room: Benton, **Thirty Years' View,** 1:342–43.

321 "When I survey, sir": Clay speech, Feb. 12, 1833, in **Register of Debates: Senate,** 22nd Cong., 2nd sess., 462–73.

325 "He who loves the Union": Calhoun speech, Feb. 12, 1833, in **Register of Debates: Senate,** 22nd Cong., 2nd sess., 477–78.

CHAPTER 32

328 "There are principles": Webster speech, Feb. 12, 1833, in **Register of Debates: Senate,** 22nd Cong., 2nd sess., 478–79.

329 "But little did the people": Calhoun speech, Feb. 15–16, 1833, in **Register of Debates: Senate,** 22nd Cong., 2nd sess., 529–53.

332 "The gentleman has terminated": Webster speech, Feb. 16, 1833, in **Register of Debates: Senate,** 22nd Cong., 2nd sess., 553–87.

CHAPTER 33

338 "If this bill": Webster speech, Feb. 25, 1833, in **Register of Debates: Senate,** 22nd Cong., 2nd sess., 727–29.

339 "I have long": Clay speech, Feb. 25, 1833, in **Register of Debates: Senate,** 22nd Cong., 2nd sess., 729–42.

CHAPTER 34

343 "Yesterday was perhaps": Clay to Barbour, March 2, 1833, in **Papers of Clay,** 8:629.

343 "I shall get some curses": Clay to James Caldwell, March 12, 1833, in **Papers of Clay,** 8:632.

344 "I have had a laborious task": Jackson to Andrew Crawford, May 1, 1833, in **Correspondence of Jackson,** 5:71–72.

345 "A year would make": Calhoun to William Preston, circa Feb. 3, 1833, in **Papers of Calhoun,** 12:38.

345 "All that I see and hear": Calhoun to Christopher Vandeventer, March 24, 1833, in **Papers of Calhoun,** 12:144–45.

CHAPTER 35

349 "Washington is no place": Harriet Martineau, **Retrospect of Western Travel** (1838), 1:235–44, 288–99.

CHAPTER 36

364 "In half an hour": Biddle to J. S. Barbour, April 16, 1833, in **Correspondence of Biddle,** 207.

365 "the exercise of a power": Clay speech, Dec. 26, 1833, in **Register of Debates: Senate,** 23rd Cong., 1st sess., 58–94.

367 "They have entered": Calhoun speech, n.d., in Benton, **Thirty Years' View,** 1:411–12.

368 "I felt an emotion": Benton, **Thirty Years' View,** 1:379.

368 "From the moment": Ibid., 1:415–20.

372 "The Bank, Mr. Van Buren": Martin Van Buren,

The Autobiography of Martin Van Buren, ed. John C. Fitzpatrick (1920), 625.

373 "Were all the worshippers": Jackson to Van Buren, Jan. 3, 1834, in **Correspondence of Jackson,** 5:238.

373 "There is no real general distress": Jackson to James Hamilton, Feb. 2, 1834, in **Correspondence of Jackson,** 5:244.

373 "Relief!" thundered Jackson: **Niles' Register,** March 8, 1834, 31.

374 "The storm in Congress": Jackson to Andrew Jackson Jr., Feb. 16, 1834, in **Correspondence of Jackson,** 5:249.

CHAPTER 37

376 "The Declaration of Independence": Adams diary, March 3, 1820, in **Memoirs,** 5:8–12.

382 "It is inexpedient": **Sons of the Fathers: The Virginia Slavery Debates of 1831–1832,** ed. Erik S. Root (2010), 13.

383 "I will be as harsh": **Liberator,** Jan. 1, 1831.

CHAPTER 38

387 "very lame account": Adams diary, Dec. 6, 1836, in **Memoirs,** 9:317.

387 "It is so": Adams diary, Nov. 17, 1837, in **Memoirs,** 9:431.

388 "Wind and tide": Adams diary, Dec. 26, 1837, in **Memoirs,** 9:457.

388 "The conduct of the executive": Adams speech, July 7, 1838, in **Speech of John Quincy Adams of Massachusetts . . . Relating to the Annexation of Texas to This Union** (1838), 115.

389 "He knows nothing": Adams speech, June 30, 1838, in **Speech of John Quincy Adams,** 79.

390 "That John Quincy Adams": Proposed censure resolution, in **Letters from John Quincy Adams to His Constituents of the Twelfth Congressional District in Massachusetts** (1837), 13.

391 "That the right of petition": Proposed censure resolution, in **Letters from Adams,** 23.

391 "Regardless of the feelings": Adams open letter to constituents, March 13, 1837, in **Letters from Adams,** 25–26.

393 "The gentleman went further": Adams speech in House, Feb. 9, 1837, in **Letters from Adams,** 48–60.

CHAPTER 39

395 "I do not belong to the school": Calhoun speech, Feb. 6, 1837, in **The Works of John C. Calhoun** (1856), 2:625–33.

CHAPTER 40

403 "My friends are very sanguine": Clay to James Clay, Jan. 22, 1838, in **Papers of Clay,** 9:133.

404 "I do not think": Clay to Porter, Jan. 26, 1838, in **Papers of Clay,** 9:135.

404 "If I am to judge": Clay to Henry Clay Jr., March 2, 1838, in **Papers of Clay,** 9:152.

405 "I handled Mr. Calhoun": Clay to Biddle, Feb. 20, 1838, in **Papers of Clay,** 9:149.

405 "Nullification, Mr. President": Clay speech, March 10, 1838, in **Papers of Clay,** 9:158.

406 "I believe in private life": Clay to Harrison Otis, June 26, 1838, in **Papers of Clay,** 9:208.

406 "I yesterday had a long interview": Clay to John Clayton, June 14, 1838, in **Papers of Clay,** 9:204.

407 "The administration party": Clay to Harrison Otis, June 26, 1838, in **Papers of Clay,** 9:205.

407 "The partiality for Mr. W.": Clay to Harrison Otis, July 7, 1838, in **Papers of Clay,** 9:212–13.

408 "There remains, then": Clipping from **Boston Atlas,** n.d., enclosed in Harrison Otis to Clay, Sept. 14, 1838, in **Papers of Clay,** 9:229n.

408 "I am mortified": Clay to Harrison Otis, Sept. 24, 1838, in **Papers of Clay,** 9:233.

409 "An opportunity exists": Tappan to Clay, June 5, 1838, in **Papers of Clay,** 9:199–200.

410 "I hope that you": Clay to Tappan, July 6, 1838, in **Papers of Clay,** 9:212.

411 "It is my clear conviction": Clay to Birney, Nov. 3, 1838, in **Papers of Clay,** 9:244.

411 "The abolitionists are denouncing me": Clay to Francis Brooke, Nov. 1838, in **Papers of Clay,** 9:246.

412 "The nomination has fallen": Clay to Harrison Otis, Dec. 13, 1838, in **Papers of Clay,** 9:252.

CHAPTER 41

414 "The third class": Clay speech, Feb. 7, 1839, in **Congressional Globe,** 25th Cong., 3rd sess., app., 354–59.

419 "I expected it would enrage": Clay to Alexander Hamilton, Feb. 24, 1839, in **Papers of Clay,** 9:291.

419 "I hope it will do good": Clay to Harrison Otis, Feb. 18, 1839, in **Papers of Clay,** 9:290.

420 "Your friends in this state": Oliver Smith to Clay, Sept. 28, 1839, in **Papers of Clay,** 9:349.

421 "I have no wish": Clay to Oliver Smith, Oct. 5, 1839, in **Papers of Clay,** 9:350.

421 "General Harrison is nominated": Porter to Clay, Dec. 16, 1839, in **Papers of Clay,** 9:365.

422 "If I have friends": Clay speech, Dec. 11, 1839, quoted in **Papers of Clay,** 9:363–64.

CHAPTER 42

423 "The whole country": Adams diary, Aug. 29, 1840, in **Memoirs,** 10:351–52.

424 "This practice of itinerant speech-making": Adams diary, Sept. 24, 1840, in **Memoirs,** 10:352–53.

425 "Mutual gratulation at the downfall": Adams diary, Dec. 4, 1840, in **Memoirs,** 10:365–66.

CHAPTER 43

429 "I hope nothing": Peter Harvey, **Reminiscences and Anecdotes of Daniel Webster** (1878), 162–63.

430 "Mr. President," he said: John Tyler Jr., in Frank G. Carpenter, "A Talk with a President's Son," **Lippincott's Monthly Magazine,** March 1888, 417–18.

431 "You are too impetuous": Harrison to Clay, March 13, 1841, in **Papers of Clay,** 9:514.

431 "I was mortified": Clay to Harrison, March 15, 1841, in **Papers of Clay,** 9:516–17.

432 "As to a Bank": Tyler to Clay, April 30, 1841, in **Papers of Clay,** 9:527–28.

433 "He has not reciprocated": Clay speech, Aug. 19, 1841, in **Congressional Globe,** 27th Cong., 1st sess., app., 364–66.

CHAPTER 44

436 "The papers will inform you": Clay to Ambrose Spencer, Aug. 27, 1841, in **Papers of Clay,** 9:594.

437 "I do not pretend": Clay speech in Senate, Sept. 2, 1841, in **Congressional Globe,** 27th Cong., 1st sess., app., 345.

438 "I am with the president": Webster to Caroline Webster, Aug. 21, 1841, in **Papers of Webster: Correspondence,** 5:145.

438 "While one says": Webster to Hiram

Ketchum, July 17, 1841, in **Papers of Webster: Correspondence,** 5:137.

439 **"I have done or said nothing"**: Webster to Tyler, Aug. 20, 1841, in **Papers of Webster: Correspondence,** 5:144.

439 "I try to keep cool": Webster to Hiram Ketchum, Aug. 22, 1841, in **Papers of Webster: Correspondence,** 5:146.

439 "I called to see Mr. Webster": Thomas Ewing diary, Sept. 3, 1841, in **American Historical Review,** Oct. 1912, 109.

440 "The conduct of the president": Address of Whig caucus, Sept. 13, 1841, in **Niles' National Register,** Sept. 18, 1841.

442 "His personal demeanor": Webster to Everett, April 25, 1842, in **Private Correspondence of Webster,** 2:120.

443 "I must at last run away": Ashburton to Webster, Dec. 3, 1842, in **Private Correspondence of Webster,** 2:157–58.

CHAPTER 45

445 "I thought at the time": Solomon Northup, **Twelve Years a Slave,** ed. David Wilson (1854), 32–39, 42–48. David Wilson was more than an editor, as he indicates in the preface. The narrative falls into the "as told to" genre common among memoirs. But the events described all came from Northup.

457 "Birch, no doubt": Ibid., 56–61, 90–92.

CHAPTER 46

462 "Senator Benton could be": John Tyler Jr., in "Talk with President's Son," 418–19.

466 "But when she goes": Calhoun to Pakenham, April 18, 1844, in **Papers of Calhoun,** 18:273–78.

CHAPTER 47

471 "I distinctly recollect": Oliver Hampton Smith, **Early Indiana Trials and Sketches** (1858), 593–96.

475 "A long cherished object": Clay speech, April 13, 1844, in **Papers of Clay,** 10:18–38.

477 "I have found a degree": Clay to Willie Mangum, April 14, 1844, in **Papers of Clay,** 10:39.

477 "Under these circumstances": Clay to editors of the **Washington Daily National Intelligencer,** April 17, 1844, in **Papers of Clay,** 10:41–46.

478 "I feel perfectly confident": Clay to John Crittenden, April 19, 1844, in **Papers of Clay,** 10:46.

479 "My venerated friend": Houston to Jackson, Feb. 16, 1844, in **The Writings of Sam Houston,** ed. Amelia Williams and Eugene C. Barker (1941), 4:265.

480 "Personally I could have": Clay to Stephen Miller, July 1, 1844, in **Papers of Clay,** 10:79.

480 "Far from having": Clay to Thomas Peters and John Jackson, July 27, 1844, in **Papers of Clay,** 10:91.

481 "My position is very": Clay to Joshua Giddings, Sept. 11, 1844, in **Papers of Clay,** 10:114–15.

482 "Could I say less?": Clay to Joshua Giddings, Sept. 11, 1844, in **Papers of Clay,** 10:114.

482 "The prospects of the Whig cause": Clay to William Taylor, Sept. 19, 1844, in **Papers of Clay,** 10:119.

482 "The great contest": Clay to Adams, Oct. 26, 1844, in **Papers of Clay,** 10:137.

483 "The sad result": Clay to Seward, Nov. 20, 1844, in **Papers of Clay,** 10:153–54.

CHAPTER 48

488 "Our reception by the noble master": Philip Hone diary, July 8–11, 1845, in **The Diary of Philip Hone, 1828–1851,** ed. Bayard Tuckerman (1910), 254–57.

490 a story that Webster had sexually assaulted the wife: Robert V. Remini, **Daniel Webster** (1997), 568–69.

491 "I have always wished": Webster speech, Dec. 22, 1845, in **Papers of Webster: Speeches and Formal Writings,** 2:357–60.

CHAPTER 49

496 "After reiterated menaces": James Polk message to Congress, May 11, 1846, in **Public Papers of the Presidents.**

496 "The question now submitted": Calhoun speech, May 11, 1846, in **Congressional Globe,** 29th Cong., 1st sess., 783–84.

497 "This war was begun": Garrett Davis speech, May 11, 1846, in **Congressional Globe,** 29th Cong., 1st sess., 794.

499 "Sir, we are in the midst": Webster speech, March 1, 1847, in **Papers of Webster: Speeches and Formal Writings,** 2:437–41.

CHAPTER 50

504 "I hold that to be": Webster speech, March 23, 1848, in **Papers of Webster: Speeches and Formal Writings,** 2:450–76.

CHAPTER 51

507 "A mournful and agitating event": **Niles' National Register,** Feb. 26, 1848.

CHAPTER 52

513 "Neither slavery nor involuntary servitude": Section 18, Article 1, California constitution (1849).

CHAPTER 53

518 "I am aware": Clay to Richard Pindell, Feb. 17, 1849, in **Papers of Clay,** 10:575.

519 "Mr. President, I hold": Clay speech, Jan. 29, 1850, in **Congressional Globe,** 31st Cong., 1st sess., 244–46.

CHAPTER 54

525 "I here assert": Jefferson Davis remarks, Jan. 29, 1850, in **Congressional Globe,** 31st Cong., 1st sess., 249.

526 "Never on any former occasion": Clay speech, Feb. 5–6, 1850, in **Congressional Globe,** 31st Cong., 1st sess., app., 115–27.

CHAPTER 55

538 "As much indisposed": Calhoun remarks, and Calhoun speech as read by James Mason, March 4, 1850, in **Congressional Globe,** 31st Cong., 1st sess., 451–55.

CHAPTER 56

549 "As soon as may be": Webster remarks, March 4, 1850, in **Congressional Globe,** 31st Cong., 1st sess., 456.

550 "The evening of my return": **A Memoir of Robert C. Winthrop,** ed. Robert C. Winthrop Jr. (1897), 111–12.

551 "Mr. President, I wish to speak": Webster speech, March 7, 1850, in **Congressional Globe,** 31st Cong., 1st sess., app., 269–76.

CHAPTER 57

566 "We are now on the opposite sides": James Freeman Clarke, **Anti-slavery Days** (1883), 138.

566 "Of all we loved and honored": Ibid., 139.

566 "Liberty! Liberty! Pho!": Ralph Waldo Emerson, **Journals and Miscellaneous Notebooks,** ed. A. W. Plumstead and William H. Gilman (1975), 11:345–46.

567 "Tell him that he": **Emerson in His Journals,** ed. Joel Porte (1982), 422.

568 "He is gone!": Clay remarks, April 1, 1850, in **Congressional Globe,** 31st Cong., 1st sess., 624–25.

570 "I have not, in public": Webster remarks, April 1, 1850, in **Congressional Globe,** 31st Cong., 1st sess., 625.

573 "We have gone through": Webster to Peter Harvey, Oct. 2, 1850, in **Papers of Webster: Correspondence,** 7:155.

CHAPTER 58

574 "I think of him with affection": Northup, **Twelve Years a Slave,** 103–11, 133–35, 163, 183, 301–2.

CHAPTER 59

586 "a covenant with death": **Liberator,** July 7, 1854.

587 "Such are the gratifying results": Clay to Citizens

of New York City, Oct. 3, 1851, in **Papers of Clay,** 10:916–25.

592 "my beau-ideal of a statesman": Abraham Lincoln in first debate with Stephen Douglas, Aug. 21, 1858, in **The Collected Works of Abraham Lincoln,** ed. Roy P. Basler (1953), 3:29.

593 "Mr. Clay's predominant sentiment": Abraham Lincoln eulogy for Clay, July 6, 1852, in **Works of Lincoln,** 2:121–32.

Index

H. W. BRANDS holds the Jack S. Blanton Sr. Chair in History at the University of Texas at Austin. He has written a dozen biographies and histories for Doubleday, two of which, **The First American** and **Traitor to His Class,** were finalists for the Pulitzer Prize in biography. Several of his books, including the most recent, **The General vs. the President**, were **New York Times** bestsellers.

LIKE WHAT YOU'VE READ?

If you enjoyed this large print edition of
HEIRS OF THE FOUNDERS,
here is another one of H.W. Brands's latest
bestsellers also available in large print.

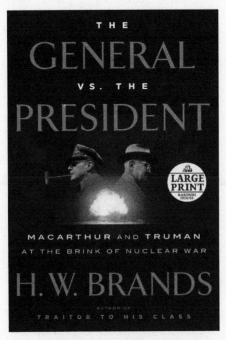

General vs. the President
(paperback)
978-1-5247-0342-4
($30.00/$40.00 CAN)

Large print books are available wherever books
are sold and at many local libraries.

All prices are subject to change. Check with your
local retailer for current pricing and availability.
For more information on these and other large print titles, visit:
www.penguinrandomhouse.com/large-print-format-books

ML   DEC   2018